# Kabuki's Nineteenth Century

# Kabuki's Nineteenth Century

*Stage and Print in Early Modern Edo*

JONATHAN E. ZWICKER

**OXFORD**
UNIVERSITY PRESS

# OXFORD
UNIVERSITY PRESS

Great Clarendon Street, Oxford, OX2 6DP,
United Kingdom

Oxford University Press is a department of the University of Oxford.
It furthers the University's objective of excellence in research, scholarship,
and education by publishing worldwide. Oxford is a registered trade mark of
Oxford University Press in the UK and in certain other countries

© Jonathan E. Zwicker 2023

The moral rights of the author have been asserted

All rights reserved. No part of this publication may be reproduced, stored in
a retrieval system, or transmitted, in any form or by any means, without the
prior permission in writing of Oxford University Press, or as expressly permitted
by law, by licence or under terms agreed with the appropriate reprographics
rights organization. Enquiries concerning reproduction outside the scope of the
above should be sent to the Rights Department, Oxford University Press, at the
address above

You must not circulate this work in any other form
and you must impose this same condition on any acquirer

Published in the United States of America by Oxford University Press
198 Madison Avenue, New York, NY 10016, United States of America

British Library Cataloguing in Publication Data

Data available

Library of Congress Control Number: 2023905965

ISBN 978-0-19-289091-7

DOI: 10.1093/oso/9780192890917.001.0001

Printed and bound by
CPI Group (UK) Ltd, Croydon, CR0 4YY

Links to third party websites are provided by Oxford in good faith and
for information only. Oxford disclaims any responsibility for the materials
contained in any third party website referenced in this work.

*For Kyongmi*

# Contents

*List of Figures*    viii
*Acknowledgments*    xii
*A Note to the Reader*    xiv

Prologue    1

1. A View from the Provinces    12
       I   A Provincial Collector    12
       II   The Shogun's Printed City    19
       III   Kabuki in an Age of Print    27

2. "Devices for Thinking about the Past": Playbills, Ephemera, and the Historical Imagination    34
       I   Playbill and Museum    34
       II   Chronology as History    38
       III   *Circa* 1811: Curiosity, Collecting, and the History of Kabuki    49
       IV   Fear of Effacement    58
       V   Curio Fever    66

3. Mapping the Stage: On Kabuki's Cartographic Archive    77
       I   Zenjirō's Maps    77
       II   The Detailed View: Mapping the Theater District    84
       III   From the Cartographic Imagination to the Parodic Imagination    101
       IV   Theater as the World/Theater in the World    121

4. The Playwright at His Desk: Imagining Authorship in Nineteenth-Century Japan    141
       I   In Search of the Shakespeare of Japan    141
       II   Archaeology of the Author's Trace    146
       III   Battlefield of the Mind: Playwriting in Early Modern Japan    158
       IV   Authorship on Trial    169

5. Individuality in an Age of Reproduction: The Image of the Actor in Nineteenth-Century Japan    179
       I   Image as Document    179
       II   Individuality in an Age of Reproduction    188
       III   Reading the Actor's Image    195
       IV   Photographing the Stage/Staging the Photograph    215

Epilogue: Stage and Print in the Digital Age                   230

*Character List*                                                246
*Biographical Appendix*                                         257
*Bibliography*                                                  261
*Index*                                                         278

# List of Figures

0.1. Utagawa Kuniyoshi: Nakamura Utaemon IV as Lord Ōtaka and Nakamura, Nakazō III as Ganzō from the play *Takagi Oriemon budō jitsuroku* ("Chidaruma"), 1848. *Source*: Tsubouchi Memorial Theatre Museum, Waseda University.   5

1.1. Utagawa Toyokuni, the audience from Shikitei Sanba, *Kakusha hyōbanki*, 1811. *Source*: National Diet Library, Tokyo.   23

2.1. Utagawa Toyokuni, the antiquarian from Shikitei Sanba, *Kakusha hyōbanki*, 1811. *Source*: National Diet Library, Toyko.   39

2.2. Katsukawa Shuntei, Ichikawa Danjūrō I and his contemporaries from Utei Enba, *Hana no Edo kabuki nendaiki*, 1811. *Source*: National Diet Library, Tokyo.   42

2.3. Creation of heaven and earth from *Shinpo Yamato nendai kōki eshō*, 1692. *Source*: Waseda University Library.   46

2.4. Katsukawa Shuntei, heaven and earth are one great theater from Utei Enba, *Hana no Edo kabuki nendaiki*, 1811. *Source*: National Diet Library, Tokyo.   47

2.5. End of Shikitei Sanba's preface and first playbill from "Sanshibai monbanzuke," 1815. *Source*: National Diet Library, Tokyo.   54

2.6. Kita Busei, fan commemorating performance by Sanshōtei Karaku in 1811 from Shikitei Sanba, "Otoshibanashi chūkō raiyu". *Source*: National Diet Library, Tokyo.   56

3.1. Map of the dressing room, *Sanshibai gakuya zassho*, n.d. *Source*: Tsubouchi Memorial Theatre Museum, Waseda University.   82

3.2. Map of the dressing room, *Shinshi Saruwaka nendaiki*, 1858. *Source*: Tsubouchi Memorial Theatre Museum, Waseda University.   82

3.3. Map of the theater district, *Shibai chōhōsho*, 1779. *Source*: Tsubouchi Memorial Theatre Museum, Waseda University.   83

3.4. Map of the Saruwaka-chō theater district, "Yobukodori waka sanchō zenzu," n.d. *Source*: Tsubouchi Memorial Theatre Museum, Waseda University.   85

3.5. Map of the Saruwaka-chō theater district, *Saruwaka saiken zu*, n.d. *Source*: Tsubouchi Memorial Theatre Museum, Waseda University.   86

3.6. Copy of "Yobukodori waka sanchō zenzu" from Ishizuka Hōkaishi's "Zoku kabuki nendaiki". *Source*: C.V. Starr East Asian Library, University of California, Berkeley.   88

3.7. "Map of Saruwaka-chō from 1847" from Kitagawa Morisada, "Morisada mankō". *Source*: National Diet Library, Tokyo.   90

3.8. Copy of map of Edo's theater district originally published in *Yarō sanza no taku* (1684) from Kitagawa Morisada, "Morisada mankō". *Source*: National Diet Library, Tokyo.     92

3.9. Map of Sakai-chō and Fukiya-chō during the Kansei period (1789–1801) from Kitagawa Morisada, "Morisada mankō". *Source*: National Diet Library, Tokyo.     93

3.10. Utagawa Kunisada, map of Sakai-cho theater district from Utei Enba, *Shibai saiken sanbasō*, 1817. *Source*: Ninjōji Bunko, Osaka University Library.     95

3.11. Utagawa Kunisada, entry for Matsumoto Kōshirō V from Utei Enba, *Shibai saiken sanbasō*, 1817. *Source*: Ninjōji Bunko, Osaka University Library.     97

3.12. Utagawa Kunisada, map of Sakai-chō theater district from Goryūtei Tokushō, *Sanbshibai yakusha saiken*, 1828. *Source*: Ebi Collection, Art Research Center, Ritsumeikan University.     99

3.13. Utagawa Kunisada, entry for Matsumoto Kōshirō V and his son Ichikawa Komazō V (right) and Nakamura Karoku I (left) from Goryūtei Tokushō, *Sanshibai yakusha saiken*, 1828. *Source*: Ebi Collection, Art Research Center, Ritsumeikan University.     100

3.14. Kitagawa Tsukimaro and Utei Enba, *Kabuki dōchū zue*, n.d. *Source*: Tsubouchi Memorial Theatre Museum, Waseda University.     102

3.15. Katsukawa Shundō, map of the interior of a theater, Hōseidō Kisanji, *Ukan sandai zue*, 1791. *Source*: Former Edogawa Ranpo Collection, Rikkyo University.     109

3.16. Utagawa Toyokuni, "Landscape of the Stage of the Three Theaters" from Kyokutei Bakin, *Yakusha meisho zue*, 1800. *Source*: National Diet Library, Tokyo.     110

3.17. Katsukawa Shunei, map of the interior of a theater presented as a map of the world from Shikitei Sanba, *Shibai kinmōzui*, 1803. *Source*: Rikkyo University Library.     112

3.18. Copy of Katsukawa Shunei's map of the interior of a theater presented as a map of the world appearing in Shikitei Sanba's *Shibai kinmōzui* from Kitagawa Morisada, "Morisada mankō". *Source*: National Diet Library, Tokyo.     114

3.19. Katsukawa Shundō, image of a horse on stage from Hōseidō Kisanji, *Ukan sandai zue*, 1791. *Source*: Kaga Bunko, Tokyo Metropolitan Library.     115

3.20. Image of a horse on stage, *Yakusha saraekō*, 1795. *Source*: Katei Bunko, University of Tokyo Library.     116

3.21. Utagawa Toyokuni, image of stage devices from Kyokutei Bakin, *Yakusha meisho zue*, 1800. *Source*: National Diet Library, Tokyo.     117

3.22. A Chinese Kabuki play from *Shinkoku yakusha kōmoku*, 1771. *Source*: National Diet Library, Tokyo.     122

3.23. Sheng or male hero role from Hatanaka Kansai, *Morokoshi kidan*, 1791. *Source*: C.V. Starr East Asian Library, University of California, Berkeley. 128

3.24. Shōkōsai Hanbē, a Chinese theater from *Shibai gakuya zue*, 1800. *Source*: National Diet Library, Tokyo. 129

3.25. Shōkōsai Hanbē, a Dutch theatergoer from *Shibai gakuya zue shūi*, 1800. *Source*: National Diet Library, Tokyo. 130

3.26. Akatsuki Kanenari, a Dutch Kyōka from *Shikankoku ichiran*, 1815. *Source*: Ninjōji Bunko, Osaka University Library. 131

3.27. Akatsuki Kanenari, map of the land of Shikan from *Shikankoku ichiran*, 1815. *Source*: Ninjōji Bunko, Osaka University Library. 132

3.28. Utagawa Kunisada, Ichikawa Danjūrō VII and Matsumoto Kōshirō V from Kimura Mokurō, *Gekijō ikkan mushimegane*, 1829. *Source*: University of Tokyo Kornaba Library. 134

3.29. Utagawa Kunisada, the six types of protagonist from Kimura Mokurō, *Gekijō ikkan mushimegane*, 1829. *Source*: University of Tokyo Kornaba Library. 136

4.1. Chikamatsu Monzaemon at his writing desk from Miki Sadanari, *Naniwa miyage*, 1738. *Source*: Art Research Center, Ritsumeikan University. 142

4.2. Shōkōsai Hanbē, copy of the image of a courtesan bearing an inscription by Chikamatsu Monzaemon, *Shibai gakuya zue shūi*, 1800. *Source*: National Diet Library, Tokyo. 149

4.3. Kitao Shigemasa, Kyokutei Bakin's study from Kyokutei Bakin, *Kyokutei ippū Kyōden bari*, 1801. *Source*: National Diet Library, Tokyo. 153

4.4. Kitao Shigemasa, Santō Kyōden's shop from Kyokutei Bakin, *Kyokutei ippū Kyōden bari*, 1801. *Source*: National Diet Library, Tokyo. 154

4.5. Ōeda Ryūhō, a scholar's writing desk, *Gayū manroku*, 1763. *Source*: C.V. Starr East Asian Library, University of California, Berkeley. 155

4.6. Sō Shiseki, table with vase containing peacock feathers, a folding fan, and a tobacco pipe, *Kokon gasō*, 1770. *Source*: Ebi Collection, Art Research Center, Ritsumeikan University. 156

4.7. Chikamatsu Monzaemon at his writing desk, n.d. *Source*: Tsubouchi Memorial Theatre Museum, Waseda University. 159

4.8. Shōkōsai Hanbē, the playwright from *Shibai gakuya zue shūi*, 1800. *Source*: National Diet Library, Tokyo. 160

4.9. Utagawa Kunisada, the dressing room of the Ichimura-za, 1811. *Source*: National Diet Library, Tokyo. 166

5.1. Tsubouchi Shōyō in his study, 1925. *Source*: Waseda University Library. 180

5.2. Photo reproduction from Sakuragawa Jihinari's 1793 *Asaina chaban Soga* from Tsubouchi Shōyō's *Shibai-e to Toyokuni oyobi sono monka*, 1920. *Source*: National Diet Library, Tokyo. 184

5.3. Utagawa Toyokuni, Kagekiyo and Dainichibō from Sakuragawa Jihinari, *Asaina chaban Soga*, 1793. Source: National Diet Library, Tokyo. 185

5.4. Katsukawa Shunshō, Ichikawa Danjūrō V as Kagekiyo and Ōtani Hiroemon III as Dainichibō from *Tsukisenu haru hagoromo Soga*, 1777. Source: Metropolitan Museum of Art. 187

5.5. Utagawa Toyokuni, the technique of the actor's likeness, *Yakusha nigao hayageiko*, 1817. Source: Art Research Center, Ritsumeikan University. 191

5.6. Utagawa Toyokuni, examples of individual actors' faces, *Yakusha nigaoe hayageiko*, 1817. Source: Art Research Center, Ritsumeikan University. 197

5.7. Utagawa Toyokuni, examples of individual actors' faces and wigs based on role type, *Yakusha nigao hayageiko*, 1817. Source: Art Research Center, Ritsumeikan University. 199

5.8. Utagawa Toyokuni, discussion of patterns of makeup from Tōshi Shōkyaku, *Yakusha sanjūnisō tengankyō*, 1802. Indicators of details added by author. Source: Nakai Collection, Art Research Center, Ritsumeikan University. 200

5.9. Utagawa Toyokuni, tableau of the plot from Shikitei Sanba, *Sono utsushie kabuki no omokage*, 1811. Source: Waseda University Library. 204

5.10. Utagawa Toyokuni, Muen Baba's discovery of Tonoinosuke and Nowakihime from Shikitei Sanba, *Sono utsushie kabuki no omokage*, 1811. Source: Waseda University Library. 206

5.11. Utagawa Toyokuni, Ichikawa Omezō as Kajiwara Kagetoki and Asao Kuzaemon as Yazaemon from Kyokutei Bakin, *Ehon Yoshitsune senbonzakura*, 1819. Source: Art Research Center, Ritsumeikan University. 208

5.12. Hairstyles used for dating prints from Sakai Matsunosuke, *Kodai ukiyo-e kaiire hikkei*, 1893. Source: National Diet Library, Tokyo. 217

5.13. Photograph of Ichikawa Danjūrō IX in 1894 from Abe Yutaka. ed., *Butai no Danjūrō* (1923). Source: National Diet Library, Tokyo. 223

6.1. Utagawa Toyokuni, the ghosts of Hōkaibō and Miyato from Shikitei Sanba, *Sono utsushie kabuki no omokage*, 1811. Source: Waseda University Library. 244

# Acknowledgments

Like most academic books, this study of kabuki's nineteenth century was conceived of, researched, and written over the course of a number of years. During that time, my work has been sustained by many individuals whose friendship and support it is a pleasure to acknowledge here.

This book would never have been written without Takagi Gen of Ōtsuma Women's University; his own work has been a model of academic rigor and innovative thinking and his friendship and mentorship for over two decades have profoundly shaped my own approach to Japan's literary past. Long before I met him in person, Akama Ryō's work on kabuki and print was an inspiration and his dedication to preserving and making accessible the theatrical past in a digital environment has profoundly shaped both the way I have done my work and my thinking about the relationship between performance and archive. I owe an enormous debt to Professor Akama and to his colleagues at the Art Research Institute at Ritsumeikan University.

Over the course of working on this study, I have also learned a great deal from colleagues across Japanese academia: Iikura Yōichi of Osaka University; Morita Teiko of Kyoto Sangyo University; Satō Yukiko of Tokyo University; Unno Keisuke, Kigoshi Shunsuke, Yamamoto Yoshitaka, Kansaku Kenichi, and Iriguchi Atsushi of the National Institute of Japanese Literature; Sasaki Takahiro, Sumiyoshi Tomohiko, and Koida Tomoko of Keiō University; Katsumata Motoi of Meisei University; Arisawa Tomoyo of Kobe University; Hashimoto Yuta of the National Museum of Japanese History; and Asahi Yoshiyuki of the National Institute for Japanese Language and Linguistics.

This book was written between two institutional settings, both of which provided research support and collegial environments that shaped and sustained my work, the University of Michigan and the University of California, Berkeley. I am grateful to my colleagues in the Department of Asian Languages and Cultures, the Center for Japanese Studies, and the East Asian Library at Michigan, where much of the initial research for this book took place: Erin Brightwell, Miranda Brown, Nancy Florida, Chris Hill, Ken Ito, Reggie Jackson, Niki Kenji, S.E. Kile, Dawn Lawson, Don Lopez, Leslie Pincus, Jennifer Robertson, David Rolston, Youngju Ryu, Kiyo Tsutsui, and Keiko Yokota-Carter. At Berkeley, I owe a great deal to Dan O'Neill and Alan Tansman, to Mary Elizabeth Berry, and to Toshie Marra. Additionally, I would like to thank Maki Fukuoka of the University of Leeds and

Hoyt Long and Melissa Van Wyk of the University of Chicago, all of whom provided feedback and ideas over the years. Finally, it is a pleasure to thank Paul Anderer, who guided my work as both and undergraduate and graduate student at Columbia University and who has always served as a model of the academic life.

Research support for this project was provided by the Centers for Japanese Studies at both Michigan and Berkeley, by the Japan Foundation, and by the National Endowment for the Humanities. I would also like to thank the two anonymous readers at Oxford University Press for the care they took reading the manuscript and giving me feedback.

My greatest debt goes to my family: my parents, Steven and Judith, have always provided unwavering love and support, as have my siblings Laura, Benjamin, and Aaron and their families. None of this would have been possible without Kyongmi, to whom this book is dedicated, and to our children, Mara and Jacob, who have been the joy of our lives.

# A Note to the Reader

All East Asian names in this book appear with surname first and given or artistic name second. Premodern figures often used a variety of names and pennames; for the sake of consistency, I have used the name by which they are most widely known. Many Japanese names were, and in some cases still are, hereditary and this is true of actors, playwrights, illustrators, and publishers. Many of the names that appear throughout the book are thus followed by a suffix (I, II, III, IV, etc.). On first appearance, I have always given the suffix and subsequently elided it when it is clear from context.

In Japanese, premodern figures are generally referred to by their given or penname, while in the modern period, the surname is generally used; thus, Shikitei Sanba (1776–1822) is referred to as Sanba, not Shikitei, while the scholar Hattori Yuiko (1932–2007) is referred to as Hattori.

For titles of plays and literary works, I have given an English translation followed by the romanized Japanese title in parentheses on its first appearance in each chapter and subsequently use the English title. For the translation of play titles and theatrical terms, I have, to the extent possible, used Samuel L. Leiter's *A New Kabuki Encyclopedia* (Westport, CT: Greenwood Press, 1997). For many premodern titles, there are variant readings; for the sake of consistency, I have used the Unified Title (Tōitsu Shomei) from the National Institute of Japanese Literature's Database of Premodern Japanese Works.

Following the Epilogue are the Character List, the Biographical Appendix, and the Bibliography. Japanese titles can be found in the bibliography as well as the Character List, which also includes proper names and common terms used in the book. The Biographical Appendix gives short entries on the most common figures who appear in the text.

All translations are my own unless otherwise noted.

# Prologue

In the summer of 1855, the kabuki actor Nakamura Nakazō III (1809–86) began writing what would become a most singular document of kabuki's nineteenth century. Part memoir, part diary, the process of writing began rather suddenly when the actor found himself at leisure in front of the mirror of his makeup stand as memories of his nearly four decades on the stage welled up.[1] For a historian (of kabuki but of the wider nineteenth century as well), the timing of Nakazō's turn toward the autobiographical is fortuitous. The two decades during which he wrote this memoir would turn out to be among the most significant years in the history of Japan, and *Self Praise* (*Temae miso*), as the book is now known, provides an extraordinary eye-witness account of the decade straddling the birth of the modern nation.

Only months after Nakazō began writing, the Great Ansei Earthquake and the fires that spread in its wake destroyed much of the city of Edo including the theater district of Saruwaka-chō. "It was the greatest calamity since the founding of the shogunate," wrote Nakazō; "the stones of the castle's various guard towers have been knocked loose," leading to speculation that "the reign of the Tokugawa might itself soon crumble."[2] In the event, this gossip proved uncannily accurate as the shogunate fell in a little more than a decade.

On the Sixth Day of the Tenth Month of the Third Year of Keiō, November 2, 1867 by the Gregorian calendar, Nakazō remembers that he began performing the role of Nagoya Sanzaemon in the play *The Straw Sandal* (*Inazuma byōshi*). "That month," he writes, "Lord Yoshinobu returned political authority to the Imperial Court."[3] And so, in one sentence, Nakazō records the most important political event of his lifetime and one of the most important events in Japanese history, the restoration of direct Imperial rule, the first step in the series of events now known as the Meiji Restoration. Over the course of his memoir, Nakazō records, often in passing, all of the major events of the late nineteenth century from the arrival of Commodore Perry's black ships in 1853, through the restoration, to the proclamation of the new era of Meiji and, in 1873, the adoption of the Western calendar.

But of more interest to Nakazō than the events of high politics were the daily successes and failures of the theater. At times, these two rather different historical

---

[1] Nakamura Nakazō III, *Temae miso*, ed. Gunji Masakatsu (Tokyo: Seiabō, 2009), p. 308.
[2] Nakamura Nakazō III, *Temae miso*, p. 312.
[3] Nakamura Nakazō III, *Temae miso*, p. 362.

registers would intersect. In the months following abdication of the last shogun, Tokugawa Yoshinobu, periodic violence would lead Edo's theaters to shut down performances. One evening, three Shogunal loyalists stormed into the Morita-za in the middle of a performance leading, eventually, to the entire theater district of Saruwaka-chō being overrun by soldiers of both sides.[4] With the outbreak of the Boshin War at the beginning of 1868, the debut of the New Year's plays was pushed back by several months. Interspersed with descriptions of violence and bloodshed in Nakazō's memoir, we find the titles of plays as well as the names of actors and the roles that they played; *Self Praise* is, for us, a strange chronicle of the Meiji Restoration in which history as event fades into the background amid an intense interest in, and preoccupation with, the everyday practices of theatrical life.

But if Nakazō's memoir can serve as a point of entry into kabuki's nineteenth century, it is not just at the level of content: the titles of plays, the names of actors and their roles, dramatic successes and failures set against the sweeping backdrop of "history." Rather, seen in a different way, the memoir itself is a particular kind of tracing of nineteenth-century theatrical culture and tells a story of how the history of kabuki has always also been a history of the ways in which the theater is constituted by writing. From the beginning, Nakazō's book crossed between the public and private spheres in suggestive ways; it documents the very public world of the theater but does so through an intense focus on the private realm of the actor's life often told through the lens of deeply personal memories. The memoir was kept in manuscript but was shared with friends such as the playwrights Segawa Jokō III and Sakurada Jisuke IV, circulating within a semi-public world defined by private sociability. Only at the very end of Nakazō's life did his memoir see print for the first time, serialized in the magazine *The Kabuki News* (*Kabuki shinpō*) beginning in 1885. Later, some time after 1893, the original manuscript was lost and our access to *Self Praise* is now largely due to a carefully edited scholarly edition based on the early printings of the memoir in the late nineteenth and early twentieth centuries. Even the history of this edition, first published in 1944 in the midst of the Second World War, is suggestive. The editor Gunji Masakatsu (1913–98) later recalled that he delivered the manuscript just before being called up to military service and it was on seeing the book in published form after the war that "I was struck by the sense that I had lived."[5]

The world to which this young theater historian returned after the war, and kabuki's place within that world, had changed in dramatic ways. As James Brandon has shown, it was in the immediate postwar years, under the Allied Occupation, that kabuki was transformed into—or, as Brandon puts it, invented as—a classical theater, "the basic nature of the art altered."[6] Emblematic of this "fossilization" is

---

[4] Nakamura Nakazō III, *Temae miso*, p. 363.
[5] Gunji Masakatsu, "Atogaki" in Nakamura Nakazō III, *Temae miso*, n.p.
[6] James R. Brandon, *Kabuki's Forgotten War 1931–1945* (Honolulu: University of Hawai'i Press, 2009), p. 353. See also Okamoto Shiro, *The Man Who Saved Kabuki: Faubion Bowers and Theatre Censorship in Occupied Japan*, trans. Samuel Leiter (Honolulu: University of Hawai'i Press, 2001).

the way that kabuki appears in Ozu Yasujirō's 1952 film *The Flavor of Green Tea over Rice* (*Ochazuke no aji*), released shortly after the end of the Occupation: the Kabuki-za Theater, the great emblem of Kabuki's modernization, is the setting for the introduction of an arranged marriage for the young Setsuko, who runs out to spend the day watching bicycle racing and playing pachinko. Like the arranged marriage, kabuki itself becomes an emblem of a staid past, a formal, middle-class sociability seemingly so distant from the postwar present.[7]

Even as kabuki would continue in this process of fossilization (it would be designated by the state as an Important Intangible Cultural Property in 1965), one of the central efforts of scholars in the decades that followed was to "rehumanize" kabuki and its history, to restore to it a sense of the lived experience of theater during the early modern period, something (to borrow the language of Ozu's film) "intimate and primitive, without reserve, more relaxed."[8] Integral to this process was a turn toward kabuki's vast printed archive (theater books and printed images and actor critiques but also playbills and ephemera of various sort), and out of this material scholars like Hattori Yukio began to fashion a new history for kabuki.[9]

It was from an encounter with such material that I came to write this book. My entry into kabuki's archive was orthogonal. I am trained as a literary historian rather than an historian of the theater and my early work was on the history of fiction but with a deep interest in the history of print and of books and their readers. From this perspective, I came to the history of kabuki, and my preoccupation has been with print and the ways in which theater circulated on the page in the nineteenth century. We know a great deal about the history of kabuki in early modern Japan and the role that print culture could play in documenting that history; we know less about the history of printed ephemera as such, not as a means of documenting the stage but as an object of historical enquiry itself. There are very good narrative histories of Japanese theater that capture the long arc of kabuki and the place of the nineteenth century in that history. My goal in writing this book is not to recapitulate that work but to ask a different set of questions, to ask how we might use kabuki's archive to resituate the theater within the broader world of nineteenth-century print culture.

An example might be useful. In *Self Praise*, Nakazō briefly mentions a performance of *The Bloodstained Bodhidharma* (*Chidaruma*) in the seventh month of 1848: "it was a great success and continued through the ninth month."[10] This is all that Nakazō records of the performance, but it is possible, and relatively easy,

---

[7] On the transformation of traditional theatrical arts like kabuki and the puppet theater into middle class or "gentlemanly" forms of leisure in the pre-war period, see the memoir of the shamisen player Tsurusawa Kanji VII, Nakano Junya, *Utakata: Nanadaime Tsurusawa Kanji ga mita bunraku* (Nishinomiya: Kansai daigaku Shuppankai, 2019), pp. 22–25.
[8] "Rehumanize" (in English) is the term that Kawazoe Yū uses to describe the work exemplified by Hattori Yukio's seminal 1986 *Ōinaru koya*. See Kawazoe Yū, "Gakujustu bunkoban kaisetsu," afterword to Hattori Yukio, *Ōinaru koya: Edo kabuki no shukusai kūkan* (Tokyo: Kōdansha, 2012), p. 398.
[9] See Kawazoe Yū, "Gakujustu bunkoban kaisetsu."
[10] Nakamura Nakazō III, *Temae miso*, p. 246.

to move from this brief entry to a fuller history of that performance. There are, for example, two different sets of actor prints—one designed by Utagawa Kunisada and the other by Utagawa Kuniyoshi—that date from the 1848 performance and show the actors in role. One of the most striking images, designed by Kuniyoshi, shows a bowed over Nakazō in the role of Ganzō providing support to the great actor Nakamura Utaemon IV (in the role of Lord Ōtaka) as he commits suicide (Figure 0.1). We also have a wide variety of theater programs from this performance: single-sheet tsuji *banzuke*, which were posted publicly as advertisements; *ehon banzuke*, short, illustrated booklets that were sold at theaters and theater teahouses and which depict the actors in role in the various scenes of the play; and *yakuwari banzuke*, booklets that detail which actors were to appear in which role and give a brief outline of the plot. We even have (unusual in the case of kabuki) several handwritten scripts—unusual because kabuki scripts were not published until the 1880s, and not many of the manuscripts have come down to us.

We might rightly use these materials to reconstruct something of the performance of this play in 1848, further situating that performance in the newly constructed theater district of Saruwaka-chō and within the ordinances of the Tenpō Reforms enacted earlier in the decade and which had come to govern theatrical life.[11] But I would like to suggest an alternate approach, one that moves away from the seemingly ineluctable draw of the stage and directs us instead toward the social lives of printed objects as they left the theater district. In a memoir he published in 1922, the poet Naitō Meisetsu records an anecdote about his mother, Yaso. Sometime shortly before Meisetsu's birth in 1847, Yaso had moved to Edo from the castle town of Matsuyama on the island of Shikoku with her husband Naitō Fusanoshin, a samurai in the service of the Iyo-Matsuyama Domain. In one of the few passages devoted to the memory of his mother, who died when he was three, Meisetsu writes:

> Shortly before her death, my birth mother went to see the theater in Saruwaka-chō. Nakamura Utaemon III [sic] was in "The Bloodstained Bodhidharma" and it was the first time for her to watch the grand kabuki after coming to Edo. At that time, most plays were quickly published as books of illustrated fiction (*kusazōshi*). She purchased a copy and cherished it. Later on, I heard that when she died my grandmother put that copy of "The Bloodstained Bodhidharma" in my mother's coffin with her.[12]

---

[11] On the direct impact, especially financial, of the Tenpō reforms on actors see Nakazō's account in Nakamura Nakazō III, *Temae miso*, pp. 206ff.

[12] Naitō Meisetsu, *Meisetsu jijoden* (Tokyo: Okamura Shoten, 1922), p. 10. After this book went into production, I became aware that Satoko Shimazaki uses a version of this quotation in her forthcoming "Stage Sounds for the Eyes: Performance and Visual-Textual Space of Gōkan," in *Graphic Narratives from Early Modern Japan: The World of Kusazōshi*, ed. Laura Moretti and Satō Yukiko (Leiden and Boston: Brill, forthcoming).

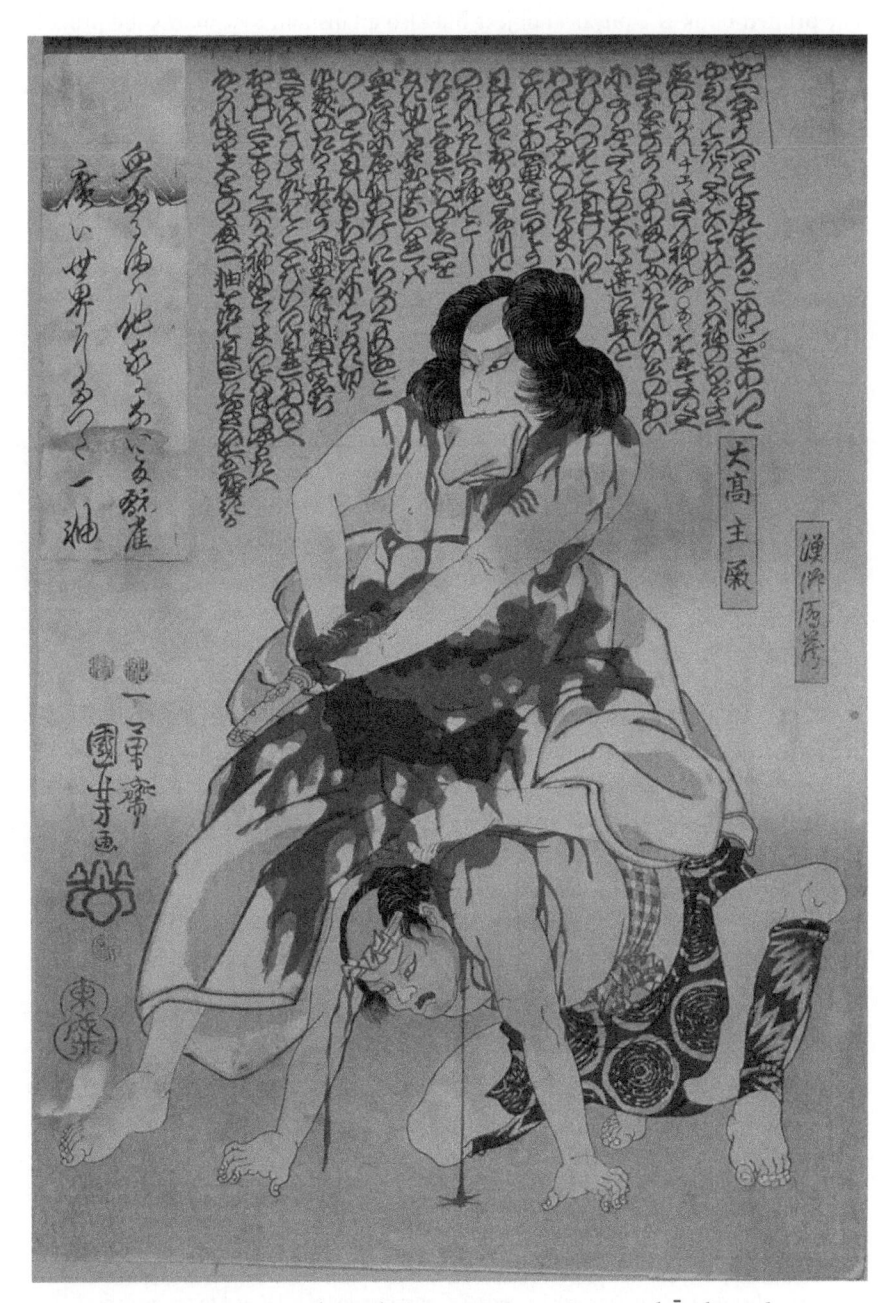

**Figure 0.1** Utagawa Kuniyoshi: Nakamura Utaemon IV as Lord Ōtaka and Nakamura, Nakazō III as Ganzō from the play *Takagi Oriemon budō jitsuroku* ("Chidaruma"), 1848.

Source: Tsubouchi Memorial Theatre Museum, Waseda University.

The printed book is a physical object but also a talisman that marks the process through which "external experience is internalized" with the "transformation of a generally purchasable, mass-produced object (the material souvenir) into private possession."[13] Moreover, this material object that is sold and bought and read and cherished becomes a kind of votive offering from mother to daughter, a keepsake to accompany a young woman on her journey in death. No longer oriented primarily to the stage, this trace of the theater can become the starting point for what the historian of British theater Jacky Bratton has described as "the mesh of connections between all kinds of theatre texts, and between texts and their users."[14]

In Chapter 1, I will turn to another young woman from the countryside who collected theater ephemera but who, to the best of our knowledge, never traveled to Edo to see, in person, that city's kabuki and its stars; rather, her experience of the plays and the great actors of the nineteenth century was entirely constituted by print. Before turning to the story of this woman, Hayashi Kuni, through which I will explore more fully how I came to this project and the approach that I have taken to its materials, I would like to lay out a few preliminaries which I hope will help the reader, especially a reader not entirely familiar with Japanese history or with the history of Japanese drama, to follow my argument and navigate the itinerary of this book.

In Japanese historiography, the nineteenth century stretches across the 1868 Meiji Restoration, which generally marks the end of the early modern period and the beginning of the modern. In 1853, at roughly mid-century, a squadron of US naval ships commanded by Commodore Mathew Perry arrived at Uraga at the entrance to Edo Bay, the first in a series of events that are colloquially described as the "opening" of Japan. These events served further to destabilize the political authority of the Tokugawa Shogunate and resulted, in 1867, in the transfer of political authority to the Meiji Emperor and, in the following year, to the relocation of the capital from Kyoto to Edo, newly renamed Tokyo. In 1889, Japan's first constitution was promulgated and its first legislature, the Imperial Diet, convened the

---

[13] Susan Stewart, *On Longing: Narratives of the Miniature, the Gigantic, the Souvenir, the Collection* (Durham, NC: Duke University Press, 1993), pp. 134, 138. A suggestive analog to this experience is offered by the film archivist Okada Hidenori, who writes of his own habits as a collector of film pamphlets:

> Flipping through the pages on the train home or in my room, I relive the story as I rest my eyes on photographs of the various scenes. I look at the introductory notes on the director and staff and actors and the names of new actors who left an impression are ingrained on my memory [...] The unifying function of the film pamphlet is as a tool which allows me to chase after the fleeting "cinematic experience" on paper, to try to bring it to my "memory" from which it will not fade.

See Okada Hidenori, *Eiga to iu "buttai X": firumu ākaibu no me de mita eiga* (Tokyo: Rittōsha, 2016), p. 214.

[14] Jacky Bratton, *New Readings in Theatre History* (Cambridge: Cambridge University Press, 2003), p. 37.

following year. And in 1894, Japan would engage in the first of what would turn out to be a series of wars of imperial expansion that would last half a century.

Although this larger political history forms the backdrop to kabuki's nineteenth century, as a reading of Nakazō's *Self Praise* suggests, the extent to which these changes affected the theater directly is uneven, and the larger implications of these decades were, in many cases, little understood by those who lived through the events. Indeed, if one were to write an account of the Meiji Restoration from Nakazō's perspective, it would hardly seem an especially significant time: from the 1850s through the early 1870s, the theater world continued to operate as it long had.

It was not until the mid-1870s that kabuki would be directly impacted by the trends of modernization. In this respect, one of the last entries of *Self Praise*, where Nakazō describes the opening of the newly built Morita-za in 1872, is striking: "The crest is copper plated and the roofing in front and back is tiled; in the center is brick and the walls are of white plaster with a skirt of namako running around the bottom half."[15] The Morita-za was the first of Edo's three licensed theaters to relocate from the walled theater district of Saruwaka-chō on the city's northeast edge. The location of the new Morita-za in Shintomi-chō was only a few blocks from its original home in Kobiki-chō, where it had been located until the 1840s. But Shintomi-chō was also located halfway between the Tsukiji Foreign Settlement in Akashi-chō and Ginza, which, beginning the following year in 1873, would become a symbol of Tokyo's modernization with a design centered around brick buildings and gas lamps. Although Nakazō lived until 1886 and was active on the stage until shortly before his death, what has survived of his account of this period ends rather abruptly in 1873, and we do not know what, if anything, he wrote about the changes within the theater world that occurred over the following decade.

Looking backward from the turbulent decades that mark the end of the nineteenth century, the first half of the century often seems a time of stasis, the endpoint of a period that stretches back indefinitely into the eighteenth century and before, part of the long "Pax Tokugawa" that covers two-and-a-half centuries. What, we might ask, suggests the opening of—a starting point for—a specifically nineteenth-century history of the intersection of stage and print when the history of both kabuki and of commercial publishing in Japan reach back to the early seventeenth century and have been deeply intertwined ever since? My own aim is not to write an outline of this longer history but to point toward a specific moment near the turn of the nineteenth century when a new set of relationships emerges between kabuki theater and its life in print.[16] This is a story about kabuki but also a story about the nineteenth century told from the vantage point of that intersection. The

---

[15] Nakamura Nakazō III, *Temae miso*, p. 383.
[16] The most extensive treatment of this broader subject is Akama Ryō, *Zusetsu Edo no engekisho: Kabuki hen* (Tokyo: Yagi Shoten, 2003).

new relationship that emerges in these years is not defined primarily by the emergence of new forms of print, although this is part of the story; rather, what reading the work of early nineteenth-century writers suggests is that the period beginning around 1800 is very much marked by new apprehensions of kabuki in relation to a set of anxieties about the nature of a society defined by the increasing commercialization, and availability, of print. What is of interest, then, is how contemporaries made sense of their own world and did so by looking at the theater as a model of the world—an idea familiar to any reader of Shakespeare but one that has a long history in East Asian thought as well.

While the culture of late eighteenth-century Japan has often been understood through the prism of the ludic, exemplified by genres of playful writing (*gesaku*) and an intense interest in the idea (or ideal) of the floating world (*ukiyo*) as a space apart from everyday reality, what we see in texts beginning in the early nineteenth century is rather a turn toward the everyday as a subject to be recorded, studied, and understood.[17] It is in this sense, too, that Nakamura Nakazō's *Self Praise* represents kabuki's nineteenth century.

An additional perspective on kabuki's nineteenth century can be found by returning to Naitō Meisetsu's memoir. After his mother's death, Meisetsu's father remarried and "because my stepmother was also from the countryside, [my father] thought she too should at least once see the kabuki so the year she married my father, when I was six, she was taken to the Kawarazaki-za in Saruwaka-chō's Ni-Chōme."[18] As souvenirs from the play she attended, Meisetsu's step-mother brought home a printed playbill and an *ōmuseki*, a booklet containing extracts of the play with a cover adorned by the likenesses of the star actors. Meisetsu himself was later taken to the theater as part of a larger family outing, and from there would come a lifelong love of kabuki. The Naitō household would soon move back to Shikoku, and this would be the only time that the family would visit the theater district. "Even though we only went this once in a decade to the grand kabuki the family was happy [...] for it was no easy thing to attend one of the great theaters."[19]

In contrast to this singular experience, Meisetsu writes that "when it came to the small theaters (*koshibai*), my grandmother would occasionally go and take me along."[20] These "small theaters" operated in shrine and temple precincts and in open spaces around the city and often staged kabuki plays although they were

---

[17] There is an extensive literature on this subject in English. In the field of literature, see Adam Kern, *Manga of the Floating World: Comic Book Culture and the Kibyōshi of Edo Japan* (Cambridge, MA: Harvard University Press, 2006); in art history, see Timon Screech, *Sex and the Floating World: Erotic Images in Japan 1700–1820* (Honolulu: University of Hawai'i Press, 1999) and *Tokyo before Tokyo: Power and Magic in the Shogun's City of Edo* (London: Reaktion Books, 2020); in intellectual history see Katsuya Hirano, *The Politics of Dialogic Imagination: Power and Popular Culture in Early Modern Japan* (Chicago, IL: University of Chicago Press, 2013).
[18] Naitō Meisetsu, *Meisetsu jijoden*, pp. 10–11.
[19] Naitō Meisetsu, *Meisetsu jijoden*, p. 13.
[20] Naitō Meisetsu, *Meisetsu jijoden*, p. 13.

not licensed to do so.[21] "Whereas having watched the grand kabuki was a point of pride," Meisetsu writes, the performances at these smaller theaters "were nothing to be proud of so people would go discretely."[22] Meisetsu's memoir is an important reminder both of the varied nature of performance and theatergoing in the nineteenth century and of the singularity of the grand kabuki. This singularity was, in some sense, as Meisetsu's autobiography makes clear, about "the experience of experience itself"; it was also about the ways that this experience came, through various printed objects, to a life beyond the theater.[23]

We find in Meisetsu's memoir another important element of the nineteenth-century stage: the life of the theater outside of the metropolis of Edo. Meisetsu writes, for example, both of watching New Year's plays staged after moving back to Matsuyama on the island of Shikoku ("how silly they seemed for someone used to the plays of Edo") and of attending a kabuki performance at the Minami-za in Kyoto ("It was, after Saruwaka-chō, my second time to watch the grand kabuki").[24] For his part, as an actor who never achieved real stardom and whose finances were always precarious, Nakamura Nakazō III spent much of his life on the road, often playing in provincial playhouses and makeshift theaters as well as plying the more traveled route between the two large urban centers of Edo and Osaka. Throughout the early modern period, the theatrical cultures of Edo and the Kamigata region of Kyoto and Osaka were overlapping—with actors traveling back and forth in both directions—but distinct.

I have outlined this varied landscape of performance because it helps to delineate my own interests and to frame the subject of my book, which is very much preoccupied with the theater culture of the city of Edo and with the ways that this culture had a life in print that often extended beyond the city's borders. In the end, this book is not about the plays, or the actors, or the stage but about the ways in which the theater took on a social life on the page: how it was imagined and written about, documented and preserved. I have not written a continuous or evenly paced history of the theater in this period, but, guided by the intersection of the theater and print in the nineteenth century, I have sought to understand why such a large and varied archive of printed theater ephemera was produced, how it was consumed, and what it meant. As I worked on these questions, new ones arose: how was this material collected and preserved in the twentieth century and why? How did it relate to new institutions like the university, the library, and the museum? How have new technologies—from photography and film in the

---

[21] See Satō Katsura, *Kabuki no bakumatsu/Meiji: koshibai no jidai* (Tokyo: Perikansha, 2010), esp. pp. 9–10. For a discussion of the terms *koshibai* and *ōshibai* (which I am here translating as "grand kabuki"), see Samuel Leiter ed., *A New Kabuki Encyclopedia* (Westport, CT: Greenwood Press, 1997), pp. 354–55.
[22] Naitō Meisetsu, *Meisetsu jijoden*, p. 14.
[23] See Joseph Roach, *It* (Ann Arbor, MI: University of Michigan Press, 2007), p. 29.
[24] Naitō Meisetsu, *Meisetsu jijoden*, pp. 69, 78.

late nineteenth century to the digital media of today—played a role in preserving and making accessible this material? And what do these changes mean for our relationship with the theatrical past?

Nakazō's memoir is emblematic: had this singular work not been serialized in the 1880s in the new medium of the magazine, it would have been lost forever.[25] But even in the case of printed objects, much of our access to the materials that allow us to understand kabuki's history in the nineteenth century is due to the work of various figures—some well-known, others not—who played a role in collecting and preserving, studying and editing this material. Perhaps working with ephemera makes the historian more conscious of the fragility and contingency of the archive, but as I worked through the various materials central to this study, ranging from playbills and historical chronologies, to maps, to portraits of authorship, to images of actors, I found myself asking questions of how the material itself has come down to us in the present. I will return to these questions throughout the body of this book, but the role of one individual, Tsubouchi Shōyō (1859–1935), in the process of kabuki's archiving, and hence his role in this book, is worth noting and here explaining.

One of the central repositories for theater ephemera in Japan is the Tsubouchi Memorial Theater Museum at Waseda University. The Museum, which opened in 1928, was conceived of by Shōyō. Today, Shōyō is best remembered for his 1885 essay on the "essence of the novel," a key document to introducing Western literary concepts to a generation of Japanese writers, but during his own lifetime, Shōyō was better known as a playwright, critic, and historian of theater. As a historian of early modern drama, Shōyō's output was enormous and catholic, and his influence on the academic study of kabuki in Japan has been immense. In my own research on nineteenth-century ephemera, I found myself coming across, and reading, Shōyō's writing at various points. At first, these encounters seemed to me almost historical curiosities. But as I continued to read Shōyō's writing on nineteenth-century kabuki, a rather more complex picture of his work emerged. I was struck by the extraordinary intelligence of many of his insights and also by a canniness, his interest in a wide variety of topics and their continuing importance to, and interest for, historians of theater and performance studies even as many of Shōyō's essays suffer from various kinds of methodological naivete and confusion, partly due to his reliance on Western methodologies which are themselves quite dated.

As I continued to write and revise this book, Shōyō's presence began to loom larger, and I felt it important to address his role—as critic, scholar, historian, and collector. I have chosen to do so by using Shōyō's work as a framing device for Chapters 2–5, beginning each chapter with a reflection on that work as a way to

---

[25] On the broader role of magazines and modern print media in the history of late nineteenth-century kabuki see Yanai Kenji, *Meiji no kabuki to shuppan media* (Tokyo: Perikansha, 2011).

frame questions that became central to this study. But before turning to these materials, I would like to offer a view of how these kinds of printed representations of the stage circulated beyond the city of Edo and are to be found, even to this day, in the private library of the descendants of a young woman who collected theater ephemera deep in the Kiso Valley.

# 1
# A View from the Provinces

## I A Provincial Collector

> Everything here in this mountain village was behind the times when compared with the neighboring province. Even the spring that came into the Kiso valley from the west each year, bringing out the buds on the zelkova along the river banks, took a full month to penetrate the hinterlands. Everything was late in arriving here.
> —Shimazaki Tōson, *Before the Dawn* (1929–35)

This is a book about the intersection of theater and print culture in nineteenth-century Edo, the forerunner of modern Tokyo. It is, therefore, very much a study of metropolitan culture, but like many intellectual projects, *Kabuki's Nineteenth Century* began elsewhere than where it ends. What first drew my attention to the relationship between stage and print in nineteenth-century Japan was the catalogue of a family's books collected over the nineteenth century in the provincial town of Tsumago in the Kiso Valley, in present-day Nagano Prefecture. And it is with a view from the provinces afforded by this catalogue that I would like to begin.[1]

In the nineteenth century, Tsumago was a post town along the Nakasendō, one of the two main highways that linked the shogun's capital of Edo in the East with the commercial city of Osaka and the imperial capital of Kyoto in the West.[2] For many readers, the image of the Kiso Valley is likely to be linked to the life and work of the great twentieth-century novelist Shimazaki Tōson, and especially to his epic novel *Before the Dawn* (*Yoake mae*), published between 1929 and 1935, much of which is set in the valley where Tōson himself was born and grew up. Tōson's novel chronicles the intellectual, social, and political transformations that occurred across the second half of the nineteenth century, from the coming of Perry's black ships in 1853 through the Meiji Restoration of 1868 and beyond.[3]

---

[1] See Suzuki Toshiyuki, ed., *Kinsei kōki ni okeru shoseki/sōshi nado no shuppan/ryūtsu/kyōju ni tsuite no kenkyū: Kiso Tsumago Hayashike zōsho oyobi Kiso Uematsu Rinsenji shozō hangi no chōsa o chūshin ni* (Hachiōji: Chūō Daigaku Bungakubu, 3833 Kenkyūshitsu, 1996).

[2] In this sense, as Kären Wigen has argued, the broader Shinshū region that encompassed Tsumago was provincial but hardly peripheral to the geography of early modern Japan. See Kären Wigen, *The Making of a Japanese Periphery, 1750–1920* (Berkeley, CA: University of California Press, 1995).

[3] Shimazaki Tōson, *Before the Dawn*, 1988.

Part of what drives the tragic narrative of *Before the Dawn* is the sense of the Valley's isolation and its "lateness" as the novel's protagonist, Aoyama Hanzō, struggles to catch up with the changes sweeping across Japan in the wake of the coming of the West.[4] But what is so striking about the view provided by the catalogue of the Hayashi library is not how it seems to represent a kind of cultural backwardness and distance from Edo but almost the opposite: it is a world into which the culture—and especially the literary and theatrical culture—of Japan's great metropolis appears to have flowed with regularity and very little impediment or delay. This culture arrives in the form of books and other printed matter.

The library of the Hayashi household, catalogued in the early 1990s by a team of researchers lead by Suzuki Toshiyuki, contains roughly 500 early modern, block-printed titles. While much is unknown about their exact provenance, the books in the library date largely from the nineteenth century and the bulk of the collection is thought to have belonged to Hayashi Kuni, the daughter of the village headman, and to her husband, who was adopted into the Hayashi family as the heir to Kuni's father.[5] The Hayashi family was designated as the auxiliary *honjin* of the region around Tsumago and Magome, a role which encompassed providing lodging for samurai and government officials who passed through the region. We know very little about Kuni's life, including her dates, though she bore a son, Hayashi Kamejurō, in 1872.[6]

The range of books in this collection is quite broad: there are a handful of Chinese classics; one book each on Buddhism and Shintō; a six-volume collection by Nakazawa Dōni (1725–1803), the popularizer of the syncretic school of Shingaku; guidebooks; and manuals for such hobbies as calligraphy, tea, and gardening. But the vast majority of the books in the library belong to what Suzuki calls books for "leisure," novels and plays.[7]

When I first encountered the catalogue of the Hayashi library, I was working on the history of fiction in nineteenth-century Japan, but I was immediately struck by what the library might tell us of the theatrical culture of the period. Indeed, the library is filled with theatrical material. One of the most prominent aspects of the theatrical works in the collection is the image they present of a dualistic structure of the circulation of the theater beyond the stage, and beyond the city,

---

[4] On this point, see Michael Bourdaghs: "[*Before the Dawn*] [...] becomes the tragedy of a man who is unable to make the transition to the new form of temporality required by the modern nation state." Michael Bourdaghs, *The Dawn That Never Comes: Shimazaki Tōson and Japanese Nationalism* (New York: Columbia University Press, 2003), p. 164.

[5] See Suzuki Toshiyuki, *Kinsei kōki ni okeru shoseki/sōshi nado no shuppan/ryūtsu/kyōju ni tsuite no kenkyū*, p. 107.

[6] There is a brief description of the Hayashi family in William E. Naff, *The Kiso Road: The Life and Times of Shimazaki Tōson*, ed. J. Thomas Rimer (Honolulu: University of Hawai'i Press, 2010), p. 601. As both Suzuki Toshiyuki and Naff note, Kuni's son married Ōwaki Yū, who was immortalized in Shimazaki Tōson's 1897 poem "First Love" ("Hatsu koi").

[7] Suzuki Toshiyuki, *Kinsei kōki ni okeru shoseki/sōshi nado no shuppan/ryūtsu/kyōju ni tsuite no kenkyū*, p. 105; see also p. 14.

in nineteenth-century Japan. On the one hand, there is a large number of scripts from the puppet theater of jōruri—both entire plays (*maruhon*) and one-scene excerpts (*nukihon*)—all but one of which were printed and published.[8] On the other hand, there are only two kabuki scripts, both of which were hand-copied. In place of scripts, however, the library contains a large collection of printed playbills, forty-two in all, from kabuki performances ranging across the Meiji Restoration from 1848 to 1874, suggesting a striking continuity across this important political divide.[9]

Here, we see one of the most Important features of the production, circulation, and consumption of drama in early modern Japan defined by a contrast between the two major theatrical forms of the period, jōruri and kabuki. While the libretti of both the nō and puppet theaters were printed or published, the scripts of kabuki circulated only in manuscript—and not very widely—until the end of the nineteenth century.[10] But as the collection of playbills hints, in contrast to this manuscript culture defined in many ways by privileged, often secret, hereditary knowledge, the world of the kabuki stage was in almost every other way dominated, even defined, by print. From the nineteenth century alone, there exist thousands of actor prints, actor critiques, illustrated playbills, and synopses; maps and guides of the theater district; and calendars, lists of salaries, rankings of actors, theatrical genealogies, and a whole array of ephemera privately commissioned and printed by fan clubs.

The archives of this material form the subject of this book and my aim is to explore what this material can tell us about not only the theater of nineteenth-century Japan but also the ways in which the culture of Edo during this period can be understood as a set of reflections (sometimes self-conscious, sometimes not) on the nature of a world defined by print. Just as the Hayashi library provides a useful way of thinking about the intersection of stage and print in nineteenth-century Japan, so too does that intersection provide a window onto a larger dynamic often manifesting itself as an anxiety over print as a mode of reproduction and dissemination, and over the relationship between print and the structures of intellectual and artistic life. That so often during this period the world was imagined as a stage and the stage as the world (a subject to which I will return in Chapter 3)

---

[8] The exception to this is a one-act excerpt of the play *Vengence at Iga Pass* (*Igagoe dōchū sugoroku*) by Chikamatsu Hanji, which premiered at the Takemotoza in Osaka in 1783. The Hayashi library holds excerpts of the two most famous scenes of the play: Act Six, "The Numazu Scene," is hand-copied from a published version while Act Eight, "The Okazaki Scene," is printed. For a translation of this play, see Stanleigh Jones, *The Bunraku Puppet Theatre of Japan: Honor, Vengence, and Love in Four Plays of the 18th and 19th Centuries* (Honolulu: University of Hawai'i Press, 2013), pp. 76–235.

[9] Suzuki Toshiyuki, *Kinsei kōki ni okeru shoseki/sōshi nado no shuppan/ryūtsu/kyōju ni tsuite no kenkyū*, p. 110.

[10] The Hayashi collection contains only one nō text, a 1685 five-volume edition of the Kanze School's *Utaibon hyakuban* (*One Hundred Nō Libretti*) preserved in a paulownia box. On the circulation of nō texts in the Edo period, see Eric C. Rath, *The Ethos of Noh: Actors and Their Art* (Cambridge, MA: Harvard University Asia Center, 2004), pp. 195ff.

is suggestive of the ways in which the theater of Edo partook in a larger discourse about the nature of social experience in nineteenth-century Japan.

In the past quarter-century, the printed archives of kabuki have re-emerged in two critical, and interrelated, ways. The first is that, through the process of digitization, these materials have become more available, literally more visible, than they had been since they first circulated in the nineteenth century. We now have the ability to call up, often with just a few strokes on the keyboard, vast quantities of images (actor prints, playbills, guidebooks, and so forth) that until quite recently were largely confined to specialist libraries or available only through modern editions. The origins of this work of digitization go back to 1993, when Akama Ryō began designing a database for the theater prints of the Tsubouchi Memorial Theater Museum at Waseda University, a project which has radically transformed the access that historians enjoy to the printed past of Japanese theater.[11] In this book's Epilogue, I will return to some of the implications that this work has had for scholarship in our digital age.

Simultaneously, scholars began turning to this material to write a new kind of theater history. In 1986, Hattori Yukio wrote a groundbreaking book which used theater ephemera to examine the history of theatrical spaces and of the audience.[12] In 1994, Timothy Clark published a remarkable essay on "Edo Kabuki in the 1780s," which used a variety of forms of printed ephemera (as well as manuscript sources such as diaries) to create a microhistory of a particular performance.[13] And in 1998, Akama edited a volume on the "various facets" of kabuki's culture which contained not only his own extensive essays on theatrical ephemera but also pioneering work on audience and reception.[14] More recently, scholars like Andrew Gerstle and Kaguraoka Yōko have used this printed register to uncover as yet little understood facets of the theatrical past from the culture of celebrity and fandom to questions of audience and reception, and Satoko Shimazaki has deftly deployed many of these materials in her study of *Edo Kabuki in Transition*.[15] This work has brought to the fore the various ways in which theatrical ephemera can be historicized and can inform the larger history of kabuki across the early modern period.

If the Hayashi library provides a useful vantage point for re-engaging with this material, it does so through a subtle shift in perspective: by locating consumption

---

[11] Akama Ryō and Kaneko Takaaki, "Ukiyo-e dejitaru ākaibu no genzai," *Jōhō shorigakkai kenkyū hōkoku* 78 (May 2008), 37–44.

[12] Hattori Yukio, *Ōinaru koya: Edo kabuki no shukusai kūkan* (Tokyo: Kōdansha, 2012).

[13] Timothy Clark, "Edo Kabuki in the 1780s," in *The Actor's Image: Print Makers of the Katsukawa School*, ed. Timothy Clark (Chicago, IL: Art Institute of Chicago, 1994), pp. 27–48.

[14] Akama Ryō, ed., *Kabuki bunka no shosō*, vol. 4 of Iwanami Kōza Kabuki/Bunraku (Tokyo: Iawnami Shoten, 1998).

[15] C. Andrew Gerstle, "Kabuki Culture and Collective Creativity" in *Kabuki Heroes on the Osaka Stage, 1780–1830*, ed. C. Andrew Gerstle (Honolulu: University of Hawai'i Press, 2005) 10–19; Kaguraoka Yōko, *Kabuki bunka no kyōju to tenkai: kankyaku to gekijō no naigai* (Tokyo: Yagi Shoten, 2002); Satoko Shimazaki, *Edo Kabuki in Transition: From the Worlds of the Samurai to the Vengeful Female Ghost* (New York: Columbia University Press, 2016).

outside the metropolis, it highlights the centrality of the printed object to the process of consumption and so, simultaneously, helps to bring forward the printed archive as an object of historical analysis.

As the work of the book historian Nagatomo Chiyoji has shown, the libretti of the jōruri puppet theater circulated widely in early modern Japan as reading material somewhat akin to fiction, and they occupied an important place in the holdings of commercial lending libraries during the nineteenth century.[16] These texts were also used by amateurs, who took up jōruri chanting as a hobby, and the physical condition of these jōruri scripts held in the Hayashi library suggests that they were likely used in this way.[17]

Playbills, by contrast, are objects of a form of attention that is defined not by *use*—for reading, for practice—but almost the opposite. "Freed from the drudgery of being useful," to recall Walter Benjamin, the playbills become objects of a kind of cathexis, proxies for the "feeling-labours" of the stage, talismans of the "secular magic" of the actor as celebrity, traces of the dreamed-of metropolis, tokens of another world, unfolding elsewhere.[18] Indeed, one of the most striking aspects of this collection is that the playbills appear to function entirely as a surrogates for the plays with no indication that anyone in the household had attended the theaters in Edo.[19]

There are other interesting ways in which these two groups of theatrical texts can be counterpointed. All of the playbills date from between 1848 and 1874, and all are for performances in the city of Edo (rather than from the theaters of the much closer castle town of Nagoya or from Osaka or Kyoto, which were roughly equidistant to Edo to the west).[20] The majority of the jōruri texts, by contrast, date from the mid-to-late eighteenth century (the 1740s through the mid-1780s) and most were published in Osaka. Part of what is reflected here is the likely provenance of the collection[21] and part the shift of the relative importance from Osaka

---

[16] Nagatomo Chiyoji has written extensively on the publishing and circulation of jōruri texts in the early modern period. See Nagatomo Chiyoji, *Kinsei Kamigata jōruribon shuppan no kenkyū* (Tokyo: Tōkyōdō Shuppan, 1999); Nagatomo Chiyoji, *Edo jidai no shomotsu to dokusho* (Tokyo: Tōkyōdō Shuppan, 2001).

[17] Suzuki Toshiyuki, *Kinsei kōki ni okeru shoseki/sōshi nado no shuppan/ryūtsu/kyōju ni tsuite no kenkyū*, p. 14.

[18] See Walter Benjamin, *The Arcades Project*, trans. Howard Eiland and Kevin McLaughlin (Cambridge, MA: Belknap Press, 2002), p. 9. On the "feeling-labours" of theater, see Erin Hurley, *Theatre and Feeling* (New York: Palgrave, 2010). On the "secular magic" of celebrity, see Joseph Roach, *It*, (Ann Arbor MI: University of Michigan Press, 2007). On celebrity and fan culture in eighteenth- and nineteenth-century Japan, see Gerstle, "Kabuki and Collective Creativity" and Yōko Kaguraoka, "Osaka Kabuki Fan Clubs and Their Obsessions," in *Kabuki Heroes on the Osaka Stage, 1780–1830*, ed. C. Andrew Gerstle (Honolulu: University of Hawai'i Press, 2005) 30–35.

[19] On this point, see Suzuki Toshiyuki, *Kinsei kōki ni okeru shoseki/sōshi nado no shuppan/ryūtsu/kyōju ni tsuite no kenkyū*, p. 110.

[20] Suzuki Toshiyuki, *Kinsei kōki ni okeru shoseki/sōshi nado no shuppan/ryūtsu/kyōju ni tsuite no kenkyū*, p. 110. While it is unclear how the playbills were procured, Suzuki notes that "It is difficult to imagine that someone in the Hayashi household traveled frequently to Edo to attend the theater."

[21] Suzuki has suggested that it is likely that the jōruri texts were originally a separate collection brought to the Hayashi house by Kuni's husband, Rokuzaemon XXIII, when he was adopted. Five

to Edo as a center for publishing and book production—and, more broadly, as a center for cultural production—as well as the relative decline of the puppet theater and the emergence of kabuki as the main theatrical genre of the nineteenth century. But the character of the collection also points to an important shift in the ways in which print provided access to theatrical culture, a shift that defines kabuki in the nineteenth century: one could read a script of a puppet play as it was performed in the theater by a chanter, but outside of the theater, kabuki could only be consumed in its constituent parts: through playbills and printed ephemera, actor critiques, actor prints, and illustrated novels. And yet, whether because of or despite this seeming fragmentation of the kabuki stage, the world of kabuki was ubiquitous and much more widely available to a broad public in print than jōruri had ever been.

Whether as scripts of the puppet theater or as playbills of kabuki, what all of this printed material asks of the historian is to consider the fundamental question of the nature of the theatrical archive. This question has gained a new urgency in recent years as emerging methodologies—performance studies on the one hand, book history on the other—have put a renewed pressure on the always-vexed relationship between performance and its record, between repertoire and archive. On the one hand, the skepticism of—even hostility toward—the archive that has characterized much work in performance studies is derived from a consciousness of the very ephemerality of the performance. "Performance's only life is in the present," Peggy Phelan wrote almost a quarter of a century ago. "Performance cannot be saved, recorded, documented, or otherwise participate in the circulation of representations *of* representations: once it does so, it becomes something other than performance."[22]

But we might also imagine that this "other than performance" constitutes a historical subject in its own right, and this is the subject of *Kabuki's Nineteenth Century*. Indeed, the nature of this other—it's ontology—is one of the central questions of this book. For, to the extent that this material is seen as or primarily "documentary," then its being is always marked by a constituent lack: the failure to capture that which cannot be saved, ephemera as the failed document of ephemerality. But if we take seriously ephemera's status as *other-than-performance*, as ephemerality's other, then we can begin to dislodge the impulse—the desire—to see this material as primarily *about* performance, a record or a document of that which has always already vanished and thus is always marked by a constitutive lack or failure.

Book history, for its part, has also taken up the problem of how print provides an afterlife to dramatic works that are, as performance, ephemeral by their very

---

of these books bear markings that they belonged to the Furuse household, the family from which Rokuzaemon XXIII was adopted. See Suzuki Toshiyuki, *Kinsei kōki ni okeru shoseki/sōshi nado no shuppan/ryūtsu/kyōju ni tsuite no kenkyū*, pp. 109–10.

[22] Peggy Phelan, *Unmarked: The Politics of Performance* (London: Routledge, 2003), p. 146.

nature. David Kastan, for example, has described the way that Shakespeare is "preserved" in print. "It is not an entirely happy metaphor," Kastan concedes; "Living beings are preferable to mummies, and print, in any case, does not preserve language as firmly as formaldehyde preserves bodies. Nonetheless, without print there is no Shakespeare for all time."[23] Kastan's point is that "'Shakespeare,' in any meaningful sense other than the biographical, is—has always been—a synecdoche for the involved mediations of the playhouse and the printing house through which he is produced."[24] My own interest, the print culture of nineteenth-century kabuki, is somewhat different: what we have left are not the plays—which were, in general, not printed and published until the late nineteenth and early twentieth centuries and now survive, if at all, often as fragmentary manuscripts—but an enormous amount of printed theater ephemera, playbills and broadsheets, actor prints and rankings, lists of salaries, illustrated novels, and so forth. For much of the twentieth century, this material was collected and preserved and was treated precisely as a form of *documentary* evidence of performance; that is to say, this material was considered as primarily indexical, always pointing elsewhere to the ever-vanishing performance of which it seems some kind of a material remainder.

The playbill provides a particularly useful point of entry into this archive. As Jacky Bratton has argued, traditionally the playbill has been "the solid, comfortable, substantive stuff of theater history [. . .] extracted and calendared, charted and published." And yet they have remained "really a very unimaginatively used resource":

> [I]n the playbill we have not only evidence for what was performed by whom and when, but also for those most difficult and evanescent aspects of theatre history— the expectations and dispositions of the audience, their personal experience of the theater. The important thing from this point of view, though, is *not* to seek for particular names and count productions of individual plays: it is to read the bill whole, and understand that every element on it is a signifier which, like all signifiers, has meaning only as part of a system of relationships.[25]

Much the same can, of course, be said for other forms of theater ephemera. This material *can* tell us a great deal about particular performances in the past but, as Bratton notes, it can also lead to a new approach to historicizing theater, one focused less on what occurs on stage and more on the relationship among printed objects and between such ephemera and their users.[26]

---

[23] David Scott Kastan, *Shakespeare and the Book* (Cambridge: Cambridge University Press, 2001), p. 15.
[24] Kastan, *Shakespeare and the Book*, p. 16.
[25] Jacky Bratton, *New Readings in Theatre History* (Cambridge: Cambridge University Press, 2003), pp. 39–40.
[26] Bratton, *New Readings in Theatre History*, p. 37.

The philosopher Henri Gouhier has suggested that a dual temporality is fundamental to theater as art—theater, that is, is of two moments, the moment of composition and the moment of performance.[27] But we might add a third moment, or really a series of moments that extend indefinitely into the future, that relate in complex ways to the moments of composition and performance: the circulation of the theater in print. It is this third moment that I take as my subject and, indeed, part of what I hope to show in this study is that ephemera need to be thought of as something more than, and more complicated than, a failed record of the ephemerality of performance. Nor, it is important to stress, are the most interesting questions we can ask of these documents necessarily related to performance at all; rather, as a particular kind of trace, these fragile objects lead us back to a complex social world in which they performed various functions: bought and sold, given and received, collected and displayed, cut up and reordered. The printed record of the theater is a record of social life as it was constituted by, through, and about ephemeral objects. What would we see, we might ask, if we used this material not to document the elusive and chimerical history of performance but to document the way in which the theater itself was documented, consumed, collected, and archived in print across the nineteenth century?

My hope is that the view provided by the Hayashi library allows us to formulate some initial questions; to answer them, we must follow the route of these printed objects back to the city in order to understand something of the world that gave birth to them.

## II  The Shogun's Printed City

At one level, the Hayashi library seems to suggest a disjuncture between the consumption of the urban theater in the provinces—always, and inevitably mediated by print—and its consumption in the city of Edo itself. A counterpoint to the provincial fan (always at a remove from the performance, which transpires elsewhere, in the city) is thus implicit: the theatergoer of Edo, whose experience of kabuki in the metropolis is unmediated and hence authentic.

And yet Shikitei Sanba's 1806 *Theater Chic This Side of the Curtain* (*Kejō suigen maku no soto*) provides an interesting contrast to the view from the provinces offered by the Hayashi library. This work of comic fiction, which presents a satire of theatergoing in Edo, opens with a group of provincial travelers, led by the suggestively named Inakamono Tarōzaemon, venturing into the city of Edo on their way to the theater district.[28] If the Hayashi library serves as a way of thinking about

---

[27] Henri Gouhier, *Le Théâtre et Les Arts À Deux Temps* (Paris: Flammarion, 1989).
[28] "Inakamono" means country bumpkin.

the consumption of the theater in the provinces, *Theater Chic This Side of the Curtain* provides an image of how provincial consumption was figured within the city and, indeed, how the urban experience of the theater was imagined in the early nineteenth century.

Just after the group of travelers has crossed into the city from the East, they stop to puzzle out an actor print posted on the doorway of a restaurant:

> "Grandma," says one of the travelers, "Isn't that Danjūrō, with that red face and small nose?" "It looks like a drunk who has drowned to death," replies Grandma [. . .] "I'll tell you who it is," interjects Tarōzaemon, "It's Segawa Hanshirō, the actor of villain roles."[29]

The humor of this scene turns on the fact that none of the travelers can decipher the print, despite the fact that it was intended to be *legible* as the likeness of a specific actor. The initial joke is that one of the travelers suggests that the actor's small nose belongs to Ichikawa Danjūrō VII, but Danjūrō, like his contemporary Matsumoto Kōshirō V, is always depicted with a rather large nose. And Tarōzaemon, despite the confidence with which he corrects his fellow travelers, appears to be as clueless as anyone, wedding together the names of the two leading actors of female roles of the time, Segawa Kikunojō and Iwai Hanshirō, but interpreting the figure as a player of male villain roles, a mistake compounded by the fact that the red makeup suggests the figure of the hero, not of a villain. It is not just that the print remains illegible to these provincial travelers but that the codes which make interpretation possible are jumbled; as the travelers puzzle over the print, they appear to be moving away from, rather than towards, an understanding of the codes on which interpretation rests.

Here, the role of print in the process of consumption is itself a subject of satire. Print can bring the stage out of the theater, but in doing so, it subjects theatrical culture to the specter of misreading and misunderstanding. As Pierre Bourdieu has written, "consumption is [. . .] a stage in a process of communication, [. . .] an act of deciphering, decoding, which presupposes practical or explicit mastery of a cipher or code";[30] the humor of this scene turns precisely on the breaking down of this process. The humor is leveraged by the fact that it plays on a gap between the (knowledgeable) reader of Sanba's work—who gets the joke—and the country bumpkin, reinforcing a distinction between cultured and non-cultured modes of consumption, a trope that Sanba uses widely in his humor. There is, moreover, an "edge" in the humor of Sanba and his contemporaries which further demarcates social dispositions (among characters in the fiction and among historical readers)

---

[29] Shikitei Sanba, *Ukiyoburo; Kejō suigen maku no soto; Daisen sekai gakuyasagashi*, ed. Satake Akihiro, Shin Nihon Koten Bungaku Taikei, vol. 86 (Tokyo: Iwanami Shoten, 1989), pp. 304–05.

[30] Pierre Bourdieu, *Distinction: A Social Critique of the Judgement of Taste*, trans. Richard Nice (Cambridge, MA: Harvard University Press, 1984), p. 2.

based on the knowledge of cultural and aesthetic codes, a subject to which I will return in Chapter 3.[31]

But beyond a set of cultural distinctions between socially constituted consumers, this passage (and others like it) also points to a different problem and one crucial to understanding the ambivalent position of print in the cultural imagination of the early nineteenth century. Even as the humor turns on a gap in cultural knowledge which seems blithely to reinforce a sense of distinction as cultural superiority, it also raises the specter of the embeddedness, and hence the contingent nature, of all cultural codes. If the act of misreading always presupposes a "proper" reading, it also exposes the fragility of that proper order. This may seem like a given (after all, humor seems always to depend on this kind of doubling), but what I would like to suggest is that this double movement—in which the very thing that creates the humorous situation also provokes an anxiety—creates a paradoxical response on the part of writers in the nineteenth century who play on the misreading of cultural codes, often for comic purposes. These writers also seem to posit a nostalgic desire for an earlier moment in which these codes were not contingent, a moment in which culture presupposes authentic experience.[32] As I will argue in Chapter 2, this impulse often manifests itself through a rejection of print in favor of manuscript, and the theater provides a particularly interesting site where writers explore this problem because it seems to *stage* this very tension: the staging of the play which can only be experienced in its fullness within the confines of the theater and then its representation in print, which always seems inadequate to the task of capturing that which is defined by its disappearance, the very problem of ephemerality to which performance studies would turn in the 1980s.

In the passage from *Theater Chic This Side of the Curtain* quoted above, the dialogue is situated within a larger scene which is immensely rich for thinking about the meanings of the actor's image in nineteenth-century Japan, a subject to which I will turn in Chapter 5. Here, we might note, the first encounter these travelers have with the theater, just as they enter the city, is mediated by a printed image. They come to Edo to view the theater, but what they encounter first is not the theater but a *representation* of the theater in print, not altogether unlike the reader in the provinces. Part of the intelligence of Sanba's work is the way it keeps circling back to the role that printed matter—actor prints, ephemera, theater books—plays in shaping the theatergoing experience even as the playgoer crosses the threshold of the theater itself.

---

[31] I have borrowed the idea of "edge" from Linda Hutcheon's work on irony in which she outlines "the often desperately 'edged'" nature of irony: "it has its targets, its perpetrators, and its complicitous audience, though these need not be three separate and distinct entities." See Linda Hutcheon, *Irony's Edge: The Theory and Politics of Irony* (London: Routledge, 1994), p. 40.

[32] In *A Theory of Parody*, Hutcheon explores the "double voicing" that is often at the heart of the pardodic. See Linda Hutcheon, *A Theory of Parody: The Teachings of Twentieth-Century Art Forms* (Urbana, IL: University of Illinois Press, 2000), esp. pp. 88ff.

Sanba himself was a devoted fan of the theater and his fiction is littered with theatrical themes and subjects. But Sanba was also, perhaps more than any of his contemporaries, a creature of the world of print and of books. In his early twenties, he became a successful author, but Sanba's relationship with print began almost at birth. His father, Kikuchi Mohē, was a woodblock carver who would, later in life, carve blocks for several of his son's works. At the age of eight, Sanba was adopted into the house of the publisher Horinoya; later, he married into another publishing family, the Yorozuya, and even spent some time as a used book dealer.[33] Yet, throughout his writing, Sanba expresses a profound ambivalence towards print and towards the ways in which the culture of writing was being shaped by increased commercialization and by the tastes and desires of new readers, especially by readers in the provinces.[34]

In Sanba's own writing on the theater, we can observe a seemingly paradoxical attitude in which, on the one hand, our experience of the theater is always mediated by print and, on the other hand, print is never fully able to represent the authentic experience of the stage. The scene in Sanba's *Theater Chic This Side of the Curtain* of the provincial playgoers attempting to puzzle out the meaning of an actor print is just one of the book's several scenes in which printed ephemera play an important role in defining the nature of the theatrical experience for theatergoers in the city of Edo. Just before this scene takes place, Sanba begins his account of the "sights" of the theater district of Sakai-chō and Fukiya-chō, by describing how the "first performances of the new year vie with one another on the walls of the barber shop, with the three theaters competing with one another to deliver broadsheets of the acting troupes to the teahouses." The theaters and their actors are embodied here in printed broadsheets and pamphlets. Or, again, when Inakamono and his companions arrive at the theater district, they encounter the public reading of a ranking of actors and their salaries from a printed broadsheet, which the grandfather mistakes for a family register. Even within the theater itself, Sanba describes a vendor selling various playbills and programs along with tea, lunchboxes, sweets, dumplings, and fruit;[35] we also overhear a discussion in which one theatergoer suggests to another that he refer to Sanba's own *Illustrated Dictionary of Theater for Beginners* (*Shibai kinmō zui*), a satirical reference work that the author had published three years earlier.[36]

In the provinces, the theater can only be consumed through its embodiment in print. But as Sanba's travelers make their way into the city of Edo, into the theater district, and even into the theater, the experience of theatergoing continues to be

---

[33] On Sanba's experience as a used bookseller see Tanahashi Masahiro, *Shikitei Sanba: Edo no gesakusha* (Tokyo: Perikansha, 1994), pp. 33–34.
[34] One of Sanba's most interesting articulations of this ambivalence can be found in the preface to *Theater Chic This Side of the Curtain*. See my discussion in Jonathan E. Zwicker, *Practices of the Sentimental Imagination: Melodrama, the Novel, and the Social Imaginary in Nineteenth-Century Japan* (Cambridge, MA: Harvard University Asia Center, 2006), pp. 85ff.
[35] Shikitei Sanba, *Ukiyoburo; Kejō suigen maku no soto; Daisen sekai gakuyasagashi*, p. 331.
[36] Shikitei Sanba, *Ukiyoburo; Kejō suigen maku no soto; Daisen sekai gakuyasagashi*, p. 341.

mediated by printed texts and images. We see something similar in Sanba's 1811, *A Critique of the Audience* (*Kakusha hyōbanki*), which contains an image of a tragic scene (at right) and a romantic scene (at left) in which we see figures with playbills (Figure 1.1). Indeed, in its own way, Sanba's work provides a catalogue of the types of material that I will be treating in this book: illustrated playbills, printed reference works, actor's images, and so forth. But what is most striking about *Theater Chic This Side of the Curtain* is that it leads not inexorably toward the performance itself; rather, as the title "this side of the curtain" suggests, the narrative focuses entirely on what takes place in front of the stage, among the audience. That is to say, there is no description of what actually happens on stage; there is no *there* there. As *readers*, we are continually anticipating but being denied access to the presence of performance.

Despite the proliferation of printed matter (or, as I will suggest in Chapter 2, in part *because* of this very proliferation), a counterpoint emerges in the writing of figures like Sanba: print can never fully capture what takes place on stage and a crucial gap opens between what is posited as the authentic experience of viewing the theater and a mediated consumption of the theater through print. In much of Sanba's writing on the stage, he points directly to the gaps and omissions that inevitably exist in any written treatment of the stage. In one of the best metaphors for understanding this, the printed page serves as a kind of shadow of the performance, like the projection of a magic lantern. In the late eighteenth and early nineteenth centuries, the magic lantern became an important trope in Japanese fiction, a way of thinking about the disjuncture of representation and reality.[37] That subject Sanba himself explored in his 1811 *Shadows of Kabuki Cast by Magic Lantern* (*Sono utsushi-e kabuki no omokage*).

**Figure 1.1** Utagawa Toyokuni, the audience from Shikitei Sanba, *Kakusha hyōbanki*, 1811.
Source: National Diet Library, Tokyo.

---

[37] Timon Screech, *The Lens within the Heart: The Western Scientific Gaze and Popular Imagery in Later Edo Japan* (Honolulu: University of Hawai'i Press, 2002), p. 112.

Roughly halfway through *Shadows of Kabuki*, Sanba disrupts the narrative flow of his work with a static image. The image, designed by Utagawa Toyokuni I, is fascinating and I will return to its meaning in Chapter 5 (see Figure 5.9). For now, I would like to focus on an apostrophe to the reader that appears at the top of the page, where Sanba notes that the page represents "An Image that Shows the Plot by Means of Etoki," etoki being a practice with a history going back to at least the tenth century in which a storyteller uses images (*e*) to explain (*toku*) a story or a Buddhist principle.[38] What is interesting about the way that Sanba uses this conceit is that he spatializes the plot, laying out on the flat page various moments in the narrative, some taking place simultaneously, some sequentially, as a way to explain the relationships among the various strands of the complex story. And while Sanba here invokes the tradition of *etoki*, what the image most closely resembles is the page of an illustrated playbill not unlike those collected by Hayashi Kuni and which Sanba himself avidly collected.

In the accompanying text, Sanba writes that the page represents a kind of suture or stitch, linking together the first and second halves of the narrative by interweaving a series of events that, Sanba claims, could not otherwise be fitted into the book:

> This work of fiction brings together in seven volumes that which ought to be a work of twelve volumes so that there are too many plot developments and not words enough. As this work is based on the plot of a kabuki play, it is quite intricate and wholly impossible to fit onto thirty-five sheets of paper and there are many places where I have had to stitch things together.[39]

The story's larger plot revolves around the work of light and shadows and how the casting of a magic lantern-like light exposes the doppelganger existence lurking within certain characters. But the magic lantern also becomes a metaphor for the written work in relation to the performance. As the title *Shadows of Kabuki Cast by Magic Lantern* suggests, the work also thinks, at some moments quite self-consciously, about the role of print as a kind of shadow cast by the play.

At one level, Sanba's work highlights the disjuncture between what transpires on stage and the capacity of print to capture performance and to preserve it. And yet, as a trope in nineteenth-century Japanese fiction, the magic lantern also serves an important function: often (and in Sanba's *Shadows of Kabuki* as well) it is the shadow cast by the magic lantern that exposes the "real" rather than that which is merely visible to the naked eye. The printed page is thus an inadequate medium for preserving performance, and yet the text suggests a different possibility: that the shadow cast by the performance is, in some ways, more real than the performance

---

[38] For an extended examination of the history and practices of *etoki*, see Ikumi Kaminishi, *Explaining Pictures: Buddhist Propaganda and Etoki Storytelling in Japan* (Honolulu: University of Hawai'i Press, 2006).

[39] Shikitei Sanba, *Sono utsushi-e kabuki no omokage* (Edo: Igaya Kanemon, 1811), 16r.

itself. Indeed, at the beginning of his preface, when Sanba urges his reader to "Take this novel in hand; its plot is that of a well written kabuki script," he seems—self-consciously—to be pointing to the printed book as a material object which can be grasped in hand and, as he notes in the preface, can be read and reread.[40]

But while Sanba invokes, and on more than one occasion, the idea that his book is an adaptation of a kabuki play, the relationship between the play and this work of illustrated fiction is far from straightforward. One of the most interesting things about Sanba's complaint, here, is that it seems intentionally misleading. Although *Shadows of Kabuki* is ostensibly based on the play *Latter-Day Reflections of the Sumida River* (*Sumidagawa gonichi no omokage*), which had been staged the previous year at the Morita Theater, Sanba's work actually seems to *add* quite a bit of material that does not appear in any of the surviving prints or playbills related to the 1810 staging. For example, there is the character of Kurikara no Kengorō, a warrior who slays the villains Kodama Hangan and Hōkaibō, recovers the famed carp scroll, and helps vanquish the possessed spirit of the priest. In *Shadows of Kabuki*, he is a central character—really *the* central character—and is depicted using the likeness of Matsumoto Kōshirō V, one of the great actors of the day, who was easily identifiable by his hooked nose. But this character does not appear in the play, nor was Kōshirō involved in the 1810 production; he was contracted that year to the rival Ichimura-za, where he played the outlaw Ishikawa Goemon during the spring staging of the play *The Temple Gate and the Paulownia Crest* (*Sanmon gosan no kiri*).

What, then, are we to make of Sanba's play of light and shadow, of a title that makes central a claim about the ontology of print and performance that has otherwise only an oblique connection to the work itself? Or of the apparent ambivalence located in Sanba's apostrophe to the reader that his own work is a kind of shadow cast by the stage but one that, perhaps, is more real than the performance on which it is based? It is tempting to imagine that Sanba saw in this play of shadows something like an ontology of the simulacrum, an intuition that the shadows are themselves real and that the hunt for the real is always chimerical. But there is also, in Sanba's work, a recurrent mourning for a lost authenticity, a subject to which I will return in the chapters that follow.

Nor, we might imagine, is it an accident that it was through the subject of shadows and ghosts that Sanba explored these questions. Historically, the ghost would be a central presence on the nineteenth-century stage.[41] But in this theme, Sanba seems also to have grasped something quite central to the theater as a particular kind of cultural form that has long played with a "ghostly quality," a sense of recurrence and return.[42] What Sanba seems to have understood is that if the

---

[40] Shikitei Sanba, *Sono utsushi-e kabuki no omokage*, 1v.
[41] See Satoko Shimazaki, *Edo Kabuki in Transition*, esp. pp. 150–93.
[42] See Marvin Carlson, *The Haunted Stage: The Theater as Memory Machine* (Ann Arbor, MI: University of Michigan Press, 2001), esp. p. 2.

theatrical stage can be thought of as a haunted space, so too can the page which sought (in fraught and ambivalent ways) to represent it in two dimensions.

Suggestively, *Shadows of Kabuki* is one of two of Sanba's works found in the catalogue to the Hayashi library, a fact that seems as if it might provide a cogent metaphor for the larger process of consuming the theater through printed images and text. At one level, the presence of *Shadows of Kabuki* in the Hayashi library is almost symbolic of the very problem the work flags: it is the embodiment of the book in print that allows the play to travel to the provinces, allows it to be preserved as part of a library, and allows it to be rediscovered by the scholar two centuries later. If the printed page is a shadow cast by the performance, a medium that seems always inadequately to grasp and represent the stage, it is still through this medium, in the form of this shadow, this *other-than-performance*, that the stage became available to the provincial consumer, to the provincial reader.

My own interest in the subject of *Kabuki's Nineteenth Century* was born out of an attempt to understand the tension inhabiting these two stances: on the one hand, the written word is an integral part of the life of the stage and, in very real ways, is the only vehicle we have for *knowing* the stage; on the other hand, there remains a skepticism on the part of Sanba and others that we can ever really *know* the stage through print which, after all, only provides us with shadows, and shadows that can easily be misunderstood. It is with an image of Sanba's *Theater Chic This Side of the Curtain* in mind that I began to conceptualize this book: rather than following the vast archives of printed theatrical material back towards the stage, I began from the question of what would happen if we, like Sanba, stopped short, if we concentrated on the world "*this side* of the curtain," a world of print. At the same time, as my research on this project developed, I was faced with a different question: what did it mean that, for writers in the nineteenth century, an appreciation of the printed life of the stage gave birth to a sense of anxiety over the meanings of cultural consumption and a nostalgia for a world of authentic experience? While the thrust of *Kabuki's Nineteenth Century* is an effort to re-examine the theater of the nineteenth century by shifting our critical focus from performance to print (embedding theater within the larger world of printed matter by means of which theatricality circulated far beyond the stage and through which performance was most often consumed), I am also concerned to understand the meanings that print had for a society attempting to make sense of itself at a historical moment when the specter of print suggested a profound transformation in the ways in which the world was approached and understood. This context, moreover, allows a project like this—historical in subject and historicist in method—to open out comparatively onto other times and places, including our own.[43]

---

[43] Ann Blair has, for example, suggested that our own anxieties about the changing nature of our relationship to information can be usefully thought about in relation to earlier moments of "information overload." See Ann M. Blair, *Too Much to Know: Managing Scholarly Information before the Modern Age* (New Haven, CT: Yale University Press, 2010). See also Andrew Piper's reflections on reading in electronic times in *Book Was There: Reading in Electronic Times* (Chicago, IL: University of Chicago Press, 2012).

My intention, then, is to offer a reconsideration of the nature of the printed archive itself, an exploration of the ways in which the array of printed material related to the theater in nineteenth-century Japan (playbills, actor critiques, theater guides, maps, actor prints, calendars, and so forth) is something more than, and more complicated than, a set of materials out of which we might recreate the always transient event of performance. Rather, the archive constitutes an object of inquiry unto itself, an object that reveals as much about the interrelations between and among various printed media and genres circulating beyond the confines of the theater as it does about what happened on stage. Even as we explore what these materials tell us about performance, a different series of questions emerge: what can the production, consumption, and collecting of this enormous archive of printed matter tell us about such problems as the construction of specialized knowledges, the role of print in everyday life, and the manner in which a culture archives itself?

These are the subjects to which I will turn in the chapters that follow, and I will begin by examining Sanba's own practices as a collector of theater ephemera. But before we turn to Sanba's collection, I would like to offer one final view of the broader landscape of kabuki's nineteenth century as a way of situating the chapters that follow within a set of questions about the intersection of print and consumption for the meanings of modern life.

## III  Kabuki in an Age of Print

For all the ways in which the Hayashi library provides a useful starting point for examining the relationship between the theater and print culture in nineteenth-century Japan, it also usefully *locates* this discussion in a specific geography, a geography, moreover, that has played, and continues to play, an important role in the discussion of the impact of print culture on Japanese society at large in the nineteenth century. In Shimazaki Tōson's *Before the Dawn*, a fictional representation of life in Kiso Valley during the nineteenth century, books play an enormously important role. In part because of the centrality of print within *Before the Dawn* and the centrality of that novel to imagining the decades that span the Meiji Restoration, Kiso (and the broader region of Shinshū) have often been the site of historical inquiries into the role that literate networks of the nineteenth century played in paving the way for the institutions of modern Japan.[44]

But if the nineteenth-century reader represented in Tōson's novel—and often *re*-presented by historians—is, in some sense, "studied for action," the Hayashi library presents the image of another kind of reader, one less active, one engaged with

---

[44] In her *Bonds of Civility*, for example, Eiko Ikegami draws a direct connection between the communities of reading depicted in Tōson's historical novel and the development of "indigenous democratic movements" in the late nineteenth century. See Eiko Ikegami, *Bonds of Civility: Aesthetic Networks and the Political Origins of Japanese Culture* (Cambridge: Cambridge University Press, 2005), p. 213.

books and printed material in a seemingly different way.[45] If it can be argued that poetry networks or reading circles can be seen to lay the ground for political action based on the spread of Nativist ideas, paving the way for the Meiji Restoration and democratic movements beyond, it seems much more difficult to imagine how a reader such as Hayashi Kuni might fit into this narrative, how we might reconcile the emergence of the provincial consumer of urban culture with a narrative of books causing revolutions or restorations.[46]

In contrast to the "studied" men of action that populate Tōson's fictional representation of the Kiso Valley in the nineteenth century, another figure appears frequently in satires written and published in the early nineteenth century: the leisure reader, especially the female reader, consumed with the superficialities and celebrity of theatrical culture, is one of the great tropes of nineteenth-century Japan and a figure of which Sanba was particularly fond. To be sure, both of these figurations of the reader are exaggerations of a historical reality that was considerably more complex. But to grasp the role that print played in nineteenth-century Japan, we need to do a better job of understanding the particular relationship between these two seemingly very different modes of reading. As Suzuki Toshiyuki puts it in his study of "reading fever" in Edo Japan, what we need is a history of the book that focuses on the "normal," "not those books in which distinctive modes of thought are piled up, nor those works of people who gathered about them many disciples in creating their own school of thought," but rather "those books that were collected normally by normal people in response to the needs of their everyday lives."[47]

One of the great virtues of the catalogue of the Hayashi library is that it provides a particularly useful means of entering this world and thus a way to reflect upon the Janus-faced position that print has always occupied in the theorizing of modern life. For all that print has been seen as an "agent of change," to borrow Elizabeth Eisenstein's term for the role of print in the spread of knowledge known as "enlightenment," printing has also, and inextricably, been tied to the spread of of mass culture, enlightenment's dialectical other.[48] In nineteenth-century Japan, perhaps

---

[45] I have borrowed this phrase from Lisa Jardine and Anthony Grafton's well-known study of Gabriel Harvey. See Lisa Jardine and Anthony Grafton, "'Studied for Action': How Gabriel Harvey Read His Livy," *Past and Present* 129 (1990), 30–78. The "purposeful reading" that they explore in the essay is a good model for the kinds of work that have been done on reading associations in early modern Japan. See, e.g. Maeda Tsutomu, *Edo no dokushokai: kaidoku no shisōshi* (Tokyo: Heibonsha, 2012).

[46] Maeda Tsutomu has made the clearest argument for reading communities in early modern Japan as a form of voluntary association that created the context through which new concepts of democracy and liberty could emerge in late-nineteenth-century Japan (see Maeda, *Edo no dokushokai*). For a discussion of the role of books in the historiography of the French Revolution, see Roger Chartier, *The Cultural Origins of the French Revolution*, trans. Lydia G. Cochrane (Durham, NC: Duke University Press Books, 1991); Robert Darnton, *The Forbidden Best-Sellers of Pre-Revolutionary France* (New York: W. W. Norton & Co., 1996), pp. 167ff.

[47] Suzuki Toshiyuki, *Edo no dokushonetsu: jigakusuru dokusha to shoseki ryūtsū*, p. 12.

[48] Elizabeth L. Eisenstein, *The Printing Press as an Agent of Change* (Cambridge: Cambridge University Press, 1980). See also the discussion of the invention of printing in Max Horkheimer and Theodor W. Adorno, *Dialectic of Enlightenment*, trans. John Cumming (New York: Continuum, 1972), pp. 3ff.

unsurprisingly, the role that print played in the spread of modes of urban culture and consumption beyond the city, and to new groups within the city, would occasion ambivalence, as we saw in Sanba, but also outright hostility.

Sanba was, of course, not alone in his unease over the ways in which print was coming to shape the culture of the early nineteenth century, what it meant for the culture of Edo to circulate beyond the city. *An Account of What I Have Seen and Heard* (*Seji kenmon roku*), written pseudonymously by a minor samurai known only as Buyō Inshi around 1816, provides another perspective.[49] To anyone who has read *An Account of What I Have Seen and Heard*, it may seem an unlikely text with which to draw a parallel with Sanba: it is a long tract about the decline of the moral fabric of society in Japan in the early nineteenth century, and among the signs of cultural decay against which its author inveighs are writers of popular fiction (*gesakusha*) such as Sanba, who "become the foundation for disorder in the Way of men and women."[50]

But there is an interesting convergence between the fears of moral decay expressed in *An Account of What I Have Seen and Heard* and what we might think of as the anxious ambivalence displayed in much of Sanba's work: both focus on the role of print in the proliferation of what has been termed "popular culture," and both have in mind someone like Hayashi Kuni, a woman and a provincial. Buyō Inshi's attack on writers who "pervert the true records and proper understanding of the past," writers such as Sanba himself, comes as part of a broader discussion of print's role in spreading the decadence of urban culture:

> These works of *gesaku* circulate widely in the world. Even if the classics of righteousness that have come down to us from the past, and indeed most books, were inexpensive, there would be few who would purchase them. But, although today's works of *gesaku* are more expensive than the books of the sages, there are many who buy them and new ones are published each year and circulate out to every province.[51]

Books are only part of the problem. Printed images, too, have become ubiquitous with "pornographic prints" (*shunga*) "treated as playthings" and "stashed away in trunks used to store clothing and passed down from mother to daughter." But even these images, Buyō Inshi concedes, are "trivial" compared with the most invidious aspects of contemporary culture: prostitution and the theater.

---

[49] Little is known about the author, who refers to himself only as Buyō Inshi, "a retired gentleman of Edo." See Buyō Inshi, *Lust, Commerce, and Corruption: An Account of What I Have Seen and Heard, by an Edo Samurai*, ed. Mark Teeuwen and Kate Wildman Nakai (New York: Columbia University Press, 2014), pp. 1–5. See also Takikawa Masajirō's note on the text's authorship in Honjō Eijirō ed., *Seji kenmon roku* (Toky: Seiabō, 1966), pp. 8–12.

[50] Buyō Inshi, *Lust, Commerce, and Corruption*, p. 330.

[51] Buyō Inshi, *Lust, Commerce, and Corruption*, p. 347.

The Hayashi library seems, in its own way, to bring alive the fears of someone like the author of *An Account of What I Have Seen and Heard* for the library is a record of the spread and popularity of this kind of "degraded" metropolitan culture circulating quite widely in the provinces. In addition to playbills, the Hayashi library is filled with works of fiction (including two by Sanba), some of which are illustrated with images of the leading actors of the day. That these books were most likely collected by a young woman only heightens the specter that various kinds of desire played in constituting the stage in print as an object of consumption for the provincial reader.[52]

If Sanba's *Theater Chic This Side of the Curtain* or *An Account of What I Have Seen and Heard* can provide a useful context for thinking about the meanings of the Hayashi library or of the intersection of print and theater more broadly, they do so because they remind us of the fundamentally ambivalent place print has always had in debates about the spread of enlightenment and of its dialectical other. *An Account of What I Have Seen and Heard* both points to this ambivalence and suggests the extent to which this problem was already central to nineteenth-century discourses on print and consumption within Japan, discourses which are familiar to any student of print culture from other times and places.[53]

Reading *Theater Chic This Side of the Curtain* or *An Account of What I Have Seen and Heard*, we should take seriously these representations of the provincial consumption of popular culture not, of course, because they provide especially compelling portrait of print culture in the early nineteenth century, or because they are in some sense "true" or "accurate," but because they situate a collection like the Hayashi library within a broader set of attitudes and dispositions in which provincial reading took place.[54] Examining discourses on reading and consumption in a polemic such as *An Account of What I Have Seen and Heard* reveals something of a society's self-consciousness, that, as in other cultural milieu, there emerged in nineteenth-century Edo an anxiety about print and reading and about their uses and misuses. In nineteenth-century Japan, as elsewhere and at other historical moments, this anxiety focused on often marginalized or excluded groups

---

[52] On this point, see Timon Screech's extensive examination of erotica, including pornographic images of actors, in Screech, *Sex and the Floating World: Erotic Images in Japan, 1700–1820* (Honolulu: University of Hawai'i Press, 1999).

[53] There is an extensive literature on the ambivalence of elite culture to the idea of mass literacy in nineteenth-century Europe. See Patrick M. Brantlinger, *The Reading Lesson: The Threat of Mass Literacy in Nineteenth-Century British Fiction* (Bloomington, IN: Indiana University Press, 1998); Richard Altick, *The English Common Reader: A Social History of the Mass Reading Public, 1800–1900* (Columbus, OH: Ohio State University Press, 1998); Jonathan Rose, *The Intellectual Life of the British Working Classes* (New Haven, CT: Yale University Press, 2010). On anxieties related to female literacy in particular see the chapter "Answering Back" in Belinda Jack, *The Woman Reader* (New Haven, CT: Yale University Press, 2012), pp. 184–227.

[54] We should be especially careful of elite representations of non-elite practices; see Roger Chartier, "Popular Appropriations: The Readers and Their Books," in Roger Chartier *Forms and Meanings: Texts, Performances, and Audiences from Codex to Computer* (Philadelphia, PA: University of Pennsylvania Press, 2007) 83–97.

(women, the provincial, the uneducated), and its two great figures are the country bumpkin and the chambermaid. And, as elsewhere, an elite concern over reading or theatergoing seems inextricably bound up with the problem of female desire.[55]

Such scholars as Maeda Tsutomu and Eiko Ikegami have argued for the role that print culture played in the creation of networks—based around intellectual movements like Nativism or around aesthetic pursuits such as poetry—and hence in fostering the contexts for the emergence of civil society or of the public sphere.[56] But the Hayashi collection represents the obverse side: the spread of literacy as the spread of urban culture dominated by consumption and leisure.[57] At a theoretical level, both of these attitudes have played an important role in thinking about the history of reading, and they present a dialectical face familiar from many contexts. But as Suzuki Toshiyuki has argued, within the discourse surrounding early modern Japan, "the image of 'the reader' has been very abstract not based on actual evidence; put uncharitably, 'the reader' has often been nothing more than a useful code at the convenience of the author."[58] For the scholar interested in the history of consumption, then, the Hayashi library can serve as a particular site for attempting to reconstitute the historical reader and, in turn, for a more nuanced understanding of these historical processes.

The reflections in Buyō Inshi's *An Account of What I Have Seen and Heard* on print and its role in promoting dissipation and indecency are themselves part of his long chapter titled "On Kabuki," a chapter in which the author repeatedly compares the vices of kabuki with the vices of the pleasure quarters, and it is important to understand these reflections on print within a broader critique of the spread of a particular kind of urban culture. The reflections recorded in "On Kabuki" are immensely rich for thinking about the meanings of kabuki in the early nineteenth-century imagination, but I would like, here, to flag one moment in the author's meditation on theatrical culture that seems startlingly modern in the way it expresses a critique of the inauthentic nature of a world dominated by cultural consumption: "it is no longer the case today that the theater imitates life; rather, the theater come first and life imitates theater."[59]

---

[55] See David Pollack, "Making Desire: Advertising and Sexuality in Edo Literature, Drama, and Art," in *Gender and Power in the Japanese Visual Field*, ed. Joshua S. Mostow, Norman Bryson, and Mirabeth Graybill (Honolulu: University of Hawai'i Press, 2003) pp. 71–88; Screech, *Sex and the Floating World*.
[56] Ikegami, *Bonds of Civility*; Maeda, *Edo no dokushokai*.
[57] On literacy in early-modern Japan, see Richard Rubinger, *Popular Literacy in Early Modern Japan* (Honolulu: University of Hawai'i Press, 2007); Peter Kornicki, "Literacy Revisited: Some Reflections on Richard Rubinger's Findings," *Monumenta Nipponica* 56, 3 (2001), 381–95; Peter Kornicki, "Women, Education, and Literacy," in *The Female as Subject: Reading and Writing in Early Modern Japan*, ed. Peter F. Kornicki, Mara Patessio, and Gaye Rowley (Ann Arbor, MI: University of Michigan Press, 2010), pp. 7–37.
[58] Suzuki Toshiyuki, *Edo no dokushonetsu*, p. 10.
[59] Buyō Inshi, *Lust, Commerce, and Corruption*, p. 335.

I say that this idea seems startlingly modern because there is something in how *An Account of What I Have Seen and Heard* lodges a critique of the inauthentic nature of a life mediated by images that seems uncannily to anticipate some of the most common, but also some of the most sophisticated and trenchant, critiques of modern life. There is a deep resonance, for example, between Buyō Inshi's description of a world in which the imitation has become the real and the real an imitation, and something of the critique of "the society of the spectacle" offered a century-and-a-half later (and half a world away) by Guy Debord: "all that was once directly lived has become mere representation."[60] Debord, of course, is talking about another place and another time, but I would like to suggest how we might use this resonance as a way of interrogating the "spectacular" nature of the culture of the stage in nineteenth-century Edo.

If such a seemingly freighted idea as the "society of the spectacle" can play a productive role in thinking through the specific history of nineteenth-century Japan, it is by taking seriously the very real problem of historicizing such an idea in the first place. As Jonathan Crary has argued:

> A striking feature of Debord's *Society of the Spectacle* was the absence of any kind of historical genealogy of the spectacle [...] For the term to have any critical or practical efficacy depends, in part, on how one periodizes it—that is, the spectacle will assume quite different meanings depending on how it is situated historically.[61]

My intention here is not to offer the outlines of such a genealogy in the case of Japan or to offer a kind of "prehistory" of the society of the spectacle as such, comparable to other such prehistories that have been sketched for Europe.[62] This would be a very different project and is beyond the scope of what I am able to do in this book. Rather, what I would like to suggest is that if we are to understand the meaning of a text like the *An Account of What I Have Seen and Heard* and to take seriously its critique of a nascent society of consumption, we must also take seriously the ways in which this critique shares, or even anticipates, similar critical ideas that emerged in other times and places.

One way of doing this is offered by Crary himself:

> The "early" work of Jean Baudrillard provides some general parameters for what we might call the prehistory of the spectacle [...] Baudrillard's account of modernity is one of an increasing destabilization and mobility of signs beginning in

---

[60] Guy Debord, *The Society of the Spectacle* [1967], trans. Ken Knabb (Berkeley, CA: Bureau of Public Secrets, 2014), p. 12.
[61] Jonathan Crary, "Spectacle, Attention, Counter-Memory," *October* 50 (1989), 98.
[62] See, e.g. Timothy J. Clark, *The Painting of Modern Life: Paris in the Art of Manet and His Followers* (Princeton, NJ: Princeton University Press, 1999); Jonathan Crary, *Techniques of the Observer: On Vision and Modernity in the 19th Century* (Cambridge, MA: MIT Press, 1992).

the Renaissance, signs which previously had been firmly rooted to relatively secure positions within fixed social hierarchies. Thus, for Baudrillard, modernity is bound up in the struggle of newly empowered classes to overcome this "exclusiveness of signs" and to initiate a "proliferation of signs on demand." Imitations, copies, and counterfeits are all challenges to that exclusivity.[63]

I have quoted Crary's analysis of Baudrillard's work at some length because the themes that he identifies—the "destabilization and mobility of signs," certain anxieties of class and status—are critical to making sense of nineteenth-century Japanese discourses on reading and print such as those we find in the writings of Sanba or Buyō Inshi, and they are themes to which I will return often in the chapters that follow. Indeed, *Kabuki's Nineteenth Century* itself takes up a history of "imitations, copies, and counterfeits"; but more broadly, this book is also an attempt to understand how a profusion of print occasioned a crisis of legitimacy in representation and what this means for understanding the history of nineteenth-century Japan. The intersection of stage and print becomes an especially rich site for examining this history because the attempt to capture the stage *in print* seems always to fail and, in this failing, to point toward something (the phantasm of an authentic experience) which might ultimately defy representation in print. Thus, if kabuki represents for Buyō Inshi the unmooring of representation from its referent, for writers like Sanba, it is something quite different, the site of a nostalgic memory of authenticity, the flip side of the shadows on the printed page.

This book, then, is meant as both a work of cultural history and as a historiographical intervention in the way we think of theater and performance history. My archive is the printed ephemera that proliferated throughout the nineteenth century but *Kabuki's Nineteenth Century* is not intended to serve as a catalogue or exhaustive description of the truly astonishing array of theater ephemera that survives from nineteenth-century Japan. That work has already been done in Japanese, and some of it is available in English. Rather, on one level, I mean to use these materials to examine the ways in which individuals and groups of writers, critics, and collectors themselves participated in the production and consumption of knowledge about the theater through the medium of print and the ways that their work intersected with other practices and modes of historical thinking. To do this requires taking seriously the printed archive in and of itself, not as an inadequate means for accessing some other history transpiring elsewhere, on stage, but as a crucial site in which the historical imagination of nineteenth-century Japan was enacted.

---

[63] Crary, "Spectacle, Attention, Counter-Memory," 98.

# 2
# "Devices for Thinking about the Past"
## Playbills, Ephemera, and the Historical Imagination

### I  Playbill and Museum

I began Chapter 1 with a discussion of playbills collected across the nineteenth century. They formed part of a private library in a town along the Nakasendō highway in the Kiso Valley. At one level, the Hayashi library is emblematic of what Suzuki Toshiyuki, who first catalogued the collection in 1992, has called, in a different context, the history of the "ordinary" reader, the record of one family's tastes and reading habits over the decades that spanned the Meiji.[1]

But if the survival of this collection seems emblematic of the ordinary or everyday, the conditions that made this survival possible hint at the rather unusual circumstances on which this preservation is predicated. The collection was kept in a storehouse within the residence of a wealthy provincial family, deep in a valley in the Japanese Alps. Suzuki writes in his catalogue:

> The magnificent residence (*yashiki*) which was rebuilt in 1877 still survives and has become a symbol of the preservation of the townscape of Tsumago. On the grounds, there is a storeroom (*bunkogura*) that preserves the construction of the Edo period as it was. There, in the oldest structure within the structure of the residence, the Hayashi family library is perfectly preserved.[2]

In one sense, the collection survives because of its fossilization and, like any process of fossilization, its preservation seems to rely on both circumstance and luck. Circumstance in the sense that the *location* of the library deep in the Kiso Valley shielded it from many of the destructive forces that marked Japan's twentieth-century history from earthquakes to firebombings, a reminder of what Wada Atsuhiko has called the importance of *place* in thinking about the

---

[1] Suzuki Toshiyuki, *Edo no dokushonetsu: jigakusuru dokusha to shoseki ryūtsū* (Tokyo: Heibonsha, 2007), pp. 9ff.

[2] Suzuki Toshiyuki, ed., *Kinsei kōki ni okeru shoseki/sōshi nado no shuppan/ryūtsū/kyōju ni tsuite no kenkyū: Kiso Tsumago Hayashike zōsho oyobi Kiso Uematsu Rinsenji shozō hangi no chōsa o chōshin ni* (Hachiōji: Chūō Daigaku Bungakubu, 3833 Kenkyūshitsu, 1996), p. 105.

history of books.[3] But also luck because so many similar collections end up lost, sold, or sometimes simply discarded.

The former Hayashi residence was first opened to the public in 1967, and in the decade after Suzuki first catalogued the library it became part of a new history museum, the Nagisomachi Museum, which highlights the Kiso Valley's early modern history as an emblem of everyday life in Edo Japan. In 2001, the residence and the *bunkogura* were named Important National Cultural Properties, enfolding the collection in a larger way of defining culture and tradition and imagining preservation and display: both the museum and the preservation of the buildings are themselves part of a trend of what Jordan Sand has called "monumentalizing the everyday," a trend that became such a central aspect of culture during the economic bubble of the late 1980s and has continued in the post-bubble decades.[4] Some of the books from the collection, which still belongs to the Hayashi family, are part of the display that represents the history of the valley, an effort to document a world remote from Japan of the early twenty-first century and a space of nostalgia for an always-vanishing tradition.[5]

In some ways, the seemingly emblematic nature of this collection also suggests how singular it is. Most private collections do not survive in the way that the Hayashi collection has been preserved, and while this is true of books, it is even more true of ephemera and broadsheets. As the theater historian Akama Ryō—who has done as much as anyone to study, catalogue, and make accessible the enormous printed archive of early modern theater ephemera—has written: "Because theater material was collected as part of a realm of personal pleasure, it is material whose fate is to be easily disposed of when, for whatever reason, that interest disappears. It is, in other words, 'ephemeral matter.'"[6] Collections, like that of the Hayashi house, are often simply discarded, but occasionally these testaments to the world of "personal pleasure" end up in the public realm in secondhand bookstores or libraries or museums.

Akama's observation comes in the preface to a catalogue of printed theater materials housed at the Waseda University Tsubouchi Memorial Theater Museum and the materials in that catalogue are themselves testament to this movement. At its

---

[3] See the preface "A Historiography of Books and Place" ("Shomotsu to basho no rekishigaku") in Wada Atsuhiko, *Ekkyō suru shomotsu: henyōsuru dokusho kankyō no naka de* (Tokyo: Shinyōsha, 2011), pp. 11–17.

[4] Jordan Sand, *Tokyo Vernacular: Common Spaces, Local Histories, Found Objects* (Berkeley, CA: University of California Press, 2013), pp. 110–41.

[5] See Carol Gluck, "The Invention of Edo," in *Mirror of Modernity: Invented Traditions of Modern Japan*, ed. Stephen Vlastos (Berkeley, CA: University of California Press, 1998), pp. 262–84; Millie Creighton, "The Heroic Edo-Ic: Traveling the History Highway in Today's Tokugawa Japan," in *Japanese Tourism and Travel Culture*, ed. Sylvie Guichard-Anguis and Okpyo Moon (London: Routledge, 2011), pp. 37–75.

[6] Akama Ryō, *Zusetsu Edo no engekisho: Kabuki hen* (Tokyo: Yagi Shoten, 2003), p. vi.

founding, in 1928, the museum's holdings were comprised almost entirely of early modern printed books and theater ephemera.[7] Tsubouchi Shōyō, in whose honor the Museum was constructed, donated his personal collection to the Museum. Shōyō's collection of kabuki ephemera was quite different in scope and composition from the collection of the Hayashi family. Indeed, there is an anecdote from Shōyō's 1920 book *Reminiscences of the Kabuki I Saw in My Youth* (*Shōnen jidai ni mita kabuki no tsuioku*) that suggests an interesting counterpoint between the basis of the Theater Museum's collections and a collection like that of the Hayashi Family:

> During the spring of the year before last, I purchased over one thousand old kabuki playbills (*banzuke*) from the Nagoya bookseller Kichūdō and among those there happened to be thirty or forty playbills of plays I had seen in my youth and so my memories, which had become hazy, suddenly became vivid and being able to talk with some certainty about the past became the motivation for my impulse.[8]

Shōyō was sixty-two at the time and deeply immersed in two of the activities that would define the later years of his life: his translation of Shakespeare's complete works and his study of early modern Japanese drama, especially kabuki. As he began writing his reminiscences, Shōyō was finishing his translation of *As You Like It* (*O ki ni mesu mama*) and reading the proofs for his study of actor prints focusing on the nineteenth-century print designer Utagawa Toyokuni and his school, two works to which I shall turn in the following chapters.

At one level, this collection of old playbills, which serves as an almost Proustian vehicle for memory, bringing alive the theater before his eyes and returning him to the "dreamlike" time of his childhood, is of a piece with the collection of playbills in the Hayashi family library.[9] In both instances, these *banzuke* have been saved from the fate of ephemeral culture, what Theodor Adorno once suggestively called "the mortality of artifacts."[10] Yet this very preservation has brought to these printed objects different fates, created out of them very different archives.

---

[7] In an article on the opening of the Museum, the *Yomiuri Newspaper* noted:
> the collections are comprised of nearly thirty-thousand woodblock prints including some eleven thousand donated by Dr. Tsubouchi, rare materials such as actor critiques from the late seventeenth through the mid nineteenth century, roughly four thousand playbills from the early seventeenth century through the early twentieth century, and approximately fifteen hundred illustrated theater books from the same period.

See "Kyō kaikanshiki no Engeki Hakubutsukan," *Yomiuri shinbun*, October 27, 1928, p. 11.

[8] Tsubouchi Shōyō, "Shōnen jidai ni mita kabuki no tsuioku," in *Shōyō senshū*, vol. 12 (Tokyo: Daiichi Shobō, 1977–78), pp. 64–65.

[9] Tsubouchi Shōyō, "Shōnen jidai ni mita kabuki no tsuioku," in *Shōyō senshū*, vol. 12, p. 72.

[10] Theodor W. Adorno, *Prisms* (Cambridge, MA: MIT Press, 1981), p. 178.

The playbills collected by Hayashi Kuni are the objects of a particular collector and her passions, and they remain within the personal domain of a home even as that home has itself become a public museum. The collection of playbills that Shōyō purchased in the 1910s is, by contrast, a collection of uncertain origin, perhaps an aggregate of smaller, individual collections, but a collection which has once more entered the marketplace, now secondhand, as antiquarian goods for a new collector. These playbills serve as prompts for Shōyō's own deeply personal memories (of his childhood, of his mother), but they are not, as it were, his own collection, his memories dependent on the mementos of others, mementos that have lost their owners. When Shōyō donated his personal collections to Waseda, these playbills were transformed again, becoming public documents and now readily available anywhere in the world as part of the Theater Museum's online archive of theater programs.

If we take these two museums together, the Nagisomachi Museum in Tsumago founded in the early twenty-first century and the Waseda Theater Museum founded in 1928, they suggest two ways that theater ephemera have served as part of historical narrative in Japan. In one instance, they become part of the fabric of an everyday past, reimagined and reconstructed, suffused with what Marilyn Ivy has called "a nostalgia for a Japan that is kept on the verge of vanishing, stable yet endangered (and thus open to commodifiable desire)."[11] In the other instance, these objects are fragments of Japan's dramatic past plotted in a global history of the theater in which the Japanese case becomes but one particular example of a universal (in both space and time) theatrical patrimony, even if this impulse toward the universal (and comparative) has largely remained an unrealized dream.

Each of these institutions seems, in some profound sense modern, offering a vantage point on the past as "other," premised on what Susan Stewart has called "a rupture in historical consciousness [. . .] creating a sense that one can make one's own culture *other*—distant and discontinuous."[12] But each institution is also, perhaps uncannily, heir to a tradition of historical thinking that can be traced back to the early nineteenth century. It was in the decades around 1800 that a new history of kabuki came to be written, and that that history was conceptualized as part of a larger world history of the theater. At the same time, amateur historians began documenting everyday life in remarkable works that even now tell us much of what we know of life in early modern Japan.

To understand the construction of kabuki as a historical object in the twentieth and twenty-first centuries, then, it is necessary first to understand how theater

---

[11] Marilyn Ivy, *Discourses of the Vanishing: Modernity, Phantasm, Japan* (Chicago, IL: University of Chicago Press, 1995), p. 65.
[12] Susan Stewart, *On Longing. Narratives of the Miniature, the Gigantic, the Souvenir, the Collection* (Durham, NC: Duke University Press, 1993), p. 142.

came to be historicized in the nineteenth century and to grapple with the transformation of ephemera into historical documents. Doing this takes us back a century before Shōyō would encounter those playbills at a second-hand bookseller in Nagoya to the world of Shikitei Sanba and his circle, to figures like Utei Enba and Santō Kyōden, and to an age of curiosity and collecting that would shape the structure and meaning of the archive of kabuki's history.

## II Chronology as History

There is an extraordinary image of a collector of theatrical material that appears in a satire of theatergoers published by Shikitei Sanba in 1811, *A Critique of the Audience (Kakusha hyōbanki)*.[13] The book's title and content parody the genre of the actor critique or *yakusha hyōbanki*, which rated and evaluated actors each year, a staple of theater publishing that goes back to the middle of the seventeenth century. In his work, Sanba substitutes the spectator (*kakusha*) for the actor (*yakusha*) and, of course, shifts his focus away from stage to audience in a repetition of the gesture he had made half a decade earlier in his 1806 *Theater Chic This Side of the Curtain (Kejō suigen makunosoto)*. At the same time, the book also pays homage to another satire published some thirty years earlier by Sanba's friend and mentor Utei Enba, *A Critique of Patrons (Kyakusha hyōbanki)* (1780), which took as its subject the patrons not of the theater but of the demimonde.[14]

Among the peculiar characters that populate the world of theatergoers that Sanba presents—from aficionados to poseurs—is an antiquarian (*kojitsusha*). The antiquarian carries the honorary title of "*nendaiki*" or "chronology" and is described by Sanba as one who "searches out old records and pursues secret writings, committing everything to memory" and thus turns his bosom into a "storehouse of the theater."[15] Sanba's text is accompanied by Utagawa Kunisada's illustration that shows an aged figure sitting in front of a charcoal brazier; he dons a *maruzukin*, a soft cap often worn by monks, and is surrounded by various theatrical objects. In the foreground of the illustration are two images: a single

---

[13] Shikitei Sanba, "Kakusha hyōbanki," in *Nihon shomin bunka shiryō shūsei*, ed. Geinōshi Kenkyūja, vol. 6 (Tokyo: Sanichi Shobō, 1973), p. 520. For a partial translation, see Jacob Raz, "The Audience Evaluated. Shikitei Samba's Kyakusha Hyōbanki," *Monumenta Nipponica* 35, 2 (1980), 199–221 and Jacob Raz, *Audience and Actors: A Study of Their Interaction in the Japanese Traditional Theatre* (Leiden: Brill, 1983).

[14] Although the title of both works is written identically in Japanese (客者評判記), Sanba's title is traditionally read with the uncommon pronunciation "kakusha" (to mirror *yakusha*) instead of "kyakusha" and is listed this way in bibliographies such as *Kokusho sōmokuroku* and databases such as the National Institute of Japanese Literature's Union Catalog of Early Japanese Books. For his part, Sanba is inconsistent and glosses the characters with both readings but uses "kakusha" more often.

[15] Shikitei Sanba, "Kakusha hyōbanki," p. 520.

sheet print of Ichikawa Danjūrō I in an *aragoto* or "rough" role for which he was famous, and, above this, a depiction of the Saruwaka-mai, the dance that Nakamura (Saruwaka) Kanzaburō I had brought with him to Edo when he founded the Nakamura-za, the first of Edo's theaters in 1624.[16] This image is mounted on a hanging scroll decorated with flying cranes, the crest of the Nakamura-za. Both of these images within the larger image would date to the earliest history of kabuki in the city of Edo in the seventeenth century (Figure 2.1).

Behind the antiquarian is a folding screen which seems to be flecked with gold and decorated with a grass pattern and onto which have been pasted various bits of theater ephemera. At the top appears to be a copy of an image of a kabuki dance but the rendition is abstract and it is difficult to read in any detail; below is an image of Ichikawa Danjūrō II in the guise of a moxa seller, a role he first played in 1719. And although they remain illegible, the screen also appears to bear tanzaku, paper strips pasted onto the screen, inscribed, one imagines, with verse dedicated to famous actors, or, perhaps, in the hand of the actors themselves.

Through this rendering of the antiquarian and his milieu run two currents. First, there is the sense of Kunisada's illustration functioning as a kind of metapicture, an image that itself meditates on the uses and functions of images in the context of the theatrical culture of early nineteenth-century Japan. Images within images are central to the composition, and the illustration seems to offer itself almost as a key to deciphering the world of the collector and the function of images in that moment around 1800 when the collecting and display of objects began to assume a particular importance. This was a world, Sanba would write in 1813, in which

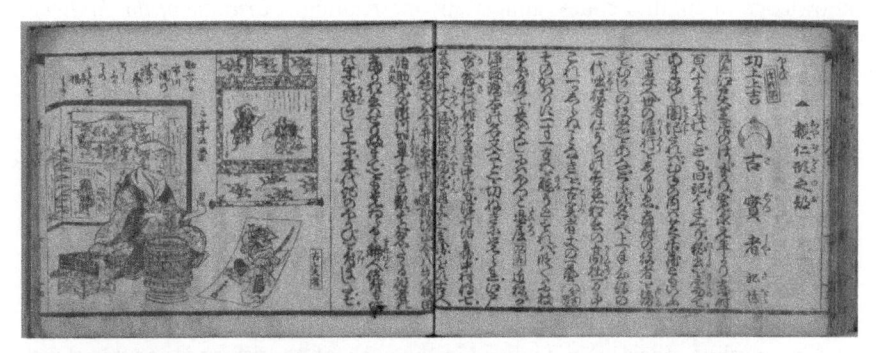

**Figure 2.1** Utagawa Toyokuni, the antiquarian from Shikitei Sanba, *Kakusha hyōbanki*, 1811.
Source: National Diet Library, Toyko.

---

[16] On *aragoto*, see Samuel L. Leiter, *A New Kabuki Encyclopedia* (Westport, CT: Greenwood Press, 1997), p. 18: "'Rough thing,' the distinctively masculine, Edo style of acting and production, in which the hero's superhuman strength and valor were stressed in a formalized manor."

"amateurs masquerade as antiques dealers who boast of their own refinement and dealers pose as amateurs sunk in the depths of greed," a world in which "neither the sellers nor the buyers have any idea which items were real and which fakes."[17] Within this world of deception and mendacity, the ability properly to read an image, and hence to understand not only its meaning but also its value, take on a critical importance.

But even as this illustration seems to appear as a guide to reading images, there is also an evocative tension at the heart of Kunisada's image between legibility and illegibility: within the overall composition, there are some images that are intentionally obscured and remain illegible while others can readily be deciphered. While the images of Danjūrō I and his son, who would become Danjūrō II, are legible within the iconography of actor prints, there is what appears to be another actor print attached to the screen, all but blocked from view by the antiquarian himself. Or the tanzaku, which are meant to evoke writing but which are completely illegible within the image, as is the signature of the print designer on the print of Danjūrō I. And the print of the dance at the top of the screen—which almost certainly shows an early seventeenth-century scene—can only be *read* as such in relation to other similar images, requiring, as we shall later see, that the viewer already know, a priori, what the image depicts or how to insert it into a series of similar images which give it meaning.

Kunisada's image, perhaps unconsciously, seems to intuit something critical to the disposition of antiquarianism both in general and as a specific set of practices that evolved in late eighteenth- and early nineteenth-century Japan. On the one hand, portions of the image are readily legible to a reader with even the most basic knowledge of cultural codes: almost anyone reading *A Critique of the Audience* would recognize Ichikawa Danjūrō I and his son and be able to understand that the images are meant to evoke the origins of kabuki in the city of Edo over a century earlier. But the image of the dance at the top of the screen cannot really be read at all; it can only be *recognized*: the reader must already have the cultural knowledge to *see* the object for what it is, a point to which I will return below. And here we have, subtly inscribed in this image, one example of a theme that recurs throughout the culture of the theater in this period: a distinction, sometimes drawn more overtly, sometimes less so, between the knowledgeable fan, whose tastes and disposition allow him access to the most refined aspects of the world of the stage, and his implied other, often depicted in the guise of boorish rustic or star-struck chambermaid, two figures who themselves appear as subjects of satire in Sanba's catalogue of theatergoers.

The tension in the composition between the legible and the illegible, however, also points in a different way to another element fundamental to collecting: its

---

[17] See Sanba's preface to Shinoda Kinji, *Kuraishō* (Edo: Nishimura Genroku, 1813). Doi: 10.11501/8929485.

inexhaustibility. There is always more to be collected. The image of the antiquarian is anchored by readily legible objects, objects that can be roughly dated by a knowledgeable reader, but it also points, and simultaneously, to the idea of endless proliferation: the illegible become a stand-in for all those scraps of writing, all those printed images, which cannot be depicted except in their abstraction as part of a larger field of the collectable. The image then gestures toward one of the central facets of collecting as an endeavor: the tension between the finite and the infinite, that which has been collected and that which, because of its boundless nature, remains the collectable or the to be collected, an emblem of the collector's "struggle against dispersion."[18]

Individually, many elements of the image are opaque, but together they mark the antiquarian as a figure of immense refinement, a curator of rare objects. The various images within the central image all date to the history of kabuki in the city of Edo from the early seventeenth century (when Nakamura Kanzaburō established the first theater in Edo) through the 1670s (when Danjūrō I invented *aragoto* acting) and on to the early eighteenth century when his son inherited the Danjūrō lineage. But if the objects in the image mark the figure as an antiquarian, the collector himself—through the very act of collecting—defines these objects and images *as collectable*, maintaining a value as antiquarian objects, and defining as the past a particular moment extending from the late seventeenth to the early eighteenth century. As we look more closely at the world of nineteenth-century collecting, questions of how—and which—objects became the subject of antiquarian interest, and of what moments in the past came to be defined as history, will emerge as critical.

But even as this image evokes the world of the antiquarian in general, it can also be read as pointing to a specific figure: Utei Enba, Sanba's friend and mentor, who had, that same year, begun publishing his enormous *A Chronology of the Kabuki of Flowering Edo* (*Hana no Edo kabuki nendaiki*), a chronology of the history of kabuki in the city of Edo from the 1620s through the early nineteenth century. The antiquarian's honorary name of "chronology" (*nendaiki*), of course, points directly to Enba and to that immense work of history; but so too do the various objects in the image: Enba was a well-known collector of theatrical artifacts and a patron of the Danjūrō line of actors.[19] Indeed, the implied possession of these objects seems to act as a guarantor of the chronology referred to in the antiquarian's title. It is only the antiquarian with access to such objects who can craft such a chronology; the objects serve as a mark of legitimacy, even authority.

And not only do the objects mark the figure *as an antiquarian* but they also point directly to Enba's *Chronology*, the first volume of which was published in 1811, the

---

[18] See Walter Benjamin, *The Arcades Project*, trans. Howard Eiland and Kevin McLaughlin (Cambridge, MA: Belknap Press, 2002), p. 211.
[19] On Enba and the Mimasuren, see Nobuhiro Shinji, *Rakugo wa ikani shite keiseisaretaka* (Tokyo: Heibonsha, 1986), pp. 85ff.

same year as Sanba's *A Critique of the Audience*, and which carries images strikingly similar to each of the objects depicted in Kunisada's illustration to Sanba's book. Here, we might return to the image of the dance affixed to the top of the folding screen behind the figure of the antiquarian in *A Critique of the Audience*: it appears to be a rough copy of an image appearing about halfway through Volume One of Enba's *Chronology* (14 recto, 15 verso) depicting Ichikawa Danjūrō I along with contemporaries such as Nakamura Denkurō, the "youth" (*wakashu*) actors Yamakawa Naiki (Hikozaemon) and Sawai Kodenji (Takamura Matashirō), and players of female roles (*onnagata*) such as Nakayama Sayonosuke (Figure 2.2).[20] This image is itself, moreover, heir to an iconography of *wakashu* kabuki dances going back to the seventeenth century, pointing to kabuki's earliest history.[21]

If the image from Sanba's *A Critique of the Audience* presents Enba in the guise of antiquarian, marked by certain practices of collecting, it also suggests, through this interplay of images, how the *Chronology*, itself the product of a particular kind

**Figure 2.2** Katsukawa Shuntei, Ichikawa Danjūrō I, and his contemporaries from Utei Enba, *Hana no Edo kabuki nendaiki*, 1811.
Source: National Diet Library, Tokyo.

[20] Utei Enba, *Hana no Edo kabuki nendaiki* (Tokyo: Kabuki Shuppanbu, 1926), pp. 16–17.
[21] See Suwa Haruo, "Kaiga shiryō ni miru shoki kabuki no geitai: wakashu kabuki no kaiga," *Kokugo to kokubungaku* 50, 5 (1973), 42–56.

of antiquarianism, is, indeed, an embodiment on the printed page of the collector's impulse. In his preface to the *Chronology*, Enba wrote of how his love of the theater went back to his childhood and how "now, approaching seventy, I have been watching plays for over sixty years and, having overheard the tales of my elders, know over a hundred years of gossip."[22] But if Enba would begin by invoking the private and the personal (that which he has seen with his own eyes, heard with his own ears), he then turns immediately to a different record, the published record provided by the printed playbill: "In addition, I have purchased, here and there, old kabuki playbills (*furuki kyōgen banzuke*) that have come down over the generations and I have been fortunate to seek the help of Yōryū Shujin in verifying these sources."[23] Here, the role of printed playbills (*banzuke*) in the way that Enba imagines his project is striking. Like Tsubouchi Shōyō's 1920 *Reminiscences of the Kabuki I Saw in My Youth*, published over a century later, Enba's *Chronology* invokes as a point of departure a collection of playbills: as with Shōyō's book, the playbills serve as an entry point into a series of historical reflections. But whereas Shōyō's reflections turn inward to the deeply personal, to his youth and to his relationship with his mother, Enba's *Chronology* pushes outward toward a tradition of print that Mary Elizabeth Berry has called "the library of public information" of early modern Japan which sought "to examine and order the verifiable facts of contemporary experience for an open audience of consumers."[24]

This *public* disposition of the *Chronology* can best be grasped in comparison to a work that Enba had compiled a decade earlier, "The Seven Heirs of Danjūrō" ("Danjūrō shichise no mago"; 1801), one section of which is a chronology, "A Theatrical Chronology of Seven Generations of Ichikawa" ("Ichikawa shichise kyōgen nendaiki"). The compilation of "The Seven Heirs of Danjūrō" was to celebrate the succession, in 1800, of the ten-year-old Ichikawa Ebizō to the name of Danjūrō VII, following the sudden death of his uncle and adopted father Danjūrō VI. The book details the biographies of the seven generations of actors to bear the Ichikawa Danjūrō name, but "The Seven Heirs of Danjūrō," while printed, was not published; rather, it was privately printed by the group of supporters (*hiiki renjū*) of the Danjūrō lineage, the Mimasuren, of which Enba was the head.[25] Furthermore, "The Seven Heirs of Danjūrō" is a composite work: the chronology of the seven Danjūrō actors is interwoven with commemorative poetry by members of the Mimasuren and with illustrations of the actors' lives copied from previously published works. Some of the material in this chronology would be later reworked and absorbed into Enba's 1811 *Chronology*, but there are some important differences between

---

[22] Utei Enba, *Hana no Edo kabuki nendaiki*, Hanrei, n.p.
[23] Utei Enba, *Hana no Edo kabuki nendaiki*. Yōryū Shujin has never been identified.
[24] Mary Elizabeth Berry, *Japan in Print: Information and Nation in the Early Modern Period* (Berkeley, CA: University of California Press, 2006), p. 15.
[25] The term "Mimasuren" comes from the three (*mi*) nested boxes (*masu*) of Ichikawa Danjūrō's crest. "*Ren*" comes from the term *hiiki renjū* meaning a group of supporters or fan club.

this earlier work, printed but not commercially published, and Enba's later work that would mark the beginning of a new chapter in the historiography of kabuki.

While both books invoke the genre of the chronology (*nendaiki*), "The Seven Heirs of Danjūrō" fashions the structure of chronology as biography, with the entries arranged around the individual careers of the seven actors to bear the Danjūrō name. Enba's later *Chronology*, by contrast, is arranged in strict chronological order, beginning in 1624 with Nakamura Kanzaburō petitioning to establish Edo's first theater, and ending in 1804 with the beginning of the Bunka Era.

In its conception of theatrical history as the history of the careers of actors, "The Seven Heirs of Danjūrō" is clearly indebted to a form of history writing that had dominated treatments of the theatrical past during the eighteenth and early nineteenth centuries, a model that came to prominence in *A Complete Book of Actors Past and Present* (*Kokon yakusha taizen*), published in 1750 by the Hachimonjiya firm in Kyoto. Hachimonjiya had pioneered, and continued to control, the market in actor critiques (*yakusha hyōbanki*), that genre satirized by Sanba in 1811.[26] After an overview of the history of kabuki in the first volume, *A Complete Book of Actors Past and Present* is arranged by actor and becomes essentially a history of kabuki told as the aggregate of individual careers, drawing heavily on the actor critiques themselves.

In Enba's *Chronology*, by contrast, the basic unit is not the career of the actor but the calendar year, and the basic archive not the actor critique but the printed playbill. Two centuries on, Enba's project—to bring together the names, dates, and places contained in ephemera and to construct out of them a detailed historical chronology—seems obvious. And yet, the seeming obviousness of the project should not blind us to the fact that although the history of printed playbills goes back to at least the late seventeenth century, it was not until Enba's chronology that the playbill came to be used as historical material in writing about the theater's past.[27] Indeed, Enba's *Chronology* represents a fundamental break in the way that kabuki's history was conceptualized; in turn, his work embodies a larger shift in the way in which amateur historians of the early nineteenth century had begun to reimagine the very practice of historical inquiry.

If one looks back from the *Chronology* to *A Complete Book of Actors Past and Present*, it becomes clear that, in addition to making the basic unit "historical time" rather than the career of individual actors, Enba had also radically changed the *scale* of history. *A Complete Book of Actors Past and Present* begins with a broad overview that first touches on the origins of drama in the Han and Tang Dynasties in China and then refers to the mytho-history of Japanese drama that goes back to the age of the gods. The subsequent five volumes treat the careers of actors

[26] On the history of *yakusha hyōbanki*, see Akama Ryō, *Zusetsu Edo no engekisho*, pp. 199–201; Raz, *Audience and Actors*, pp. 155–57.

[27] On the history of printed playbills, see Akama Ryō, *Zusetsu Edo no engekisho*, pp. 160–80. According to Akama, the oldest extant printed playbill dates to 1675.

arranged not strictly by chronology but first and foremost by role type, beginning with male leads and followed by villains and players of female roles (*onnagata*). Entries for individual actors draw on the actor critiques, and lineages of actors are treated in a single entry. The first entry of *A Complete Book of Actors Past and Present*, for example, treats both Ichikawa Danjūrō I and his son, Danjūrō II. Furthermore, the histories of kabuki in Edo, Kyoto, and Osaka are all treated as a single field.[28]

Enba's *Chronology*, by contrast, radically shrinks the scope of his history: he treats only the city of Edo and only the period from 1624 to 1804, completely ignoring the mytho-history that had pervaded publications on kabuki; yet, he produces from this a much longer work because the detail is so much finer. This is especially visible in the composition of the individual volumes: Volume One covers the 103-year period from 1624 to 1727, but then each of the subsequent 7 volumes covers a period of only 9–15 years.[29]

As Nagatomo Chiyoji has noted, the emergence of the chronology along with other forms of historical writing in the Genroku period (1688–1703) "reflects the deepening of scholarly thought and a tendency towards positivism" of society in general. In the century-and-a-half that followed, the chronology would appear in an extraordinary variety of forms, from all sizes and format of printed books to various kinds of broadsheets.[30] By the nineteenth century, when "a historical consciousness was widely shared as both common sense and consensus," the chronology had become ubiquitous.[31]

At one level, Enba may have drawn inspiration for the idea of a theatrical chronology from a 1727 chronology of the puppet theater, *A Chronology of Puppetry Past and Present* (*Ima mukashi ayatsuri nendaiki*) by Nishizawa Ippū (1655–1731), to which he would likely have had access through a pirated edition published in Edo in 1797.[32] But in his *Chronology*, Enba borrows his basic framework and the structure of his approach to the past directly from a different source, a widely reprinted illustrated chronology of Japanese history, *The Illustrated and Annotated Chronology of Japan* (*Nendaiki ōeshō*). *The Illustrated and Annotated Chronology of Japan* was first published in 1692 and circulated widely in the late

---

[28] For a general overview of *A Complete Book of Actors Past and Present* and the context for its publication, see Hirose Chisako, "Hachimonjiya gekisho no seiritsu: 'Shinsen kokon yakusha taizen' o megutte," *Geinōshi kenkyū* 45 (1974), 44–64.

[29] On the issue of scale in Enba's chronology, see Hirose Chisako, "*Hana no Edo kabuki nendaiki* no seiritsu," *Kinsei bungei* 41 (1984), 45.

[30] Nagatomo Chiyoji, *Edo jidai no shomotsu to dokusho* (Tokyo: Tōkyōdō Shuppan, 1999), p. 231. On the ubiquity and the variety of formats of *nendaiki* in early modern Japan, see Suzuki Toshiyuki, "'Nendaiki' oboegaki," *Mō hitotsu no kotenchi: zenkindai Nihon no chi no kanōsei*, ed. Maeda Maeda Masayuki (Tokyo: Bensei shuppan, 2012), p. 215.

[31] Suzuki, "'Nendaiki' oboegaki," p. 219.

[32] Fujii Otoo, "*Gedai kagami* oyobi *Ayatsuri nendaiki* no ihan," in Fujii Otoo *Edo bungaku sōsetsu* pp. 6–7.

eighteenth century, with versions printed in 1760, 1770, 1773, and 1781 amid the emergence of a deep and abiding interest in Japan's past among Nativist scholars.

And a comparison of Enba's *Chronology* with the *Illustrated and Annotated Chronology of Japan* is suggestive. The *Illustrated and Annotated Chronology of Japan* begins with an enumeration of the seven generations of heavenly deities, (*tenjin shichidai*) followed by the five generations of earthly deities (*chijin godai*), and bears an illustration at the top of the page which depicts the creation of heaven and earth (*tenchi kaibyaku*); at the center of the image is Kunitokotachi no Mikoto followed by the beginnings of the Japanese (*Nihonjin no hajimari*) and the birth of the gods. The subsequent pages bear illustrations of the successive generations of both heavenly and earthly gods (Figure 2.3).[33]

The illustrations to Enba's *Chronology* begin with a different kind of origin: the first image is labeled "Heaven and Earth are One Great Theater"—a phrase critical to the ontology of the theater in the nineteenth century—and shows the sun (heaven) over Mount Fuji (earth). To this fundamental dualism between

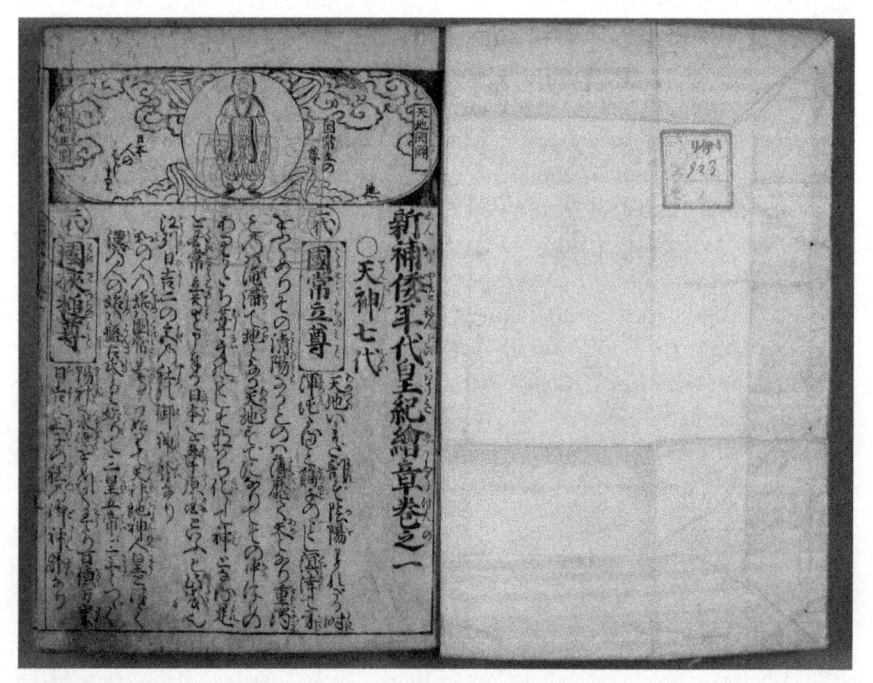

**Figure 2.3** Creation of heaven and earth from *Shinpo Yamato nendai kōki eshō*, 1692.
*Source*: Waseda University Library.

---

[33] For an easily accessible edition of *Nendaiki ōeshō*, see *Shinpo Yamato nendai kōki eshō* (Kyoto: Fushimiya Hyōaemon et al., 1692), http://www.wul.waseda.ac.jp/kotenseki/html/ri04/ri04_00923/index.html.

heaven and earth is added a flying crane, the symbol of the Nakamura-za, the first of Edo's theaters, founded in 1624. The second illustration, labeled origins (*kaibyaku*), directly imitating the *Illustrated and Annotated Chronology of Japan*, shows Nakamura Kanzaburō I, the founder of the Nakamura-za, with a dancer of Saruwaka-mai, below a curtain adorned with the ginkgo leaf, the crest of the Nakamura-za (Figure 2.4).

In place of the lineage of gods which follows in the *Illustrated and Annotated Chronology of Japan*, Enba's *Chronology* offers 100 illustrations of actors from the early history of kabuki, taken, Enba notes, from a copy in his personal collection of the 1693 *A Beauty Contest of One Hundred Actors Past and Present* (*Kokon shibai irokurabe hyakunin isshu*), which was illustrated by Torii Kiyonobu. As Ihara Toshirō notes in his preface to the modern reproduction of *A Beauty Contest of One Hundred Actors Past and Present*, the book was banned shortly after its publication in 1693, and all copies as well as the woodblocks were ordered to be collected and destroyed.[34] In this context, Enba's use of these illustrations

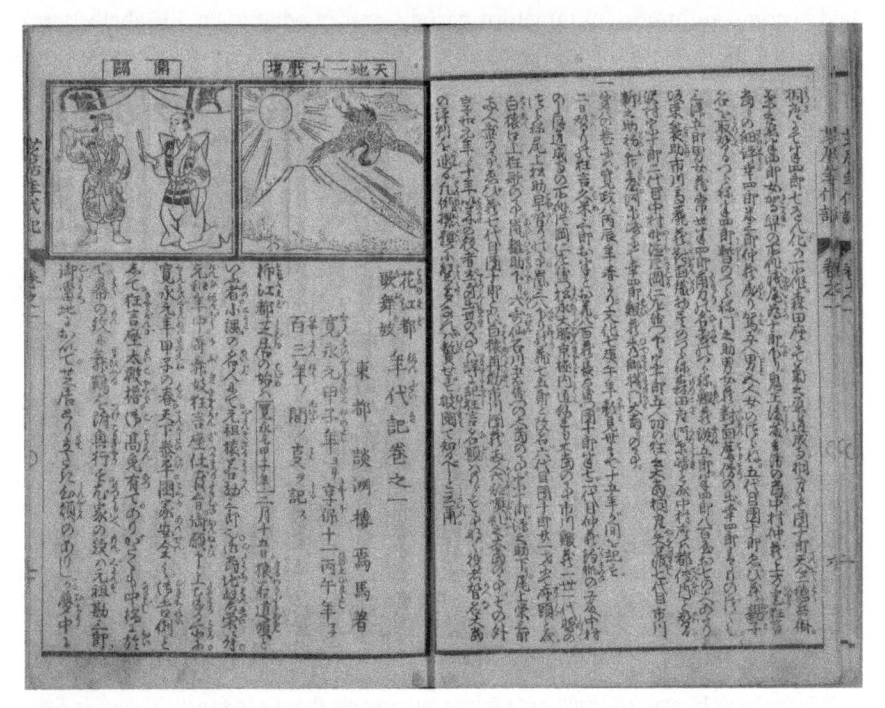

**Figure 2.4** Katsukawa Shuntei, heaven and earth are one great theater from Utei Enba, *Hana no Edo kabuki nendaiki*, 1811.
Source: National Diet Library, Tokyo.

---

[34] See Ihara's preface to Dōgedō Shiten, *Shibai hyakunin isshu*, ed. Ihara Toshirō (Tokyo: Engei Chinso Kankōkai, 1914). Doi: 10.11501/1088269.

reproduced from his own collection allow for these rare images to circulate in public for the first time in over a century; however, the inclusion of these illustrations also, and especially, used in counterpoint with the images of gods from the *Illustrated and Annotated Chronology of Japan* suggests a subversive edge.

At a moment when Nativism had begun to occupy a central place within the intellectual discourse of Japan, leading to a renewed interest in accounts of the earliest history of the archipelago, Enba self-consciously invokes the origin myth and models his *Chronology* on one of the most widely available accounts of the mythohistory of Japan. Given this contrast, it is difficult not to see the 1811 *Chronology* as something deeply parodic: Enba was a master of playfulness and humor and in Chapter 3, I will turn to a parodic map of the world of the theater that he created in the opening years of the nineteenth century. The juxtaposition of high and low fundamental to Enba's opening gesture seems, then, part of a broader cultural landscape of "inversion" which, as Katsuya Hirano has suggested, is a critical part of the intellectual and social world of the late eighteenth and early nineteenth centuries.[35] By the early nineteenth century, the chronology as a genre had become an important target for parody, part of what Mary Elizabeth Berry has called the guise of the "playground" in which history appeared in early modern texts.[36] And yet, despite the irreverence of the gesture of modeling a history of a theatrical art performed by outcasts, and, for much of its history, tied to both female and male prostitution on a chronology of the imperial lineage that returns to the divine origins of the Japanese people, Enba's chronology is actually a work of great scholarship and erudition, entirely devoid of humor. Indeed, after this initial parodic gesture, a striking gap opens between the *form* of the *Chronology*, which copies directly the format of the *Illustrated and Annotated Chronology of Japan*, most noticeably in the layout of the pages and illustrations, and its *content*, which completely eschews the parodic for the historical, the quotidian, and the antiquarian.[37]

It is here, in the tension between parody and antiquarianism, that we can see most clearly the way in which this work represents a broader intellectual shift in the early nineteenth century, a shift that is largely unobserved in treatments of the late Edo period, treatments which still too often present the culture of this period as one defined entirely by play. To understand how the antiquarian imagination of the early nineteenth century diverged from, and became a critique of, the parodic

---

[35] See Katsuya Hirano, *The Politics of Dialogic Imagination: Power and Popular Culture in Early Modern Japan* (Chicago, IL: University of Chicago Press, 2013), esp. Chapter 3: "Comic Realism: A Strategy of Inversion."

[36] Berry, *Japan in Print*, pp. 235–40. In 1802, both Shikitei Sanba and Kyokutei Bakin published short works that took the chronology as target of parody, *Kusazōshi kojitsuke nendaiki* and *Shijū Kara ryōken nendaiki*, respectively. On Sanba's work, see Marcia Yonemoto, *Mapping Early Modern Japan: Space, Place, and Culture in the Tokugawa Period, 1603–1868* (Berkeley, CA: University of California Press, 2003), pp. 149–54.

[37] Hirose Chisako has noted that the "dry and boring" nature of the work is unusual for Enba's oeuvre. See Hirose, "*Hana no Edo kabuki nendaiki* no seiritsu," 40–41.

sensibility that had dominated the literary culture of the late eighteenth century, we might return to 1811. It was within this world that both Enba and Sanba fashioned their own collections of theater ephemera and participated in a genealogy of collecting that would continue to shape approaches to theatrical history for over a century after their deaths.

## III *Circa* 1811: Curiosity, Collecting, and the History of Kabuki

In the fourth month of 1811, the same year in which he began to publish his *Chronology of Edo Kabuki*, Enba was invited to participate in a gathering of collectors held at the Unchaten, a teahouse located between the Yushima Seidō and the Kanda Myōjin Shrine.[38] The Unchakai, as the group of collectors was known, was hosted by the publisher and book dealer Kariganeya Gisuke, a protégé of Ōta Nanpo and a noted collector with "a penchant for the love of the past (*kōko no kuse*) who collects all manner of antiques such as old paintings, calligraphy, and ceramics without regard to whether they are popular or refined."[39]

The men who gathered at the Unchaten came from a variety of backgrounds: they included doyens of the literary world like Ōta Nanpo and Santō Kyōden (and Kyōden's brother Kyōzan) but also amateur literati like the host Kariganeya, the physician Katō Ebian, and the taphophile Nakao Choken. Much of what we know of the gathering we owe to a detailed account left by Nanpo, and this source, in turn, allows us to conjure up a world of sociability centered on *things* even when all that is left of those things is a record constituted of words.[40]

What is especially interesting about this gathering for our understanding the emergence of a new mode of historicism informing theatrical history in the early years of the nineteenth century is the way in which theatrical objects are located within a broader world of collectables. Santō Kyōden, for example, brought to the gathering a variety of objects related to the history of the demimonde: a note in the hand of the great seventeenth-century courtesan Manji Takao, a doll of a "beautiful youth" made by the seventeenth-century doll maker Hinaya Ryūho, and an image of the Yoshiwara from the 1670s by Hishikawa Moronobu.

One of Enba's objects, too, was from the history of the pleasure quarters, a guidebook or "view" (*saiken*) of the Yoshiwara from the early eighteenth century. But like Enba's other objects, this booklet had a connection to the history of theater for it supposedly contained the signatures, on its endpaper, of the forty-seven retainers who had participated in the 1703 vendetta against Kira Yoshinaka

---

[38] On the Unchakai, see Satō Yukiko, *Santō Kyōden: kokkei share daiichi no sakusha* Kyoto: Mineruva Shobō, 2009), pp. 272–74.

[39] This is Shikitei Sanba's description, quoted in Satō Yukiko, *Santō Kyōden*, p. 273.

[40] Ōta Nanpo, "Ichiwa ichigen," in Hamada Giichirō ed. *Ōta Nanpo zenshū* vol. 16 (Tokyo: Iwanami Shoten, 1988), pp. 89–111. The following description of the items presented at the Unchakai are based on Ōta's record of the event.

immortalized in the 1748 play *Chūshingura: The Storehouse of Loyal Retainers* (*Kanadehon chūshingura*). Enba also brought two other objects with a connection to the vendetta: a short spear said to be that of Ōishi Yoshio, the leader of the forty-seven retainers, and a candleholder used in the night attack on Lord Kira.

Along with these objects, Enba also displayed a seemingly more mundane piece of theatrical history, a scroll bearing an image of actors dating to the late seventeenth or early eighteenth century, perhaps, one imagines, the model for the dance image found in his *Chronology* and appearing on the screen depicted in Sanba's *A Critique of the Audience*. Nor was Enba the only collector to bring with him objects related to theatrical history. Another collector brought a ticket for entrance to *sajiki* seating from the Yamamura Theater which had been abolished in 1714 following the Ejima-Ikushima Affair in which a lady-in-waiting to the Shogun's mother was discovered to have had a rendezvous with the actor Ikushima Shingorō. And at a second gathering, at the beginning of the following month, Nakao Choken displayed his collection of playbills from the 1740s and '50s and a print of the actor Ōtani Jicchō II; and Katō Ebian brought an image of kabuki actors from the Genroku period (1688–1704). What these various objects and images, and image-bearing objects, share is that almost all date from the late seventeenth and early eighteenth centuries, 100 years before the gathering itself and roughly the same time span covered by the images at the beginning of Enba's *Chronology*. The past for these collectors was a very specific and local past, both in time and place; for them, theatrical history was one node, and a critical one, in a cultural history of the city of Edo.

In many ways, the Unchakai is heir to a tradition of sociability that revolves around collecting and displaying that goes back to the 1770s and emerges out of *kyōka* poetry circles. Indeed, both Enba and Ōta Nanpo had participated in a "*takara awase*," or treasure showing, thirty years earlier in 1783 at the Kawachiya restaurant near Yanagibashi in Ryōgoku, and the young Santō Kyōden would be employed to provide illustrations for the published record of the gathering just at the time his own writing career was beginning to take off. But if these two gatherings stand in a genealogical relationship one to another, the distance between them also suggests how much had changed in the decades between 1780 and the period around 1810.

As Yamamoto Hirofumi has written, the "treasures" of *takara awase* gatherings of the 1770s and '80s were themselves fakes and were simply there to provide opportunities for poets and writers to "show off to one another their comic prose which details the origins [of the 'treasures']."[41] The objects displayed at the Kawachiya in 1783, for example, included a golden egg, the umbrella used by the

---

[41] Yamamoto Harufumi, "Kaidai: takara awase kai to 'Kyōbun takara awase no ki,'" in *"Kyōbun takara awase no ki" no kenkyū*, ed. Kobayashi Fumiko and Nobuhiro Shinji (Tokyo: Kyūko Shoin, 2000), p. 290.

ninth-century poet Ono no Komachi, and the famed bell of the Dōjōji Temple. The gatherings invoked a form of antiquarian sociability, but they were, in fact, premised on the fanciful and the ludic, with fantastical objects purporting to come from legend and myth described in a poetic language that embedded them in a complex literary fabric of intertextuality so important to the poetry circles of the late eighteenth century. All of this was absent from the Unchakai and, as Satō Yukiko has suggested, "while it might recall the *takara awase* gatherings in which comical treasures were brought together, the Unchakai was not a gathering with such a humorous bent but rather an occasion to share nostalgic remains of Edo."[42]

Among the participants of the Unchakai, Santō Kyōden was most self-conscious about a turn away from the world of play and a rejection of his past work as a writer of playful fiction. As Satō has argued in her biography of Kyōden, the period around 1810 marked a moment of disillusionment with the parodic and an increasing turn toward forms of evidentiary scholarship.[43] Such an ambivalence toward the playful world of the late eighteenth century can also be seen in the work of Kyōden's friends and contemporaries including Sanba, who is best remembered even today as a master of the comic and whose work is suffused by satire and parody.

And Sanba's case is emblematic. In 1815, the same year that Enba published the final volumes of his chronology of kabuki, Sanba, his friend and protégé, set about putting in order his own substantial collection of broadsheets and playbills in a series of scrapbooks: one scrapbook (*harikomichō*) devoted to ephemera related to the history of storytelling and a further sixteen albums into which Sanba pasted *banzuke*, programs from Edo's three kabuki theaters. It seems possible, even likely, that, at some level, Sanba saw the creation of these albums as preparatory to his own succession to Enba as the chronology's editor: Enba was in his early seventies, thirty-three years Sanba's senior, and the coincidence of Sanba's creation of his scrapbooks with the publication of the final volumes of Enba's chronology is suggestive.

In the event, Sanba died in 1822, five months before Enba, but his scrapbooks would remain as the record of a set of practices of collecting and of engagements with the archiving of ephemeral culture; they are of immense historical interest, shedding light on both Sanba's own historical concerns and those of his circle, including Enba. Enba's project to create an ongoing chronology of kabuki's history would be continued by the hands of others for over half a century after the Meiji Restoration of 1868. I will return to the meandering history after Enba's death of the *Chronology* and to its subsequent iterations under Ishizuka Hōkaishi and Tamura Nariyoshi. But first, Sanba's own habits as a collector demand our

---

[42] Satō, *Santō Kyōden*, p. 272.
[43] On Kyōden's turn toward historical scholarship, Satō, *Santō Kyōden*, pp. 237–89.

attention as a way to think about a set of transformations in historical inquiry and a method out of which Enba's work grew and in which that work would participate.

In his manuscript preface to "The Origins of the Revival of Storytelling" ("Otoshibanashi chūkō raiyu"), the scrapbook devoted to storytelling, Sanba wrote that he had been "hiding away" this material for some years. He couches the production of the scrapbook in the rhetoric of making visible what was hidden and of providing a record of the "origins" of the nineteenth-century revival in storytelling, even if that record must, inevitably, remain incomplete with "not an inconsiderable number of items already lost or having escaped me."[44] The scrapbooks are products of this tension between the desire to collect, collate, and preserve—broadly speaking, to archive—and the knowledge that this project of documentation would remain incomplete and imperfect.

As he wrote in the 1815 manuscript preface to his collection of theater programs, "Programs of Edo's Three Theaters" ("Edo sanshibai monbanzuke"), his project might serve as a resource for historians of the future looking back on his own world:

> As for these play programs, countless numbers have been produced between when I began my project and now, with those of old mostly scattered and lost and rarely existing today. From our own time, I have sought out examples here and there and have, over time, amassed a large number and have now taken the occasion to put them in order, mend any tears, and form these sixteen volumes. I will continue to search out the many that have eluded me and add them as I do.[45]

More material was being produced each day and so rapidly that it was impossible for the collector to keep pace even as the fragile record of the past was gradually eroded by time. Sanba was caught up in the impossible dream of archiving the present and arresting time.

It is easy to imagine that Sanba's impulse to collect and preserve was in part driven by personal circumstance; roughly a decade earlier, in 1806, Sanba's home was destroyed by fire and, as he would later recall, "the majority of my library was reduced to nothing."[46] The earliest ephemera collected in "The Origins of the Revival of Storytelling" (invitations, broadsheets, mementos) date from 1808,

---

[44] Shikitei Sanba, "Otoshibanashi chūkō raiyu," manuscript, Kotenseki Shiryōshitsu, national Diet Library, http://dl.ndl.go.jp/info:ndljp/pid/1288373?__lang=en. For a transcription of Sanba's preface see Shikitei Sanba, "Otoshibanashi ezuri gachō," in Geinōshi Kenkyūkai ed., *Nihon Shomin bunka shiryō shūsei* vol.8 (Tokyo: Sanichi Shobō) 127.

[45] Shikitei Sanba, "Edo sanshibai monbanzuke," manuscript, Kotenseki Shiryōshitsu, National Diet Library, http://dl/ndl.go.jp/info:ndljp/pid/1288373?__lang=en. For a transcription of Sanba's preface, see Hattori Yukio, "Shikitei Sanba no shibai banzuke shūshū," *Nihon kosho tsūhin* 49, 2 (February 1984), 4. Both "Otoshibanashi chūkō raiyu" and "Edo sanshibai monbanzuke" contain ephemera that postdate Sanba's preface as well as blank pages suggesting the ongoing nature of his projects.

[46] Shikitei Sanba, "Shikitei zakki," in *Zoku enseki jusshu*, ed. Ichijima Kenkichi and Iwamoto Kattōchi, vol. 1 (Tokyo: Kokusho Kankōkai, 1908), p. 61.

after the fire, and surely there is something poignant about the idea of a collector's obsessions being reduced to ashes. Sanba, however, would come to understand that the fire that claimed his library was itself only part of a much larger cultural phenomenon of disappearance and dispersal. It was symptomatic, of course, but the problem had as much to do with the sheer quantity and ephemeral nature of printed matter that was so easily "scattered and lost" as it did with the occasional, if devastating, effects of fire. After the fire, Sanba worked as a used book dealer, and this experience no doubt heightened both his awareness of the fragile nature of the book as a material object and his keen sense that the progressive commercialization of print had led to a debasement of literary culture in the first decade of the nineteenth century, with publishers "prizing most above all else works that will sell among the boorish and rustic."[47]

Sanba's scrapbooks, particularly the smaller book containing materials on the history of storytelling, preserve much material that would otherwise have been completely lost. Sanba himself seems to have understood this. As he writes in the 1815 manuscript preface to his collection of theater programs, his project might serve as a resource for historians of the future looking back on his own world: "Certainly, those of some refinement will sneer that this is a useless and wasteful endeavor, but I hope that perhaps this collection might become a meager piece for the study of the past (*inishie manabi*), shedding some light, no matter how dim, onto the customs of that world."[48] Yes, Sanba's preface tells us of a broad impulse to collect and preserve ephemeral material that is being scattered and lost even as it is being produced, but it also reveals his understanding of the status of this material as a historical record, a record of the recent past but also, ultimately, a record for the future of Sanba's own historical moment.

The playbills and ephemera Sanba collected provide a form of documentary evidence of the cultural practices of the past: they show, often in minute detail, the proximate worlds of storytelling and of the theater and are filled with names and dates and places, allowing for a rich reconstruction of an otherwise ephemeral aspect of nineteenth-century social life. But to understand Sanba's albums only, or even primarily, as evidence of the practices they record is to overlook these albums as themselves a particular kind of document, one whose interest lies as much in how it was constituted as a physical object as the witness it bears to other phenomena. In this regard, to think of these albums in relation to Enba's *Chronology* is instructive. There is, no doubt, a shared impulse between the published chronology and Sanba's scrapbooks, but they are also very different. Enba's *Chronology* is synthetic, culling and bringing together information from various sources but presenting it as a single chronology of kabuki beginning in 1624. In the *Chronology*,

---

[47] Shikitei Sanba, *Ukiyoburo; Kejō suigen maku no soto; Daisen sekai gakuyasagashi*, ed. Satake Akihiro, Shin Nihon Koten Bungaku Taikei, vol. 86 (Tokyo: Iwanami Shoten, 1989).
[48] Shikitei Sanba, "Edo sanshibai monbanzuke."

the data are regularized into a kind of table and arranged in chronological order as a single history, and this vision of kabuki's history would serve as the template for the various timelines of theater history that would become ubiquitous in nineteenth-century broadsheets and ephemera.

In Sanba's albums, we encounter the materials of theater history in a rather different form: not as they were first produced and consumed, to be sure, but not either as wholly synthesized, collated data, entirely independent of their material expression. Rather, the albums are composed entirely of printed playbills that have been cut into single sheets and then pasted in chronological order into the albums. There is, then, a sense of *inbetweenness* that characterizes the albums; they preserve a huge amount of information but also, in somewhat altered states, they preserve the material forms in which this information was embedded (Figure 2.5). Indeed, there is in Sanba's preface an ambiguity of motive. He writes that he seeks to preserve these programs now "mostly scattered and lost," but to what end? For the data they contain and, hence, for what they tell us of the theater? Or as examples of a particular kind of material object, as historical artifacts that might serve as what Sanba himself calls in his preface to his collection of playbills "devices for thinking about the past"?[49]

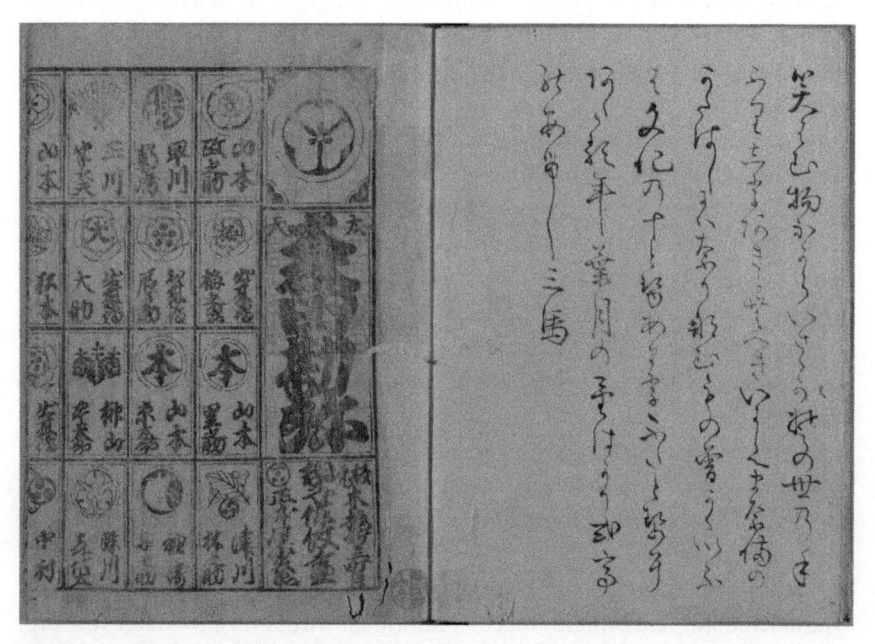

**Figure 2.5** End of Shikitei Sanba's preface and first playbill from "Sanshibai monbanzuke," 1815.
Source: National Diet Library, Tokyo.

[49] Shikitei Sanba, "Edo sanshibai monbanzuke."

It is this *inbetweenness* that is most striking about these albums and most suggestive about their place within the cultural economy of the fist decades of the nineteenth century. Instead of keeping the playbills as independent pamphlets—as they were kept in the Hayashi library and in other collections—Sanba first disassembles and then reassembles them as single sheets pasted into albums. The albums, then, are peculiar artifacts that maintain a status somewhere between unique objects and the infinitely repeatable. Each album is unique but is created out of material that was intended to be reproduced and was reproducible; each is a handmade book composed almost entirely of printed matter reshaped and annotated by hand. Usually, we think of the "original" preceding the copy: here, the assemblage of copies produces what is unique. As material objects, then, the albums occupy a strange place in the economy of the book in the nineteenth century, being neither wholly manuscript nor printed book, they are stitched together using pieces of material scavenged and collected, collated and annotated, composed entirely of foreign parts.

At one level, however, Sanba's two collections of ephemera are also quite different from each other. The scrapbook in which he collected materials on the history of storytelling, "The Origins of the Revival of Storytelling," is visually much more striking and contains an array of material in different shapes and sizes and colors: a fan printed to commemorate a performance by Sanshōtei Karaku, invitations, and various *surimono*, the privately issued prints so popular with collectors in the late Edo period (Figure 2.6). As in albums of *surimono* compiled in these decades, the material in Sanba's "The Origins of the Revival of Storytelling" is essentially occasional and commemorative. His scrapbook is striking in its impulse specifically to document the history of storytelling and, in this respect, it is unique. Or almost so: the scrapbook was twice copied out by hand in painstaking detail. Each copy literally traces over the original printed matter—preserving its contours—as well as Sanba's own manuscript notes. Of course, the copies, which replicate the entire scrapbook by hand, lose the clear and visceral distinction in Sanba's scrapbook between the printed matter pasted onto the page and the notes. Sanba's original, clearly pastiche, becomes, in the two manuscript copies, seamless. One can sense an almost devolutionary impulse at work in which, through the intervention of the human hand, the technically more advanced text, printed and yet ephemeral, is salvaged from time, fixed and preserved by being translated, in stages, *backward* into manuscript.[50]

---

[50] This process, of course, evokes the larger resonances between the souvenir and the book to which Susan Stewart has pointed:

It is significant that such souvenirs [as scrapbooks] often appropriate certain aspects of the book in general; we might note especially the way in which an exterior of little material value envelops a great "interior significance," and the way both souvenir and book transcend their particular contexts. Yet, at the same time, these souvenirs absolutely deny the book's mode of mechanical reproduction. You cannot make a copy of a scrapbook without being painfully aware that you possess a mere representation

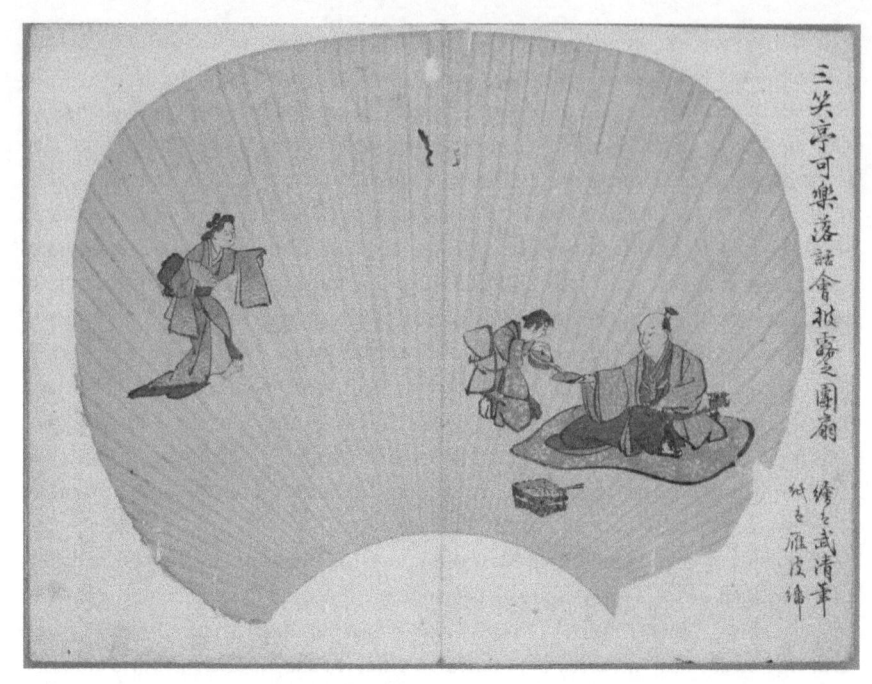

**Figure 2.6** Kita Busei, fan commemorating performance by Sanshōtei Karaku in 1811 from Shikitei Sanba, "Otoshibanashi chūkō raiyū".
*Source*: National Diet Library, Tokyo.

The albums in Sanba's scrapbook of theater programs, collectively titled "Programs of Edo's Three Theaters," are visually much less arresting than "The Origins of the Revival of Storytelling" and much of the material they contain—theater programs dating from the 1730s and onward—has been preserved in other collections. At the level of data, these albums are made redundant by works such as Enba's *Chronology* and its sequels and now increasingly by databases. Thus while "Programs of Edo's Three Theaters" is of less inherent interest to the historian of early modern culture than "The Origins of the Revival of Storytelling," these albums nevertheless present a case that is, in some ways, more interesting still for thinking about the ambiguities and complexities of the status of such handmade albums in an age of print. While "The Origins of the Revival of Storytelling" collects material that was occasional and commemorative, printed in small runs but not published and sold, the sixteen volumes of "Programs of Edo's Three Theaters" are composed entirely of printed booklets that *were* published and sold in and around Edo's theaters. These booklets occupy, then, a different place within

of the original. The original will always supplant the copy in a way that is not open to the products of reproduction.
See Stewart, *On Longing*, p. 139.

the contours of the private and the public and within the general cultural economy of early nineteenth-century Edo than do objects like *surimono*, images that were printed but not commercially published.

The public and commercial nature of these playbills is illustrated in Sanba's 1806 *Theater Chic This Side of the Curtain*, his satirical novella that depicts the world of the theater "beyond the stage curtain," the world, that is, of the audience. In *Theater Chic This Side of the Curtain*, there is a scene in which a vendor appears in the theater selling various playbills and programs along with tea, lunchboxes, sweets, dumplings, and fruit. The insertion of such printed matter among other consumables is suggestive of what the theater historian Akama Ryō has called the "commodification" of this kind of printed theater ephemera in the late Edo period.[51] Sanba's own writing on the theater in the first decades of the nineteenth century forms a series of very self-conscious reflections on commodification. *Theater Chic This Side of the Curtain* begins with a meditation on the special place of Edo's three theaters within what Sanba calls the "marketplace of Edo" (*Ō-Edo no shōkinjō*), and everywhere in the text appear references to the prominent place occupied within this economy by printed matter: broadsheets and flyers, playbills, programs, and actor prints, even lists of actors' salaries.

On one level, of course, the collector repeats the acquisitive impulses of the consumer, which Sanba himself observes in the opening lines of his preface to "Playbills of Edo's Three Theaters": "Since the study of the past has recently become quite popular, if something is merely said to be antique, no matter how trifling an object, it is highly prized and there have come to be many who amuse themselves at the expense of thousands of pieces of gold." The fetishistic character of the commodity is not only preserved but also augmented, and hence these albums pose a new problem: what becomes of the commodity nature of these items—designed to be consumed in the theater alongside tea and sweets—when they are removed from circulation, when they no longer function within the economy for which they were designed, when they are fixed in a collection, pasted into albums? Here, the collector undertakes what Walter Benjamin once so eloquently described as "the Sisyphean task of divesting things of their commodity character by taking possession of them."[52] Sanba's albums precisely bear witness to this process: the reproducible is turned into the unique, the ephemeral is fixed,

---

[51] Shikitei Sanba, *Ukiyoburo; Kejō suigen maku no soto; Daisen sekai gakuyasagashi*, p. 331. In his satirical encyclopedia of the theater, *Shibai kinmō zui* (1803), Sanba similarly lists illustrated playbills (*kyōgen banzuke*), picture books (*ehon*), and digests of the scripts (*ōmuseki*) alongside lunchboxes, tea, sweets, and tangerines as goods that vendors (*nakauri*) sold in theaters. Shikitei Sanba, *Shibai kinmo zui: Kyōwa sannen shohanbon*, Kabuki no Bunken 3 (Tokyo: Nihon Geijutsu Bunka Shinkōkai, 2001). On the commodification of theater ephemera, see Hattori Yukio, "Shibaihon taishūka no seiki (1)," *Nihon Kosho tsūhin* 58, 10 (October 1993), 10–11; Hattori Yukio, "Shibaihon taishūka no seiki (2)," *Nihon Kosho tsūhin* 58, 11 (November 1993), 8–11; and Akama Ryō, "Kabuki no shuppanbutsu (4): kabuki no engekisho," vol. 4 of Iwanami Kōza Kabuki/Bunraku, ed. Akama Ryō (Tokyo: Iwanami Shoten, 1998) pp.55–60.

[52] Benjamin, *Arcades Project*, p. 19.

the consumable is preserved, cheap printed matter is raised to the status of historical archive.

These opening lines from "Playbills of Edo's Three Theaters" also suggest a broader world of interest in collecting and documenting the past within which Sanba was operating. Sanba was, after all, not alone in what he called his "affection for the past" (*inishie konomu kokoro*) nor in his desire to archive both the recent past and the present in anticipation of the future. Indeed, the late eighteenth and early nineteenth centuries saw an explosion of interest in the past: from the extraordinary work of the late eighteenth-century antiquarian Fujiwara Sadamoto (1732–97) to the salons and circles that grew up around figures such as Kimura Kenkadō (1736–1802), Morishima Chūryō (1756–1810), and, later, Yamazaki Yoshishige (1796–1856). Underlying this early nineteenth-century passion for collecting, however, was a larger shift in the way history was imagined and through which the practices of the collector came to be refigured as the work of the archivist. And one of the central figures in this development was Santō Kyōden, who had participated in the late-eighteenth-century world of curiosity but who would turn his interests, in the opening years of the nineteenth century, to recording less fantastical, more mundane facets of Japan's past.

## IV  Fear of Effacement

In 1804, roughly a decade before Sanba compiled his scrapbooks, Kyōden published a compendium of lore and anecdote; the preface to that work, *Thoughts on Extraordinary Things of Recent Times* (*Kinsei kisekikō*), is an immensely rich document for thinking about the historical imagination in early nineteenth-century Japan, self-consciously reflecting on both the methods and the motives of the historian:

> Those who are fond of the past have shed some light on things past through the study of those eras. Even things of a thousand years before come to light from time to time. The examination of the recent past has, on the other hand, been neglected and many facts have been lost. What has happened to be passed down by word of mouth contains much that is false. When it once occurred to me that, in the future, there would no doubt be those who think fondly of the present as the past, I set out to rectify this problem, seeking material in secret coffers and searching for items in arcane books, visiting ancient ruins and tombs; when I had ascertained some truths, the scraps of paper upon which I had scribbled notes came, in the course of things, to fill my old leather case.[53]

---

[53] Santō Kyōden, "Kinsei kisekikō," in Nihon Zuihitsu Taisei Henshūbu ed. *Nihon zuihitsu taisei*, ser. 2, vol. 6 (Tokyo: Yoshikawa Kōbunkan, 1974), p. 256.

Like Sanba, writing a decade later, Kyōden is keenly aware of the fragile nature of the historical record and of the irony that it is often the recent past that is most vulnerable to neglect and indifference. Kyōden is intent on preserving this record both for his own time and for a future generation for whom his own present would serve as a future past. Like Enba and Sanba, Kyōden seemed to sense that he was living at an important historical juncture from which the near horizons of the recent past were still visible but growing ever distant and in real danger of being forever lost. What is especially interesting about Kyōden's approach—and what makes *Thoughts on Extraordinary Things of Recent Times* and Kyōden's later *A Collection of Curiosities* (*Kottōshū*; 1814–15) such fascinating reading—is his turn toward the history of culture. It is a turn, of course, implicit in the works themselves, which treat all manner of cultural practices; it is a turn of which Kyōden is also himself aware and on which he self-consciously reflects in his 1804 preface:

> In general, official histories record the general import of things but are of little help in seeing the details. But just as anyone wishing to examine the Heian era draws upon *The Tale of Genji*, though it be a work of fiction, so too someone wishing to write about the recent past would see it come alive in the works of Ihara Saikaku and Asai Ryōi—though they be popular books—and of Hinaya Ryuho and Hishikawa Moronobu—though they be playful pictures (*zare-e*). There is much in them to serve as evidence.[54]

Kyōden's invocation of *The Tale of Genji* and of scholars who elucidate the distant past while ignoring the recent past was a timely intervention. This is 1804, five years after the publication of Motoori Norinaga's extended mediation on *The Tale of Genji* as a historical document, *The Tale of Genji: A Little Jeweled Comb* (*Genji monogatari tama no ogushi*), and Kyōden's ambivalent relationship with Nativisim (*Kokugaku*) is well known.[55] So Kyōden's references to antiquarians who shed light on the distant past of 1,000 years ago and to the historical uses of *The Tale of Genji* clearly resonate with the historical practices of Nativisim and suggest the place of the work of Kyōden, Enba, and Sanba within a broader intellectual field.

But Sanba's phrase "the study of the past" (*inishie manabi*) recalls not just the Nativist project but, more directly still, the Ancient Learning (Kogaku) school of Confucianism and Ogyū Sorai's turn away from orthodox Neo-Confucian cosmology and toward history and philology. Though Enba's chronology and Sanba's scrapbooks may seem distant from the scholasticism of Sorai, the historical work

---

[54] Santō Kyōden, "Kinsei kisekikō," p. 256.
[55] On Kyōden's interest in Nativism, see Yamamoto Harufumi, "Santō Kyōden no kōshō zuihitsu to gesaku," *Kokugo to kokubungaku* 63, 10, 1986 pp. 50–65; Yamamoto Kazuaki, "Santō Kyōden to 'kōshō,'" in Nakanishi Chikai Sensei Kanreki Kinen Ronbunshū Kankōkai ed., *Bukkyō to ningen* (Kyoto: Nagata Bunshōdō, 1994), pp. 229–46.

of these writers is very much defined by—we might even say made thinkable by—the emergence of what Maruyama Masao called the "historical consciousness" of Ancient Learning and by the "awareness of the historical mutability of norms" that Nativism borrowed from and shared with Sorai's work.[56]

It thus becomes possible to see the early nineteenth century, the present of Enba, Sanba, and Kyōden, as a particular historical moment in which debates between Nativists and Confucian scholars (however widely their own texts circulated) over history and its uses had become "part of the social environment itself."[57] How we might situate the work of figures like Enba, Sanba, and Kyōden within this larger epistemological field is suggested by Sanba in a wonderful scene from *Theater Chic This Side of the Curtain* in which "a man who seemed very much to be a Confucian scholar of *The Classics without Teachers* (*Keiten yoshi*)" and "a dogmatic Nativist who is prone to speak in archaisms about even the most trifling matters" quite literally bump heads in the theater.[58] The humor of the scene turns on the fact that each labors to interpret his own everyday reality through the lens, and importantly the language, of his respective dogma and its archaisms, and is thus able neither to understand nor to be understood by the world around him. In this scene, just as in Kyōden's preface to *Thoughts on Extraordinary Things of Recent Times*, the present is overlooked in favor of a distant past, and those who self-righteously cloak themselves in the mantle of the past are rendered not only irrelevant but also objects of ridicule.

Enba's approach in his chronology, Kyōden's essays in *Thoughts on Extraordinary Things of Recent Times* and *A Collection of Curiosities*, and Sanba's practices as a collector are novel in that, even as each draws on the shared methods of ancient learning and Nativism, and especially Nativism's use of the literary and the vernacular as a textual record to be read against the grain of orthodox history, they are not interested in the distant past, the objects of 1,000 years before, so much as in the recent past and their own historical present as a future past. Here, then, the present emerges as what Georg Simmel has called "a combination of a fragment of the past with a fragment of the future" and becomes thinkable *as history*.[59] Susan Burns has suggested that Nativist discourse be seen not as "an exercise in

---

[56] Maruyama Masao, *Studies in the Intellectual History of Tokugawa Japan* (Tokyo: University of Tokyo Press, 1974), pp. 99, 163. On the methodological debt of Nativism to Sōrai, see pp. 135–76 and Momokawa Takahito, *Uchinaru Norinaga* (Tokyo: Tōkyō Daigaku Shuppankai, 1987), pp. 212–33. On the emergence of historicism, see Tetsuo Najita, "History and Nature in Eighteenth-Century Tokugawa Thought," in *The Cambridge History of Japan Volume 4. Early Modern Japan*, ed. John Whitney Hall and James L. McClain, The Cambridge History of Japan (Cambridge: Cambridge University Press, 1991), pp. 596–659.

[57] Tetsuo Najita, "Method and Analysis in the Conceptual Portrayal of Tokugawa Intellectual History," in *Japanese Thought in the Tokugawa Period, 1600–1868: Methods and Metaphors*, ed. Tetsuo Najita and Irwin Scheiner (Chicago, IL: University of Chicago Press, 1978), pp. 6, 11.

[58] Shikitei Sanba, *Ukiyoburo; Kejō suigen maku no soto; Daisen sekai gakuyasagashi*, pp. 337–38. On *Keiten yoshi*, see Peter Kornicki, *Languages, Scripts, and Chinese Texts in East Asia* (Oxford: Oxford University Press, 2018), p. 181.

[59] Georg Simmel, "Fashion," in *Georg Simmel on Individuality and Social Forms*, ed. Donald N. Levine (Chicago, IL: University of Chicago Press, 1971), p. 303.

antiquarianism or nostalgia" but as "a moment of social formation in which one set of representations, one 'imaginary,' was beginning to fail and another was taking form."[60] To understand the historical significance of Enba's chronology, of Kyōden's compendia, or of Sanba's albums, we need, similarly, to look beyond the obviously antiquarian impulses of the collector and to locate the practices of collecting, collating, and preserving within the broad social moment in which they participate. This is a moment of uncertainty, on the one hand, yes, but a moment, too, of an active engagement with times past looking toward a possible future.

For writers like Kyōden, Enba, and Sanba, the historical present was marked by a sense of urgency, an urgency driven by a new understanding of the quotidian as an object of historical inquiry and of the role that ephemeral culture could play as "a device for thinking about the past." The same year that Sanba wrote these words, Kyōden would write of his habit of commonplacing: "From a young age, whenever I read, I copy out and collect passages that might serve as a means for thinking about the past."[61] Just as Sanba would lend order to his collection of ephemera in a series of albums, Kyōden would order his chaotic notes in a book he called *A Collection of Curiosities*. Two decades later, Kyokutei Bakin would echo Sanba's call for a record of the present as a future past in his great catalogue of fiction writers. Bakin began to record the biographies of authors and illustrators as a way to "keep them from oblivion," though he had at first thought that these writings were "not something to be shown to others but to be hidden away in a chest to become the dwelling place of bookworms."[62] Bakin eventually relented and allowed his manuscript to circulate and to be copied, imagining that "a hundred years from now were there someone such as myself, what a marvelously precious book this would be and a means of endless enjoyment."[63]

If the contemporary world was to be documented and "kept from oblivion" by printed broadsheets, playbills, and novels, by commonplacing and copying, then the very nature of this material meant that the historical record was itself quite fragile. And if that record were scattered or lost, there would be no archive of the present as a past for the future. For these writers and their contemporaries, the danger was that their own time would leave behind no traces that could be recovered by historians in the future. What they feared was effacement.[64]

---

[60] Susan L. Burns, *Before the Nation: Kokugaku and the Imagining of Community in Early Modern Japan* (Durham, NC: Duke University Press Books, 2003), p. 3.

[61] Santō Kyōden, *Kottōshū*, vol. 3 (Edo: Tsuruya Kiemon, 1815), 1r. The précis (ōmune) of *Kottōshū*, printed at the beginning of Volume 3, does not appear in modern editions of the text, which are likely based on later nineteenth-century printings. On this point, see Satō Miyuki, "Santō Kyōen: tenkaki no kōshōka," *Kokubungaku kaishaku to kanshō* 57, 3 (1992), 145. I have used the copy from the Mitsui Collection, C.V. Starr East Asian Library, University of California, Berkeley.

[62] Kyokutei Bakin, *Kinsei mono no hon Edo sakusha burui: chosha jihitsu hokibon*, ed. Kimura Miyogo (Tokyo: Yagi Shoten, 1988), p. 23.

[63] Kyokutei Bakin, *Kinsei mono no hon Edo sakusha burui*, p. 23.

[64] I have borrowed the idea of a "fear of effacement" from Roger Chartier, *Inscription and Erasure: Literature and Written Culture from the Eleventh to the Eighteenth Century*, trans. Arthur Goldhammer (Philadelphia, PA: University of Pennsylvania Press, 2007).

To an extent, the fears of Sanba and his contemporaries were well founded, but the effacement of their culture would occur in a manner rather different from what they anticipated. They were victims not of effacement so much as indifference, though apathy led to an effacement of sorts. The materials these writers assembled and recorded—Enba's chronology, Sanba's albums, Kyōden's compendia of lore and arcana, Bakin's catalogue of fiction writers—did preserve a record of the culture of nineteenth-century Japan, and in many ways, a cultural history of this period is unthinkable without recourse to the materials preserved by amateur historians of the nineteenth century. And yet, though the record was preserved, it would be largely ignored, even forgotten, in the century that would follow the Meiji Restoration of 1868.

In one of the earliest post-Restoration attempts to theorize the practice of history, *An Outline of a Theory of Civilization* (*Bunmeiron no gairyaku*) (1875), Fukuzawa Yukichi wrote:

> until the present, all of the history carried out in Japan was concerned with researching the genealogy of the royal family, or arguing the historical merits of particular lords and officials, or recording the outcomes of wars like the warrior tales of the storytellers. There is virtually nothing outside of such matters [. . .] To put it simply, there was no history of Japan, only a history of the Japanese government.[65]

Yet, it was precisely this register of history outside the realm of government that Enba, Sanba, Kyōden, and Bakin sought to preserve. As Kyōden put it in his *A Collection of Curiosities*, "What is recorded in official histories (*seishi*) and records is primarily concerned with the public realm and bears virtually no relationship with matters of private life so that there is little in them to serve as devices for thinking about the manners and customs of the people of the past."[66]

Kyōden imagined a different kind of history written from a different archive, and in Kyōden's hands, these other materials of the past—the vulgar, the fictional, the decorative—become not only objects of historical inquiry in their own right to be collected, studied, and archived but also, more fundamentally, what he calls "evidence" (*shō*) for the construction of a broader and more detailed picture of the past than what was to be found in "official histories."[67] What is so interesting about Enba chronicling the history of kabuki, Sanba collecting playbills and ephemera, Kyōden compiling volume after volume of early modern lore and anecdote, and, in

---

[65] Quoted in Katsurajima Nobuhiro, "Ikkokushi no seiritsu," in *Seiki tenkanki no kokusai chitsujo to kokumin bunka no keisei*, ed. Nishikawa Nagao and Watanabe Kōzō (Tokyo: Kashiwa Shobō, 1999), p. 105. For a translation, see Fukuzawa Yukichi, *An Outline of a Theory of Civilization*, trans. David Dilworth and G. Cameron Hurst (New York: Columbia University Press, 2009).

[66] Santō Kyōden, *Kottōshū*, vol. 3, 1r–1v.

[67] Santō Kyōden, "Kinsei kisekikō," pp. 256–57.

the 1830s, Kyokutei Bakin writing a detailed history of early modern authors is that they all seem to anticipate what they could not have known. In a little over a half a century, the world in which they lived would be radically altered and, while the practices they documented would live on beyond the Meiji Restoration, they were indeed documenting for the future a culture that would grow ever more remote and inaccessible. Even now, the work of these nineteenth-century collectors and amateur historians provides the basis for much of what we know of early modern culture, and it is sobering to think of how much of that culture would have been lost without their efforts, a fact that Enba, Sanba, Kyōden, and Bakin clearly grasped.

Of course, the reflection cast backward from 1868 obscures the much more interesting fact that these writers all sensed—independent of black ships and imperial loyalists—that their cultural moment was gradually vanishing even as it was in the process of emerging and that, without properly being documented, it was in danger of slipping into the abyss of history. Here, we might return to the odd nature of Sanba's albums because it is their status as material objects that most powerfully suggests the impulses that underlie the historical imagination of the early nineteenth century: Sanba's albums are, after all, an attempt to arrest the ephemeral, to transfigure the reproducible as the unique, an attempt, almost, to fashion an original out of a copy. The art historian Craig Clunas has used the suggestive idea of "the work of art in an age of woodblock reproduction" to write of the visual culture of late imperial China;[68] and while it is tempting to see in the practices of collecting of the discourses of Nativism an impulse to seek out and recover an auratic presence, it is also useful to recall Theodor Adorno's remark, in the opening pages of *The Jargon of Authenticity*, that "it is hardly an accident that Benjamin introduced the term at the same moment when, according to his own theory, what he understood by 'aura' became impossible to experience."[69] It is precisely the phantasmagoric nature of the aura, that it should become visible only at the moment of its disappearance, that seems most useful to understanding the status of collecting in early nineteenth-century Japan, that it was in this moment of the expansion of commercial publishing and the proliferation of all manner of printed objects that there emerged a profound sense of anxiety over documenting that culture even as it was being dispersed.

Sanba's preface to "Playbills of Edo's Three Theaters" reveals his own anxiety over the disappearance and the fragility of the historical record "with those [playbills] of old mostly scattered and lost" and his continuing preoccupation with collecting new material even as it appeared. In this, Sanba would be echoed by his contemporaries Enba, Kyōden, and Bakin. There is a clear resonance between Sanba's intentionally unfinished albums, with pages left blank to anticipate the

---

[68] Craig Clunas, *Pictures and Visuality in Early Modern China* (London: Reaktion Books, 1997).
[69] Theodor W. Adorno, *The Jargon of Authenticity* (Evanston, IL: Northwestern University Press, 1973), p. 9.

future, and the unfinished nature of the monumental works of Enba and Bakin, their histories of kabuki and fiction, respectively.

And yet, whereas Enba and Bakin both attempted synthetic works, drawing on a variety of contemporary sources, Sanba produced something very different: a collection of objects that, in turn, formed a new object. What is most striking about Sanba's albums is that while they seek to preserve ephemeral objects, the playbills, invitations, and broadsheets, the process of collecting itself enacts a kind of crude violence on these materials that are cut, pasted, annotated. Would it not have been enough, one wonders, simply to collect these objects, like the playbills collected in the Hayashi family library or those purchased by Tsubouchi Shōyō in 1920, without, in the process, creating entirely new objects? But at some level, Sanba's intuition seems to have been correct; he feared the materials being scattered and lost. And their very existence today suggests that the albums achieved exactly what Sanba had envisioned; they have preserved the material in a single place and have become "devices for thinking about the past."

Sanba's relationship with print was deeply ambivalent. He grew up in the book trade and worked variously as a publisher, writer, and bookseller. But Sanba also sensed that he had been born too late, that the urbane world of wit of men like Santō Kyōden and Utei Enba had ended in the 1790s and that his own work was out of place in a market dominated by sentimental and historical fiction. He blamed publishers and booksellers and, above all, the provincial reader. There is a special place of ridicule in Sanba's fiction for the country traveler unable to navigate Edo's cultural landmarks, such as Inakamono Tarōzaemon from *Theater Chic This Side of the Curtain* or the provincial playgoers in *A Critique of Audiences*.

Kyōden's, Enba's, and Sanba's approaches to collecting in the early nineteenth century seem born of, and conditioned by, a historical moment dominated by the simultaneous proliferation of all manner of printed material, on the one hand, and an accompanying anxiety of effacement on the other. "Paradoxically," Roger Chartier has written of Europe, the very success of print in recording the past and staving off loss "could lead to a danger of another sort: that of uncontrollable textual proliferation, of a discourse without order or limits. The excess of writing [...] [creates] a peril no less ominous than the threat of disappearance."[70] For Sanba, collecting became a means of attempting to control the proliferation of printed matter, of ordering and fixing information within a framework constructed around the idea of a history. In the opening decades of the nineteenth century, an antiquarian approach to the recent past sought both to preserve the documents of an ephemeral culture as a record for the future and simultaneously to archive those documents in a way that provided shape and coherence.

Santō Kyōden died in 1816, Sanba and Enba in 1822. Only Kyokutei Bakin lived to participate in one of the most extraordinary gatherings of collectors and

[70] Chartier, *Inscription and Erasure*, p. vii.

antiquarians from this period, the monthly meetings of the Society of Curiosity Lovers (Tankikai) hosted by Yamazaki Yoshishige (1796–1856) from the middle of 1824 to the end of 1825. Over the course of a year-and-a-half, the gatherings drew participants from a diverse group of intellectuals including Bakin, the painter Tani Bunchō (1763–1841), and Ogyū Korenori (n.d.), Ogyū Sorai's great-grandson. Yoshishige had written a manifesto of sorts for the group at its first meeting:

> Though when one yearns for the past, it is the way of the world to read books, in order to see the changing world as if before one's eyes there is nothing better than objects of the past. In the case of distant foreign lands as well, the best way to know the customs of those lands is to see objects actually made in those countries.[71]

"Each day," Yoshishige continued, "old objects are lost and foreign objects are always rare and difficult to come by" so a group of "friends who share an interest in such things" would come together once a month to share the objects they had "stored away."[72]

At one level, the Society of Curiosity Lovers recalls the late-eighteenth-century salons of figures such as Ōta Nanpo and Morishima Chūryō that gathered poets, scholars, and writers to "share treasures" (*takara awase*). But like the 1811 Unchakai, the Tankikai is different from these earlier iterations: gone from the meetings are the fantastical objects that purport to come from legend and myth. Gone, too, is the playful and poetic language that embedded these objects in a literary fabric of intertextuality. In their stead, we have a more prosaic approach to history and curiosity: coins, ceramic shards, bits of the Japanese past together with bits of the non-Japanese present. The merging of the curious and the fabulous has been replaced with a turn toward a more obviously material interest in documenting the world.

Importantly, the Society of Curiosity Lovers also reveals a deep ambivalence toward print: books allow access to the past, Yoshishige notes in his manifesto, but how much better are *things*. The Society of Curiosity Lovers did create a book as a record of its meetings, just as the "treasure-sharing" groups had done in the late eighteenth century: a collection of things transformed into a collection of words and images on the page. But unlike the earlier gatherings, the Society of Curiosity Lovers did not publish the record of its gatherings; instead, this record circulated in manuscript like Bakin's catalogue of fiction writers and Sanba's albums. Manuscript had its own currency in an age of print: it was one of the surest ways of circumscribing access to privileged knowledge. More importantly, the privileged

---

[71] For a transcription of Yoshishige's manifesto, which served as a preface for the record of the gatherings, as well as for a broader discussion of the Tankikai, see Koide Masahiro, "Tanki manroku kaidai," in *Tanki manroku*, ed. Nihon Zuihitsu Taisei Henshūbu, *Nihon zuihitsu taisei: bekkan*, vol. 1 (Tokyo: Yoshikawa Kōbunkan, 1994), pp. 1–2.
[72] Koide Masahiro, "Tanki manroku kaidai," pp. 1–2.

status of this knowledge was itself constituted through, and dependent on, the very restriction that manuscript assured. If print had come to be dominated and debased by the demands of a boorish and unlearned reading public, one of Sanba's favorite topics of comment, manuscript allowed for the reaffirmation of a world of private erudition separate from the public world of the printed page.

Two centuries on, the work of Sanba, Enba, and Kyōden feels both irrevocably distant and uncannily proximate. On the one hand, their work seems to belong to a different world of historical thinking in which the archiving of the arcane and the curious becomes an end in itself. On the other hand, these figures, each in his own way, clearly apprehended the role that collecting can play in recasting history away from established themes and ossified protocols and toward an engagement with neglected registers of the past. For anyone interested in the cultural history of early modern Japan, it is hard not to see the activities of these figures in the early nineteenth century as a kind of cultural history *avant la lettre*.

The genealogy of historical inquiry begun in the early nineteenth century—and the historical practices that accompanied it—would themselves live on beyond the Restoration and, in a new century, they would intersect with new institutions of knowledge—the museum, the library, the university—that would both preserve much of the archive of the nineteenth century as a record for the future and also situate the act of collecting within new institutional settings. Indeed, in the early twenty-first century, our own access to this historical record, to these "devices for thinking about the past," is very much dependent on the ways in which the printed record of the nineteenth century came to be preserved in the early twentieth century.

## V  Curio Fever

Both the albums of ephemera that Sanba collected and Enba's *Chronology* have had curious fates in the two centuries since the two men died in 1822. As singular objects, Sanba's scrapbooks, which are all now housed in the National Diet Library in Tokyo, have a provenance which can be traced, albeit piecemeal, and which allows us to understand something of how these artifacts of a collector's passions themselves became objects of collection and possession in the decades after Sanba's death. I will return to a more detailed account of these scrapbooks in the Epilogue to explore the vexed relationship between objects and their digital copies and what that relationship means for the process of research in our own time.

Enba's chronology presents a different problem, not the tracing of a unique set of objects through time but the following out of various strands that point Enba's work forward to different projects that would create, for a century after his death, an ongoing chronology of the theater. This history, which unfolds in fits and starts, tells a story of the survival and archiving of the printed culture of early modern theater in the twentieth and now twenty-first centuries, a story no less rich than the case of Sanba's scrapbooks for thinking about the status of books as material objects and the ambivalences and anxieties that marked the relationship between manuscript and print, public and private, across the nineteenth and into the twentieth centuries. Sanba's albums of theater programs seem to suggest a kind of devolution from print to manuscript, with mass-produced printed ephemera being transformed into a unique, handmade object. The history of the *Chronology* for the century after Enba's death similarly traces a movement of historical knowledge out of the public realm and into the hands of a more narrowly circumscribed group of enthusiasts and collectors, a trajectory almost opposite to Enba's making a public record of his own collection of playbills.

It seems strangely symbolic that the final supplemental volume to the *Chronology*, compiled during the 1910s by the theater impresario Tamura Nariyoshi (1851-1920), has never been published but exists only in a fragmentary manuscript copy in the holdings of the Tsubouchi Memorial Theater Museum. The manuscript for this volume was thought to have been lost in the Great Kanto Earthquake of 1923 and was rediscovered only in 1991.[73] The 1923 earthquake has long served as an important marker for understanding Japan's cultural history and the country's relationship with its own past. The destruction of some of the great collections of books—so memorably noted by Akutagawa Ryūnosuke in the direct aftermath of the earthquake—became symbolic of a culture in danger of losing its past and the printed record that early modern collectors and amateur historians had worked so hard to preserve.[74]

Enba's *Chronology* was reprinted in its entirety in 1841 amid the Tenpō Reforms (1830-43), a quarter of a century after Enba had published the final volumes of his *Chronology* in 1815, which covered the history of kabuki only up through 1804. It was not until a century later, in 1907, that a new supplement to the *Chronology* covering the period from 1805-59 would be published. The compiler of that volume was Ishizuka Hōkaishi (1799-1862).[75]

That Hōkaishi's supplement to the chronology circulated only in manuscript during his lifetime, and for almost half a century after his death in 1862, should not be surprising. The Tenpō Reforms radically transformed the climate surrounding publishing, and the censorship policies that governed commercial publishing during and after the Reforms led to a drastic drop in the number of titles published in

---

[73] Terada Shima, "Engeki Hakubutsukan shozō no 'Zoku zoku kabuki nendaiki' ni tsuite," *Engeki kenkyū* 19 (1995), 13-27.
[74] See Akutagawa Ryūnosuke, "Taishō jūninen kugatsu tsuitachi no daishin ni saishite," in Itō Sei ed. *Akutagawa Ryūnosuke zenshū* vol. 7 (Tokyo: Kadokawa Shoten, 1968), pp. 174-85.
[75] See Kurahashi Masae, "Ishizuka Hōkaishi 'Kakōto kabuki nendaiki zokuhen': kinsei kōki ni okeru kabuki kōgyō kiroku no ichi yōsō," *Ronkyū nihonbungaku* 100 (2014), 111-26.

the middle decades of the nineteenth century.[76] And we should note, too, that the world of the theater would itself be a particular target of the Reforms: it was during the Reforms that the theaters and the actors were exiled to the area of Saruwaka-chō on the northeastern edge of the city, close to the pleasure quarters of the Shin Yoshiwara.

Hōkaishi was a prolific diarist and amateur historian but published very little during his lifetime.[77] His great friend, Shibue Chūsai, who, at one point, came into ownership of Sanba's scrapbook of storytelling ephemera, similarly wrote extensively but published almost nothing during his lifetime; in many ways, the literary culture of this moment is defined by a distance from print and publication, a withdrawal into manuscript culture.[78] The Tenpō Reforms provide an immediate context for this retreat, but this stance toward print is itself an extension of the unease and ambivalence toward print and publishing that can be seen going back to the 1820s in the Tankikai gathering or in Bakin's "Catalogue of Recent Fiction Writers of Edo" ("Kinsei mono no hon Edo sakusha burui") as explored above.

Hōkaishi's manuscript was left to the playwright Kawatake Mokuami (1816–93) and was eventually destroyed in 1923 in the Great Kantō Earthquake.[79] The first published version of his chronology, which appeared in 1907, almost half a century after Hōkaishi's death, was based on a manuscript copy in the possession of Tamura Nariyoshi, the great Meiji theatrical impresario who had founded the Kabuki-za in 1889 and who was himself working to extend the chronology into the twentieth century. The 1907 edition of Hōkaishi's work was printed under the title *A Chronology of the Kabuki of Flowering Edo Part II* (*Hana no Edo kabuki nendaiki zoku hen*) and appeared as Volume 4 of the New Classified Collection of Japanese Classics and Documents (Shin Gunsho Ruijū), a collection of previously unpublished or obscure works primarily related to the history of literature and the theater modeled on Hanawa Hokiichi's (1746–1821) Classified Collection of Japanese Classics and Documents (Gunsho Ruijū), a massive project that published 530 volumes between 1793 and 1819.[80]

---

[76] See Peter Kornicki, *The Book in Japan: A Cultural History from the Beginnings to the Nineteenth Century* (Leiden: Brill, 1998) and Satō Yukiko, *Edo no shuppan tōsei: danatsu ni honrō sareta gesakushatachi* (Tokyo: Yoshikawa Kōbunkan, 2017).

[77] One of the two exceptions to this is *The Complete Book of Fukagawa* (*Fukagawa taizen*), an 1833 essay on the Suzaki pleasure quarter in Fukagawa in Edo's southeast. In the book's preface, Hōkaishi claims that the book was a manuscript of Santō Kyōden's that he had found in a used bookstore and that he had edited and revised for publication. See Miyazaki Shōzō ed., *Fukagawa taizen* (Tokyo: Chinshokai, 1917).

[78] Today Shibue Chūsai is best remembered as the subject of Mori Ōgai's 1916 historical novel *Shibue Chūsai*. See Edwin McClellan, *Woman in the Crested Kimono: The Life of Shibue Io and Her Family* (New Haven, CT: Yale University Press, 1985).

[79] Kurahashi Masae, "Ishizuka Hōkaishi 'Kakōto kabuki nendaiki zokuhen,'" 113.

[80] See Kumata Atsumi, *Sandai hensanbutsu: Gunsho ruijū, Koji ruien, Kokusho sōmokuroku no shuppan bunkashi*, pp. 19–30; Masayuki Sato, "A Social History of Japanese Historical Writing," in *The Oxford History of Historical Writing*, vol. 3, ed. Daniel Woolf and Axel Schneider (Oxford: Oxford University Press, 2011), pp. 90–91.

That it was in this fashion that Hōkaishi's work would end up being published is suggestive. The New Classified Collection of Japanese Classics and Documents was begun in 1906 by the Society for the Publication of the Nation's Books (Kokusho Kankōkai), established just after the Russo-Japanese War by the former Prime Minister Ōkuma Shigenobu (1838–1922), who had founded the Tōkyō Senmon Gakkō, the forerunner to Waseda University. The editor of the series was Ichijima Kenkichi (1860–1933), the head of Waseda's library, who would work closely with Tsubouchi Shōyō to plan the Theater Museum in the 1920s, and the volume contained a preface by Mizutani Futō (1848–1953), an 1894 graduate from Waseda's forerunner and a student of Shōyō's. Study of the theater was no longer the province of amateurs and theater fanatics but was now encompassed within the new elite institutions of knowledge whose birth marks late-nineteenth-century Japan.

But if Hōkaishi's manuscript was rescued from obscurity after half a century by its publication, it is not the case that publication made it widely available. The New Classified Collection of Japanese Classics and Documents was printed in limited runs and was only available as part of a subscription service for the cost of two yen a month and required a three-year contract. In this sense, the fate of the book is emblematic of the new institutionalization of knowledge in the Meiji period: what had been originally designed by Enba in the early nineteenth century to be a published and public record was now the province of professional editors and scholars, circulating on a limited basis not unlike the ways in which manuscript circumscribed access during Hōkaishi's own lifetime.

There is, moreover, a resonance with the final volumes of the chronology compiled during the first two decades of the twentieth century by Tamura Nariyoshi, which he imagined as an extension of the project that had begun a century earlier with Enba and that was continued by Hōkaishi. When Tamura's son, Toshijirō, printed the first volume of his father's work in 1922, it would have a circulation more limited still than Hōkaishi's volume. In the preface to the volume, Toshijirō wrote that his father "had no intention of making [the volume] public, it was only something to be kept by his side," and the son, too, seemed ambivalent about publication. He settled on an unusual compromise, privately printing 1,000 copies, which he distributed as gifts to friends and acquaintances.[81] Toshijirō had intended to print a second volume of his father's chronology, which covered the period up until 1920 when Tamura had died, but the manuscript was thought to have been lost during the fires that followed the Great Kanto Earthquake of 1923 and Toshijirō himself died the following year.[82]

It was not until 1991 that a trace of the manuscript would resurface when a partial copy was found, uncatalogued, in the holdings of the Waseda Theater Museum,

---

[81] Tamura Nariyoshi, *Zokuzoku kabuki nendaiki* (Tokyo: Ichimura-za, 1922), n.p.
[82] Terada Shima, "Engeki Hakubutsukan shozō no 'Zoku zoku kabuki nendaiki' ni tsuite," p. 13.

but the contents of the manuscript, which comprises some 3,600 pages in 10 volumes, has never been published, a strange reminder of the vexed relationship this project has had with print in the two centuries since Enba's death.[83]

If the Great Kanto Earthquake marks a moment of crisis in which the fragility of the printed past became impossible to ignore, it also leads, in very concrete ways, to new attempts to preserve that past. When the earthquake hit just before noon on September 1, 1923, Tsubouchi Shōyō was at Waseda University finishing up a discussion with Takata Sanae (1860–1938), the university's president, and Ichijima Kenkichi, the head of the library, about an exhibition of theater material that was to be held at the university in October.[84] Within days of the earthquake, Shōyō had decided to donate his own private collection of books and theater ephemera to Waseda, and it was in the wake of the earthquake that he began to develop in earnest an idea that he had nurtured for some time of creating at theater museum on the grounds of the university.[85]

Shōyō had begun to imagine a theater museum as early as 1916, but it was only in the wake of the 1923 earthquake that a plan to open what would become the first university museum in Japan would begin to move forward.[86] The idea of the museum, as Hayashi Kimio, the head of the Waseda University Library, put it in announcing the university's plan to establish the museum in February of 1927, was to "preserve, as a form of history, Japan's theater which is incomparable in form in the world and which has developed along a unique path."[87] In practice, what this meant was that the Theater Museum would become a giant archive of printed matter: books, actor prints, playbills, and other print ephemera.

But if Hayashi stressed the museum's role as a repository for the nation's theatrical patrimony, the museum itself, as a built structure, suggests how Japanese history came to be enveloped in a conception of universalism filtered through the prism of the European example. The building was designed by the architect Satō Kōichi (1878–1941) based on the plans for the Elizabethan Fortune theater that had been reconstructed by W. H. Godfrey using the original contract between the Fortune's manager Philip Henslowe and the carpenter Peter Street.[88] Shōyō knew of Godfrey's reconstruction from Sir Walter Raleigh and Sir Sidney Lee's 1916

---

[83] Terada Shima, "Engeki Hakubutsukan shozō no 'Zoku zoku kabuki nendaiki' ni tsuite," p. 13.
[84] Shōyō Kyōkai ed., *Mikan Tsubouchi Shōyō shiryōshū*, vol. 3 (Tokyo: Shōyō Kyōkai, 2001), p. 58.
[85] Shōyō Kyōkai ed., *Mikan Tsubouchi Shōyō shiryōshū*, vol. 3, p. 58.
[86] Morishige Noburō, "Wagakuni hatsu honkakuteki daigaku hakubutsukan no tanjō ni tsuite," *Nihon Daigaku Daigakuin Sōgō Shakai Jōhō Kenkyūka kiyō* 11 (2010), 129–38; Waseda Daigaku Engeki Hakubutsukan, *Engeki Hakubutsukan gojūnen* (Tokyo: Waseda Daigaku Tsubouchi Hakushi Kinen Engeki Hakubutsukan, 1978).
[87] Hayashi Kimio, "Engeki Hakubutsukan no keikaku," *Asahi shinbun*, February 22, 1927.
[88] See Ōtsuka Takanobu, "Gurōbu-za: sono fukugen mokei to kōshō," in *Engeki* hakubutsukan *shiryō monogatari*, ed. Waseda Daigaku Engeki Hakubutsukan (Tokyo: Waseda Daigaku Tsubouchi Hakushi Kinen Engeki Hakubutsukan, 1988), p. 316.

*Shakespeare's England*, and he included a copy of the plans in his own 1928 *An Introduction to Shakespeare for Japanese Students* (*Shēkusupiya kenkyū shiori*).[89]

Although it had been Shōyō's dream to create a repository for theatrical materials and an institution to support research on the theater, he was ambivalent about the idea of creating a museum and had originally wanted to call it a theatrical library. When the Theater Museum opened in 1928, Shōyō remarked, "Although it is called a museum, it is really a center for research on historical materials of the theater and is certainly not some place for the collecting of curios (*kottō*)." Shōyō then gives a specific example: "we are certainly not interested in boasting that we have a first edition of a woodblock print by so and so."[90] At one level, Shōyō, here, is explicitly rejecting what he considered the aestheticization and museumification of Japanese woodblock prints, a point to which I will return in Chapter 5. For Shōyō, the theater prints of nineteenth-century Japan were first and foremost "historical material" (*shiryō*), and their transformation into art objects housed in European and American collections had robbed researchers of access to these important archives.[91]

But for Shōyō, the term "curio" (*kottō*) had a particular meaning and resonance, deeply embedded within the politics of collecting. In 1912, Shōyō had written a play with the suggestive title "Curio Fever" (*Kottōnetsu*). In one scene, a young man watches a German couple cart off their purchases in a rickshaw and remarks to his uncle:

They say that there are no longer any of the ordinary run of the mill curios left and these days it seems that there are many searching for tea rooms complete with accompanying trees and garden rocks or Buddhist altar rooms complete with the family's mortuary tablets, altar fittings, and decorations.

It seems, the young man continues, that "Japan itself has become one faded sacred, great big and old art object. Or put differently, it is a unique antique, one giant curio."[92] But if Japan had itself been turned into one great curio for Western collectors, it was just at this moment that Japanese collectors and art dealers had begun to turn their attention to China and Korea in the wake of China's 1911 revolution and Japan's formal annexation of Korea in 1910. Indeed, as Kuchiki Yuriko has shown in her book on the "house of Yamanaka," it was Japanese art dealers like Yamanaka

---

[89] Tsubouchi Shōyō, *Shēkusupiya kenkyū shiori* (Tokyo: Waseda Daigaku Shuppanbu, 1928), p. 160; Walter Alexander Raleigh, Sidney Lee, and Charles T. Onions, eds, *Shakespeare's England; an Account of the Life & Manners of His Age. An Introduction to Shakespeare for Japanese Students* (Oxford: Clarendon Press, 1916) is the English title that Shōyō gave to *Shēkusupiya kenkyū shiori* when it was published.
[90] "Kyō kaikanshiki no Engeki Hakubutsukan," p. 11.
[91] See Tsubouchi Shōyō, "Shibai-e to Toyokuni oyobi sono monka," in *Shōyō senshū*, vol. 7 (Tokyo: Daiichi shobō, 1977–78), 1–268.
[92] Tsubouchi Shōyō, "Kottōnetsu," in *Shōyō senshū*, vol. 2 (Tokyo: Daiichi shobō, 1977–78), p. 803.

Sadajirō (1836–1936) who played a critical role in shaping the vogue for Orientalia in Japan and in the West during these early years of the second decade of the twentieth century.[93]

This reflection on the "curio-ification" of Japan was followed immediately, in Shōyō's play, by a dialogue between a middle school principal and a Buddhist monk; as the principal notes, the bronze statue of Confucius on display stood as a testament to "the honor and power of the Japanese empire," a sentiment interrupted by the appearance of a so-called "madman"—a Chinese exile who cries: "My country, China, was once proud. But now there is a revolution. The country has collapsed [...] Today everything down to the bronze statue of Confucius, the great shining sun of rectitude for our country, has been bought up by the Japanese."[94]

Shōyō's play seems cannily to understand Japan's ambivalent place within the world during the age of empire: Japan as collected and collector, as object of Western fetishism but itself casting an Orientalist gaze fixed upon other nations of Asia.[95] The Buddhist monk and the school principle *ape* the rhetoric and practices of Western collectors, uncomfortably calling to mind the late-nineteenth-century cartoons by Western artists like Georges Bigot that depict Japanese with distinctly simian features in Western dress.

For Shōyō, the term *kottō*, or curio, had another point of reference: the work of Lafcadio Hearn, who had published his *Kotto: Being Japanese Curios, with Sundry Cobwebs* in 1902. Shōyō and Hearn had briefly been colleagues after Hearn had joined the faculty at Waseda University in 1904, and the two men would carry on a correspondence, in English, until the latter's death in September of that year. In many ways, the arc of the relationship of these two men is critical for understanding Shōyō's own intellectual development and the increasing ambivalence which he would show to the West, as in "Curio Fever," but it is also emblematic of a longer trajectory of Japanese intellectuals as they grappled with the "spectre of comparisons" that has so haunted the history of the non-West in the twentieth century. In Shōyō's own correspondence with Hearn, as well as comments he confided to others, we see an initial excitement and enthusiasm followed by disappointment and a growing sense of ambivalence.[96] On the one hand, Shōyō expressed an admiration for Hearn's work and was eager to serve as a kind of "native informant" on the history of Japanese drama. On the other hand, Shōyō came to see Hearn as essentially shallow, an aesthete more interested in his own interpretations of Japan and

---

[93] Kuchiki Yuriko, *Hausu obu Yamanaka: Tōyō no shihō wo Ōbei ni utta bijutsushō* (Tokyo: Shinchōsha, 2013).

[94] Tsubouchi Shōyō, "Kottōnetsu," p. 805.

[95] See Stefan Tanaka, *Japan's Orient: Rendering Pasts into History* (Berkeley, CA: University of California Press, 1995).

[96] On the relationship between mimicry and ambivalence, see Homi K. Bhabha, "Of Mimicry and Man: The Ambivalence of Colonial Discourse," in *The Location of Culture*, Routledge Classics (London: Routledge, 2004), pp. 121–31.

its past than in attempting to understand what Shōyō would consistently refer to as a scientific approach to history. In this sense, Japan was very much a curio for Hearn, whose attitude was more that of collector than scholar.

Shōyō's own expressions of this unease were themselves almost emblematically ambivalent. In a short note on Hearn at the time of his death in 1904, for example, Shōyō would write how, when he read Hearn's work, he would "feel as I do towards my dear mother," describing his work as "overly subjective" but moving nonetheless.[97] Hearn's work was shot through "with the tenor of a late nineteenth-century romanticist," and, for Shōyō, Hearn would always remain "a genius of the *fin de siècle*."[98]

In private, Shōyō would be more explicit about his frustrations. His friend Ichijima Kenkichi, then head of the Waseda University Library, would record Shōyō's impressions meeting with Hearn:

[Hearn] had said he was interested in hearing about Japanese drama so I did quite a bit of research and made various charts and had planned to thoroughly introduce Japanese theater but it seems that he had a different idea [. . .] [Hearn] was in the end a poet [. . .] He is not someone who would spend enough time to study about something systematically and scientifically and then write about it later [. . .] He was the type who wanted to take pen in hand as soon as he felt something.[99]

But in addition to this ambivalence, Shōyō's relationship with Hearn was also marked by a deep sense of anxiety over language, over his ability to express himself, over whether or not he would be heard. In his letters to Hearn, he returns again and again to this theme, noting his unease with written English but noting as well that he was more comfortable writing than speaking. Hearn's own relationship to the Japanese language was complicated: in the early twentieth century, he was one of the great interpreters of Japan to the Western world, but much of his work was based on stories told to him by his Japanese wife Koizumi Setsuko, as she would vividly recall after his death, a process emblematic of the ethnic and gender politics that often underwrote Western knowledge of the non-West at this time.[100]

For Shōyō, there was thus a structural asymmetry to his relationship with Hearn, the same asymmetry that would mark the Theater Museum a quarter of a century later, that would mark most of Shōyō's work from this point on, and that

---

[97] Tsubouchi Shōyō, "d Yakumo," in Tsubouchi Shōyō ed. *Shōyō senshū*, vol. 12 (Tokyo: Daiichi shobō, 1977–78), p. 471.
[98] Tsubouchi Shōyō, "Koizumi Yakumo," pp. 474, 475.
[99] Ichijima Shunjo [Kenkichi], "Seikaroku" quoted in Sekita Kaoru, "Tsubouchi Shōyō to Koizumi Yakumo: shinshiryō kara mite," *Kokubungaku kaishaku to kyōzai no kenkyū* 43, 8 (1998), 86.
[100] Setsuko Koizumi, *Reminiscences of Lafcadio Hearn* (New York: Houghton Mifflin, 1918), p. 36.

would become a hallmark of many of Japan's intellectuals' relationship to the West across the twentieth century: the Japanese subject *could* speak, but to be *heard*, the Japanese subject would need to speak in the language of the West and even then might not be listened to. Indeed, when Shōyō spoke both in the language *and* the scientific idiom of the West, he found himself ignored, unable to represent Japan in a way that could easily be digested by the poet Hearn. "Japan" would always, or so it seemed in the early twentieth century, need to be spoken for, an object of interpretation, the "native informant" elided in the process.

Shōyō wanted to create a "scientific" and "systematic" history, but Hearn was more interested in the mythical and mystical, like so many others who came over from America in the Gilded Age. In Hearn's case, there was another dimension, owing, one imagines, to his own complex sense of identity as Anglo-Irish born of a Greek mother, himself very much a son of empire. As Hearn's biographer Elizabeth Stevenson has written, "he wished, under gray Irish skies, to be Greek, to be pagan, to be even 'Oriental.'"[101] For his part, in "mimicking" the language of scientific history, Shōyō would cease to play the role of the "native informant" and begin to mount a critique of what he saw as the Eurocentrism of Western historians of Japan like Hearn or the German art historian Friedrich Succo. Indeed, Shōyō's critique of Succo in 1920, to which I will turn in Chapter 5, can be read as an extension of the frustrations he felt toward Hearn's dilettantism, which, more than any event in his life, seems to have inflected his relationship with the West.[102]

And here we might return to Shōyō's 1912 play "Curio Fever" for in it we see not just the Western collectors who have turned Japan into "one giant curio" but also the Japanese who mimic them, who replicate their habits and rhetoric, who turn China and Korea into fantasies to be collected just as Japan had been.[103] But Shōyō is in no sense an anticolonial nationalist, nor did his sympathies lie with the kind of Pan-Asianism that imagined Asian solidarity in the face of Western empire, such an important intellectual thread in Japan during his lifetime. Rather, despite his encounter with Hearn, he remained drawn toward, and committed to, the systematic and the scientific, an Occidentalism around which all of his ideas of scholarship revolved.

But if, for Shōyō, Hearn seemed to belong to the romanticism of the fin de siècle, so far removed from the "scientific" historiography to which he was committed, Hearn would, in a most uncanny way, return to Shōyō's consciousness in 1920, at the very time when Shōyō came to develop the intellectual underpinnings of a universal theatrical history that would inform the opening of the Theater Museum at the end of the decade. In 1920, Shōyō began reading Albert Mordell's 1919 *The*

---

[101] Elizabeth Stevenson, *The Grass Lark: A Study of Lafcadio Hearn* (New Brunswick, NJ: Transaction Publishers, 1999), p. 5.
[102] See Tsubouchi Shōyō, "Shibai-e to Toyokuni oyobi sono monka," in *Shōyō senshū*, vol. 7.
[103] On this point, see Kim Brandt, *Kingdom of Beauty: Mingei and the Politics of Folk art in Imperial Japan* (Durham, NC: Duke University Press, 2007), esp. ch. 5.

*Erotic Motive in Literature*—through which Shōyō discovered Freud; Mordell's approach to the idea of universal themes in literature would have a profound impact on Shōyō's idea of a "sociological" or "anthropological" approach to the origins of theater in humanity's shared past, the idea on which the Theater Museum was founded. And Hearn plays an important role in Mordell's argument; indeed, Mordell would argue that "Hearn anticipated many of Freud's conclusions," especially with Hearn's emphasis on "unconscious memory"—what Mordell calls "one of the axioms of psychoanalysis, or rather one of its pillars"—and an idea that seems to inhabit Shōyō's own work in the 1920s.[104]

Here, a decade-and-a-half after his brief correspondence with Hearn, the "poet" of the fin de siècle returns as a kind of structuring presence in Mordell's argument. Shōyō's reading of Mordell, and through him of Freud, is symptomatic of the politics of academic disciplines in Japan and elsewhere in the non-Western world for much of the twentieth century. Shōyō was a figure of deep learning and erudition, unable to escape the structural Eurocentrism of the very disciplines to which he was committed in making sense of the Japanese past, a figure who turns repeatedly, almost compulsively, to Western models to understand Japan as a specific example but who finds at the center of those models not the scientific rigor he imagines but rather yet another layer of mythos often indebted to the spirit of eighteenth- and nineteenth-century Orientalism.

Shōyō would never abandon his Western models and his debt to Western methods, and if he could see this structural asymmetry for what it was, he could not see himself clear of it. If Japanese history were to be spoken, it would need to be spoken of in the language of the Western academy, understood in the idiom of the universal, through likeness and analogy to the Western example, even if one of Shōyō's insights was that such analogies were often unhelpful in making sense of historical reality.

"Curio Fever" displays both Shōyō's awareness of the colonial world and of the ugly nature of Japanese colonial attitudes that mimicked the West, but he was unable to break free of his intellectual commitment to Western historical thinking and to the image of "science" on which, he believed, such thinking was founded. In this sense, as both built structure and as collection, the Waseda Theater Museum, in which so much of the materials addressed in this book are now housed, stands as a monument to this configuration of knowledge that emerged during the late nineteenth and early twentieth centuries: an institution built on the notion of the universal and the comparative in which the Japanese past is, quite literally, encased within a Western-style shell. That structure in no way negates or compromises the extraordinary work done at the museum or the immense value of its collections

---

[104] Albert Mordell, *The Erotic Motive in Literature* (New York: Boni and Liveright, 1919), pp. 237, 239. For the influence of Mordell on Shōyō, see especially Shōyō's discussion of eroticism in kabuki and its relationship with the unconscious in Tsubouchi Shōyō "Shōnen jidai ni mita kabuki no tsuioku," in *Shōyō senshū*, vol. 12, esp. pp. 262ff.

for thinking about Japanese, or world, theater. Indeed, as we near the centennial of the Theater Museum, it is possible, and necessary, to recognize how, as Jacques Derrida put it in his late meditation on Freud, "archivable meaning is also and in advance codetermined by the structure of the archive."[105] And yet, meanings can exceed the structures imposed by the archive when new questions are posed to the objects that the archive contains, questions unimaginable to Shōyō himself because they take as a point of departure a critical stance towards the very disciplinary commitments from which Shōyō was never finally able to free himself. When Shikitei Sanba had imagined his own collections of ephemera serving as "devices for thinking about the past," this is what he meant.

[105] Jacques Derrida, *Archive Fever: A Freudian Impression*, trans. Eric Prenowitz (Chicago, IL: University of Chicago Press, 1997), p. 18.

# 3
# Mapping the Stage
## On Kabuki's Cartographic Archive

### I Zenjirō's Maps

In the preface that he wrote to a collection of theater prints in 1919, Tsubouchi Shōyō suggested that "the map and the timeline are the binoculars of the historian."[1] As we have seen in Chapter 2, the compilation of timelines as tools for research into the history of kabuki goes back a century before Shōyō to the work of Utei Enba and his contemporaries in the second decade of the nineteenth century. But maps and other spatial diagrams, too, are common in nineteenth-century theater materials, and they appear in a diversity of forms ranging from insets in printed broadsheets and prefatory matter in actor critiques to large-format, multi-sheet, and multi-chromatic prints. To be sure, then, the archive of nineteenth-century printed theater ephemera is replete with all kinds of maps; but what might Shōyō have imagined as to their historical import? And how might we train this other lens on the history of the theater?

In Chapter 2, I explored the ways in which writers at the turn of the nineteenth century began to imagine a history of kabuki intimately bound up with the practices of collecting. This chapter examines the cartographic archive in order to explore how many of the same writers and collectors used the form of the map as a vehicle for both parody and history and how, at the same time, a deep interest in the theatrical practices of China created a new lens and idiom through which that history came to be conceptualized.

As the historian of cartography, J. Brian Harley has written, "When a historian reaches for a map, it is usually to answer a fairly narrow question about location or topography and less often to illuminate cultural history or the social values of a particular period or place."[2] If we step back and survey the broad archive of maps and other spatial diagrams related to Japan's early modern theater, it is immediately apparent that some of the maps *can* tell us about narrow questions of location; but many more cannot and—marked by what Harley once called "the pregnancy of the

---

[1] Tsubouchi Shōyō, "'Shibai nishikie shūsei' jo," in *Shōyō senshū*, vol. 7 (Tokyo: Daiichi shobō, 1977–78), p. 292.
[2] John B. Harley and John H. Andrews, *The New Nature of Maps: Essays in the History of Cartography*, ed. Pau Laxton, new ed. edn (Baltimore, MD: Johns Hopkins University Press, 2002), p. 34.

opaque"—these maps can only be read as a particular kind of document of social and cultural history.[3] This is especially true of maps that do not purport to chart any real, physical space in the first place but rather use cartographic techniques to plot more abstract aspects of the theater: a late-eighteenth-century book which takes the form of a gazetteer to introduce the history and practices of kabuki, an early nineteenth-century map that shows theatrical practice imagined as its own kind of space, or an image from the second decade of the nineteenth century that displays the career of an actor as a map.

But beyond reading any particular map, the historian of nineteenth-century theater ephemera is also faced with a broad set of questions about the nature of cartographic evidence itself as a *form* of theatrical archive. Why is it that from the late eighteenth century onward, maps became so central to envisioning, and plotting, the theater and its history?

Looking at the broad archive of printed theater ephemera from the late eighteenth and early nineteenth centuries, three things are immediately striking. First, maps and spatial diagrams of all sorts begin to proliferate during this period; second, while some chart real, physical spaces, others use the techniques of cartography to envision abstract aspects of theater practice and history; and third, all of this mapping, both real and imagined, was taking place just at a time when an intense interest emerges in the histories and practices of non-Japanese theatrical forms, that is, of situating Japanese theater *in the world*. During this time, we also see a systematic elaboration of the idea of the *sekai*—literally "world"—as a constituent element of dramaturgy, indicating the historical but also geographic setting of a dramatic composition.[4]

In many ways, Tsubouchi Shōyō's own work on theater in the twentieth century was also preoccupied with questions of place and space. Very early in his career, Shōyō developed an interest in, and a commitment to, the comparative method that informed and even structured his approach to theater history. And his lifelong engagement with Shakespeare, both as a translator and as a director, meant that, throughout his career, Shōyō's approach to Japan's theatrical past was haunted by what Benedict Anderson has suggestively called the "spectre of comparisons."[5]

Emblematic of these interests is the Waseda University Tsubouchi Memorial Theater Museum, the history of which I outlined in Chapter 2. Above the entranceway to the museum, an inscription in thick gothic lettering reads "Totus Mundus Agit Histrionem," colloquially rendered in English as "All the world is a stage." The

---

[3] J. B. Harley and J. H. Andrews, *The New Nature of Maps*, p. 159.

[4] For a concise explanation of *"sekai"* as it pertains to kabuki, see Samuel Leiter, *A New Kabuki Encyclopedia* (Westport, CT: Greenwood Press, 1997), p. 564. See also Satoko Shimazaki, *Edo Kabuki in Transition: From the Worlds of the Samurai to the Vengeful Female Ghost* (New York: Columbia University Press, 2016), esp. pp. 66–81.

[5] Benedict Anderson, *The Spectre of Comparisons: Nationalism, Southeast Asia, and the World* (London: Verso, 1998).

museum is housed in a faux Elizabethan reconstruction of the Fortune Theater and Shōyō had chosen the inscription because he believed it to have been the motto of Shakespeare's Globe Theater.[6] For the visitor to the museum, or for the researcher using its collections, the inscription serves a kind of talismanic function, shaping one's experience even if one is unable to decipher its message, perhaps even if one is unaware of its presence.[7]

Indeed, the inscription and the building itself are suggestive of the work that Shōyō had envisioned for the museum in several ways. The first is the role that comparison was always meant to play in the intellectual mission of the museum and also, one imagines unintentionally, the asymmetric nature of the reality of comparison: the building *as replica* stands in for the "missing" objects from the Western theatrical tradition that Shōyō envisioned eventually supplementing its Japanese collections.[8] The second is the suggestion of a homology between world and stage, a homology that gives to the study of the theater a particularly important place in the study of mankind, the theater serving as a kind of scale model for all of humanity and thus embodying human history in miniature.[9] Shōyō's increasing attention, in the last decade of his life, to Freud, and, more broadly, to psychoanalysis and psychology as a way to investigate the theater is revealing of his impulse to seek in the theater the deep structures of humankind—the "motives" and "motifs" that explained human history writ large, with the theatrical archive serving as the archive of the human psyche.

But the motto also suggests the work of the museum in a less obvious way. At one level, through its association with the Globe, the inscription invokes an entire history of Western thought on the relationship between the theater and the world that stretches from the Elizabethan era back through the notion of *theatrum mundi* to the Latin Middle Ages and the classical tradition and links up with discourses within the fields of geography and cartography in which this conceit played a central role in the early modern European imagination.[10] But if the motto seems but

---

[6] On the historical question of the relationship of this motto to the Globe, see Richard Abrams, "Oldys, Motteux and 'the Play'rs Old Motto': The 'Totus Mundus' Conundrum Revisited," *Theatre Notebook* 61, 3 (2007), 122–31.

[7] In a letter that he sent on August 4, 1928 to Kawatake Shigetoshi, with whom he was working closely at the time, Shōyō stressed that the Latin lettering should be decorative and floral and that it was fine if it was difficult to read. See Tsubouchi Shōyō, *Tsubouchi Shōyō shokanshū*, ed. Shōyō Kyōkai, vol. 3 (Tokyo: Waseda Daigaku Shuppanbu, 2013), pp. 118–19. Kawatake, who was adopted by Yoshimura Ito, the daughter of the playwright Kawatake Mokuami, at Shōyō's behest, was a professor at Waseda at the time and would go on to become the second director of the Theater Museum, serving in that capacity from 1934 to 1960.

[8] When the museum opened in October 1928, Shōyō was quoted in the *Yomiuri Newspaper* as saying, "As we do not yet have the funds, [the collections] are not ideal but filling them out is our work going forward": "Kyō kaikanshiki no Engeki Hakubutsukan," *Yomiuri shinbun*, October 27, 1928.

[9] On this point, see Morishige Noburō, "Wagakuni hatsu honkakuteki daigaku hakubutsukan no tanjō ni tsuite," *Nihon Daigaku Daigakuin Sōgō Shakai Jōhō Kenkyūka kiyō* 11 (2010), 133.

[10] John Gillies, *Shakespeare and the Geography of Difference* (Cambridge: Cambridge University Press, 1994), pp. 76ff.

one more example of a classic "specter of comparisons" in which "the West" provides a lens through which non-Western histories come to be understood and refashioned, the rendering of the motto into Japanese in a 1928 account of the opening of the Theater Museum suggests a different history of this metaphor, a history that provides an example of a kind of comparison that, in its own ways, deeply resonates with Shōyō's project.

In an account of the opening of the Theater Museum in the *Yomiuri Newspaper*, the motto is described as follows: "on the crossbeam above the main entranceway, designed by Shōyō himself, is the phrase written in gold lettering in Latin 'tenchi ichidai gijō.'"[11] These six characters—literally "Heaven and earth are one great theater"—are not so much a translation of the Latin as a phrase with its own rich semantic history. As we saw in Chapter 2, the phrase appears on the opening page of Enba's 1811 *Chronology*, and it was used widely in the early nineteenth century by writers like Shikitei Sanba and Kyokutei Bakin and provided a governing metaphor for thinking about the relationship between the theater and the world. And just as the Globe motto points outward toward continental Europe and backward to a rich history extending into the classical period, so too does "*tenchi ichidai gijō*" point toward the Asian continent and to a connection between world and stage with a long history in Chinese thought.

The metaphor of life as a play extends back to the Song Dynasty (960–1279 C.E.) and is important in Zen (Ch'an) Buddhist thought, but the phrase becomes especially widespread during the late Ming and early Qing periods. Indeed, as Gōyama Kiwamu has argued, "it is the phrase that perhaps best symbolizes the thought of the late Ming and early Qing," and it is in this guise that the phrase enters Japanese discourse on the theater in the eighteenth century.[12]

In Japan, the idea of heaven and earth as a stage came into wide currency in writing about theater in the early nineteenth century and provided a guiding cognitive metaphor for writers like Enba, Sanba, and Bakin. From the late eighteenth century onward, the very language of the Chinese theater comes to saturate Japanese discourse on the stage. As I will explore later in this chapter, that language would provide a conceptual grid through which the particularity of the history of kabuki was understood by inserting that particularity within a universal discourse on "the theater" as such furnished by the Chinese example in just the way the European example would serve a century later.

More broadly if, in the early nineteenth century, writers like Enba and Sanba were keenly interested in recording the history of kabuki, they were equally preoccupied with imagining a geography of kabuki; just as writers turned to the tools of the historical imagination like the chronology, so too did they turn to the tools

---

[11] "Kyō kaikanshiki no Engeki Hakubutsukan," October 27, 1928.
[12] Gōyama Kiwamu, "Minmatsu Shinsho ni okeru 'jinsei wa dorama de aru' no setsu," in Aoki Kyōju Taikyū Kinenkai ed. *Chūgoku tetsugakushi ronshū kenkyū* (Fukuoka: Asahi Shobō, 1982), p. 622.

of what Marcia Yonemoto has called "the vivid geographic imagination" of this period (maps, atlases, gazetteers) as a way to situate the theater in the world.[13]

One of the challenges of conceptualizing, and historicizing, these maps as a field is that, by their very nature, they are widely, and seemingly haphazardly, dispersed. To be sure, there are important works that foreground this "vivid geographical imagination," such as the parodic encyclopedias produced by Hōseidō Kisanji in 1791, *An Illustrated Encyclopedia of U and Kan's Three Stages* (*Ukan sandai zue*), and by Shikitei Sanba in 1803, *Illustrated Dictionary of Theater for Beginners* (*Shibai kinmō zui*), two texts to which I shall return below. But theatrical maps are found in a whole range of other publications, where they appear together with an assortment of other material such as chronologies, calendars, and lists of famous plays or famous playwrights.

There is, for example, a gyōki-style map of the second-floor dressing room found in Edo's three theaters that appears as an inset in both *Miscellaneous Notes from Behind the Stage of the Three Theaters* (*Sanshibai gakuya zassho*) (n.d.) (Figure 3.1) and *A Newly Printed Chronology of Saruwaka* (*Shinshi Saruwaka nendaiki*) (1858) (Figure 3.2), two broadsheets from the mid-nineteenth century. *A Treasury of the Theater* (*Shibai chōhōsho*) (1779) (Figure 3.3), another single-sheet print, also contains a gyōki-style map, this one depicting as a fictional island the historical theater district of Sakai-chō and Fukiya-chō in the area around Nihonbashi before the theaters were moved north to Saruwaka-chō beginning in 1841.[14] These examples are not chosen at random; rather, each comes from a piece of ephemera now part of an enormous collection of scrapbooks of early modern broadsheets compiled by Yasuda Zenjirō II, the scion of the Yasuda financial conglomerate, and, in the early twentieth century, one of the foremost collectors of early modern books and ephemera.[15]

It was in the course of looking through microfilms of Zenjirō's collection, now housed at the Waseda Theatre Museum, primarily for examples of theatrical chronologies, that I first began to recognize the questions posed by these maps. They are decorative, of course, sometimes fanciful and playful, but they are also widespread, and it is clear that they played an important role in how theater was imagined. How, then, do we account for this cartographic turn? And what

---

[13] Marcia Yonemoto, *Mapping Early Modern Japan: Space, Place, and Culture in the Tokugawa Period, 1603–1868* (Berkeley, CA: University of California Press, 2003), p. 4.

[14] "Shinpan sanshibai gakuya zassho," in *Waseda Daigaku Engeki Hakubutsukan shozō Yasuda Bunko kyūzō kinsei kindai fūzoku shiryō harikomichō*, vol. 5, 14 microfilm reels (Tokyo: Yūshōdō Shuppan, 2001), R–5, 31–006; "Shinshi Saruwaka nendaiki," in *Waseda Daigaku Engeki Hakubutsukan shozō Yasuda Bunko kyūzō kinsei kindai fūzoku shiryō harikomichō*, vol. 5, 14 microfilm reels (Tokyo: Yūshōdō Shuppan, 2001), R–5, 31–010; "Shibai chōhōsho," in *Waseda Daigaku Engeki Hakubutsukan shozō Yasuda Bunko kyūzō kinsei kindai fūzoku shiryō harikomichō*, vol. 5, 14 microfilm reels (Tokyo: Yūshōdō Shuppan, 2001), R–5, 31–005.

[15] On Yasuda Zenjirō's collection, see Waseda Daigaku Engeki Hakubutsukan, ed., *Engeki Hakubutsukan gojūnen* (Tokyo: Waseda Daigaku Tsubouchi Hakushi Kinen Engeki Hakubutsukan, 1978), pp. 215–17.

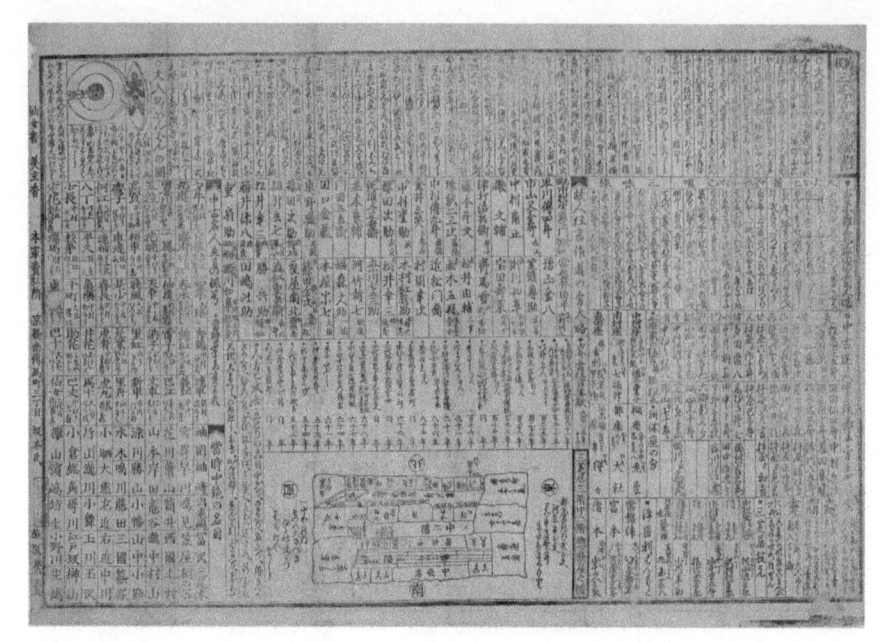

**Figure 3.1** Map of the dressing room, *Sanshibai gakuya zassho*, n.d.
*Source*: Tsubouchi Memorial Theatre Museum, Waseda University.

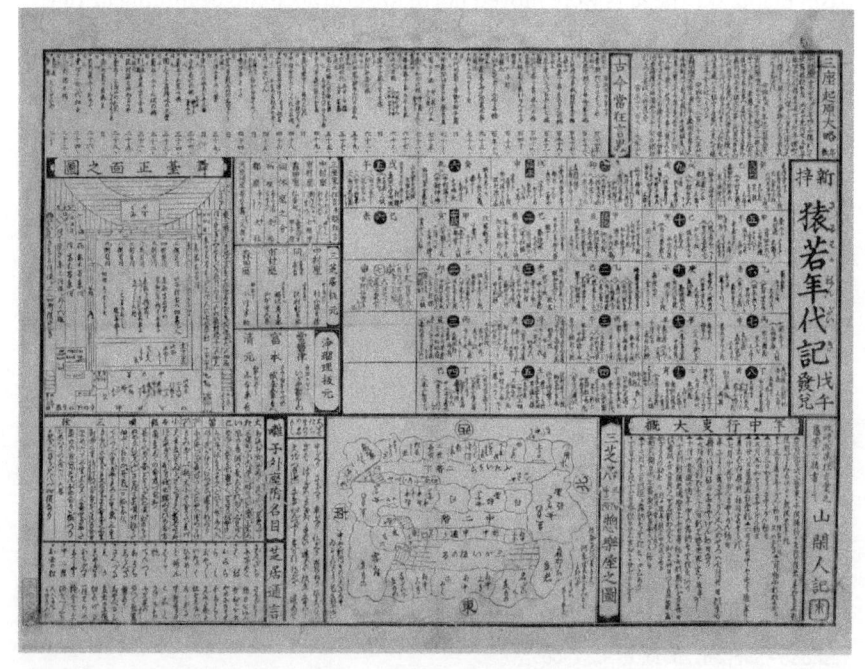

**Figure 3.2** Map of the dressing room, *Shinshi Saruwaka nendaiki*, 1858.
*Source*: Tsubouchi Memorial Theatre Museum, Waseda University.

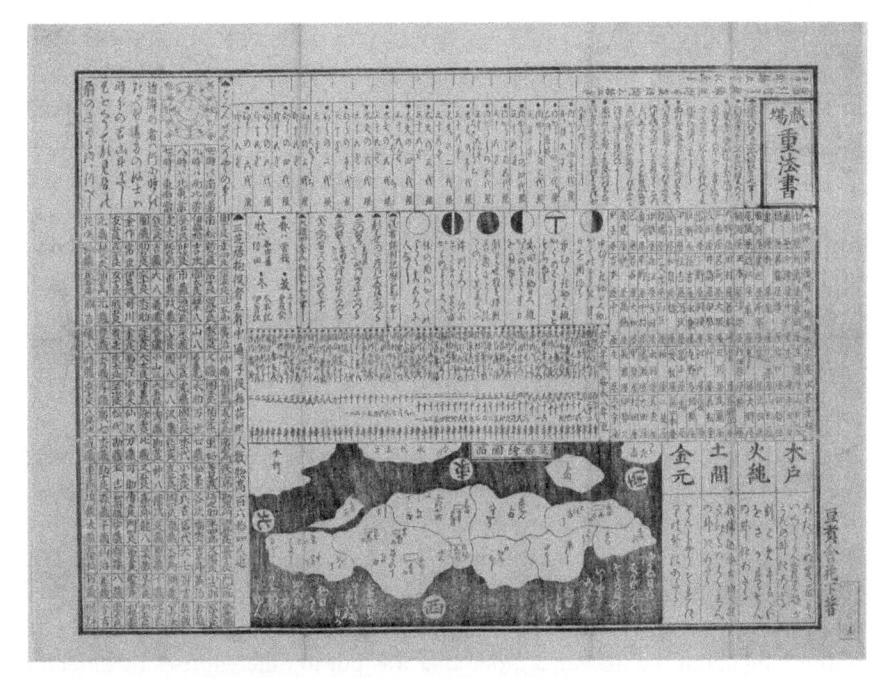

**Figure 3.3** Map of the theater district, *Shibai chōhōsho*, 1779.
*Source*: Tsubouchi Memorial Theatre Museum, Waseda University.

does it mean to our understanding of both the history and the historiography of nineteenth-century kabuki that it was so often to the cartographic idiom that writers turned to convey that history?

I would like to begin to answer these questions by turning to Yasuda Zenjirō's scrapbooks. By 1920, Zenjirō's library, the Matsunoya, was one of the most important private collections of books in Japan, but the collection was completely destroyed in the fires following the Great Kanto Earthquake of 1923, and all that is left of the Matsunoya is a kind of ghostly imprint in the form a partially reconstructed catalogue that the historian and bibliographer Kimura Senshū compiled in 1958.[16]

After the Earthquake, Zenjirō returned to collecting, and although he would die in 1936, just over a decade later, his second library, known as the Yasuda Bunko, would itself become one of the most important book collections in pre-war Japan. The scrapbooks, part of the Yasuda Bunko, were in turn donated to the Waseda Theater Museum in 1940 by Zenjirō's son, Hajime;[17] they contain, in 92 volumes, roughly 5,000 discreet items, primarily printed broadsheets from the nineteenth

---

[16] See Kimura Senshū, "Matsunoya Bunko no zōsho," in Kimura Sutezō ed. *Kimura Senshū shū*, Nihon Shoshigaku Takiei, vol. 31-3 (Tokyo: Seishōdō Shoten, 1983), pp. 115–48.
[17] Waseda Daigaku Engeki Hakubutsukan, *Engeki Hakubutsukan gojūnen*, pp. 214–16.

century. And although the Yasuda Bunko would be destroyed during the Second World War, the scrapbooks and other theatrical materials that had been donated to the Theater Museum have survived, virtually the only remnants of Zenjirō's bibliomania.[18]

The scrapbook collection—which contains an extraordinary range of printed ephemera about all aspects of the social and cultural life of early modern Japan—includes three volumes of kabuki material, primarily single-sheet playbills and lists of actor ranks and salaries. Interspersed with other kinds of material are a number of maps of varying size and form. Most, like the examples given above, are set within printed broadsheets that contain other information, including chronologies of the theater. But Zenjirō's collection also contains three stand-alone maps: one dating from the first decade of the nineteenth century and the other two from some time near mid-century. These maps provide an entryway for thinking about the role of the geographic imagination in nineteenth-century discourse on kabuki.

Part of any engagement with the printed archive of the nineteenth-century theater is the imperative to grasp the meanings of its rich and varied objects. The maps in Zenjirō's scrapbooks, as well as other maps contained in books and on printed broadsheets, demand that we take seriously the *form* of the map as a mode of thinking about the theater, a mode that was put to different uses by different "cartographers" and at different times. Zenjirō's maps, that is, allow for an entry into a broader discourse about the theater, and so it is to "reading" and historically situating these maps that I now turn.

## II The Detailed View: Mapping the Theater District

One of the most arresting pieces of theater ephemera contained in Zenjirō's scrapbooks is a large-format (380 by 729 mm), three-sheet, color-printed map designed by the printmaker Utagawa Yoshifuji, which depicts the theater district of Saruwaka-chō on the northeastern edge of the city (Figure 3.4).[19] The map bears the cryptic title "Yobukodori waka sanchō zenzu." The title plays on a series of what, in the Japanese poetic tradition, are called pivot words (*kakekotoba*), words that link two meanings. Yobukodori is one of the three birds (*sanchō*) of Japanese poetry (*waka*) delineated in treatises on poetics. "*Waka*," however, also calls to mind Saruwaka-chō, the new theater district which is depicted in the map and

---

[18] The only other books that have survived were given by Yasuda Hajime to the scholar Kawase Kazuma, who had worked as his father's assistant at the Yasuda Bunko and which are now part of the Daitōkyū Memorial Library at the Gotoh Museum in Tokyo. In 1998, the Daitōkyū Memorial Library published a reconstruction of the collection of Yasuda Bunko based on surviving sources. See "Kyū Yasuda Bunko zōsho no fukugen," *Kagami* 32/33 (1998), 58–170.

[19] "Yobukodori waka sanchō zenzu," in *Waseda Daigaku Engeki Hakubutsukan shozō Yasuda Bunko kyūzō kinsei kindai fūzoku shiryō harikomichō*, vol. 2, 14 microfilms (Tokyo: Yūshōdō Shuppan, 2001), R-2, 8–037.

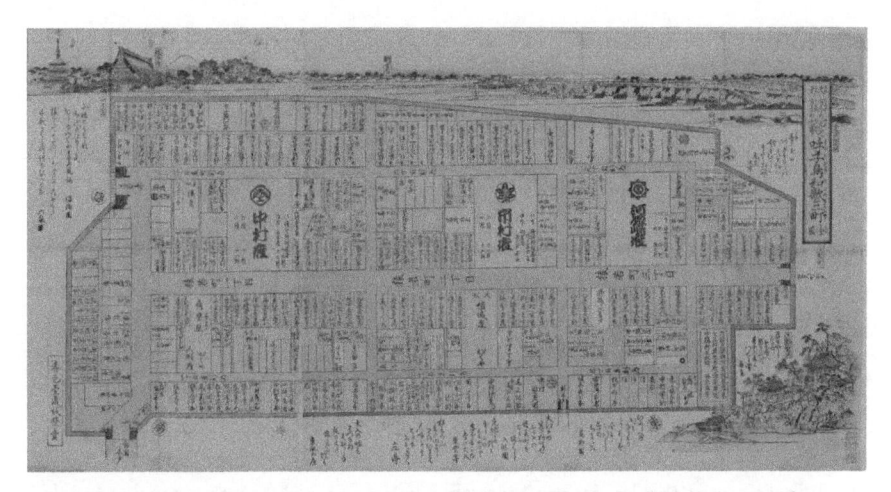

**Figure 3.4** Map of the Saruwaka-chō theater district, "Yobukodori waka sanchō zenzu," n.d.
*Source*: Tsubouchi Memorial Theatre Museum, Waseda University.

which was comprised of three blocks (*sanchō*). The print is a map of the stockaded area to which the theaters were moved beginning in 1841 as part of the Tenpō Reforms; based on internal evidence—the map does not bear a date—it can be roughly assigned to the years between 1843 and 1855.

"Yobukodori" is oriented with the north–south axis running diagonally across the print, North at the viewer's upper right and South at the lower left. This orientation puts the main gate to the district at the right edge of the map and has the main street, which the theaters abut, running across the map from right to left, an orientation that clearly evokes the genre of the *saiken* or detailed view of the pleasure quarter of the Shin Yoshiwara, a genre with a history that goes back to the seventeenth century. The city's three kabuki theaters—the Kawarazaki-za, the Ichimura-za, and the Nakamura-za—appear on the upper half of the map, each marked with the theater's crest; below are the two puppet theaters which moved to Saruwaka-chō: The Satsuma-za (a jōruri theater) and the Yūki-za, a theater which used marionettes (ayatsuri ningyō).[20]

The rest of the map depicts an extraordinary array of information: various classes of theater teahouse, liquor stores and tobacconists, a public bath and barber shop, pawn shops, confectioners, and noodle and sushi vendors. These central commercial spaces are surrounded by properties bearing the names of various actors and denoting the residence of the actors and theater managers, now forced

---

[20] In contrast to the puppets used in jōruri, the marionettes of the Yūkiza were much smaller and controlled by a single puppeteer using strings from above the puppet.

to live within the confines of the district.²¹ Indeed, although "Yobukodori" includes purely decorative elements, including a panorama of the area from Asakusa through the demimonde of Shin Yoshiwara to Nihon Zutsumi on its upper edge, the map is very much a map of a real space and draws heavily on the cartographic conventions and visual grammar of the detailed views (*saiken*) of the city's pleasure quarters of Shin Yoshiwara to which the theater district was now physically proximate.²²

In Zenjirō's scrapbook, "Yobukodori" is paired with a second map of the same district, *A Detailed View of Saruwaka* (*Saruwaka saiken zu*), which makes this reference to the genre of the *saiken*, or guides to the pleasure quarters, explicit (Figure 3.5).²³ This map bears a striking resemblance to "Yobukodori" and, at first sight, the two appear to be perhaps two versions of the same map, possibly even based on the same set of printing blocks. There are differences in coloration, subtle differences in the landscape view that serves as a decorative border around

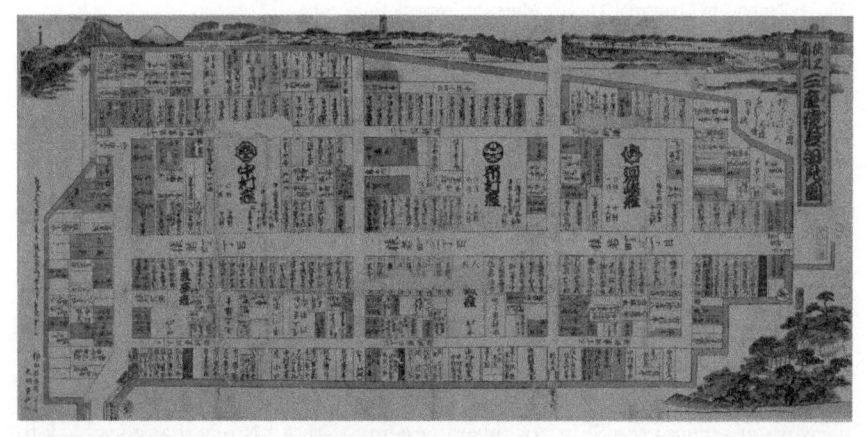

**Figure 3.5** Map of the Saruwaka-chō theater district, *Saruwaka saiken zu*, n.d.
Source: Tsubouchi Memorial Theatre Museum, Waseda University.

---

²¹ Although actors, as members of an outcast group, were technically supposed to live within the theater district before the move to Saruwaka-chō, this seems to have gone largely unenforced. There is a long description of the lavish residences and lifestyle that some of the most famous actors enjoyed (before the theaters moved to Saruwaka-chō) in the 1816 *Seji kenmonroku*, in which actors are described as living in "exceptional splendor [...] their extravagance in everything is beyond compare." See Buyō Inshi, *Lust, Commerce, and Corruption: An Account of What I Have Seen and Heard, by an Edo Samurai*, ed. and trans. Mark Teeuwen and Kate Wildman Nakai (New York: Columbia University Press, 2014), p. 332.
²² Edo's theaters moved to Saruwaka-chō, along the Sumida River northeast of the Sensōji Temple in Asakusa, beginning in 1841. The Yoshiwara pleasure quarter had similarly moved from its original location near Nihonbashi in the center of Edo to north of the Sensōji following the 1657 Meireki Fire.
²³ "Kōsei shinkoku Saruwaka saiken zu," in *Waseda Daigaku Engeki Hakubutsukan shozō Yasuda Bunko kyūzō kinsei kindai fūzoku shiryō harikomichō*, vol. 2, 14 microfilm reels (Tokyo: Yūshōdō Shuppan, 2001), R-2, 8-036. On the genre of *saiken*, see Peter Kornicki, *The Book in Japan: A Cultural History from the Beginnings to the Nineteenth Century* (Leiden: Brill, 1998), pp. 71–72.

each map, and minor differences in the details contained within the central plan each offers of Saruwaka-chō. But the two maps appear almost completely identical, suggesting a likely relationship of filiation. *A Detailed View of Saruwaka*, like "Yobukodori," however is undated, making it difficult to know for sure which iteration is earlier and which later.

Through their visual and cartographic grammar, both maps evoke a parallelism between the theater district and the pleasure quarter, a parallelism with a long but vexed history. For while the history, especially the early history, of kabuki and of its spaces was intimately bound up with both female and male prostitution, by the late eighteenth century and into the nineteenth, this relationship had become largely historical since government regulation of both sex work and entertainment became more intrusive.[24]

And yet, despite the extraordinary similarity of "Yobukodori" and *A Detailed View of Saruwaka* at the cartographic level, the two maps are actually quite distinct from one another *as objects*, a difference derived from their production and circulation and marked on each at the lower left edge. *A Detailed View of Saruwaka* bears the name and address of the publisher, Ōtaya Sakichi, along with a note to "please inform the publisher quickly of any changes to the streets"; "Yobukodori" bears the inscription: "Blocks owned by Shunshokudai. Not for Sale." Shunshokudai was a pen name used by the retired kabuki playwright Hanagasa Bunkyō, and the map also bears a poem in Bunkyō's name on the upper right of the first sheet. While almost identical at the level of what is represented and *how* it is represented, the maps in fact belong to very different social worlds, inhabiting different spaces in relation to print and the public sphere, a subject that I began to explore in Chapter 2.

Like maps and guidebooks of the Shin Yoshiwara, on which it was modeled, the published *A Detailed View of Saruwaka* is intended to be a living document, both to be used and to be updated, a map whose value is largely dependent on the extent to which it continues to reflect the physical spaces it represents. But "Yobukodori" has an entirely different purpose. Produced by Bunkyō and his circle, "Yobukodori" is celebratory and commemorative, marking the beginning of a new era of the theater in a new space, with the central map surrounded by panegyric verse written by a small circle of theater enthusiasts. The two maps also have subtly different orientations toward time: *A Detailed View of Saruwaka* points toward an unfolding future, changes yet to come, whereas "Yobukodori" is celebratory, marking a new phase in the history of kabuki.

---

[24] See Donald H. Shively, "Bakufu versus Kabuki," *Harvard Journal of Asiatic Studies* 18, 3/4 (1955), 326–56; Gary Leupp, *Male Colors: The Construction of Homosexuality in Tokugawa Japan* (Berkeley, CA: University of California Press, 1997), p. 78; Gregory Pflugfelder, *Cartographies of Desire: Male-Male Sexuality in Japanese Discourse, 1600–1950* (Berkeley, CA: University of California Press, 2007), pp. 117ff.

Indeed, the similarity of these maps highlights the ways in which identical, or almost identical, objects can lead very different social lives in different circumstances or historical moments. A map that may be designed as a commodity, primarily informational and utilitarian, can be transformed into a commemorative and celebratory memento or keepsake and then again become an object for collection and display. Time itself would impart to both maps an uncanny sense of ghostliness, for the district of Saruwaka-chō would collapse shortly after the Meiji Restoration of 1868 when the theaters were once again permitted to move out of the district. By the time Zenjirō would collect these maps in the 1920s, they were not guides to a living space but historical relics of a vanished past. But, suggestively, the transformation of these maps into historical artifacts began much earlier, prior to the Meiji Restoration and prior to the demise of Saruwaka-chō.

Indeed, in the nineteenth century, maps are themselves intimately part of the process of creating a history of the present for the future: already, there is a copy of "Yobukodori" included in Ishizuka Hōkaishi's manuscript continuation of Enba's *Chronology of Kabuki*, which, like "Yobukodori," was compiled in the wake of the Tenpō reforms during which the culture of kabuki was so much a target for public censure. Hōkaishi, who had taken up the continuation of Enba's chronology sometime after the latter's death, includes a hand-drawn copy of Bunkyō's map after the entry for the year 1842—the year in which the last of the three kabuki theaters, the Kawarazaki-za, was moved to Saruwaka-chō (Figure 3.6).[25] But Hōkaishi's

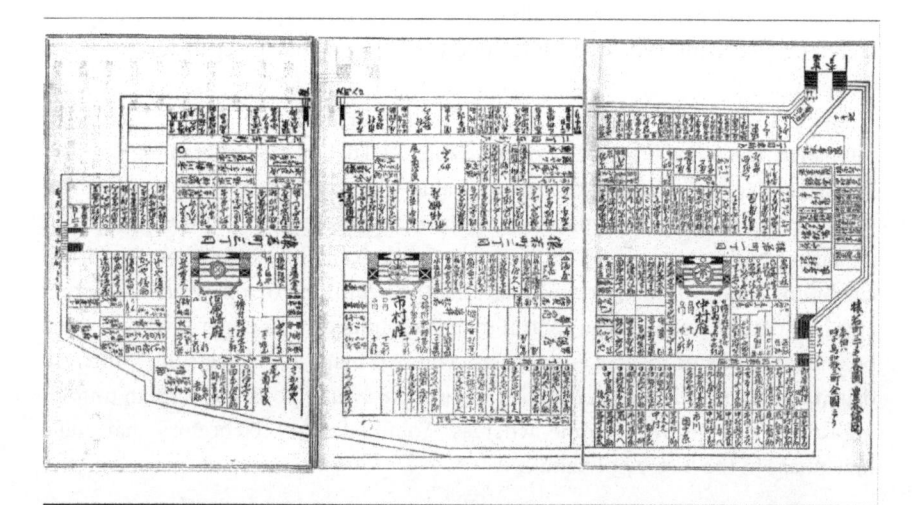

**Figure 3.6** Copy of "Yobukodori waka sanchō zenzu" from Ishizuka Hōkaishi's "Zoku kabuki nendaiki".
Source: C.V. Starr East Asian Library, University of California, Berkeley.

---

[25] Ishizuka Hōkaishi, *Hana Edo kabuki nendaiki zokuhen*, ed. Mizutani Futō and Ichijima Kenkichi, vol. 4, Shin Gunsho Ruijū (Tokyo: Kokusho Kankōkai, 1907), pp. 425–27.

manuscript map is also different from "Yobukodori" in one important respect: the decorative elements included as part of the original map, its panoramic border and panegyric verse, are stripped away and all that is left is the central plan of Saruwaka-chō as a physical space. Although Hōkaishi could not have known that the district would vanish in less than a generation, there is a kind of prescience to including a copy of the map as a record of the district at this particular historical moment; as part of the chronology, the map becomes a piece of documentary evidence, almost a snapshot of the theater district at this point of transition.

The celebratory poems that adorn Bunkyō's map are collected in Hōkaishi's chronology but are removed from the map itself and placed at the end of the entry.[26] Hōkaishi, that is, retains both the map as image and the poems, but he severs their direct connection and each becomes its own kind of record of the year 1842 but with the relationship between the two altered. The verse remains as a record of a particular kind of sociability set apart from the commercial sphere, a mode of connoisseurship and collecting to which Hōkaishi's own manuscript, itself a product of this post-Tenpō moment, belonged. Indeed, Hōkaishi himself adds his own poem, which predicts that the prosperity of the district will increase day by day and that the banners of the three theaters will fly for generations. The map of Saruwaka-chō as it was in 1842 thus captures one moment within an ongoing history of Edo's theater world, the subject that the *Chronology* itself seeks to document as it unfolds.

Another manuscript copy of a very similar map of Saruwaka-chō can be found in volume twenty-four of "Morisada's Miscellany" ("Morisada mankō") (Figure 3.7). This is an extraordinary compendium of notes on contemporary life compiled by Kitagawa Morisada over an almost thirty-year period beginning in 1837.[27] Like the copy of "Yobukodori" in Hōkaishi's chronology, the map in "Morisada's Miscellany," which simply bears the title "Map of Saruwaka-chō from 1847," is completely devoid of decorative elements; it is meant to record the actual spaces of the district at a discreet historical moment, part of Morisada's attempt to write the history of the world as he knew it and, in turn, to record the history of kabuki as part of that world. In the preface he wrote to his manuscript in 1853, Morisada described the overall purpose of his project as "to record the everyday life of the people (*minkan no zatsuji*) and pass it on to my descendants";[28] and he describes his project in language that explicitly invokes works of a previous generation such as Santō Kyōden's *Thoughts on Extraordinary Things of Recent Times* (1804) and *A Collection of Curiosities* (1814–15), with the thousands of pages of his manuscript recording, in often meticulous detail, the habits and practices of early modern Japan.

---

[26] Ishizuka Hōkaishi, *Hana Edo kabuki nendaiki zokuhen*, p. 428.
[27] Kitagawa Morisada, *Morisada mankō*, ed. Asakura Haruhiko and Kashikawa Shūichi, vol. 4 (Tokyo: Tōkyōdō Shuppan, 1992), p. 27.
[28] Kitagawa Morisada, *Morisada mankō*, vol. 1, p. 3.

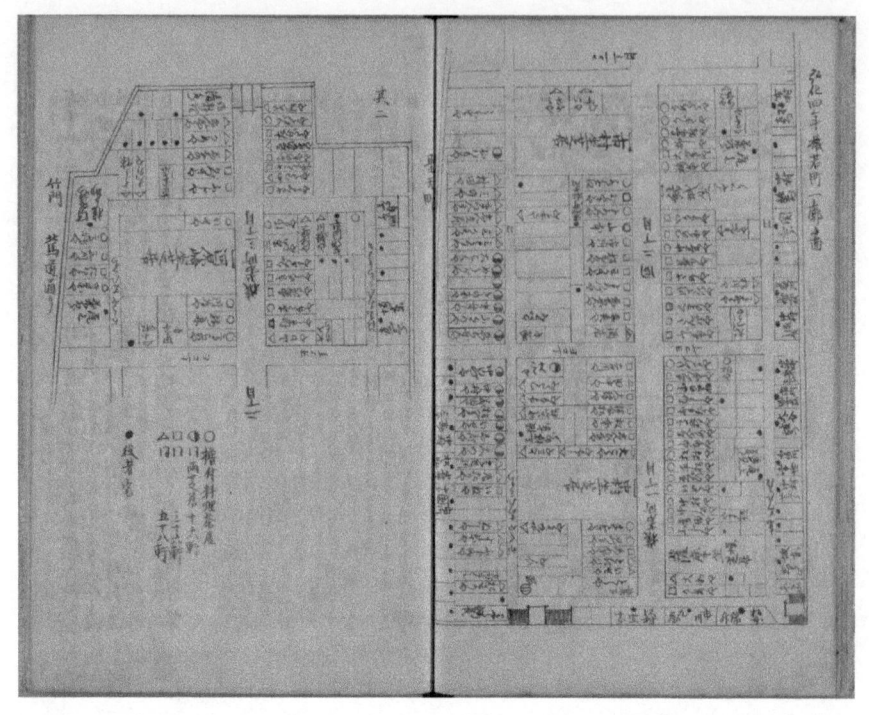

**Figure 3.7** "Map of Saruwaka-chō from 1847" from Kitagawa Morisada, "Morisada mankō".
*Source*: National Diet Library, Tokyo.

As part of a broad archive of theater ephemera, these different versions of the Saruwaka-chō map suggest two important roles that cartographic convention played in thinking about the theater across the nineteenth century. The first focuses not on what is internal to the maps but rather on the maps as material objects: how these cartographic images—published or private, printed or hand copied—participated in the broader world of a nascent historicism that I addressed in Chapter 2. Although they may not have imagined the map and the timeline as forming a pair of historical lenses, by the mid-nineteenth century, maps were used repeatedly both to investigate kabuki's past and to document its present as a future past.

The second role that maps play in thinking about the theater in the nineteenth century derives from *what* is represented and *how* it is represented. The printed maps of Saruwaka-chō found in Zenjirō's scrapbooks evoke a parallel between the theater and the pleasure quarters, what the literary historian Hirosue Tamotsu has called the twin "spaces of vice" (*akubasho*) of early modern Edo.[29] These images allow us to see how contemporaries—observers, critics, and fans but also playwrights—used maps to negotiate the spatial and the historical complexities of this relationship and also how that relationship was not static in the way that Hirosue imagined but rather changing and evolving over time.

At one level, Morisada's map of Saruwaka-chō is, like so many of the other images and quotations found throughout the manuscript, a bit of miscellany documenting a world that Morisada saw vanishing before his eyes, even before the portentous arrival of American Perry's black ships.[30] But Morisada's hand-drawn map of Saruwaka-chō is also one of a series of three maps of Edo's theater district, a series which inserts this map of the 1840s into a longer genealogy of maps going back to the late seventeenth century that Morisada uses to document changes in Edo's theater district. For Morisada, maps are a form of historical evidence, and he uses these diagrams to illustrate how the theater district has evolved over a century-and-a-half.

Chronologically, the earliest of the maps of Edo's theater district that Morisada includes is a copy of a map originally published in the 1680s (Figure 3.8).[31] As Morisada notes, this map is hand copied from Saitō Gesshin's 1847 *Anthology of Pieces for Voice* (*Seikyoku ruisan*), which had, in turn, reproduced it from the 1684 *An Apologia for the Fellows of the Three Theaters* (*Yarō sanza taku*).[32] *An Apologia for the Fellows of the Three Theaters* is a "fellows critique" (*yarō hyōbanki*), a genre of actor critique that emerged in the late seventeenth century in tandem with the *Yoshiwara saiken* and courtesan critiques (*yūjo hyōbanki*) but served as a guide to the comeliness of "fellows" (*yarō*), male actors whom patrons could hire for sexual purposes.[33] Thus, the seventeenth-century map which Morisada had copied from a mid-nineteenth-century source is itself a document not just of the theater district in the late seventeenth century but also of the deep interconnections between the theater and sex work that very much mark the early history of kabuki, even if Morisada himself seems not to have completely understood these connections.

---

[29] Hirosue Tamotsu, *Shinpen akubasho no hassō* (Tokyo: Chikuma Shobō, 1988).
[30] "Morisada mankō" was composed between 1837 and 1853, but in 1867, Morisada added a note to his preface stating that, following the arrival of the Commodore Matthew Perry and the threat of war, he had made a number of additions and emendations to his text in black ink. See Kitagawa Morisada, *Morisada mankō*, vol. 1, p. 4.
[31] Kitagawa Morisada, *Morisada mankō*, vol. 4, pp. 23–24.
[32] Kitagawa Morisada, *Morisada mankō*, vol. 4, pp. 22–24.
[33] For a discussion of the broader context of male–male sexuality in the Edo period, see Pflugfelder, *Cartographies of Desire*, pp. 23–96; Leupp, *Male Colors: The Construction of Homosexuality in Tokugawa Japan*.

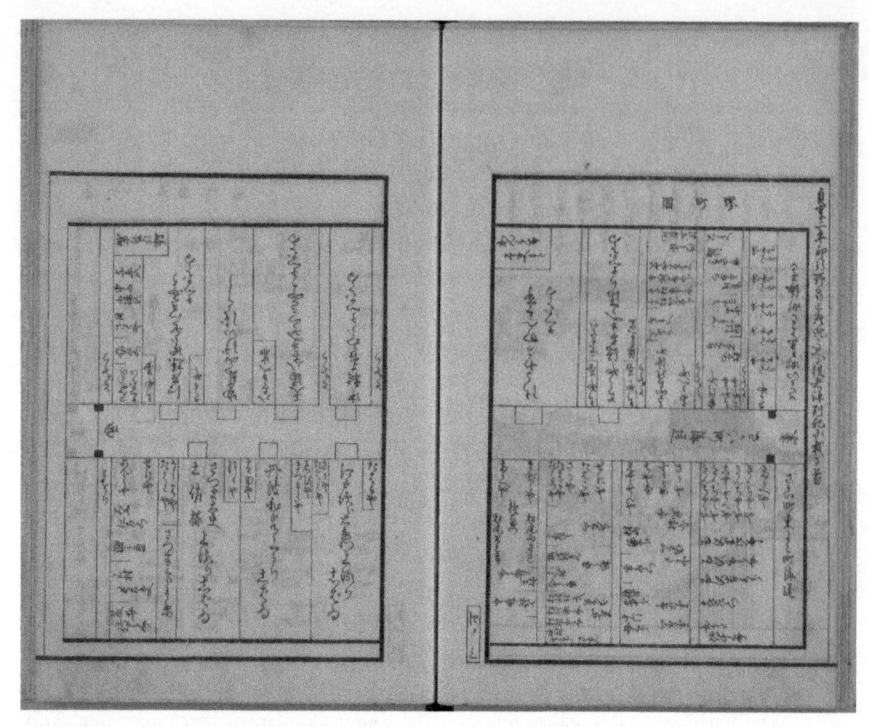

**Figure 3.8** Copy of map of Edo's theater district originally published in *Yarō sanza no taku* (1684) from Kitagawa Morisada, "Morisada mankō".
*Source*: National Diet Library, Tokyo.

The map registers not only the location of the various theaters operating in the district, as well as tobacconists, noodle shops, and teahouses, but also a large number of establishments marked "*kinchakuya*," a term referring to houses of male prostitution, though Morisda himself seems unsure what this term meant, writing:

> Throughout the map there are many places marked "*kinchakuya*." It seems like these are not in fact stores that sold purses (*kinchaku*). They seem to be a type of teahouse but there are other establishments marked teahouse. They are perhaps a type of establishment that provides a guide to the theater operating under the name *kinchakuya*. I will need investigate this matter further.[34]

In this early map of the theater district, the intimacy of the theater with the spaces for sex work is clearly visible and, indeed, serves as an important purpose of the map. In the mid-eighteenth century, Hiraga Gennai would produce much more detailed guides to the *kagema jaya*, the male brothels, of the district in works that were explicitly modeled on the *Yoshiwara saiken*, the detailed views or guides of

---

[34] Kitagawa Morisada, *Morisada mankō*, vol. 4, p. 21.

the pleasure quarters. Gennai's maps cover not just the central thoroughfare of Sakai-chō and Fukiya-chō but also the so-called Fukiya-chō Gaidō, which abutted a canal, and Gakuya Shinmichi to the north of the theaters and Yoshi-chō to the south, the areas around which the houses of male prostitution were concentrated. The prefaces to, though not the maps from, Gennai's *Detailed View of Edo Male Love* (*Edo nanshoku saiken*; 1775) and *The Chrysanthemum Garden* (*Kiku no sono*; 1764), both guides to the way of the youth, were reproduced in Kimura Mokurō's 1829 *A View of the Theater through a Microscope* (*Gekijō ikkan mushimegane*), a work that took substantial interest in the geography of the theater and to which I will return below in a different context.[35]

The second map of the Edo theater district in Morisada's manuscript is a diagram of Sakai-chō and Fukiya-chō during the Kansei period, 1789–1801 (Figure 3.9).[36] No source is listed for the map, and it appears to be a composite sketch of Morisada's own making rather than a copy of a single original source.

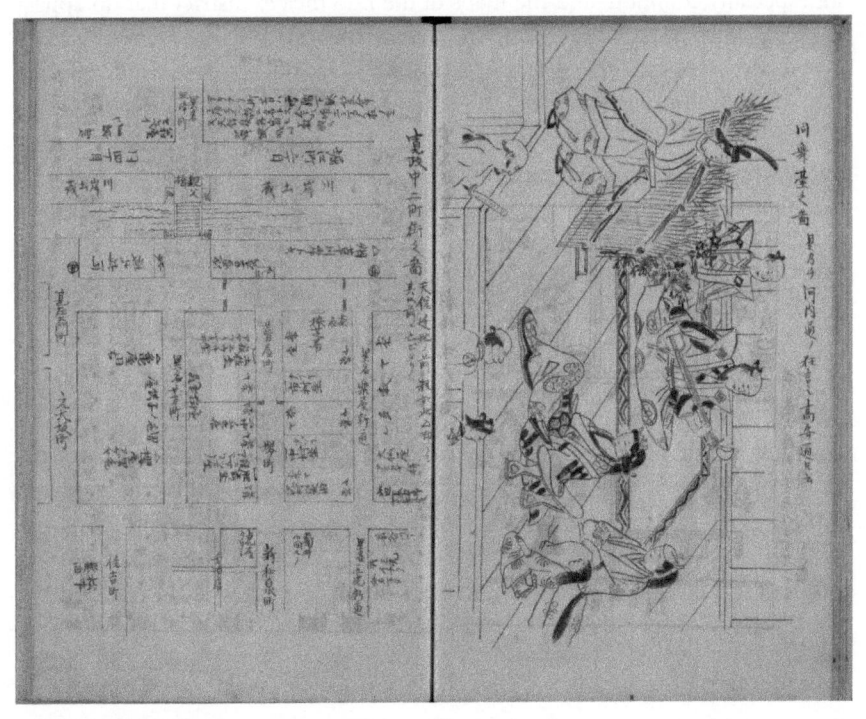

**Figure 3.9** Map of Sakai-chō and Fukiya-chō during the Kansei period (1789–1801) from Kitagawa Morisada, "Morisada mankō".
Source: National Diet Library, Tokyo.

---

[35] Kimura Mokurō, "Gekijō ikkan mushimegane," in *Engeki bunko*, ed. Engei Chinsho Kankōkai, reprint. vol II, (Tokyo: Gannandō Shoten, 1973), pp. 40–43.
[36] Kitagawa Morisada, *Morisada mankō*, vol. 4, p. 26.

The map is oriented with west at the top and includes, in addition to a plan of the main district, some of the surrounding neighborhood: not only Gakuya Shin-michi and Yoshi-chō to the north and south, respectively, but also Sumiyoshi-chō and Shin Izumi-chō to the east and Horie-chō across the canal to the west. What is interesting about Morisada's sketch is not the expansiveness of the area depicted in the map, which, after the move of the theaters north to Saruwaka-chō in the 1840s, locates and positions this recently displaced space within the city for an imagined reader in the future; rather, what is striking is that it was during the very years depicted in this map that mappings of the theater district in publications would become rather more tightly focused on the main thoroughfare of Sakai-chō and Fukiya-chō, excluding the surrounding areas that Morisada himself includes—that is, the cartographic strategy of Morisada's map is quite different from that of maps dating from the period that the map itself seeks to depict.

Although maps of Edo's theater district, as well as the theater districts of Osaka and Kyoto, appear occasionally in late-eighteenth-century actor critiques, they are not especially common, and the maps of the Edo theater district that do appear are more tightly focused on the main thoroughfare of Sakai-chō and Fukiya-chō than was the 1684 *An Apologia for the Fellows of the Three Theaters*. In the map of Edo's theater district that is found in the widely reproduced 1795 actor critique *A Disquisition on the Customs of Actors* (*Yakusha saraekō*), for example, all we are given is the main thoroughfare that runs from Fukiya-chō in the west to Sakai-chō in the east; but Yoshi-chō, the center of male sex work at the time, is completely absent from the map. Had Morisada simply copied a contemporary source from the late eighteenth century such as the map found in *A Disquisition on the Customs of Actors*, what he would have produced would have been rather narrower in focus and scale.[37]

Almost a century earlier, with the publication of the 1699 *The Actor's Vocal Shamisen* (*Yakusha kuchi jamisen*), actor critiques had begun to shift their focus to acting rather than the physical appearance of the actors, and in many ways, the history of kabuki in the eighteenth century can be seen as a struggle for legitimacy, a struggle that was in part predicated on distancing itself from origins intimately bound up with various forms of sex work.[38] Maps of the theater district seem to reflect this; the spaces of male prostitution, once central to guides to the theater district, are absent on later maps, rendering invisible this historical relationship.

---

[37] *Yakusha saraekō*, also romanized *Yakusha saraikō*, was republished in 1800 under the title *Zōho gekijō ichiran* and is reproduced under that title in Geinōshi Kenkyūkai ed., *Nihon shomin bunka shiryō shūsei*, vol. 6 (Tokyo: Sanichi Shobō, 1973), pp. 373–430. The map of Edo's theater district appears on p. 414. On the different editions of *Yakusha saraekō*, see Satō Chino, "Yakusha hyōbanki no kaihan: *Yakusha saraekō* shoshi hoi," *Engeki kenkyūkai kaihō* 41 (May 2015), 20–30.

[38] On the history of *hyōbanki*, see Akama Ryō, *Zusetsu Edo no engekisho: Kabuki hen* (Tokyo: Yagi Shoten, 2003), pp. 199–200. On kabuki's struggle for legitimacy see Shively, "Bakufu versus Kabuki"; Katherine Saltzman-Li, *Creating Kabuki Plays: Context for Kezairoku, "Valuable Notes on Playwriting"* (Leiden: Brill, 2010).

MAPPING THE STAGE: ON KABUKI'S CARTOGRAPHIC ARCHIVE    95

One striking example of this can be found in the map of the same district included at the beginning of a work written by Utei Enba in 1817, just after he had finished the final volumes of his *Chronology*. Like the much later *A Detailed View of Saruwaka*, the map of the Saruwaka-chō theater district of the Tenpō period collected in Yasuda Zenjirō's scrapbooks, Enba's book, *A Detailed View of the Theater: The Three-Leafed Clover* (*Shibai saiken sanbasō*), explicitly and self-consciously calls on the example of the *saiken*, the guidebooks to the pleasure quarters published since the early eighteenth century.[39]

For example, *The Three-Leafed Clover* opens with a preface in which Enba explicitly compares his project with the Yoshiwara *saiken*, noting that even the title he chose for his work, the three-leafed clover (*sanbasō*), plays on the title often used in guides to the pleasure quarters from the 1780s forward, the five-leafed pine (*goyō no matsu*).[40] The map of the theater district is, moreover, clearly modeled on the map of the Shin Yoshiwara included in *saiken* like *The Five Leafed Pine* (*Goyō no matsu*) and suggests a parallel between these two spaces (Figure 3.10).

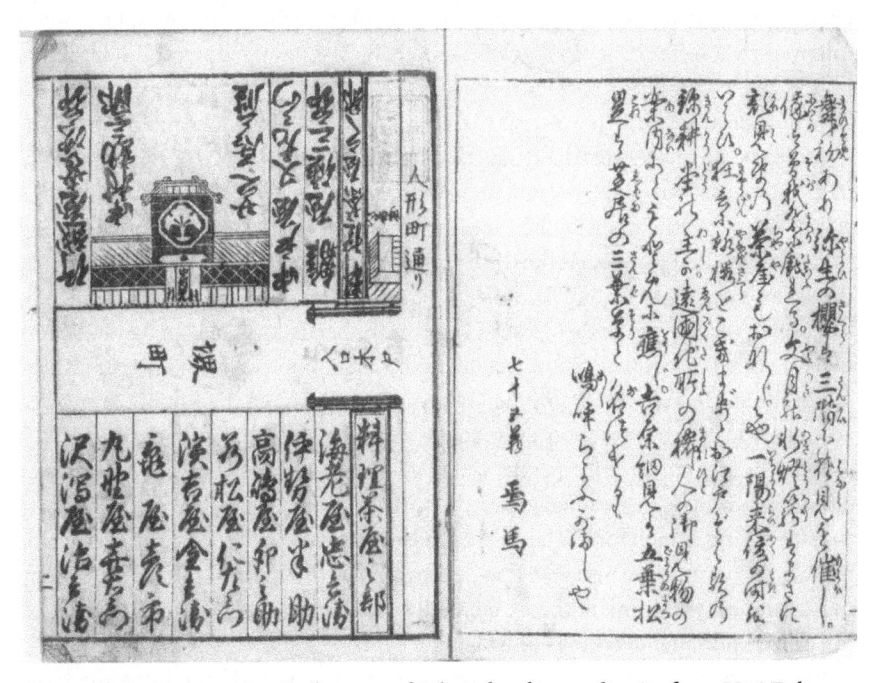

**Figure 3.10** Utagawa Kunisada, map of Sakai-cho theater district from Utei Enba, *Shibai saiken sanbasō*, 1817.
Source: Ninjōji Bunko, Osaka University Library.

[39] Utei Enba, *Shibai saiken sanbasō* (Edo: Moriya Jihē and Yamaguchiya Tōbē, 1817).
[40] Utei Enba, *Shibai saiken sanbasō*, 1v. In both instances, there is a pun in the title: the five-leafed pine (*goyō no matsu*) of the guide to Shin Yoshiwara referred to the five (*go*) districts (*machi*) of the quarter while the three-leaf clover (*sanbasō*) of Enba's title refers both to the *sanbasō* dance of the kabuki theater, a ritual dance derived from the *nō* theater, and to the three theaters of Edo.

But there are two important elements to note about the map: first, because of the narrow focus on the main thoroughfare that ran from Sakai-chō to Fukiya-chō, the larger area including Gakuya Shinmichi and Yoshi-chō is excluded. Even as the *form* of the map draws a parallel with the pleasure quarters, the map itself excludes the male brothels surrounding the theaters. The theater district is a space *like* the Shin Yoshiwara, the map seems to suggest, but the relationship is one only of analogy.

The second important feature of the map is that it is not really a *map* at all, despite both its appearance and Enba's own claims that it would serve as a guide to the traveler unfamiliar with the district. This is clear especially when comparing the map in Enba's book to maps from detailed views of Yoshiwara. Maps of the Shin Yoshiwara, like that found in *The Five-Leafed Pine*, give a detailed plan of the pleasure quarter along what amounts to two axes. First is the main axis that runs essentially north–south along Naka-no-chō starting at the main gate, the Ōmon, and which bisects the district. Then, perpendicular to this, are a series of smaller streets running east–west, which contain the main courtesan houses which are presented sequentially with a map of the smaller teashops lining Naka-no-chō followed by a series of maps showing the brothels running along the side streets of Edo-chō, Sumi-chō, and Kyō-machi.

At first glance, Enba's map seems to follow a similar pattern. The main thoroughfare bisects the theater district from the entrance to Sakai-chō at Ningyō-chō dōri in the northeast down to the canal that abuts the back of Fukiya-chō. Spatially, this is very similar to the maps of the Shin Yoshiwara, with the theaters plotted among the teahouses that populated the district. But what is strange about the map is that the various classes of teahouses appear to be given on the map not by their actual location in relation to the theaters but simply grouped by type in lists.[41] Enba seems to have done this because of the dictates of the larger choices he and his publishers made about the map. By excluding Gakuya Shinmichi, there is simply no way of accurately locating the teahouses, many of which lined that alleyway.

But a second constraint emerges when we look at how Enba constructs the second axis we find in the detailed views, the spatial plan of the brothels running along the side streets, which forms the bulk of those guidebooks. The detailed views plot these brothels in space and give detailed entries recording the various courtesans of each house with rank and cost denoted by an intricate series of chevrons and other markings, the meanings of which are explained at the front of the book.

Enba, however, transforms this section entirely. While still retaining the basic spatial layout and the form of a map, what he plots here are not real, physical spaces but the actors themselves ranked by fame and skill. While the structure of these entries is copied directly from the detailed views, the function is entirely

---

[41] The map gives three types of teahouse, each listed in a section (*bu*): *ryōri jaya* (restaurants), *kojaya* (smaller teahouses serving food), and *mizujaya* (teahouses that only served tea).

different. For example, *The Five-Leafed Pine* gives a map of the first district of Edo-chō that begins with an establishment called the Tamaya and lists its courtesans marked by rank. Here, we find the courtesans Kasugano and Tamagawa followed by Komurasaki and Hanamurasaki, who have the highest rank. *The Three-Leafed Clover* gives an analogous "map," but what is listed in place of the Tamaya is the Kōraiya, the yagō or "shop name"[42] of the actor Matsumoto Kōshirō V, and what is given in place of the individual courtesans are the roles for which he was known, ranked in order of skill, beginning with Fuwa Banzaemon, Taira no Masakado, and Banzui Chōbē (Figure 3.11).[43]

This "map" requires of the reader a certain amount of knowledge otherwise it is essentially unintelligible. In this sense, Enba's "guide" functioned very differently from the guides to the Shin Yoshiwara that it parodied. Those guides were practically oriented and offered maps to the real spaces of the district. But this, of course, is, in some ways, the point: for Enba, the knowledgeable reader will "get" the various allusions and the overall structure of the extended comparison of the theater district and the pleasure quarters. And yet, this parodic impulse, which underlies

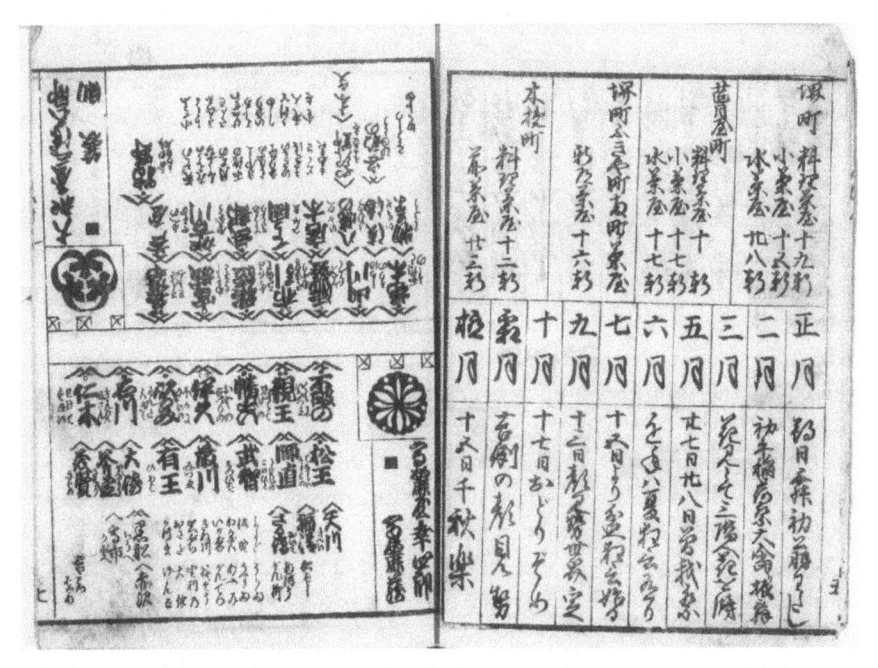

**Figure 3.11** Utagawa Kunisada, entry for Matsumoto Kōshirō V from Utei Enba, *Shibai saiken sanbasō*, 1817.
Source: Ninjōji Bunko, Osaka University Library.

---

[42] On yagō, see Leiter, *A New Kabuki Encyclopedia*, p. 692.
[43] Utei Enba, *Shibai saiken sanbasō* (1817), 6r.

the book's structure, stands in contrast to the idea of the book as it is laid out by both Enba in his preface and by his publishers Moriya Jihē and Yamaguchiya Tōbē in an afterward. As Enba notes, he had created the book in response to a request by the publishers to provide a "guide for travelers from distant provinces and foreign lands" (*engkoku tasho no marebito*) a phrase that the publishers themselves echo in a postscript to the book.[44]

But if a book like *The Five-Leafed Pine* could serve as a practical guide to the Shin Yoshiwara, it is impossible to imagine how *The Three-Leafed-Clover* could have functioned in a similar way; the map of Sakai-chō and Fukiya-chō is hardly a functional guide to the area other than in the most basic sense. *The Three-Leafed Clover* is more like a list in map form and understanding the entries on individual actors relies on deep knowledge of the actors, the plays, and the roles. And while Enba retains the iconic system of chevrons used to rank courtesans by price, he nowhere explains what the system means or how it ought to be read, despite a legend of this kind being common in guides to the pleasure quarters themselves. A reader, that is, would only understand these rankings if they were already familiar with the system from guides to the pleasure quarter. Although there is an indication in the publisher's postscript that the book was intended to be updated and reissued, like the detailed views of the Yoshiwara, this project seems to have been abandoned until some years after Enba's death, when it was revived by Goryūtei Tokushō working with the original publishers Moriya Jihē and Yamaguchiya Tōbē.[45]

Tokushō's book, *A Detailed View of the Actors of the Three Theaters* (*Sanshibai yakusha saiken*), which was issued yearly between 1826 and 1828, is self-consciously modeled on Enba's earlier work, but it differs from that work in several important ways. First, despite retaining *Detailed View* in the title, and using the basic structure of the detailed views of the Shin Yoshiwara, including the iconic ranking system, in contrast to Enba's work, Tokushō makes no references to that genre or to the Yoshiwara itself in his preface, which focuses entirely on the practices of the theater. The book no longer explicitly compares the theater district with the pleasure quarters, even if that comparison is implied by the structure. Even the title, which retains the word *saiken*, suggests an important distinction: the *saiken*, or detailed view, is, here, explicitly of the *actors* rather than the theater district.

Second, the map Tokushō includes is a much more accurate representation of the actual spaces of the theater district: the teahouses are marked in their locations both on the main thoroughfare and on Shinmichi, and the different types of teahouse are marked by corresponding symbols (Figure 3.12). Tokushō also includes a map of Kobiki-chō, the area to the south of Sakai-chō and Fukiya-chō where the

---

[44] Utei Enba, *Shibai saiken sanbasō*, 1v.
[45] See Goryūtei Tokushō, *Sanshibai yakusha saiken* (Edo: Moriya Jihē and Yamaguchiya Tōbē, 1826), https://www.dh-jac.net/db1/books/SB4064/portal.

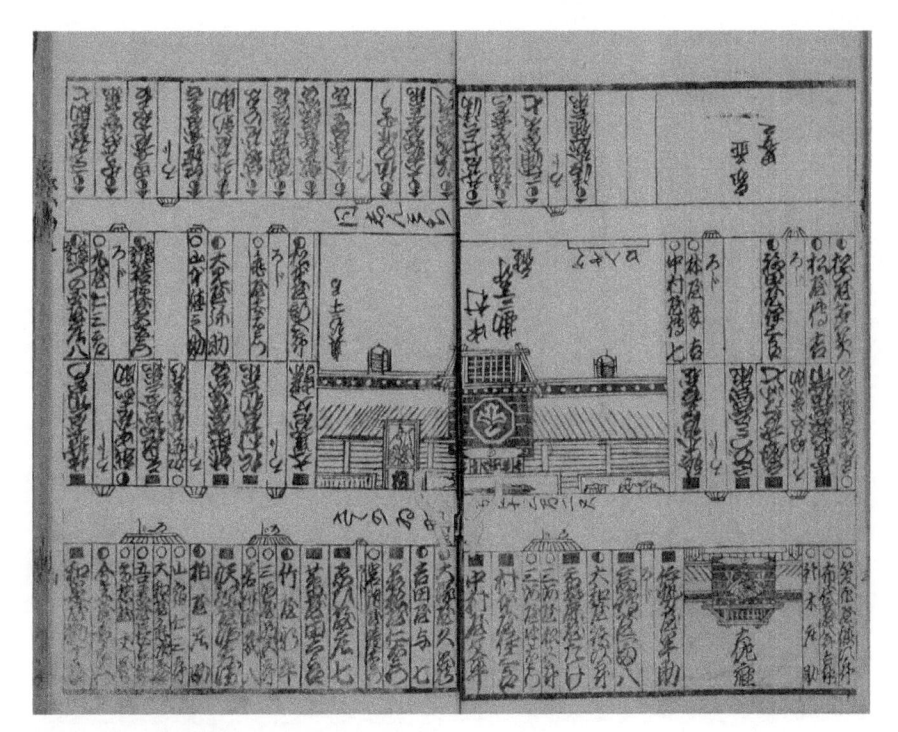

**Figure 3.12** Utagawa Kunisada, map of Sakai-chō theater district from Goryūtei Tokushō, *Sanbshibai yakusha saiken*, 1828.
*Source*: Ebi Collection, Art Research Center, Ritsumeikan University.

third licensed theater was located. What was a fairly rough and abstract approximation of the district in Enba's *Three-Leafed Clover* is here a rendered as a more practical guide.

But the biggest difference between the two works is how Tokushō transforms the body of the work, which lists actors and rank. Gone almost entirely is the pretense of following the structure of the detailed views of the pleasure quarter in which competing houses are arrayed on either side of the street. The conceit of having this section of the book approximating a map is entirely abandoned, and instead, the entries for the most famous actors are dominated by likenesses drawn by the famed print designer Utagawa Kunisada (Figure 3.13). Although, in many ways, *A Detailed View of the Actors of the Three Theaters* resembles *A Detailed View of the Theater: The Three-Leafed Clover*, the book seems differently oriented. Central now are images of the actors and there is, moreover, a subtle gendering of the books: in contrast to Enba's work, which foregrounded its connections with guidebooks to the masculine space of the *demimonde*, these later editions contain advertisements for a popular brand of make-up and eschew any explicit reference to the pleasure quarter.

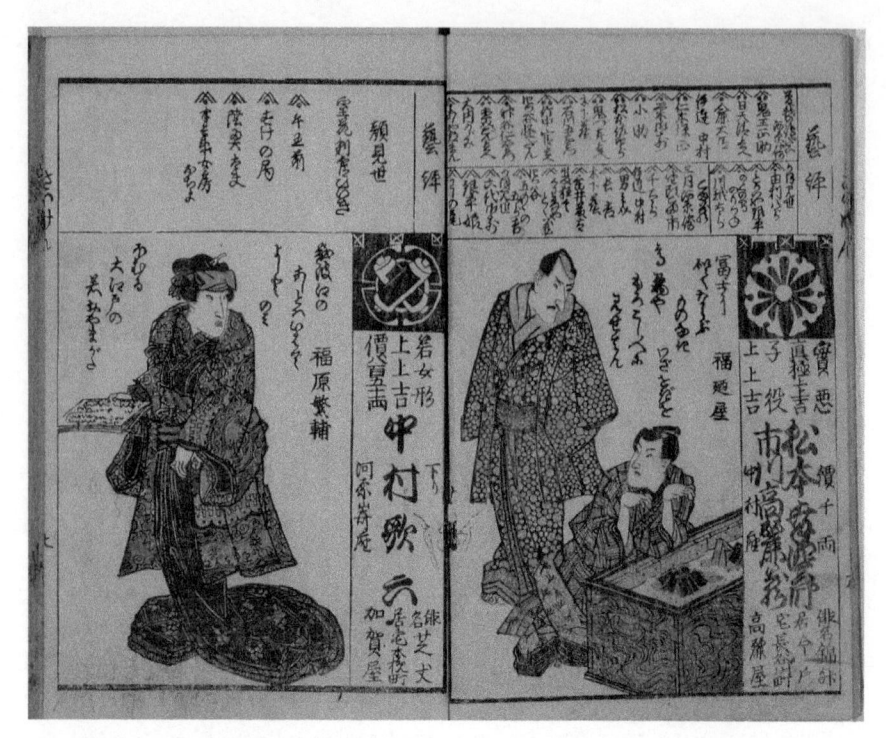

**Figure 3.13** Utagawa Kunisada, entry for Matsumoto Kōshirō V and his son Ichikawa Komazō V (right) and Nakamura Karoku I (left) from Goryūtei Tokushō, *Sanshibai yakusha saiken*, 1828.
Source: Ebi Collection, Art Research Center, Ritsumeikan University.

In 1832, exactly a decade after Utei Enba's death, the publishers of the original *A Detailed View of the Theater: The Three-Leafed Clover* began to issue a new series of books under that title, issued yearly at least until 1836.[46] But these books were now almost completely different from Enba's original 1817 edition. These Tenpō-era editions of *A Detailed View of the Theater: The Three-Leafed Clover* were published annually in six volumes, two volumes for each of Edo's three licensed theaters. Like Enba's original version, the books do contain maps of the area surrounding the theaters (although the maps themselves are taken from Tokushō's later edition), and they also include updated editions of the "maps" based on the detailed views of the Shin Yoshiwara that Enba had created to rank the various actors and their roles. But in these later editions, all of this material that explicitly calls to mind the genre of the guide to the pleasure quarters comes at the end of the second volume for each theater. What constitutes the entire first volume and the bulk of second is an illustrated synopsis—replete with famous lines—of the most important plays of the year for each theater, drawn with actor's likenesses

---

[46] Utei Enba, *Shibai saiken sanbasō*, 6 vols (Edo: Moriya Jihē and Yamaguchiya Tōbē, 1832).

and meant to approximate the format of *gōkan*, the genre of illustrated fiction so popular at the time. While traces of the original conceit of the project survive, what we are left with in the 1830s is completely different both in form and in purpose, as if two decades after first embarking on the project of creating a "view" of the theater, the publishers, Moriya and Yamaguchiya, had finally figured out what it was that the market would bear: not a practical guide to the theater district as space, nor a parody of the guides to the pleasure quarters, but a digest of the theatrical season lavishly illustrated with printed likenesses of actors.

These books from the 1830s and the world they represent form the most immediate context for the two maps of Saruwaka-chō from the 1840s found in Zenjirō's scrapbooks. Those maps of Saruwaka-chō were created less than a decade after the Tenpō-era editions of *The Three-Leafed Clover*, but, of course, a great deal had changed in the intervening years. Most importantly, the theaters were themselves moved out of the central downtown area near Nihonbashi and to the area of Saruwaka-chō, northeast of Asakusa and close to the Shin Yoshiwara, making the parallelism of these two areas of the city more explicit, perhaps inescapable. And, we might imagine, it was this new physical remoteness of the theaters from everyday commerce and life that necessitated something like the detailed "views" that appeared for the pleasure quarter after it was similarly moved from the central area around Ningyō-chō to north of Asakusa at the edge of the city in the 1650s.

While the maps of Saruwaka-chō that begin to appear in the 1840s seem to be heir to a longer tradition of "detailed view" maps going back through the books published in the decades from 1817 to the 1830s to earlier examples found in actor critiques in the 1780s and even further back to the maps to the same district that appeared in guides to male brothels in the late seventeenth and eighteenth centuries, it is also necessary to see this genealogy as one of discontinuity and disruption in which similarities in basic form also belie the fundamental, even radical, differences in function. And indeed, it is in the decades between the Kansei Reforms, beginning in the late 1780s, and the Tenpō Reforms, beginning in the early 1840s, when mappings of the physical spaces of the theater are least frequent, that a conceptual space seems to open up in the cartographic imagination for a different approach to the geography of the theater, one dominated by the impulses not of information but of parody.

Enba was himself one of the great masters of parody in nineteenth-century Japan, and so it is perhaps fitting that it is one of his own maps that will serve as a guide into this other cartographic universe.

## III From the Cartographic Imagination to the Parodic Imagination

A decade before writing the original *A Detailed View of the Theater: The Three-Leafed Clover* in 1817, Utei Enba had already begun to experiment with the map as form. Working with the illustrator Kitagawa Tsukimaro, Enba created a

**Figure 3.14** Kitagawa Tsukimaro and Utei Enba, *Kabuki dōchū zue*, n.d.
Source: Tsubouchi Memorial Theatre Museum, Waseda University.

two-sided broadside consisting of a map entitled *An Illustrated Road Guide to Kabuki* (*Kabuki dōchū zue*) and a second sheet which contains two sections: "A Registry of Historic Sites of Departed Actors" at top and "A Road Guide to Kabuki Travel" at the bottom (Figure 3.14).[47] The broadsheet, like the two later maps of Saruwaka-chō discussed above, is contained in Zenjirō's scrapbooks; it is undated but internal evidence suggests that it was produced in the early nineteenth century.[48]

If "Yobukodori" and *A Detailed View of Saruwaka* point us to the physical spaces of the theater district, *An Illustrated Road Guide to Kabuki* is entirely different. Coming across *An Illustrated Road Guide to Kabuki* in Zenjirō's scrapbooks, it offers an arresting image. At first, the map is difficult to make sense of: it is faded,

---

[47] Utei Enba, "Kabuki dōchu zue," in *Waseda Daigaku Engeki Hakubutsukan shozō Yasuda Bunko kyūzō kinsei kindai fūzoku shiryō harikomichō*, vol. 5, 14 microfilm reels (Tokyo: Yūshōdō Shuppan, 2001), R-5, 31–002.

[48] A copy of the map is also contained in the "Kyota kyakushokuchō," a forty-two-volume scrapbook of theater ephemera that the playwright and illustrator Hamamatsu Utakuni compiled for the collector Yoshino Goun, an Osaka druggist, in the early nineteenth century, which is now housed in the Waseda Theater Museum. In the reproduction of the "Kyota kyakushokuchō" in *Nihon shomin bunka shiryō shūsei*, the date of the map is given as 1801. See Geinōshi Kenkyūkai, *Nihon shomin bunka shiryō shūsei*, vol. 14, p. 643.

illegible in parts, and it does not appear to represent any immediately intelligible space. But quickly (and more quickly, no doubt, for Enba's contemporaries), the map emerges as a kind of a puzzle, almost a game. The broadsheet's title, *An Illustrated Road Guide to Kabuki* is meant literally: it offers a guide not to the real spaces of the theater but a road map to kabuki as a set of ideas, practices, and institutions. The topographical markings on the map, that is, correspond not to places but to aspects of the theater itself, some with a spatial component, others without.

The top of the map is dominated by a structure called the *Sanza Daigongen* or the Great Spirit of the Three Theaters, referring to the three licensed theaters of Edo but punning on the Sanja Daigongen shrine in Asakusa. To the right of the *Sanza Daigongen*, from the viewer's perspective, for example, is the Rock of Great Success (*Ōatari no iwa*), marked by an arrow hitting a bullseye, the standard iconography within kabuki for a commercial hit (*ōatari*). This central scene is bordered on each side by a waterfall (the Waterfall of the Skillful (*Jōzu no taki*) to the left and the Waterfall of the Greats (*Meijin no taki*) to the right), which then lead to a set of peaks: the Peak of the Peerless and the Peak of the Head of All Arts, to the left and right, respectively, terms that had been employed since the eighteenth century to refer to the greatest of actors such as the legendary *onnagata* Yoshizawa Ayame.[49]

At the bottom of the map is the *Inarimachi*, a term used within kabuki to refer to the lowest rank of actor. On the map, *Inarimachi* bears the following inscription: "if one proceeds from here, one will reach the Crossroads of Fame after some time." The Crossroads of Fame is just below the *Sanza Daigongen* and lies just beyond Mount Bandachi, referring to the opening skit performed by the lowest-rank actors at the beginning of the day's program of plays. The "Road Guide to Kabuki Travel" printed on the lower half of the print's second sheet explains how the aspiring actor would make the journey up the Hanamichi or Road of Flowers, the term used for the walkway in kabuki theaters that leads through the audience to and from the stage. To ascend the path from *Inarimachi* to the Crossroads of Fame, the aspiring actor must first pass through the Gates of the Curtain Opener (*Jobiraki no mon*), which takes him past a shrine to the Acala of the Novice Actor (*Arashaba Fudō*) and the Pass of Despair (*Kurayami tōge*) up to the Peak of the Third Floor (*Sankai no Mine*), beyond which point women are forbidden to enter, referring to the historical practice of prohibiting women from entering the dressing room. Here, the actor finds the entry point for Mount Aichū, referring to the rank at which the actor's name begins to appear on the play sign. To reach the peak of Mount Aichū, the traveler must negotiate the perils posed by *sarugaeri* and *michigaeri*, referring to two acrobatic somersaults performed in fight scenes.[50]

---

[49] Utei Enba, "Kabuki dōchu zue."
[50] Utei Enba, "Kabuki dōchu zue."

By the early nineteenth century, a large body of published guidebooks (*dōchūki*) had emerged to help travelers on a variety of routes, including the main highways that connected Edo with Kyoto and Osaka, the Tōkaidō and the Nakasendō. These booklets contained a wealth of practical information from the distance between post stations and the cost of lodging to what famous places could be found along the route. At the same time, travel also became an important literary subject with the serialized publication of Jippensha Ikku's (*Tōkai dōchū hizakurige*) beginning in 1802. In *An Illustrated Road Guide to Kabuki*, moreover, the sense of movement along a route to a fixed goal calls to mind the dice game of *sugoroku* in which players vie with one another to move along byways towards a set goal. Elaborately illustrated and printed *sugoroku* boards began to proliferate during the early nineteenth century and, indeed, these game-boards are dominated by the subjects of travel and the theater. But in its form, the map appears to be based not on a board game but on a different kind of print that was also common in the early nineteenth century, pictorial tourist maps to the famous sites of cities such as Edo or Kamakura. *An Illustrated Road Guide to Kabuki*, for example, bears a striking resemblance to tourist maps of Kamakura, which were published regularly across the Edo period beginning in the middle of the seventeenth century.[51]

If we take this comparison seriously, rather than a participant in the journey of the actor, then, the viewer of the map is positioned more as a tourist in an unfamiliar land. But there is also an odd tension to this map *as* a tourist map: a tourist map seeks to make the unfamiliar familiar through recourse to a shared cartographic grammar. The specific and the individual—this mountain or river, that shrine or temple—are denoted as examples of general categories and rely on a shared iconography. A map such as the tourist map of Kamakura translates the specificities of the local into a general language of convention, which allows the viewer to *read* the map. But *An Illustrated Road Guide to Kabuki* functions rather differently, almost in an opposite way: a mountain does not represent a mountain but points only inward toward a joke or word play. The reader cannot really *learn* anything about the world of the theater from Enba's map but rather must bring to bear his or her own knowledge of theatrical practice and convention to *get* the jokes embedded in the broadsheet. This same tension, of course, inhabits Enba's later *A Detailed View of the Theater: The Three-Leafed Clover*, which had also claimed to be a guidebook but which required of the reader knowledge both of the form and conventions of the detailed views of the Shin Yoshiwara and a deep familiarity with the conventions of kabuki and with individual actors and roles.

Rather than using convention to plot the specific within a general framework, like a tourist map, and thus make it legible, the parodic nature of *An Illustrated*

---

[51] See, e.g. *Kamakura ezu* (Kamakura: Ōsakaya Magobē, n.d.), http://www.wul.waseda.ac.jp/kotenseki/html/bunko10/bunko10_08464/index.html.

*Road Guide to Kabuki* demands of the reader knowledge both of the object of parody and of the codes on which the humor relies. In this sense, the map is not unlike that portrait of Enba that Shikitei Sanba includes in *A Critique of the Audience*: in that image (see Chapter 2), readers can only understand the references embedded in the picture if they already know what the references mean.

Taken alone, out of context, as a single image in Zenjirō's scrapbooks, it is difficult to make sense of the historicity of Enba's map—why it existed and what it means. But, as Marcia Yonemoto has argued, beginning in the mid-eighteenth century, the tools of the cartographic imagination became broadly subject to parody, with "writers of comic fiction [. . .] taking the spatial frameworks and categories established in maps and travel accounts and putting them to decidedly playful uses" by applying "'serious' mapping tropes to seemingly frivolous subject matter."[52] In the history of kabuki, the appearance and then disappearance of these "documents of *dis*order," as Yonemoto calls them, seem to coincide almost exactly with a moment when we have a kind of blank space in the archive for real maps of the theater district—almost as if one could map the theater in reality or in imagination but not both at the same time.[53]

Why should this be the case? Why, that is, does a literal mapping of spaces of the theater district, which we see from the seventeenth century through the mid-eighteenth century, essentially disappear as a subject of interest in the decades around 1800 only to appear again in the mid-nineteenth century? And why, in those intervening decades, do we find in the place of these maps something rather different, playful and parodic mappings that take as their subject not concrete spaces but abstract ideas or theatrical practices?

For more than a quarter of a century from the late 1780s through the beginning of the second decade of the nineteenth century, a wide variety of parodic maps of the theater appear. Some, like Utei Enba's *An Illustrated Road Guide to Kabuki* were printed as broadsheets; others, like the maps that appear in the 1788 *A Guide to the Provinces of Actors* (*Yakusha jinkokuki*) were published in actor critiques; still others were published as parts of parodic reference works such as Hōseidō Kisanji's 1791 *An Illustrated Encyclopedia of U and Kan's Three Stages* or Shikitei Sanba's 1803 *Illustrated Dictionary of Theater for Beginners*. Taken as a whole, theses maps, and others like them, suggest a historical moment in which the parodic impulse seems to cohabit with, and in some cases to have displaced, the function of maps to record, and *order*, reality. Parody *as form* inhabits a particular moment in the production of knowledge about kabuki, and about the world more generally, and in this sense can be historicized. That is to say, we may rightly ask why, between the 1780s and the 1810s, parody becomes such an important tool for imagining the world and theater's place within it?

---

[52] Yonemoto, *Mapping Early Modern Japan*, p. 6.
[53] Yonemoto, *Mapping Early Modern Japan*, p. 6.

In a legend that appears in *An Illustrated Road Guide to Kabuki*'s cartouche, Enba offers an account that situates the map's origins not in the culture of the early nineteenth century but in that of the early eighteenth century. The map, Enba writes, was based on a work "created in jest" by the late Ichikawa Danjūrō II (1688–1758) and Sawamura Sōjūrō I (1675–1734), two of the great actors of the first half of the eighteenth century, which, he claims, had been given to him by his friend Ichikawa Danjūrō V (1741–1806). Enba himself had merely amended the map, he writes, in response to the urging of the publisher Shūseikaku, who was now printing the map for the enjoyment of theater fans.[54]

Nothing like the original "A Record of the Kabuki Highway" ("Kabuki kaidō ki") described by Enba has survived and, two centuries on, it is hard to know if this was always a piece of apocrypha that added to the map a layer of historical depth and perhaps also obscured the conceptual debt Enba owed to contemporary writers who had already begun to use parodies of maps, guidebooks, and gazetteers to map the theater world as an imagined space. The story recalls the often fantastic items displayed at the late-eighteenth-century "treasure showings," in which Enba had participated, but also those items of theatrical history collected and shared at gatherings like the Unchakai: rare objects of kabuki's past, materials out of which the history of kabuki might be fashioned.

A more plausible origin for Enba's map can be found in a series of works that began to appear at the end of the eighteenth century, including the 1791 *An Illustrated Encyclopedia of U and Kan's Three Stages* (*Ukan sandai zue*) written by Hōseidō Kisanji, one of the foundational texts for understanding the role of the parodic imagination in mapping the theater and one of the earliest works to make an extended play on the idea of the theater as its own world. Kisanji was a senior samurai from the Kubota Domain in northern Japan who had begun publishing poetry and fiction after moving to Edo in the 1780s. Kisanji had, in fact, contributed the preface to the 1783 *The Five-Leafed Pine*, the detailed view of the Shin Yoshiwara on which Enba had modeled *A Detailed View of the Theater: The Three-Leafed Clover*. Kisanji had written extensively on the pleasure quarters and, in 1777, had published *A Geographical Guide to Courtesans* (*Shōhi chiriki*).[55] The book, as Marcia Yonemoto has noted, brings together "the conventions of history, geography, and comic fiction, [creating] a mock guide to an 'unknown' land called Gepponkoku, the 'Land of the Rising Moon,' which on closer inspection turns out to be the Yoshiwara."[56]

Like *A Geographical Guide to Courtesans*, *An Illustrated Encyclopedia of U and Kan's Three Stages* is a parody of a reference work, the important Sino-Japanese encyclopedia *An Illustrated Japanese–Chinese Encyclopedia of the Three Realms*

---

[54] Utei Enba, "Kabuki dōchu zue."
[55] Yonemoto, *Mapping Early Modern Japan*, pp. 142ff.
[56] Yonemoto, *Mapping Early Modern Japan*, p. 143.

(*Wakan sansai zue*; 1712) and is based on the conceit that the theater, like the Shin Yoshiwara before it, is its own world. The book's title puns on the *Wakan* (Japan and China) of the original title, with *Ukan* derived from the first characters of the given names of the founders of Edo's two oldest theaters: Ichimura Uzaemon and Nakamura **Kan**zaburō, the founders of the Ichimura-za and the Nakamura-za, respectively.[57] The book purports to provide an extended introduction to this world complete with sections on climate, geography, and the customs of the people of the world. The opening pages, for example, which give the history of Edo's three theaters—literally, the "Origin of the Three Stages" ("Santai no kigen") and the "Meaning of the U and Kan" ("Ukan jigi")—are written in a dense mock Chinese style that mimics the encyclopedia on which the book is based. But quickly, the humor—if not the writing style—becomes less arch. In a description of the inhabitants of this world, Kisanji writes that "this country is a land of extremes":

> The good are exceptionally good, the wicked exceptionally wicked. The wise have extraordinary wisdom while the foolish are extremely foolish. The women are all chaste and sincere and there are absolutely no women who are beautiful in appearance but who harbor a wicked heart. In general, the good all have the outward appearance of good and the wicked the outward appearance of wickedness.[58]

The world of the theater is a world of extremes, a Manichaean world in which the melodramatic imagination of the age comes alive, a subject to which I will return in Chapter 5.

At this point, Kisanji provides a section on the geography of the three lands of this world with the three licensed theaters each treated as its own country, though these countries, he notes, are all the same in terms of "topography, climate, and the character of their population." This imaginary geography is overlain on the real geography of the theaters in the city of Edo: "Although the land of Chū and the land of Ichi are not distant from each other, there is a great mountain called Fukuyama between them and they are separated by four or five other countries, one of which is called Korea."[59] The Nakamura-za (Chū) in Sakai-chō and the Ichimura-za (Ichi) in Fukiya-chō were just a block away from each other, but they were separated by a series of tea houses including the Fukuyama (literally the mountain of fortune) and the Kōraiya, whose name is derived from the Korean kingdom of Koryo. A similar conceit was used in *A Treasury of the Theater*

---

[57] For an overview of *Ukan sandai zue*, see Hōseidō Kisanji, *Ukan sandai zue*, Kabuki no Bunken, vol. 4 (Tokyo: 1971), pp. 83–92. For a broader discussion of the work including its connections with *Shōhi chiriki*, see Hamada Keisuke, "Kokkeibon toshite no gekisho," in Hamade Keisuke *Kinsei shōsetsu: eii to yōshiki ni kansuru shiken* (Kyoto: Kyōto Daigaku Gakujutsu Shuppankai, 1993), pp. 205–08.

[58] Hōseidō Kisanji, *Ukan sandai zue*, pp. 98–99.

[59] Hōseidō Kisanji, *Ukan sandai zue*, pp. 97–98.

(*Shibai chōhōsho*), a broadsheet published a decade earlier in 1779, which contains a map of the theater district in *gyōki* style intended to resemble the Japanese archipelago and which marks the Fukuyama teahouse between the Nakamura-za and Ichimura-za (see above Figure 3.3).[60]

That earlier map is part of a two-sided printed broadsheet. On one side is a chronology of kabuki with the title *A Chronology of Kabuki* (*Kabuki nendaiki*) some three decades before Enba would write his own chronology with that title. On this side of the broadsheet, we have an overview of the origins of kabuki, a section on the yearly calendar of the theaters, and a chronology presented as a table beginning with the founding of the Nakamura-za in 1624 and running through 1779.

The map is printed on the obverse side, which is titled *A Treasury of the Theater* and which contains an array of information: a list of 100 teahouses operating in the theater district, a list of 164 actors currently performing, and a timeline marking the deaths of famous actors beginning in the seventeenth century with Murayama Matasaburō (1605–52) and ending with Ichikawa Danzō III (1719–72). The map itself, which appears at the bottom of the sheet, is quite simple: it is oriented with east at the top and shows the area running from Izumi-chō in the north (on the left) through Sakai-chō and Fukiya-chō down through Kobiki-chō in the south at the right-hand of the map. But this area is depicted not as a real space but as an imagined world, an island surrounded by water resembling *gyōki*-style maps of Japan, not unlike the map of the Shin Yoshiwara that Kisanji had published in *A Geographical Guide to Courtesans* two years earlier. As in that map, the imaginary world is itself overlain onto the real spaces of Edo: the islands of Eitaijima and Tsukudajima are marked on the map and to the theater district's east is a body of water that would correspond to the Sumida River with Honjo (on the eastern bank of the Sumida) roughly where contemporaneous maps of Japan located the Korean peninsula.

But in *An Illustrated Encyclopedia of U and Kan's Three Stages*, the map that Kisanji provides is quite different. Rather than using a *gyōki*-style map to show the theater district, like the one he had used a decade-and-a-half earlier in his *A Geographical Guide to Courtesans* to map the pleasure quarters, Kisanji includes a map of "the Land of Chūkan," which is actually a diagram of the interior of the Nakamura-za designed to look like the map of a country (Figure 3.15).[61] This focus on the interior of the theater, as well as the backstage and dressing room, as the subject of mapping as opposed to the larger theater district as physical space is striking

---

[60] For a brief discussion of this map, see Hattori Yukio, *Ōinaru koya: kinsei toshi no shukusai kūkan* (Tokyo: Kōdansha, 2012), pp. 45–46.

[61] Hōseidō Kisanji, *Ukan sandai zue*, pp. 16–17.

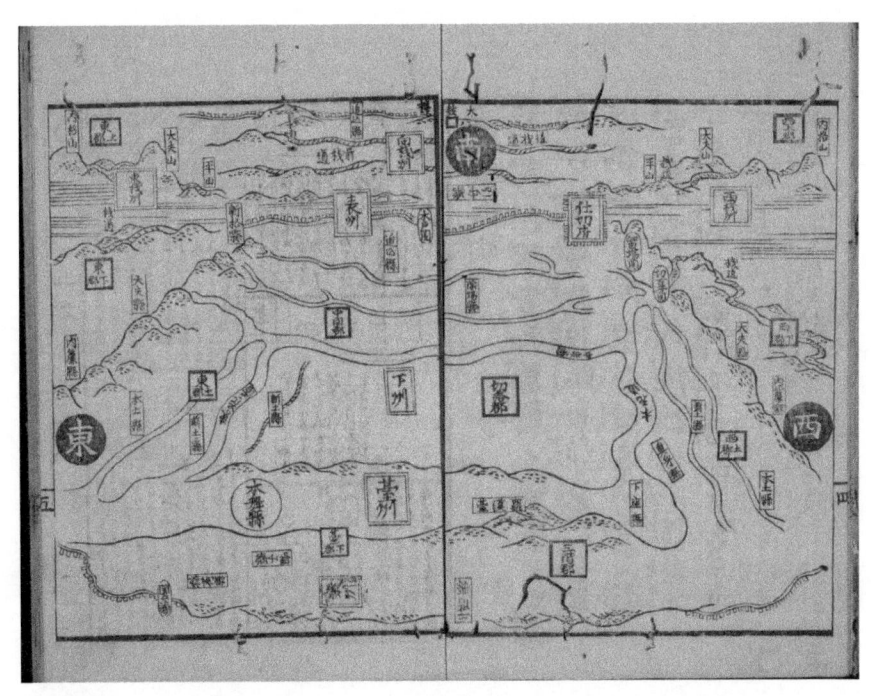

**Figure 3.15** Katsukawa Shundō, map of the interior of a theater, Hōseidō Kisanji, *Ukan sandai zue*, 1791.
*Source*: Former Edogawa Ranpo Collection, Rikkyo University.

and seems symptomatic of the broader trend I have already noted: that maps of the theater district are actually quite uncommon in the decades surrounding the turn of the nineteenth century. What we find, in their stead, are these "maps," which depict the interior of the theater as its own world.

Kisanji's map is oriented with north at the bottom of the page, where the main stage is located. Thus, at the center of the bottom of the map is the "Province of the stage" (*Taishū*), which is comprised of the "Domain of the Main Stage" (*Honbu ken*) and the "Domain of the Musicians" (*Geza ken*); just below the main stage is the "Province of the Dressing Room" (*Gakushū*), which includes the "Domain of the Novice" (*Inari ken*), the "Domain of the Second Floor," and the "District of the Third Floor," the area of the backstage reserved for the star actors. The accompanying text explains "since the Province of the Dressing Room is forbidden to foreigners, what kind of a land it is is difficult to know." Moving outwards on the map, we come to the various sections of seating depicted as domains (*ken*) and districts (*kōri*) with the *uchigōshi* or second floor boxes depicted as mountains at the upper edges of the map.

A decade later, Kyokutei Bakin would present a similar image, designed by Utagawa Toyokuni, in his 1800 *An Illustrated Collection of Actors* (*Yakusha meisho zue*), which also depicts the interior of the theater.[62] Here, however, the theater is presented not as a map as such but as a landscape of a famous place, drawing on the conventions of the emerging genre of *meisho zue* or gazetteer of famous places. Thus, *An Illustrated Collection of Actors* functions as a strategic hybrid in which "Bakin plays the straight-faced chronicler, as it were, by mimicking the commentaries of conventional illustrated gazetteers, but he lets the reader in on the joke."[63]

In "The Landscape of the Stage of the Three Theaters" (Sanza butai fūkei no zu) (Figure 3.16), Toyokuni fashions, in the guise of what looks like an ordinary landscape, a detailed diagram of the interior of a kabuki theater very similar to the

**Figure 3.16** Utagawa Toyokuni, "Landscape of the Stage of the Three Theaters" from Kyokutei Bakin, *Yakusha meisho zue*, 1800.
Source: National Diet Library, Tokyo.

---

[62] See Kyokutei Bakin, *Bakin no yakusha meisho zue o yomu*, ed. Daichō o Yomu Kai, Chikamatsu Kenkyūjo Sōsho 4 (Osaka: Izumi Shoin, 2001), pp. 32ff.
[63] Robert Goree, "Publishing Kabukiland: Late Edo Culture and Kyokutei Bakin's Yakusha Meisho Zue," in Keller Kimbrough and Satoko Shimazaki ed. *Publishing the Stage: Print and Performance in Early Modern Japan*, Boulder Books on Asian Studies 1 (Boulder, CO: Center for Asian Studies, University of Colorado, 2011), p. 205.

map from Kisanji's *An Illustrated Encyclopedia of U and Kan's Three Stages*, but with the orientation changed so that the main stage is at the viewer's right marked by the "Pine of the Minister's Pillar," a reference to the tradition that had originated in *nō* theater of having a pillar made of pinewood to mark the boundaries of the stage. Extending outward is a plank bridge, which represents the *hanamichi*, the iconic walkway that leads through the audience used for entrances and exits in kabuki. This rises above the "Inland Sea of Doma," referring to the least expensive seating boxes at the center of the theater.

Bakin, however, was not the first to use the idea of the actor as famous place (*meisho*): in 1792, an actor critique also titled *An Illustrated Collection of Actors* (*Yakusha meisho zue*) was published by Hachimonji Jishō III, which already deploys a parody of the illustrated gazetteer just as that genre was becoming an extraordinary commercial success.[64] While this earlier work uses only the basic idea of the "illustrated collection of famous places" (*meisho zue*), the conceit goes largely undeveloped. Each of the three volumes of the critique for Kyoto, Osaka, and Edo contains a register of famous sites that plays on the names of the actors, but the parody is confined to this initial list (*mokuroku*).

In each volume of the 1792 actor critique, there is a list of places divided into districts (*kōri*) with a list of famous places for each district. Thus, for Edo, the "District of the House of Shibaraku" (*Shibaraku-ke no kōri*)—reference to the Ichikawa line of actors whose house was associated with the play *Just a Minute!* (*Shibaraku*)—contains the "Grotto of Sanshō," the "Crossing of Chūsha," the "Hill of Shinsha," the "Bay of Kinshō," and the "Village of Hakuen" which play on the pen names of Ichikawa Ebizō I, Ichikawa Yaezō III, Ichikawa Omezō I, Ichikawa Komazō III (later Matsumoto Kōshirō V), and Ichikawa Danjūrō V.

Bakin's 1800 *An Illustrated Collection of Actors* elaborates and extends this idea. The first volume of Bakin's two-volume *An Illustrated Collection of Actors* depicts the "famous places" of the theater (much as Enba's map would), and it is in this volume that we find the image of the theater as landscape. Thus, in this volume, we find entries that pun on the names of the owners of Edo's three licensed theaters: Nakamura Kanzaburō, Ichimura Uzaemon, and Morita Kanya: the first entry is for "the founding of the Kanza Tower" (*Kanzaburō*), with the "*rō*" of tower punning on Kanzaburō's name; this is followed by a description of "the story of the Bamboo Castle (Take-no-jō) of Ichi Village (Ichimura)"; finally, we find "the legend of the Morita Shrine (kanya)."[65] Each of these imagined places is given an entry that is itself composed of an extraordinarily dense set of puns that play with the history of the three theaters.

---

[64] On the history of the genre of *meisho zue*, see Robert Goree, *Printing Landmarks: Popular Geography and Meisho Zue in Late Tokugawa Japan* (Cambridge MA: Harvard University Press, 2020).
[65] Kyokutei Bakin, *Bakin no yakusha meisho zue o yomu*.

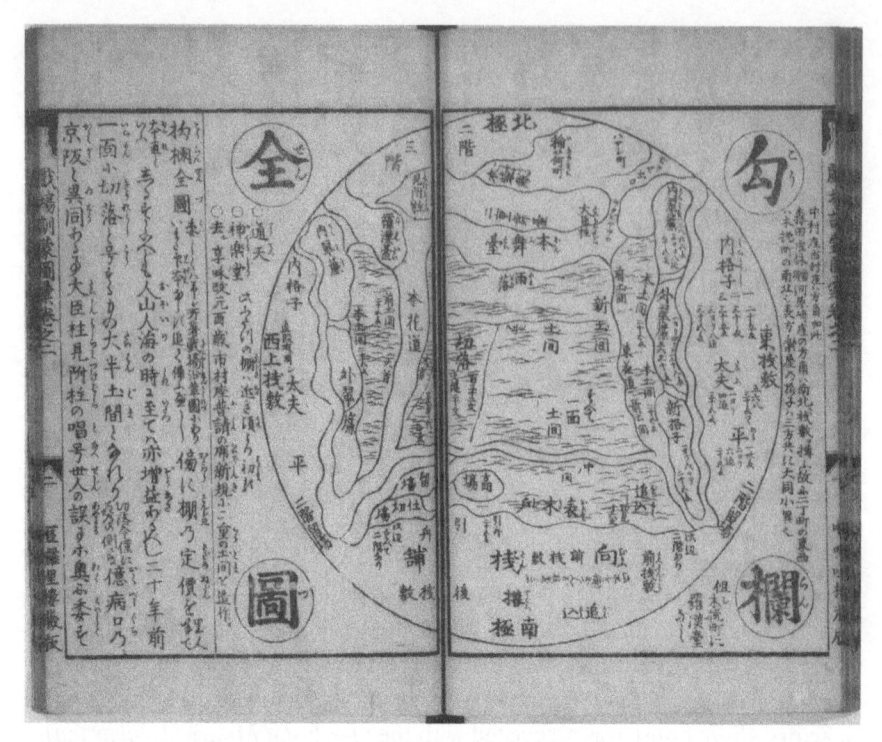

**Figure 3.17** Katsukawa Shunei, map of the interior of a theater presented as a map of the world from Shikitei Sanba, *Shibai kinmōzui*, 1803.
Source: Rikkyo University Library.

Another "map" which bears a heavy conceptual debt to Kisanji's *An Illustrated Encyclopedia of U and Kan's Three Stages* is the iconic image of the interior of the theater presented as a map of the world found in Shikitei Sanba's 1803 *Illustrated Dictionary of Theater for Beginners* (*Shibai kinmō zui*) (Figure 3.17).[66] Here, the orientation is the reverse of Kisanji's image, with the main stage at the top of the page (north according to the legend); the sides and the bottom are filled in by various seats marked by price, and the center of the image is dominated by the *doma* seating area in the center of the theater, depicted as a body of water.

Sanba's work is, like Kisanji's *An Illustrated Encyclopedia of U and Kan's Three Stages*, a parody of a well-known reference work, the *Illustrated Encyclopedia* (*Kinmō zui*), first published in 1666. And Sanba draws heavily on Kisanji's earlier work, even plagiarizing it at points. Like the original, seventeenth-century *Illustrated Encyclopedia*, Sanba's parodic encyclopedia is broken into sections covering

---

[66] Shikitei Sanba, *Shibai kinmo zui: Kyōwa sannen shohanbon*, Kabuki no Bunken 3 (Tokyo: Nihon Geijutsu Bunka Shinkōkai, 2001).

heaven (*ten*), earth (*chi*) and man (*jin*), imaging the theater as its own world consisting of two lands: the land of the theater (*gekijō kuni*) and the land of the play (*kyogen kuni*), drawing a distinction between the physical world of the theater and the diegetic world of the play.

The book opens, for example, with a section on *Tenmon* that puns on astronomy (*Tenmon*) but substitutes the character for crest (*mon*) for the character for writing (also read *mon*). Thus, Sanba notes, while the *I Ching* explains that *tenmon* (天文) is the position of the sun, moon, and stars in the heavens (ten), in the theater *tenmon* (天紋) refers to the actors' crests (*mon*) on the lanterns that hang from the ceiling (*tenjō*) of the theater.[67]

Looking at these three parodic "maps" together, there are a number of striking features that they share and that define the ways in which the cartographic imagination came to function in parodic texts in the decades surrounding the turn of the nineteenth century. The first is the subject of the mapping itself: not the spaces of the wider theater district—the kabuki and puppet theaters, the teahouses, or the district's location within the city—but the physical space of the theater's interior ranging from the stage to the seating for the audience and also, in the case of Kisanji and Sanba, including the backstage areas. Second, the *technique* of mapping is not the realistic depiction of physical spaces we find in the detailed views offered by *saiken*-style maps both of the eighteenth and of the later nineteenth centuries but abstract maps of the physical spaces of the theater imagined as the natural features of landscape. The third is the obviously parodic nature of these maps, that they employ cartographic technique from well-known works of Edo's "information library," but here, the texts can only be "read" if the reader already possesses all of the "information."

Sanba's map from his 1803 *Illustrated Dictionary of Theater for Beginners* is a particularly interesting case, in part because it was more widely copied and commented upon than the works of Kisanji, Bakin, and Enba. There is, for example, a hand-copied version of Sanba's "Map of the Theater" ("Kōran zenzu") among other maps and diagrams, including the copy of the Saruwaka-chō map discussed above, in volume twenty-four of the "Morisada mankō" (Figure 3.18).[68] Morisada uses Sanba's map entirely for the information it contains on the prices charged for various types of seating, and he discusses the *form* of the map only in passing and only to note that because Sanba had modeled the map on maps of the globe (*chikyūzu*), the circular form of the map distorts the spatial layout of the theaters.[69] For Morisada, the form of parody becomes an impediment to knowledge, and this is largely how *Illustrated Dictionary of Theater for Beginners* and similar works

---

[67] Shikitei Sanba, *Shibai kinmo zui*, p. 19.
[68] Kitagawa Morisada, *Morisada mankō*, vol. 4, p. 32.
[69] Kitagawa Morisada, *Morisada mankō*, vol. 4, p. 32.

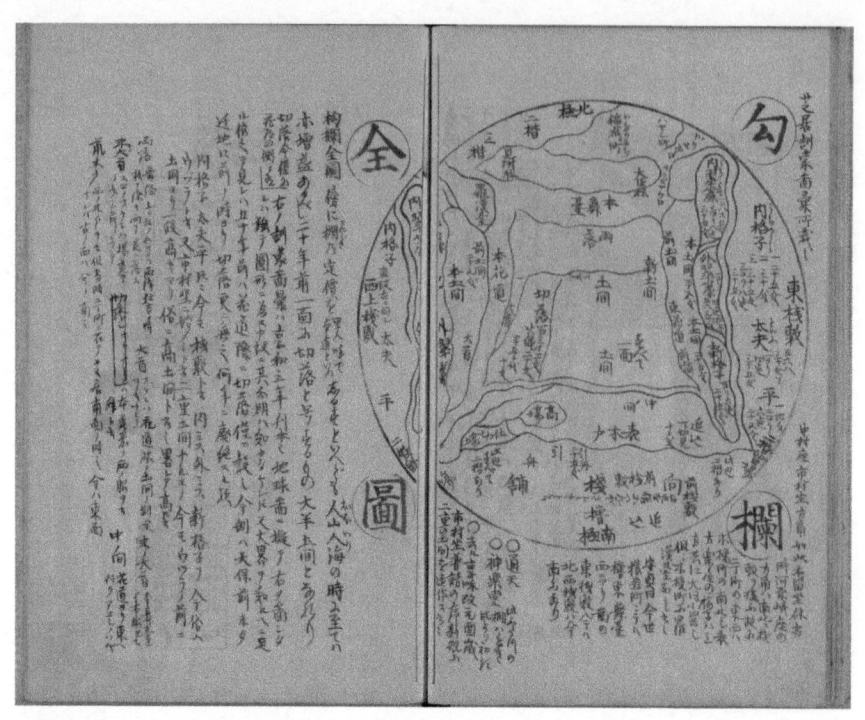

**Figure 3.18** Copy of Katsukawa Shunei's map of the interior of a theater presented as a map of the world appearing in Shikitei Sanba's *Shibai kinmōzui* from Kitagawa Morisada, "Morisada mankō".
Source: National Diet Library, Tokyo.

have been treated for the past 200 years, as if the parodic form in which information is embedded is something that distorts and must be ignored or overcome rather than a constituent part of information itself.

One of the most important elements of these parodic maps is the tension between their *form* and their impulse to convey information. Hamada Keisuke has noted that this is one of the most striking features of parody in the theater books of this period, that "knowledge and humor are difficult to separate out, like two sides of a coin."[70] And we can go further and say that not only are they difficult to separate out but they also appear, at times, to be working at cross purposes. The humor and parody distort, as Morisada suggests, by embedding information within often dense and complex settings that require of the reader an intimacy with the theater and its social world. The question is why? Why, that is, does this particular *form* of information become so important in the decades that surround the turn of the nineteenth century?

---

[70] Hamada Keisuke, "Kokkeibon toshite no gekisho," p. 206.

Part of the answer to this question can be seen in the way that these texts treat information. An especially clear example of this appears in the discussions of stagecraft that we find in *An Illustrated Encyclopedia of U and Kan's Three Stages* and *An Illustrated Dictionary of Theater for Beginners*. In Kisanji's 1791 book, the accompanying images drawn by Katsukawa Shundō show the obviously "staged" nature of the theater: birds are suspended by ropes, for example, and under the costumes used for animals like horses, boars, or cows, human legs are clearly visible. Kisanji's text points to the artificial nature of the stagecraft but does so *as if* recording an observable world. For horses, *An Illustrated Encyclopedia of U and Kan's Three Stages* has an extended entry, with Kisanji writing how the horses of this world are exceedingly slow: "these are exceedingly calm horses. Thus, as one would expect, they are slow of foot. When you are in a hurry it is perhaps more efficient to get off the horse and run" (Figure 3.19).[71] Kisanji observes "both the forelegs and the back legs resemble those of humans," and, he continues in his entry on cows and boars, these animals too have "four legs that resemble those of a human and they

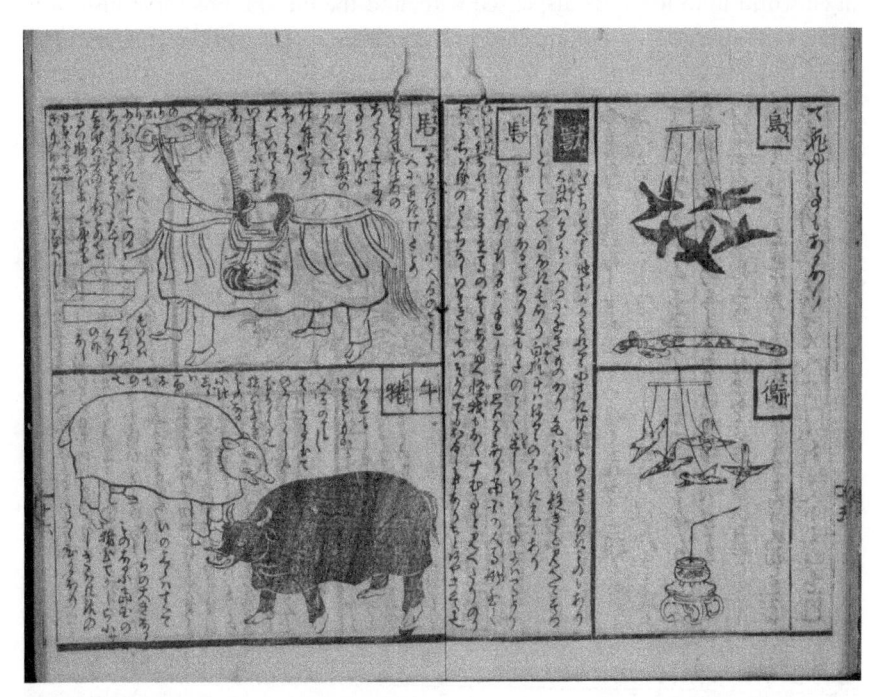

**Figure 3.19** Katsukawa Shundō, image of a horse on stage from Hōseidō Kisanji, *Ukan sandai zue*, 1791.
*Source*: Kaga Bunko, Tokyo Metropolitan Library.

[71] Hōseidō Kisanji, *Ukan sandai zue*, p. 119.

are exceedingly slow. Although cows are naturally slow, the boar is fast and so these boars are quite unusual."

The humor of these passages derives from the *knowing* nature of these observations; we can see, quite clearly in the illustrations, the artificial nature of costumes, but we are meant to pretend that this is a world unto itself. Moreover, both *An Illustrated Encyclopedia of U and Kan's Three Stages* and *Illustrated Dictionary of Theater for Beginners* point to an important gap between what the audience sees and what is seen by the characters on stage, who are entirely part of this fictional world.

This disposition stands in stark contrast to a work published four years after *An Illustrated Encyclopedia of U and Kan's Three Stages*, a 1795 actor critique *A Disquisition on the Customs of Actors (Yakusha saraekō)*.[72] *A Disquisition on the Customs of Actors* includes an extended series of illustrations that explain the mechanics of the special effects used on the kabuki stage, and these are clearly taken from the illustrations to *An Illustrated Encyclopedia of U and Kan's Three Stages*. But, in *A Disquisition on the Customs of Actors*, parody (and the pretense of describing a world unto itself) is dispensed with, and the illustrations serve instead to inform the reader as to the mechanisms at work. Thus, accompanying the entry for "Crows," *A Disquisition on the Customs of Actors* uses exactly the same illustration from *An Illustrated Encyclopedia of U and Kan's Three Stages* but adds a simple explanation: "controlled from the ceiling." And in *A Disquisition on the Customs of Actors*, the illustrations for horses, boars, and cows are explained very simply: "Horse: there are two people inside constituting the forelegs and the hind legs"; "One person goes in the boar"; "a cow is the same as a horse" (Figure 3.20).[73]

While Bakin does not himself turn to an explanation of stage effects in his work, *An Illustrated Collection of Actors* does contain a striking image drawn by Utagawa

**Figure 3.20** Image of a horse on stage, *Yakusha saraekō*, 1795.
Source: Katei Bunko, University of Tokyo Library.

[72] See Geinōshi Kenkyūkai, *Nihon shomin bunka shiryō shūsei*, vol. 6, pp. 373–430.
[73] Geinōshi Kenkyūkai, *Nihon shomin bunka shiryō shūsei*, vol. 6, p. 383.

Toyokuni that shows the actor Matsumoto Kōshirō V on stage surrounded by various examples of stage mechanics: next to Kōshirō, there is a stage hand making the sound of footsteps; to the viewer's right is another stagehand, behind a black screen, manipulating a snake; and a third can be seen, suspended from the ceiling on a cloud, with a flock of birds. The image also depicts a drum used for the sound of thunder noting that "not all thunder comes from above and rather tends to emanate from below" where the musicians were located (Figure 3.21).[74] Here, the mechanics of stagecraft are completely exposed in an especially artificial way: not in their constituent parts, as in *An Illustrated Encyclopedia of U and Kan's Three Stages* and *Illustrated Dictionary of Theater for Beginners*, but as a kind of tableau with the actor on stage.

For his part, Sanba takes his treatment of stage effects directly from Kisanji and even, at times, plagiarizes that earlier text. But Sanba also introduces a new element: a chatty and intrusive narrator who jokes and makes asides and explains things to the uninitiated. For example, in his section on astronomy at the beginning of his book, Sanba includes a "Chart of the Great Ultimate" (*Daigoku no zu*)

**Figure 3.21** Utagawa Toyokuni, image of stage devices from Kyokutei Bakin, *Yakusha meisho zue*, 1800.
Source: National Diet Library, Tokyo.

[74] Kyokutei Bakin, *Bakin no yakusha meisho zue o yomu*, p. 46.

modeled on the *taiji-tu* depicting the relationship among the five elements of fire, water, earth, metal, and wood. Sanba replicates the chart but then adds that if one is not careful one might mistake the orbs for *dango*, round dumplings made from rice flower. Sanba next explains what the various elements mean for the theater: wood (*ki*) for the *kidoban*, the guard at the entrance way; fire (*hi*) for the *hinawa*, the wick used by audience members to light tobacco; earth (*do*) for the *doma*, the seating area in the middle of the theater; and metal (*kin*) for the *kanemoto*, the financier or theater proprietor. But then the narrator is unsure what to do with the fifth element, water: "Water, hmm, what should we do about water? Oh, how 'bout this? It stands for the 'tea seller' (chauri) who sells tea as cold as water. I think I've done a pretty good job of stretching things to fit."[75]

At first sight, this narrative technique seems like a minor change, but it fundamentally alters the reader's relationship to the text. Both Kisanji's *An Illustrated Encyclopedia of U and Kan's Three Stages* and Bakin's *An Illustrated Collection of Actors* function as "straight" parodies: they are presented *as if* the reader were reading a real encyclopedia or almanac to another world—the world of the stage. Sanba's work, too, takes this as its starting point but then repeatedly points out to the reader parodic nature of the book. It is as if, not contented with revealing the mechanics of the stage, Sanba is also interested in revealing the mechanics of the joke.

How are we to understand this seeming tension between parody as form and the role of these books as guides to the theater? Sanba himself suggests a way of approaching this problem in the opening lines of the preface to *Illustrated Dictionary of Theater for Beginners*: "Although many view the theater, those who are capable of seeing it are few."[76] This framing distinction between the knowledgeable reader marked by his or her familiarity with both the aesthetic and social codes of the theater and the uninitiated reader capable of only viewing the theater at a surface level pervades *Illustrated Dictionary of Theater for Beginners*. As Hattori Yukio has observed about Sanba's book:

> In a sense, this is humor and satire (*ugachi*) that would only be gotten by "those in the know." It is literature of the "in the know" (*tsū*), and a book like this could emerge as a comic novel only when the author could imagine that all readers were in the know.[77]

There is, however, a different way to understand Sanba's relationship with the reading public: that he did not imagine *all* of his readers would be "in the know," that they would *get* all of the jokes; rather, the book itself, like Enba's map, is

---

[75] Shikitei Sanba, *Shibai kinmo zui*, p. 19.
[76] Shikitei Sanba, *Shibai kinmo zui*, p. 13.
[77] Hattori Yukio, "Kaidai," in *Shibai kinmo zui: Kyōwa sannen shohanbon*, ed. Shikitei Sanba, Kabuki no Bunken 3 (Tokyo: Nihon Geijutsu Bunka Shinkōkai, 2001), p. 6.

predicated on the opposite: that only certain readers would get certain jokes, that the book itself would not only rely upon on social distinction but also, in a fundamental way, serve to enact that distinction.

This distinction between the knowledgeable audience member capable of truly appreciating the theater (and of getting the jokes) and the naive viewer, who only sees surfaces, is critical to understanding how parody functions in these works. As Marcia Yonemoto has written about Kisanji's 1777 *A Geographical Guide to Courtesans*, "Kisanji makes maps and other geographical texts work on many different levels, and he challenges the reader to 'get' his multilayered joke."[78] But herein lies the inherent tension of parody: it only works if the reader does, indeed, *get the joke*. Or more exactly if they are capable of getting the joke. "Parodic codes," Linda Hutcheon has argued, "have to be *shared* for parody—as parody—to be comprehended."[79] When the reader does not get the parody, the parodic grammar breaks down, but a new comic element emerges in its place: readers who do not *get* the joke become, themselves, the object of ridicule.

Within these parodic books, there are a number of overlapping points of view in the interplay between text and illustration. At the most basic level, there is the diegetic world of the stage in which the characters on stage cannot see that they are living in an entirely fictional world. Both Kisanji and Sanba come back to this point again and again, noting the distance between what the characters can see and what the audience sees: the ropes and pulleys in the illustrations or, in *Illustrated Dictionary of Theater for Beginners*, the images that show how the revolving stage and trapdoors work. But there is a further disjunction, one not spelled out, between the audience, who in some ways participate in the diegetic illusion, allowing themselves to be "fooled" by obviously fake suns and moons and stars, and the reader of the book, for whom the stage mechanics are exposed. As readers, we are let in on the joke and can laugh along with the author, who is allowing us a peek behind the curtains, who knowingly shows us the mechanics of the stage.

Parody as form seems born out of a moment of tension in which the writer must reveal the world of the theater to the general reading public and do so in a way that acknowledges, and reinforces, distinctions in the socially constituted nature of that public, distinctions between the knowledgeable reader (the reader who is truly *capable* of seeing the theater) and a newly constituted reading and viewing public that is emerging just in the decades surrounding the turn of the nineteenth century.

Parody is a strategy, then, to deal with these conflicting tensions, and it is marked by an impulse of disavowal: I will show you the inner workings of the theater, but I will not reveal too much. Or as Sanba puts it in his preface to *Illustrated*

---

[78] Yonemoto, *Mapping Early Modern Japan*, pp. 147–49.
[79] Linda Hutcheon, *A Theory of Parody: The Teachings of Twentieth-Century Art Forms* (Urbana, IL: University of Illinois Press, 2000), p. 93.

*Dictionary of Theater for Beginners*: "in compiling this book, I have not recorded the most secret of knowledge [...] and thus there is much that has been omitted. Those with great knowledge of the theater must not deride the shortcomings which mark this work from beginning to end."[80] Here, we see a remarkable doubling of the structure that pervades Sanba's work and that of Kisanji before him: the knowledgeable reader is supposed to laugh not just at the cleverness of the author but also, it is implied, at the foolishness of the audience member who succumbs to—or willingly participates in—the diegetic illusion of the stage, opening up a space of *knowing laughter* between the viewer capable of truly seeing the theater and the broader viewing public. "In laughter," Henri Bergson has written, "we always find an unavowed intention to humiliate" and there is no other way to make sense of Sanba's repeated use of the trope of the naive theater enthusiast who misreads or misunderstands other than as such a figure of ridicule and humiliation.[81]

This same stance seems to dictate the very subject matter of the maps themselves: they do not show the spatial layout of the theater district, a publicly accessible space in the heart of Edo's commercial district only a short distance from the city's center at Nihonbashi; rather, the diagrams in cartographic form show the inaccessible spaces of the interior of the theater, the stage and the dressing room but also the areas for the audience. The reader *could* go to the theater, but as the prices that accompany Sanba's "map" show, actually attending the theater was out of reach for many; for them, the only access they would have to the world of the stage was through the medium of the printed page. The map then becomes no longer a guide to the actual spaces of the theater district broadly; rather, it functions more as a proxy for the interior, a world beyond the reach of many.

This tension seems to run from *An Illustrated Encyclopedia of U and Kan's Three Stages* through Bakin's *An Illustrated Collection of Actors* to Sanba's *Illustrated Dictionary of Theater for Beginners* and Enba's *An Illustrated Road Guide to Kabuki*. But there are also two striking features that *An Illustrated Collection of Actors* and *Illustrated Dictionary of Theater for Beginners* share that are absent from *An Illustrated Encyclopedia of U and Kan's Three Stages*, written a decade earlier. The first is their heavy emphasis on the likenesses of actors, a subject to which I will turn in Chapter 5. Bakin would later recall how the immense popularity and commercial success of his book led the publisher to reissue it with color illustrations, and both *An Illustrated Collection of Actors* and *Illustrated Dictionary of Theater for Beginners* would be issued with separate volumes featuring color-printed images of actors.[82] The second is the suffusion of both texts with the language of the Chinese stage. Just as theatrical writing turned repeatedly to the cartographic idiom of maps and gazetteers in the nineteenth century, so too did a different geography of the

---

[80] Shikitei Sanba, *Shibai kinmo zui*, p. 17.

[81] Henri Bergson, *Laughter: An Essay on the Meaning of the Comic*, trans. Cloudesley Brereton and Fred Rothwell (Mineola, NY: Dover Publications, 2005), p. 67.

[82] Kyokutei Bakin, *Kinsei mono no hon Edo sakusha burui: chosha jihitsu hokibon*, ed. Kimura Miyogo (Tokyo: Yagi Shoten, 1988), pp. 170–71.

theater emerge from contact with writings about theatrical practices beyond Japan. Indeed, it was in the very years when we see a turn to parodic mapping that the theater of China became a source of fascination for connoisseurs, commentators, and historians of kabuki, and the image that emerged of Chinese theater provided a conceptual grid through which—and a vocabulary by means of which—kabuki could be refashioned and re-conceptualized: understood no longer as "the basis for fostering debauchery in our world" as the author of the "An Account of What I have Seen and Heard" put it in 1816, but as a local iteration of the universal phenomenon of theater.[83] And at the heart of the intersection of geography and theater in this period lay the metaphor that "heaven and earth are one great theater" or, rendered more colloquially, that "all the world's a stage," an image of the relationship between the theater and the world that would come to be central in conceptualizations of the theater across the nineteenth century.

## IV Theater as the World/Theater in the World

Kyokutei Bakin's 1800 *An Illustrated Collection of Actors* provides a particularly useful entry point for thinking about the confluence of the parodic impulse and the actor's likeness with the idiom of the Chinese stage. In the image, discussed above (see Figure 3.21), which shows Matsumoto Koshirō V, one of the most easily identifiable actors of his age, on stage surrounded by the various mechanics of theatricality, Utagawa Toyokuni's likeness of the actor is central to this image; but in the background, just off stage, we see an engagement with the newly emerging idiom of Ming-Qing drama: to Kōshirō's left is a sign hung from a peg onto which is written a Chinese couplet: "The hero and heroine draw near to one another, their roles executed masterfully./The villain and the clown act out their comic antics, making quite a disruptive scene."[84] The couplet, which specifically draws on the defined role types of the Chinese theatrical genre of *chuanqi*, seems to mark a subtle disjuncture in the scene between legibility and illegibility, clarity and opacity. On the one hand, foregrounded is the image of Kōshirō V, which is premised on the readily legible likeness of the actor; this is coupled with a depiction of stagecraft, which similarly foregrounds clarity and ready legibility (here, what we are shown, is how the stage tricks actually work); in contrast, the opacity of the couplet blends into the background and seems to enact an *illegibility* or a different kind of legibility which very much depends on the *habitus* of the reader.

The tension which marks this image is emblematic of a broader set of tensions that we find in the theatrical culture of the early nineteenth century, a culture which seems beset by the pressures of a print market seeking to appeal to a broad public (the centrality of actors' likenesses, the revealing of the mechanics of the

---

[83] Buyō Inshi, *Lust, Commerce, and Corruption*, p. 330.
[84] Kyokutei Bakin, *Bakin no yakusha meisho zue o yomu*, pp. 46–47.

stage) while, at the same time, marking modes of distinction based on specialized knowledge and an intimacy with theatrical culture. The couplet in this image itself has an interesting history that suggests the manner in which the Chinese theater came to occupy the minds of Japanese writers at the end of the eighteenth century. The proximate source for Bakin's text is a 1771 book titled *Important Facts about Actors, Newly Printed* (*Shinkoku yakusha kōmoku*),[85] the first volume of which contains two scenes from the Chinese dramatist Li Yu's (1610–80) play, *The Mirage Tower* (*Shen zhong lou*), which the text describes as a "Chinese kabuki play" ("Morokoshi kabuki kyogen").[86] The play, printed in vernacular Chinese with Japanese reading glosses, is accompanied by two illustrations: one depicts the so called "Dance of the Four Heroes" from *The Mirage Tower*; the second image depicts a Chinese stage above which are emblazoned two phoenixes. The verse that we see in the image of Kōshirō from Bakin's *An Illustrated Collection of Actors* appears as a pair of couplets that flank the stage (Figure 3.22).[87]

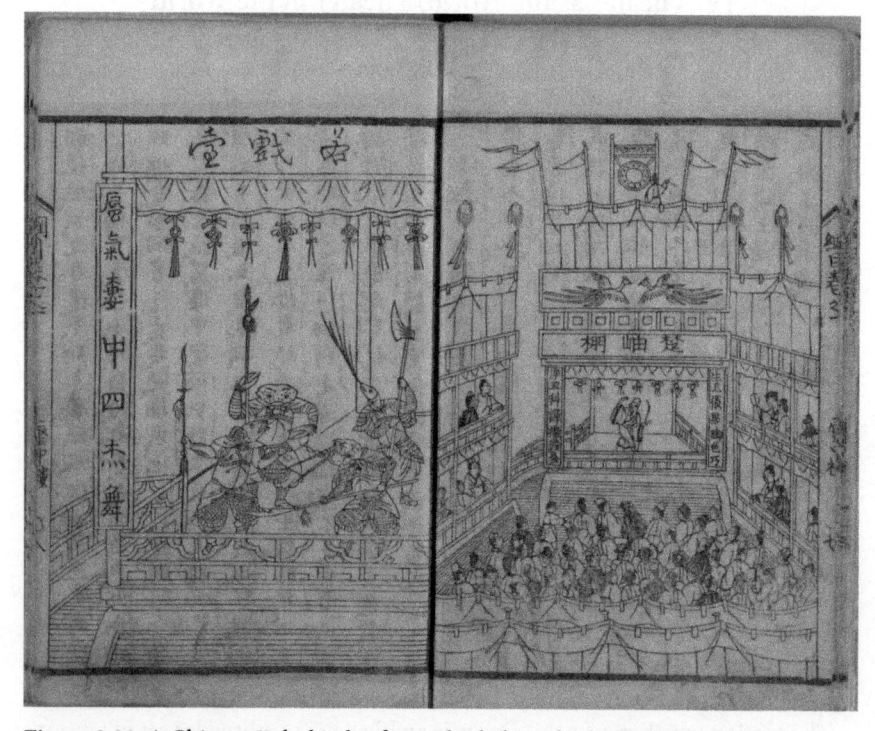

**Figure 3.22** A Chinese Kabuki play from *Shinkoku yakusha kōmoku*, 1771.
*Source*: National Diet Library, Tokyo.

---

[85] Kyokutei Bakin, *Bakin no yakusha meisho zue o yomu*, p. 47.
[86] Hachimonjiya Jishō III, ed., *Shinkoku yakusha kōmoku*, vol. 1 (Kyoto: Hachimonjiya Hachizaemon, 1771), 2v.
[87] Hachimonjiya Jishō III, *Shinkoku yakusha kōmoku*, vol. 1, 11r–12v.

Although this couplet has come to be associated with Li Yu and the *The Mirage Tower*, there is no attested source for the couplet in Li Yu's work nor is there a readily identifiable source for the image itself, neither among early editions of Li Yu's plays and fiction that circulated in early modern Japan nor in other works from this period. Bakin, for his part, would develop a deep and abiding interest in the playwright, and the image of Li Yu that Bakin and his contemporaries would help construct played a critical role in emerging notions of authorship in the nineteenth century, a subject to which I will return in Chapter 4.

But if we think about the *function* of the couplet in Toyokuni's image of Kōshirō from Bakin's 1800 *An Illustrated Collection of Actors*, it suggests something of the peculiar place that the Chinese stage occupied in early-nineteenth-century Japan. To the knowledgeable reader, who might have access to, or know of, *Important Facts about Actors, Newly Printed* (published over a quarter of a century earlier), the couplet may have served as a marker of erudition and taste, both of Bakin and of the reader. But to a reader without some knowledge of Chinese role types and theatrical convention, the couplet itself is opaque, its purpose decorative, perhaps vaguely evocative of the foreign and the continental.

Nor is this the only point in *An Illustrated Collection of Actors* where Bakin refers to the Chinese stage; indeed, in many ways, the idiom of Chinese theater pervades Bakin's work. The very title of the work uses the Chinese term for actor *huzi* (J. keshi 戯子) as a graphic stand-in for the common Japanese term *yakusha* (役者) and in his preface, Bakin writes how "in the forms of their gestures and speech [the actors of China] are no different from those of our own country."[88] The book also contains a prefatory note in literary Chinese that bears the name of Santō Kyōden's younger brother Santō Kyōzan: "the sun and moon are lanterns, the rivers and seas the oil, the wind and thunder the drums and all of heaven and earth one great theater."[89]

Central to this passage, of course, is the idea that heaven and earth are like a stage and that the theater, therefore, provides a model of the human world. This same passage also appears, rendered in Japanese, at the beginning of the preface that Morishima Chūryō contributed to Sanba's 1803 *Illustrated Dictionary of Theater for Beginners*, but in that text, these lines are attributed to the Kangxi Emperor and quoted from the preface to a work called the *Hikōden (Feihong chuan)*.[90] That preface can, in turn, be traced back to a 1717 Japanese biography of Coxinga, the half-Japanese Ming Loyalist who had been immortalized by the playwright Chikamatsu Monzaemon in 1715; the preface contains the same quotation with one minor variation.[91]

---

[88] Kyokutei Bakin, *Bakin no yakusha meisho zue o yomu*, p. 11.
[89] Kyokutei Bakin, *Bakin no yakusha meisho zue o yomu*, p. 15.
[90] Shikitei Sanba, *Shibai kinmō zui*, p. 13.
[91] Ukai Nobuyuki, *Kokuseiya chūgiden* (Kyoto: Tanaka Shōbē, 1717), 1r.

How this particular idea of the world as a stage, which first surfaces in Japan in the early eighteenth century, came to circulate among writers like Bakin and Kyōzan, Sanba and Chūryō the better part of a century later is not entirely clear, but it is part of a much broader interest in, even fascination with, the image of the world as a theater and the theater as a world in miniature that becomes intimately bound up with ideas of the Chinese drama that began to consume Japanese intellectuals at the turn of the nineteenth century. If the deploying of lavishly colored actor images in works like *An Illustrated Collection of Actors* and *Illustrated Dictionary of Theater for Beginners* suggests an attention to, even an indulging of, the tastes of the popular reader, the suffusion of these works and others from the early nineteenth century in the vernacular of Chinese drama points in a different direction entirely: an image of refinement rooted in a sense of worldliness, even a kind of cosmopolitanism, that comes to pervade the literature of drama in Japan's nineteenth century.

While the parodic elements of works like Bakin's *An Illustrated Collection of Actors* and Sanba's *Illustrated Dictionary of Theater for Beginners* trace their origins back to the 1790 *An Illustrated Encyclopedia of U and Kan's Three Stages*, the origin of this fascination with Chinese drama can similarly be found in a work published in the early 1790s, Hatanaka Kansai's 1790 *Strange Tales from China* (*Morokoshi kidan*). The book is a primer of Chinese theater and included what Kansai claimed to be a partial translation of Li Yu's *Thousand Character Classic Willow of the West Lake* (*Senjimon seiko no yanagi*).[92]

*Strange Tales from China* was the first work systematically to introduce the theatrical world of Late Imperial China to Japanese readers and to *translate* its practices into the language of Japanese theater. The primary purpose of Kansai's text may have been to introduce Chinese theater to the Japanese reader, but its most important contribution to theatrical discourse in Japan was something ancillary: a process of establishing equivalences between the theatrical practices of Japan with those of China and thus creating a conceptual framework for thinking of Japanese theater as a particular, local example of a general phenomenon—the *theater* as such. When Bakin wrote, in his preface to *An Illustrated Collection of Actors*, that "in the forms of their gestures and speech [the actors of China] are no different from those of our own country," he was suggesting not just analogy but commensurability, and this commensurability, in turn, allowed for the emergence of a framework for understanding the place of Japanese theater in the world.[93]

In the decades that would follow the Meiji Restoration of 1868, this process would continue, but its terms would change and the project of imagining kabuki through the language of Chinese drama initiated with *Strange Tales from China*,

---

[92] Itō Sōhei has pointed out that while *Thousand Character Classic Willow of the West Lake* is presented in *Morokoshi kidan* as the work of Li Yu, this is actually a misattribution. See Itō Sōhei "Ri Ryū ō no shōzōga," *Kyūko* 14 (1988) and 15 (1989).

[93] Kyokutei Bakin, *Bakin no yakusha meisho zue o yomu*, p. 11.

and extended in a range of works from the early nineteenth century, would be largely forgotten as the theatrical idiom of the West would come not only to dominate discourse in the late nineteenth century but also to provide a foundational vocabulary for the new discipline of theater history as it came to be established in the early twentieth century.

Although *Strange Tales from China* would be a pivotal work in introducing Ming-Qing theater to the Japanese reading public, there is a genealogy of interest in Chinese theater that extends back another century. Arai Hakuseki (1657–1725)—the scholar, shogunal advisor, and economist—had sketched, in his "Notes on Actors" ("Haiyūkō"), a framework for a comparative history of the theater, noting, at the opening of the essay, that "the origins of acting in the different courts is a matter that is not yet known" and proceeding with a detailed philology of particular instances of acting in classical texts. But even Hakuseki's essay, which circulated in manuscript until the early twentieth century, lacks a unified concept of theater that encompasses and articulates the variety of practices he details.[94] It is the concept of actor rather than of theater that provides the essay with its framework and unity; this is what allows Hakuseki to link the histories of theatrical traditions like Chinese *zaju* and the Japanese *sarugaku* together and to translate the one into the other. Hakuseki's work is based entirely on a philological approach to texts like the *Mencius*, the *Records of the Grand Historian* (*Shiji*), and the *Discourses of the States* (*Guoyu*) or, in the Japanese case, the *Chronicles of Japan* (*Nihon shoki*) and the *Tale of Genji* (*Genji monogatari*), but over the course of the eighteenth and early nineteenth centuries, there is an enormous growth in exposure to, and knowledge of, foreign theatrical practices in Japan. The most immediate site of this exposure was Nagasaki, the only port open to foreign trade at the time, and the dictionaries compiled by the Nagasaki interpreters are filled with references to theatrical terms and role types, some even devoted entirely to theatrical subjects.

One of the most striking accounts of an interest in the drama of China comes from the record of a conversation held in 1725 (the year of Hakuseki's death) between Ogyū Hokkei (1673–1754), the jurist and younger brother of Ogyū Sorai, and Zhu Peizhang, a Chinese physician resident in Nagasaki.[95] Hokkei, serving as a liaison for the eighth Shogun, Tokugawa Yoshimune, enquires about a range of topics and issues including theatrical practices, subject matter, the construction of plots, the composition of signs and advertising, and the names of various role types. The record of the exchange between Hokkei and Zhu Peizhang, mediated by the interpreter Fukami Arichika, suggests how intimately the abstraction of particular practices into general categories is tied to the process of translation

---

[94] Arai Hakuseki, "Haiyūkō," in Kokusho Kankōkai ed. *Arai Hakuseki zenshū*, vol. 6 (Tokyo: Kokusho Kankōkai,1907), pp. 524–35.
[95] Tessō Dōjin, "Kyōhō nenjū Fukami shirabegaki," in "Kaihyō ibun," manuscript, Dōshisha University Library, Komuro-Sawabe Bunko, Co81.K5 vol. 38 (n.d.), https://dgcl.doshisha.ac.jp/digital/collections/MD00000040/?lang=0.

and the positing of "tropes of equivalence."[96] Hokkei asks whether there are specific areas designated for the performance of "*shibai kabuki, jōruri, karakuri* and such" to which Zhu responds that "*shibai* and *odori kyōgen*"—that is theater and dance plays—"are known collectively as *ju* or colloquially as *xi*" and that there are no fixed theater districts in China.[97] It is precisely in these sorts of translingual exchanges that the categories of theater begin to be freed of specific and local references and enabled to act as taxonomic categories that would become crucial in the early nineteenth century.

One of the most suggestive aspects of this exchange is how little of contemporary Chinese theatrical practice seems to be known in Japan in the early eighteenth century, and how, a century later, many of Zhu Peizhang's answers had become common knowledge. Kansai's *Strange Tales from China* would be a key text in creating this framework of knowledge, making broadly accessible the practices of the contemporary Chinese stage to the Japanese reader for the first time.

*Strange Tales from China* is comprised of two volumes. The first offers a brief overview of the history of Chinese theater, a list of popular plays from the Tang, Song, Jin, Yuan, and Ming Dynasties and a kind of primer of Chinese theatrical terms and role types. Volume One also introduces the playwright Li Yu and a play called the *Thousand Character Classic of the Willow of the West Lake* (*Senjimon Seiko no yanagi*), which is misattributed to Li Yu and which is partially translated in Volume Two. In the decades that followed, Kansai's book would lead to an extraordinary interest in Li Yu. A spate of adaptations of his work by writers like Santō Kyōden, Kyokutei Bakin, and Ishikawa Masamochi were produced in the nineteenth century, making Li Yu the best-known Chinese playwright in early modern Japan and something of a model for how authorship, and especially dramatic authorship, came to be imagined.[98]

But in many ways, the most important impact of *Strange Tales from China* would be in providing a framework, and a vocabulary, through which Japanese theater could be reimagined. It is the book's role as a kind of dictionary of theatrical terms and practices that would lead to a revolution in the ways in which kabuki was understood, described, and historicized in the nineteenth century. Indeed, the first line of the text reads: "If we inquire as to what is the theater (*gou lan/shibai*) of China, it is no different from the theater (*shibai*) of Japan."[99] But in this simple sentence, an interesting act of translation occurs: the Chinese term "*gou lan*" (勾欄) is glossed with the reading "*shibai*," which then also serves as a functional equivalent in the sentence. The two are equated (i.e. both semantically and also

---

[96] See Lydia Liu, *The Clash of Empires: The Invention of China in Modern World Making* (Cambridge, MA: Harvard University Press, 2004), p. 110.
[97] Tessō Dōjin, "Kyōhō nenjū Fukami shirabegaki."
[98] See Shiau Han Chen, "Ri Gyo no sōsaku to juyō," doctoral thesis, Division of Asian Studies, Graduate School of Humanities and Sociology, University of Tokyo, 2013. Doi: https://doi.org/10.15083/00006193.
[99] Hatanaka Kansai, *Morokoshi kidan* (Kyoto: Kōseikaku, 1933), 3r.

graphically), allowing for the Chinese characters to be read in Japanese (as *shibai*) and thus for the Chinese term to represent the Japanese case.

This positing of hypothetical equivalence between Chinese and Japanese terms, this creating of a common vocabulary, is one of the primary elements of the text and occupies much of the first volume. A lexicon of sorts is included and begins with a translation of terms for the theater itself: "In China, what we call theater (shibai) is called yanchang (J. enjō 演場), huchang (J. kejō 戯場), juchang (J. gekishō 劇場), goulan (J. kōran 勾欄), or hutai (J. kedai 戯臺)." Kansai then includes terms for various elements of the physical theater: "the stage (butai) is called hupeng (J. kehō 戯棚)"; "the dressing room (gakuya) is called hugang (J. kebō戯房)." He also includes terms for the play itself: "what we call a play (kyōgen) is called yinhu (J. inke 引戯), yanhu (J. enke 演戯), huchu (J. keku 戯齣), or huwen (J. kebun 戯文)"; terms for acting: "acting (miburi o suru) is called jie (J. kai介) or ke (J. ka 科)"; terms for the physical script: "the script (shibaihon) is called yuanben (J. inhon 院本) or yanduan (J. endan 檨段)"; and for the actor: "the actor (yakusha) is called huzi (J. keshi 戯子) or liyan zidi (J. rien shitei 梨園子弟)." These Chinese terms, would, in turn begin to overlay Japanese theater in a wide variety of publications in the nineteenth century. In the title for his *An Illustrated Collection of Actors*, Bakin, for example, uses the Chinese characters *huzi* (J. *keshi* 戯子) in place of the standard Japanese term for actor, and the book is more broadly suffused with Chinese theatrical terms.

In *Strange Tales from China*, this functional lexicon is followed by a detailed discussion, with illustrations, of the various role types that are so critical to Chinese theatrical tradition. As Yoshida Eri has pointed out, these illustrations are not actually of actors or even of theatrical subjects but, with one exception, are copied directly from *A Catalogue of Peerless Historical Figures* (*Wu shuang pu*), a collection of images of historical figures broadly copied in illustrations for both books and decorative objects in Late Imperial China.[100] In this section, the positing of equivalences continues with equivalencies found between Chinese and Japanese role types; thus the *sheng*, or male hero of Chinese drama, is translated as the *tachiyaku*, or hero of kabuki; *dan*, the heroine, is translated as *onnagata*; and *jing*, villain, is translated as *katakiyaku*. The use of these Chinese terms, often glossed by Japanese readings, would, like other Chinese theatrical terms, become widespread in the early nineteenth century.

But in *Strange Tales from China*, there is also the positing of *historical* equivalencies. Thus, in the discussion of *sheng/tachiyaku* we find the following:

> There are many famed [sheng] from the past but in the present world of the Qing Liu Ziqing (J. Ryū Shikei 劉子卿) is the greatest actor. He is also a player of villain roles and is like Fujikawa Heigorō or Kanō Hinasuke of our country. To play

---

[100] Yoshida Eri, "Nihon 'bunjinga' kenkyū nōto: Edo chūki no Ri Gyo (Ri Ryūō) no imēji ni kan suru kōsatsu," *Gakushūin Daigaku jinbunkagaku ronshū* 8 (September 1999), p. 51, n. 32.

both hero and villain is called liangjiao (J. ryōkyaku 両脚). The famed actor Yang Yunwu (J. Yō Ungo 楊雲伍) is greatly skilled and is like Nakamura Utaemon or Onoe Kikugorō.[101]

What was until this point largely abstract (the positing of hypothetical equivalences) here becomes concrete in a particular way (Figure 3.23). At one level, the role played by this concretization is intuitive: it is by analogy to contemporary Japanese actors that the reader is asked to imagine the great actors of the Qing stage. But this equivalence functions in another way as well: Fujikawa Heigorō or Kanō Hinasuke themselves become *like* their Chinese counterparts, become, for the first time, not merely kabuki actors but *actors* just like their Qing counterparts. In the nineteenth century, it would become common to imagine an adoring foreign audience for the stars of the kabuki stage. For example, there is a poem by Fukunoya Uchinari that accompanied the image of Matsumoto Kōshirō V and his son Ichikawa Komazō V in Goryūtei Tokushō's *A Detailed View of the Actors of the Three Theaters* discussed above: "Like mount Fuji, Kōraiya is peerless. How I would like to show off his acting to the inhabitants of foreign lands."

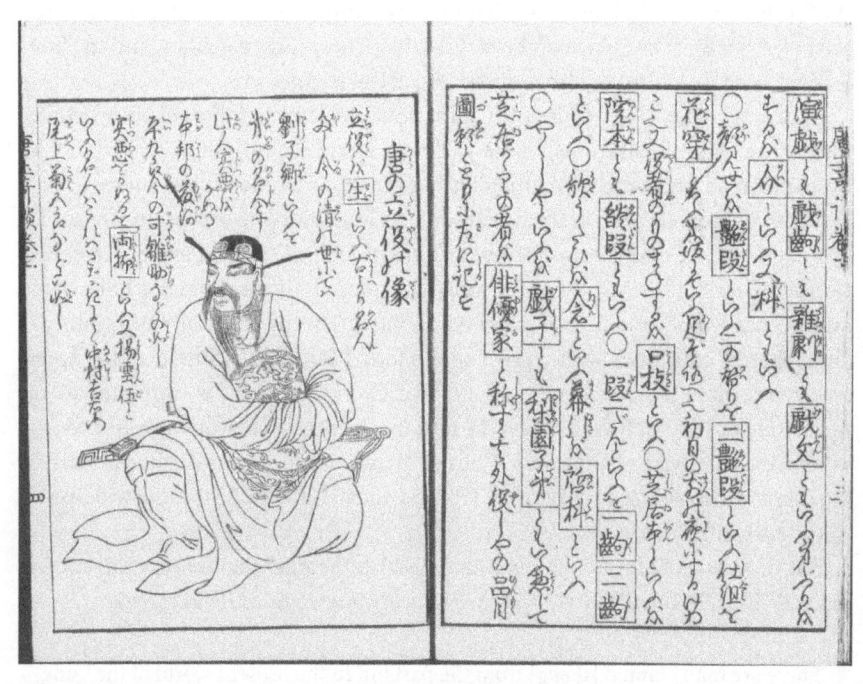

**Figure 3.23** Sheng or male hero role from Hatanaka Kansai, *Morokoshi kidan*, 1791.
Source: C.V. Starr East Asian Library, University of California, Berkeley.

---

[101] Hatanaka Kansai, *Morokoshi kidan*, 6v.

Nor was this conceit limited to actors. In 1820, a book was published under the title of *Strange Tales from Abroad* (*Kaigai kidan*) which claimed to be a translation into Chinese of the Japanese play *Chūshingura: The Storehouse of Loyal Retainers* (*Kanadehon chūshingura*), the 1748 puppet play that first dramatized the story of the forty-seven loyal retainers.[102] Although there are earlier examples of Japanese plays being translated into Chinese, such as Tsuga Teishō's 1771 *Four Chirping Cicadas* (*Shimeizen*), in which he rendered two *nō* plays and parts of two *jōruri* plays into the style of *Yuan* drama,[103] what is remarkable about *Strange Tales from Abroad* is the conceit that it was originally published in China and is being reissued in Japan with Japanese glosses on the Chinese original.

In 1800, the same year in which Bakin published *An Illustrated Collection of Actors*, a book titled *An Illustrated Guide to the Dressing Room: A Supplement* (*Shibai gakuya zue shūi*) was published in Osaka, which contains not only a striking image of a Chinese theater (Figure 3.24) but also a likely apocryphal account

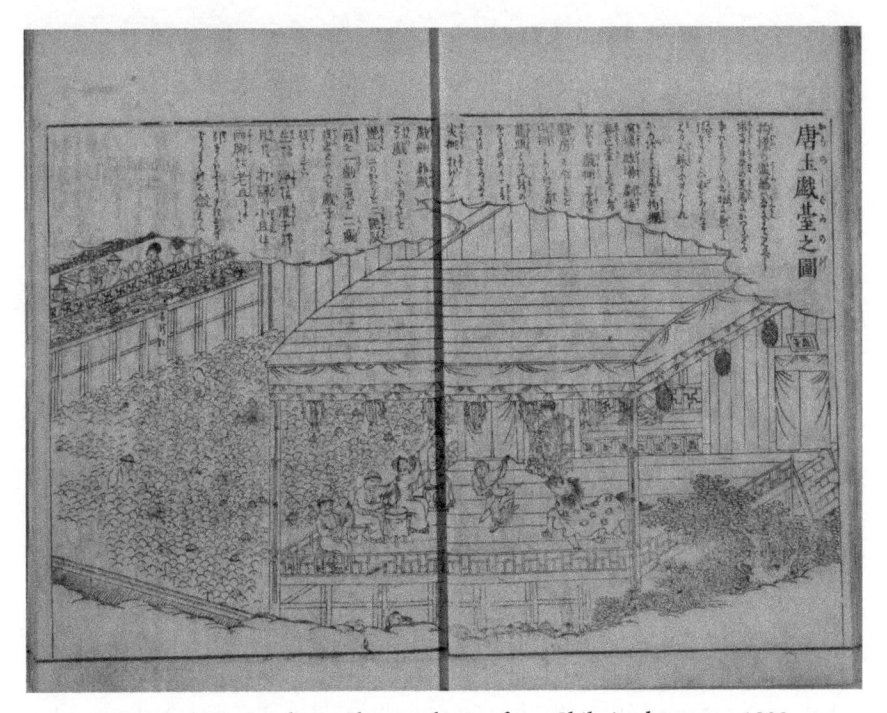

**Figure 3.24** Shōkōsai Hanbē, a Chinese theater from *Shibai gakuya zue*, 1800.
*Source*: National Diet Library, Tokyo.

---

[102] See Okumura Kayoko, "Chūgokugo yaku *Chūshingura* no shosō: *Kagai kidan* no honyakusha zō to honyaku taido shotan," *Kansai Daigaku tōzai gakujutsu kenkyūjo kiyō* 43 (April 2010), 131–42.
[103] Takada Mamoru ed., *Tsuga Teishō/Itami Chinen shū*, Edo kaii kisō bungei taikei, vol. 2 (Tokyo: Kokusho Kankōkai, 2001), pp. 273–329.

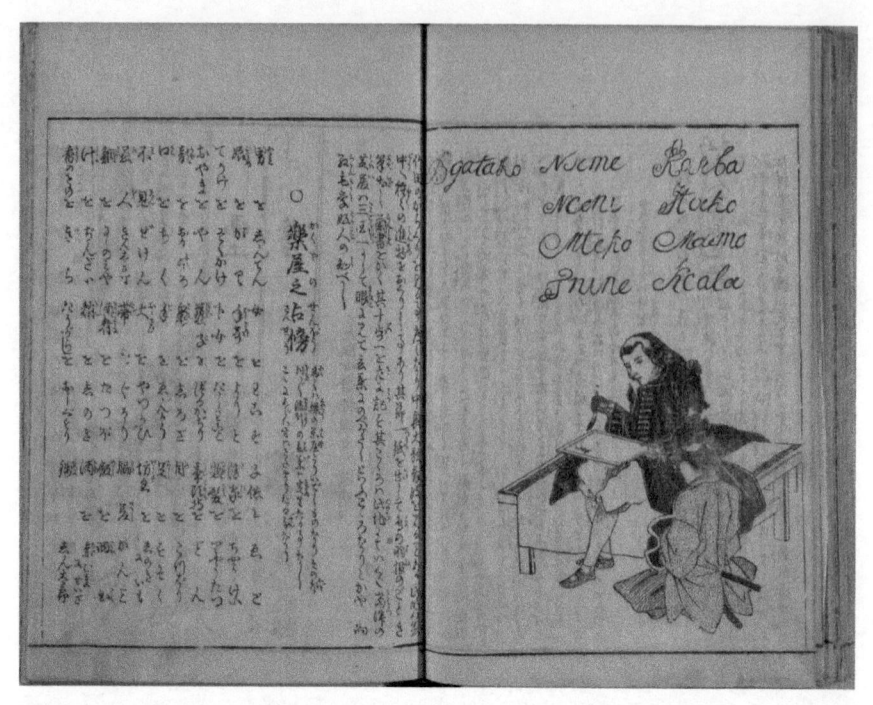

**Figure 3.25** Shōkōsai Hanbē, a Dutch theatergoer from *Shibai gakuya zue shūi*, 1800.
*Source*: National Diet Library, Tokyo.

of a Dutch theatergoer who had visited Dōtonbori in Osaka (Figure 3.25) and provided a number of gifts to the actors, including a handwritten note in Dutch in which he had praised the theaters of Osaka over those of Edo and Kyoto.[104]

Nor was *An Illustrated Guide to the Dressing Room* the only work to deploy the conceit of a Dutch appreciation for the Osaka stage. A decade-and-a-half later, in 1815, *A View of the Land of Shikan* (*Shikankoku ichiran*)—written, illustrated, and printed by members of Nakamura Shikan's (Utaemon III) fan club—contains a framed Western portrait of the great Osaka actor along with what is described in the text as a "Dutch kyōka" (Figure 3.26).[105] At the same time, throughout the text, *A View of the Land of Shikan* is shot through with the idiom of the Chinese stage, creating a peculiar structure in which the universality of Japanese theater as theater is guaranteed by hypothetical equivalence with the conventions of Chinese theater. What is most striking about *A View of the Land of Shikan*, however, is the way that this text blends together a number of elements from geography, ethnography, and cartography to create a playful portrait of its subject, Nakamura Shikan. Indeed,

---

[104] Shōkōsai Hanbē, *Shibai gakuya zue shūi* vol. 2 (Osaka: Kawajiya Tasuke, 1800), https://dl.ndl.go.jp/info:ndljp/pid/2605334.
[105] Dōrosai Hyakki, *Shikankoku ichiran* (Osaka: Morimoto Tasuke, 1815), 9r.

Figure 3.26 Akatsuki Kanenari, a Dutch Kyōka from *Shikankoku ichiran*, 1815.
Source: Ninjōji Bunko, Osaka University Library.

the entire text is framed by, and its subject comprehended through, the language of geography. *A View of the Land of Shikan* is a biography of the actor written as if it were a guidebook to a foreign land, presenting an overview of the "famous places, historical spots, products, and language" of the Land of Shikan complete with a map and entries of ethnographic detail (Figure 3.27).[106] The conceit is the same as we find in Sanba's *Illustrated Dictionary of Theater for Beginners* or in the earlier *A Guide to the Provinces of Actors*: the actor imagined as a country. But here, the idea is extended, taken to its logical conclusion, with the book serving as a guide to the single land. In this text, the actor is at once placed within the real world of historical geography and the emergent, comparative category of the theater; simultaneously, the tools of the geographic imagination are redeployed to frame their subject anew, providing a way of understanding biography as if it were synchronic rather than diachronic: the actor's life and career mapped, comprehended through the metaphors of space and place.

At one level, there is something modish about the widespread use of Chinese terms in the early nineteenth century, as there would be for the vogue in using

[106] Dōrosai Hyakki, *Shikankoku ichiran*, 9r.

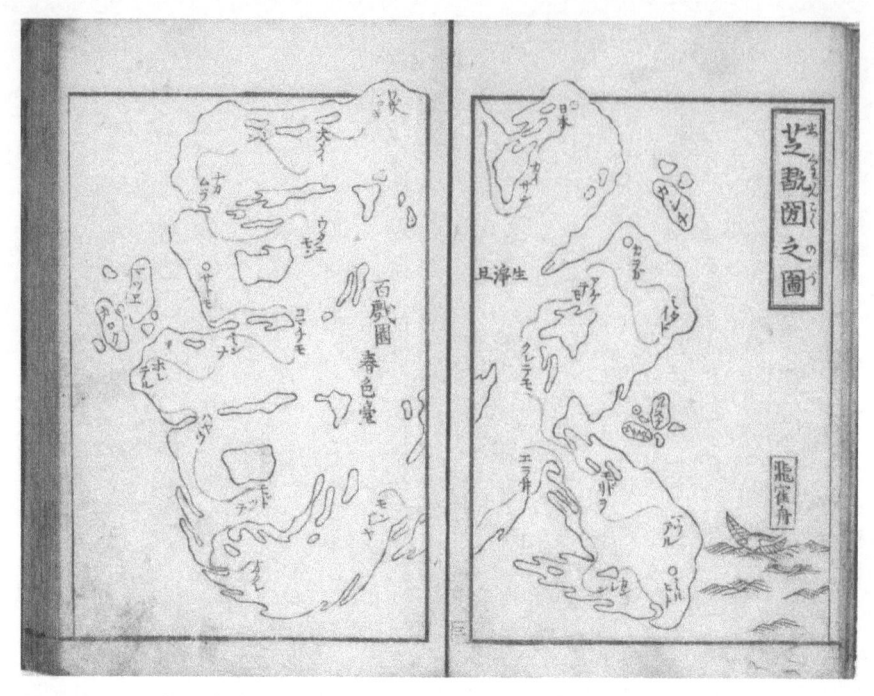

**Figure 3.27** Akatsuki Kanenari, map of the land of Shikan from *Shikankoku ichiran*, 1815.
*Source*: Ninjōji Bunko, Osaka University Library.

Western concepts in the decades following the Meiji Restoration. But just as Western aesthetic and literary concepts would have a profound impact on how drama came to be thought and written about in the late nineteenth and twentieth centuries, so texts like *Strange Tales from China* cannot be reduced to a surface reading in which the widespread use of the idiom of the Chinese stage is either a form of playful comparison or as a fashionable embrace of the foreign. Indeed, the use of Chinese theatrical terminology would lead to broader attempts to use Chinese theatrical discourse as a way to systematize knowledge of the Japanese theater, and in this sense, we need to see the decades of the early nineteenth century as a moment in which various conceptual schemes overlapped, and sometimes competed, just as they would the better part of a century later.

The conceptual framework provided by the Chinese theater allowed writers both to understand kabuki's place within a broad history of world theater and to use the abstract categories provided by the Chinese model to detail the history of kabuki itself. These abstract categories find their clearest expression in *A View of the Theater through a Microscope* (*Gekijō ikkan mushimegane*), a work written in 1829 by Kimura Mokurō, essayist, literary historian, and confidant to Kyokutei Bakin. *A View of the Theater through a Microscope* was intended, wrote Mokurō, for "theatrical novices" to provide an introduction to "viewing the theater," and the microscope of the title, Mokurō explains, was meant to convey both the introductory nature of the work and the level of detail at which he would present his findings.[107] But the figure of the microscope, which also appears on the book's frontispiece, suggests a different aspect of the work as well: Mokurō's taxonomic impulse, his drive, that is, to understand his subject—kabuki—within a larger classificatory system—the theater.

In many ways, Mokurō's book needs to be seen against the backdrop of the parodic works that appeared over a quarter of a century earlier. While *A View of the Theater through a Microscope* includes a bibliography which lists twenty-two of the best known titles, beginning with Sanba's *Illustrated Dictionary of Theater for Beginners*, Mokurō completely ignores the parodic framework of this work, and the body of *A View of the Theater through a Microscope* becomes a systematization of those earlier works only on an informational level, which aims to record, explain, and define various theatrical "practices" (*kojitsu kisoku*).[108] It is as if, by the 1820s, in the struggle between parody as form and the impulse to convey information, the latter has completely won out.

In his preface, Mokurō frames his study in a very different way to Sanba, not as an imaginary geography of the theater but as a quite literal emplotting of kabuki against a grid made up of both temporal and spatial axes. "The theater originated in the distant past," writes Mokurō, "with the ancient customs of kagura, turning, in the Heian period, into shirabyōshi and then into sarugaku, was later called dengaku, and has recently transformed into kabuki."[109] Nowhere in *A View of the Theater through a Microscope* does Mokurō present the *terminus a quo* of most previous histories of kabuki, the figure of Okuni. And in Okuni's place, we have not another figure, a different figure, but rather a genealogy, a slow transformation of theatrical practice over a millennium.

Even as he establishes a genealogy of theatrical practice within Japan, however, Mokurō also frames the history of Japanese theater as belonging to yet a more general phenomenon of *theater* of which the Japanese case is but a particular example. "Nowhere is theater not performed," continues Mokurō, "whether in distant foreign countries—as recorded in the Tales of the Seven Indias—in the various lands of China—as recorded in News from Abroad—or, more close by, in the various provinces and islands of Japan."[110] Here, in addition to a historical genealogy, Mokurō offers a spatial framework, and in each instance, the impulse is the same: to move both diachronically and synchronically in order to create a frame of reference within which he can departicularize the theatrical practices of nineteenth-century Japan, seeing the history of kabuki not as the history of a

---

[107] Kimura Mokurō, "Gekijō ikkan mushimegane," p. 2.
[108] Kimura Mokurō, "Gekijō ikkan mushimegane," p. 2.
[109] Kimura Mokurō, "Gekijō ikkan mushimegane," p. 2.
[110] Kimura Mokurō, "Gekijō ikkan mushimegane," p. 2.

discreet phenomenon but as an instance of a broader set within which it is encompassed. What emerges in Okuni's place, what emerges we might say in place of the particular history of kabuki, is something rather profound: an abstract concept of the theater (*shibai* 芝居・劇場・雑劇), a concept able to articulate the connections between and among theatrical practices across time and space, a concept that sees kabuki as a particular instance of a general category.

The primary purpose of *A View of the Theater through a Microscope*, Mokurō writes, is to provide a comparison between the theatrical practices of kabuki in Edo and the Kamigata region of Kyoto and Osaka. But to allow for this comparison, Mokurō makes recourse to a classificatory system entirely based on *Chinese* theater. The influence of *Strange Tales from China* on Mokurō's project is immense. The book, for example, contains eight color frontispieces designed by Utagawa Kunisada that depict the kabuki stars of the age in role, but the images are framed by the language of Chinese role types. The first image depicts Ichikawa Danjūrō VII and Matsumoto Kōshirō V: the image of Danjūrō is labeled "Canggu: a martial hero" ("Sōkotsu: eibu no hito") while the image of Kōshirō is labeled "Jing: a villain" (Figure 3.28). The images are framed using Chinese role types but then

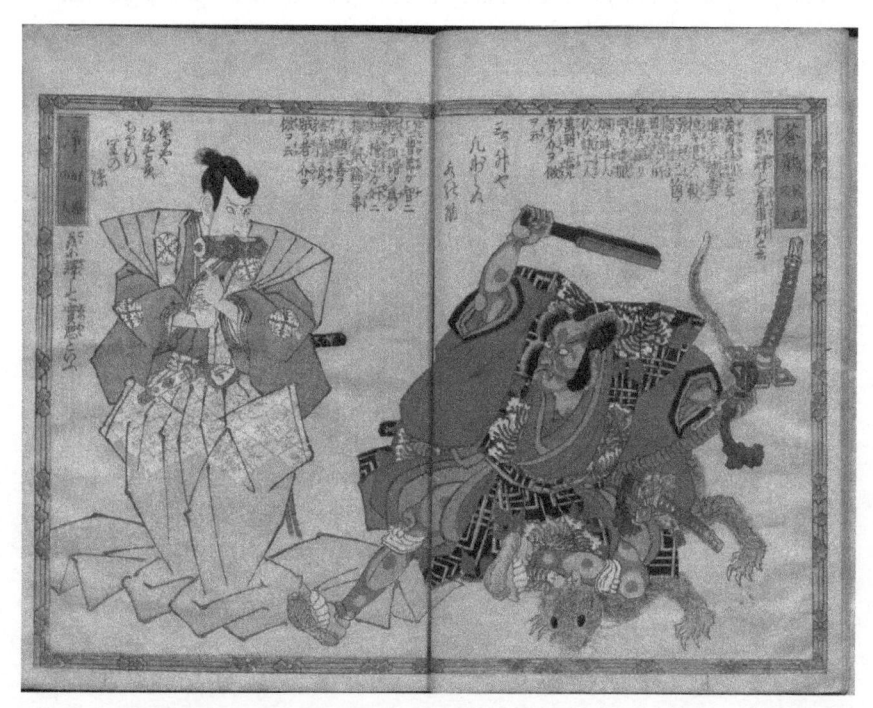

**Figure 3:28** Utagawa Kunisada, Ichikawa Danjūrō VII and Matsumoto Kōshirō V from Kimura Mokurō, *Gekijō ikkan mushimegane*, 1829.
Source: University of Tokyo Kornaba Library.

each contains a "translation" back into Japanese using a role type from kabuki: *aragotoshi* for Danjūrō and *jitsuaku* for Kōshirō, a pattern that is repeated for all of the frontispieces.

The images themselves—which blend together the appeal of a full color actor's likeness with the erudition of Chinese discourse and which use Chinese role types to frame the understanding of Japanese examples—are not unusual. The use of terms like *sheng, dan,* and *jing* as equivalents to kabuki's *tachiyaku, onnagata,* and *jitsuaku* had become widespread in the early nineteenth century after the publication of *Strange Tales from China*. What is striking, however, is how Mokurō then develops an elaborated taxonomy of kabuki roles based on the Chinese model. Thus, Volume 2 of *A View of the Theater through a Microscope* contains sections on *tachiyaku* (protagonist), *katakiyaku* (antagonist), and *onnagata* (female lead), each of which bears an elaborate taxonomic chart explaining the particulars of kabuki theatrical practice within a framework provided by Chinese drama.[111]

The chart for "The Six Types of Protagonist" ("Tachiyaku mushina no zusetsu") (Figure 3.29) has at the top three Chinese terms glossed with Japanese readings: *canggu*, or martial hero, is glossed as *aragotoshi; zheng sheng*, or hero, is given as the Japanese role type *jitsugoto*; and *xiao sheng*, or youthful hero, as *wagotoshi*, an actor who plays primarily romantic roles. Below this primary taxonomy, derived from Chinese theater, are role types specific to kabuki with examples given from particular plays. Thus, in column one, headed by *canggu/aragotoshi*, we have *aragoto* with specific examples of the characters Watōnai from *The Battles of Coxinga* and Asaina from *The Mirror of the East*. The column for *zheng sheng*, is subdivided into *sabakiyaku* (the wise hero) and *shinbōyaku* (the hero who endures suffering) with a third, hybrid role type, *wajitsu*, positioned between *zheng sheng* (*jitsugoto*) and *xiao sheng* (*wagotoshi*), thus sharing attributes of each. In explaining his chart, Mokurō writes:

> If one classifies (*bunbetsu*) the category (*shurui*) of the protagonist (*tachiyaku*) as in the chart, there are three large classes (*ōmoto*): *jitsugoto* (*zheng sheng*), *aragoto* (*canggu*), and *wagoto* (*xiao sheng*). Within these [three classes], there are six families (*shina*), the *sabakiyaku, shinbōyaku, wajitsu, wagoto, aragoto,* and *pinto kona*. In order for the amateur to quickly understand, I have noted them in the diagram of roles at the left.[112]

What is striking about this passage is both the general use of the language of categories (*shurui*) and classification (*bunbetsu*) but also the specific use of the terms "class" and "family" through which Mokurō introduces taxonomic principles

---

[111] Kimura Mokurō, "Gekijō ikkan mushimegane," pp. 13–26.
[112] Kimura Mokurō, "Gekijō ikkan mushimegane," pp. 17–18.

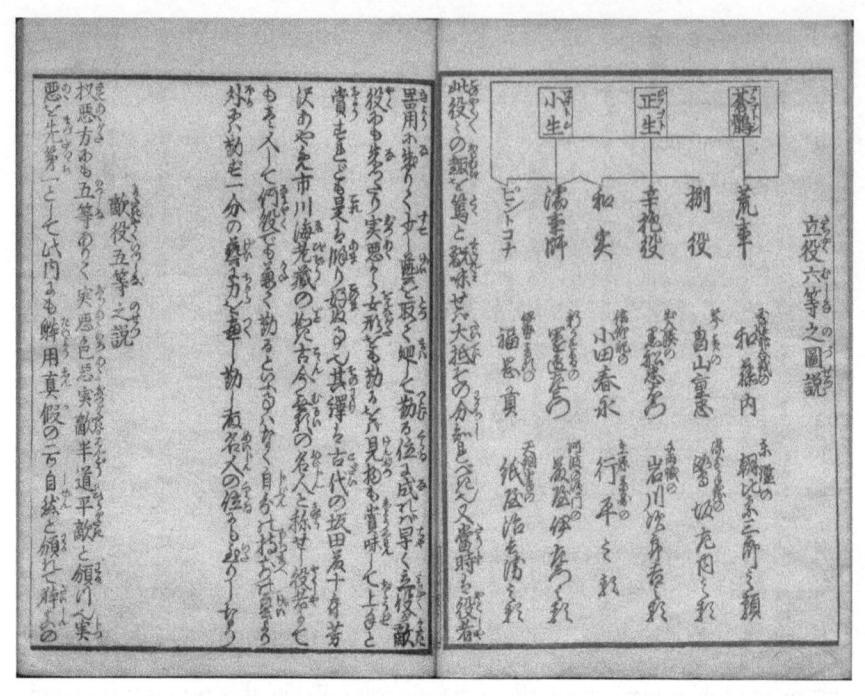

**Figure 3.29** Utagawa Kunisada, the six types of protagonist from Kimura Mokurō, *Gekijō ikkan mushimegane*, 1829.
Source: University of Tokyo Kornaba Library.

from natural history and pharmacology, fields with which Mokurō was himself tangentially involved.

Mokurō's book was published the same year as Itō Keisuke's *Taisei honzō meiso*, the first book systematically to introduce the Linnaean system to Japanese readers, and while it is not clear that Mokurō would have been aware of the interest that had emerged in the work of Linnaeus among his contemporaries, his use of this taxonomic language reflects two aspects of his approach to theatrical history in his "microscopic" view.[113] The first is an attempt to lend a systematic approach to the enterprise of theatrical history too often dominated by what Mokurō calls "pedantry" (*ugachi*): "pedantry is being knowledgeable about things which serve no use whatsoever. For example, knowing how old such and such an actor is and his wife's name or that the costume used in the fourth act of *Chūshingura* was reused in the third act of *Twenty-Four Paragons of Filial Piety*."[114] Rather than

---

[113] See Maki Fukuoka, *The Premise of Fidelity: Science, Visuality, and Representing the Real in Nineteenth-Century Japan* (Stanford, CA: Stanford University Press, 2012).

[114] Kimura Mokurō, "Gekijō ikkan mushimegane," p. 36.

simply enumerating these kinds of "useless" facts, Mokurō tries to synthesize and systematize.

Second, and more suggestive, Mokurō seems to have understood the role that binomial nomenclature could play in establishing classificatory hierarchy. Beginning with *Strange Tales from China*, a kind of functional binomialism begins to pervade writing on kabuki's history and culture with the broad use of Chinese theatrical terms glossed with Japanese readings pointing toward a set of hypothetical equivalences. Mokurō understood that this use of Chinese terms could provide the same type of systematic framework to drama as Chinese terms had played in the development of the study of *materia medica* in Japan.[115] In other words, what is critical about Mokurō's use of Chinese terms is not that they suggest *equivalence* but classificatory *hierarchy*, with Japanese terms becoming local examples of universal categories represented by Chinese terms.

After all, the purpose of Mokurō's book is *not* to compare Japanese and Chinese theater but primarily to compare the theatrical practices of Edo and of the Kamigata region of Kyoto and Osaka. The Chinese theater does not serve as a *point of comparison* but rather functions as a governing classificatory system that allows for the comparison of two *local* examples, much in the way that Chinese pharmacological texts would provide a lens through which the local *materia medica* of Japan could be understood in a systematic fashion.

The influence of this way of thinking about the theater was both profound and short-lived: profound because the advent of an abstract vocabulary for examining the theater would allow for a basic framework for comparative thinking about theatrical practice that in some ways survives to this day; short-lived because within a half-a-century, the taxonomy derived from Chinese theater by way of *Strange Tales from China* would be displaced by a new way of thinking about comparison dominated by a vocabulary indebted to Western concepts.

Indeed, as Kamiyama Akira has pointed out, it was in 1878, almost exactly a half-century after Mokurō published *A View of the Theater through a Microscope*, that the modern term for the theater, *engeki*, would first come to prominence in a speech read aloud by the actor Ichikawa Danjūrō IX at the opening of the newly remodeled Shintomiza, the first kabuki theater to open with a Western facade and stage. "The theater (engeki)," said Danjūrō, "is not a useless plaything."[116]

The actors and the playwright Kawatake Mokuami all appeared on stage in formal Western coat-tails as Danjūrō read the panegyric that had been written by Fukuchi Ōchi, who had served as an interpreter on Japan's first mission to Europe in 1861 and as first secretary on the Iwakura Mission to the United States and Europe in 1870. Fukuchi would argue for theater reform as one of the central

---

[115] Fukuoka, *The Premise of Fidelity*.
[116] Akira Kamiyama, *Kindai engeki no raireki: kabuki no "isshin nisei"* (Tokyo: Shinwasha, 2006), p. 8.

tenets of modernization and would become one of the leading advocates of the theater reform movement that sought to find in kabuki an official theater modeled on Western theater.[117] As Takahashi Yūichirō has argued, the opening of the new Shintomiza can be thought of as "a historical node at which point the changes within kabuki—the introduction of a new theater architecture, a new mode of theatergoing, and efforts to attain respectability—became perceptible."[118]

It is within this larger context that we need to locate a shift in the very language through which kabuki, and Japanese theatrical practice more generally, came to be understood. This shift was not accomplished in a single moment on stage in 1878, but it was profound and it gradually resulted in the wholesale adoption of a new vocabulary to comprehend drama and its history, resulting in what Kamiyama Akira has called the "aporia" of modern Japanese theater through which terminology and concepts that were formed after the Meiji period, such as "traditional" and "theater" (*engeki*) are deployed to historicize Japan's theatrical past in such a way that they appear to have always already existed.[119] "We think of the 'modernization' of theater," Kamiyama has argued, "when in reality 'the theater' (engeki) is itself formed and made into an image within the various institutions of 'modernity' and then projected backward to the period before the Tokugawa era" so that the abstract concept of "the theater" itself becomes "a self-evident premise" of historical research."[120]

In many ways, there is no clearer embodiment of this aporia than Waseda University's Tsubouchi Memorial Theater Museum itself, which opened exactly half a century after the remodeled Shintomiza and a century after Mokurō published *A View of the Theater through a Microscope*. As we have seen in Chapter 2, both as an intellectual enterprise and as a physical structure, the Theater Museum embodies that "spectre of comparisons" that has marked historical thinking about Japanese theater since the late nineteenth century, a museum and research institute dedicated to the comparative study of theater, which understands the Japanese dramatic past as but one example of the universal set of the theater or *engeki*.

And here we might return to the most literally outward-facing expression of this stance, the building itself and the Latin inscription it bears, "Totus Mundus Agit Histrionem." Shōyō would return to variants of this phrase repeatedly over the last decades of his life. In 1920, he would, for the first time, publish a translation of *As You Like It* and render in Japanese Jaques's line from Act 2 Scene 7 "All the world's a stage,/and all the men and women merely players." At the time, Shōyō was completely immersed in the world of nineteenth-century kabuki,

---

[117] See M. Cody Poulton, *A Beggar's Art: Scripting Modernity in Japanese Drama, 1900–1930* (Honolulu: University of Hawai'i Press, 2010), p. 3.

[118] Yūichirō Takahashi, "Kabuki Goes Official: The 1878 Opening of the Shintomi-Za," in *A Kabuki Reader: History and Performance*, ed. Samuel L. Leiter (Armonk, NY: M. E. Sharpe, 2002), p. 126.

[119] Kamiyama, *Kindai engeki no raireki*, p. 10.

[120] Kamiyama, *Kindai engeki no raireki*, pp. 8–9.

deeply involved with cataloguing the material that would become the basis for the Theater Museum as well as writing a book on the nineteenth-century print designer Utagawa Toyokuni and his school. But rather than drawing on the Chinese idiom that we see so widely deployed in nineteenth-century Japan by writers like Bakin, Sanba, and Enba, Shōyō invents an entirely new idiom: "ningen sekai wa kotogotoku butai desu, sōshite subete no danjo ga haiyū desu."[121] For a writer so broadly erudite in Japanese theatrical tradition, so deeply immersed in the culture of early nineteenth-century kabuki, and so attuned to phrasing and language, the dry formality of Shōyō's rendering seems oddly out of pitch and certainly flattens out one of Shakespeare's most memorable lines. How could he not, one wonders, hear the echo of that governing image of the early-nineteenth-century stage in Shakespeare's language? How could he have so completely cut off his translation from any reference to, or acknowledgement of, this uncanny resonance?

Shōyō's ambivalent relationship with this phrase seems emblematic: the Latin could stand in for the larger category that contained—quite literally in the case of the physical building—the Chinese and Japanese examples, but the Chinese phrase that first came to Japan in the eighteenth century could no longer play this role. On the façade of the Theater Museum, just as in the Linnaean taxonomic structure, Latin had come to replace Chinese. But Shōyō *would* return to the Chinese rendering of the phrase, leaving behind several examples of calligraphy in his own hand in which he copied out this phrase with subtle variations. One was published posthumously in 1936 in a reproduction of a calligraphic album that Shōyō created towards the end of his life.[122] A second, written by Shōyō in 1930, hangs, framed, in the Shōyō Memorial Room on the second floor of the Theater Museum.

These various expressions of the staged nature of the world and the worldliness of the stage seem emblematic: the outward-facing, public expression in Latin adorning the faux Elizabethan building and the more private versions in Chinese calligraphy. The version now housed in the Shōyō Memorial Room of the Museum seems especially evocative for it finds a home in an eclectic room full of various objects that point toward the complexities of Shōyō's own interests in the history of drama: from miniature versions of Shakespeare's first folios and a replica of Yorick's skull from Hamlet to a small wooden statue, carved by Hasegawa Eisaku, of Shōyō himself sitting at his writing desk, book open. The desk, here modeled in miniature, is itself a replica that Shōyō had made in 1917 of the writing desk of the great playwright of the puppet theater Chikamatsu Monzaemon.

Shakespeare and Chikamatsu: for Shōyō they form a pair that would define his approach to the history of drama, an approach that made central the figure of the author and the play script as a form of literature. Strikingly absent from

---

[121] William Shakespeare, *Okinimesumama*, trans. Tsubouchi Shōyō (Tokyo: Waseda Daigaku Shuppanbu, 1920), p. 87.

[122] See Tsubouchi Shōyō, *Ninkōjō* (Tokyo: Daiichi Shobō, 1936), https://archive.wul.waseda.ac.jp/tomon/tomon_18727/tomon_18727_0001/tomon_18727_0001_p0028.jpg.

the room is any trace of Li Yu, the Chinese playwright who came to prominence in Japan with the publication of *Strange Tales from China* in 1790. In the Meiji period, Chikamatsu would come to be called the Shakespeare of Japan, but a century earlier he was imagined differently, as the Li Yu of Japan and this shift from Chinese to Western model itself tells a broader story about how playwriting was defined and redefined over the course of the nineteenth century. It is to the complex relationship among the images of these three men that I shall now turn.

# 4
# The Playwright at His Desk
## Imagining Authorship in Nineteenth-Century Japan

### I In Search of the Shakespeare of Japan

In 1897, the *Curio Magazine* (*Kottō zasshi*), a journal of antiquarianism edited by Miyatake Gaikotsu, ran a short note introducing an item of interest to its readers: a small writing desk once owned by the late-seventeenth- and early-eighteenth-century playwright Chikamatsu Monzaemon. This is, as far as I am aware, the first reference to the survival of the desk depicted in a famous image of Chikamatsu published in *A Souvenir of Naniwa* (*Naniwa miyage*) in 1738, a decade-and-a-half after the playwright's death (Figure 4.1).[1]

In the antiquarian note, the desk is transformed from a mere physical object—a meter in length, it is noted, and made of zelkova wood—into something more profound:

> When one imagines that it was at this simple and elegant desk where those marvelously exquisite passages were composed that made millions both past and present feel happiness or anger, laughter or sadness, one feels suddenly moved and it must be said that this is one of the rare treasures of this world.[2]

As a material object, the desk has a social life that can be traced piecemeal, a provenance that situates the desk within a genealogy of collecting that stretches from the late eighteenth century through the middle decades of the twentieth century. But as it is envisioned in 1897, in the pages of the *Curio Magazine*, the desk was also an emblem of the writerly imagination, the physical site a synecdoche for artistic creativity.

The portrait of Chikamatsu at his desk from *A Souvenir of Naniwa*—a copy of which was long displayed along with the small wooden statue of Tsubouchi Shōyō sitting at his replica of the desk in the Waseda Theater Museum—is one of a handful of published images of Chikamatsu to circulate during the Edo period, and it came to define how he was imagined: a solitary figure, brush in hand, ink stone at

---

[1] *Namiwa miyage* was published in 1738 by Miki Sadanari. A reprint of the text can be found in Nishizawa Ippū, *Ima mukashi ayatsuri nendaiki*, *Jōruri kenkyū bunken shūsei*, ed. Engeki Bunken Kenkyūkai, Vol. 2 of *Nihon engeki bunken shūsei* (Tokyo: Hokkō Shobō, 1944).
[2] Miyatake Gaikotsu, *Kottō zasshi*, vol. 17 of *Miyatake Gaikotsu kono naka ni ari* (Tokyo: Yumani Shobō, 1994), p. 164.

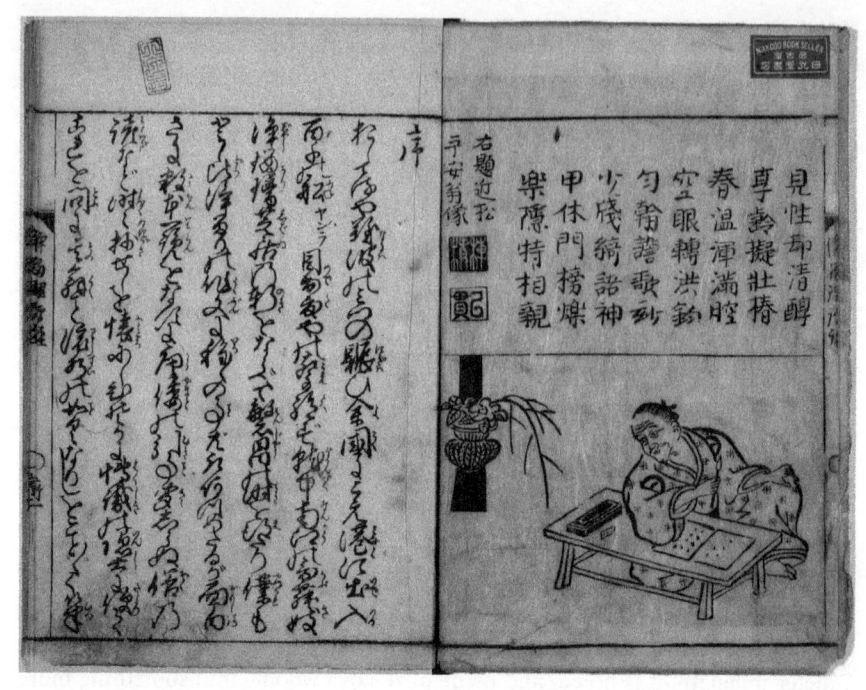

**Figure 4.1** Chikamatsu Monzaemon at his writing desk from Miki Sadanari, *Naniwa miyage*, 1738.

*Source*: Art Research Center, Ritsumeikan University.

his side, half reclining but seemingly deep in thought, in the act of composition. By the time the *Curio Magazine* published the note on Chikamatsu's desk, the image had been reprinted in Tsukagoshi Yoshitarō's 1894 biography of Chikamatsu for the series "Twelve Men of Letters" ("Jūni bungō") published by Minyūsha in the 1890s (which included volumes of Carlyle, Macauley, Goethe, and other Western writers). It was in this volume that Tsukagoshi would make what appears to be the earliest comparison of Chikamatsu and Shakespeare; the book's conclusion is titled simply "He Was in Many Respects the Shakespeare of Japan."[3] The modern circulation of this image provides a context in which the desk could emerge as a particular emblem of the author who was in the midst of being "rediscovered" and reimagined and, like so much else in the 1890s, refracted through the prism of the West.

---

[3] See Tsukagoshi Yoshitarō *Chikamatsu Monzaemon* (Tokyo: Kenyūsha, 1894). Doi: 10.11501/872073. In 1900, Tsubouchi Shōyō would use this same portrait as one of the frontispieces for a volume of essays on Chikamatsu he published with his students, *Chikamatsu no kenkyū*. See Tsubouchi Shōyō and Tsunashima Ryōsen, eds, *Chikamatsu no kenkyū* (Tokyo: Shunyōdō, 1900). Doi: 10.11501/991478.

According to the article in *Curio Magazine*, the desk was, at the time, in the possession of Ryūtei Enshi, one of the great professional storytellers of the late nineteenth century, whose lineage can be traced back to Utei Enba. Like Enba before him, Enshi was not only a professional raconteur but also a prominent member of the Mimasuren, the group of fans that supported the actor Ichikawa Danjūrō, and a collector of theater material.[4] Where the desk came from and how and when Enshi acquired it are unclear, but it seems likely that it came into his possession shortly before the article was published. Only two months earlier, together with the actor turned theater-manager Sakano Kyūjirō, Enshi had held an exhibit of rare theater material at the exhibition hall of the Nihon Bijutsu Kyōkai at Ueno Park.[5] According to a contemporary account, the exhibition included several hundred rare historical items ranging from a pair of golden dice and a war mantle given to Nakamura Kanzaburō I by the shogun Tokugawa Hidetada to a floor plan of the Nakamura-za given to the city magistrate of Edo by the carpenter Hasegawa Kanbē. The actor Ichikawa Danjūrō IX also lent several items including the great sword and wig used in Shibaraku. Enshi himself exhibited a number of objects including a rare likeness of the actor Ichikawa Danjūrō V made in charcoal and an early eighteenth-century doll of the actor Ikushima Shingorō, who was put to death for an alleged affair with a court lady in the service of Shogun Tokugawa Ietsugu's mother.[6] Chikamatsu's writing desk, however, is not mentioned.

As to its origins, one obvious possibility is that the desk was a fake, a possibility that Tsubouchi Shōyō himself entertained when he decided to have a replica of the desk made.[7] It also seems possible that the desk had somehow emerged in tandem with the exhibition. According to Hayashi Kyōhei's account of the provenance of the copy that Tsubouchi Shōyō had made in 1917, the desk had once belonged to Senba Tarōbē, a wealthy merchant who had made his fortune in overland trade in the 1850s and '60s and had become a collector of tea ware.[8] Senba had gone bankrupt in 1891,[9] and it is possible to imagine that the desk had come onto the market as part of the revival of interest in Chikamatsu and in the broader context of the trade in antiques that marked the decades after the Meiji Restoration.[10]

---

[4] See the obituary published in the *Asahi shinbun* at the time of Enshi's death in 1900. "Ko Danjūrō Enshi no koto," *Asahi shinbun*, Feburary 13, 1900, p. 5.
[5] "Gekijō onko hakurankai," *Asahi shinbun*, February 27, 1897, p. 3.
[6] "Gekijō onko hakurankai ga kaijō," *Yomiuri shinbun*, Feburary 26, 1897, p. 3.
[7] Shōyō expressed these doubts ("whether it is authentic or not, it's structure is interesting") in a note that he wrote in 1926 that is affixed to the bottom of the replica of the writing desk currently held by the Waseda Theater Museum, the second copy of the desk he had made. See Waseda Daigaku Engeki Hakubutsukan, ed., *Engeki hakubutsukan shiryō monogatari* (Tokyo: Waseda Daigaku Tsubouchi Haushi Kinen Engeki Hakubutsukan, 1988), pp. 240–41.
[8] See Tanihata Akio, *Cha no yu jinbutsushi* (Kyoto: Tankōsha, 2012).
[9] "Senba-shi shindaikagiri," *Asahi shinbun*, December 20, 1891, p. 1.
[10] On the trade in antiquities, see Suzuki Hiroyuki, *Kōkokatachi no jūkyūseiki: Bakumatsu Meiji ni okeru "mono" no arukeorojī* (Tokyo: Yoshikawa Kōbunkan, 2003), p. 20.

By the time Tsubouchi Shōyō first encountered the writing desk in 1917, it had passed into the hands of Matsuyama Yonetarō, one of the great collectors of Chikamatsu materials during the pre-war period. Like Senba, before him, Matsuyama, too, was an important figure in the circles of the tea ceremony. Matsuyama's father, Matsuyama Kitarō, was an antiques dealer active in Tokyo in the 1890s and likely knew of the desk from that time, although it appears that the family may not have acquired the desk until 1909.[11]

Two decades after the desk first surfaces in the pages of the *Curio Magazine*, Tsubouchi Shōyō's encounter with this artifact of the writer's life suggests its status as a kind of talisman, an object of cathexis. Shōyō visited Matsuyama on July 1, 1917 to view his collection; in a follow-up letter dated July 5, he asked to be able to make a copy of the desk.[12] A month later, on August 5, when he first sat at his new desk, Shōyō turned, emblematically, to work on a translation of Shakespeare's *Measure for Measure*.[13]

For Shōyō, and for others of his generation, Shakespeare and Chikamatsu would form a tangled pair, the great Elizabethan playwright serving as a strange mirror from which Chikamatsu and dramatic authorship more generally would be reflected:

> It has become custom since the nineteenth century to label whoever is a country's most accomplished dramatist, in other words the most highly regarded playwright, as that country's Shakespeare. We see this, for example, in the pronouncements over who is the Shakespeare of France or the Shakespeare of Germany. I do not know who was the first to say this but for some time now our own Chikamatsu has been called the Shakespeare of Japan.[14]

As William Lee has written, for Shōyō and his students, "the examination of the Japanese tradition is always haunted by the question of national identity and by the example of the west":

> Shōyō's research into Japan's theatrical traditions and his study of foreign models [...] must be seen in the context of an ideological and discursive environment in which considerations of the native culture were always accompanied and shaped by an awareness of the west.[15]

---

[11] Waseda Daigaku Engeki Hakubutsukan, ed., *Engeki hakubutsukan shiryō monogatari*, p. 239.

[12] Letter from Tsubouchi Shōyō to Matsuyama Yonetarō, July 5th, 1917 quoted in Waseda Daigaku Engeki Hakubutsukan, ed., *Engeki hakubutsukan shiryō monogatari*, p. 240.

[13] Shōyō Kyōkai ed., *Shōyō nikki* vol. 1 (Tokyo: Shōyō Kyōkai, 2002), p. 99.

[14] Tsubouchi Shōyō, "Chikamatsu tai Shēkuspiya tai Ibusen," in *Shōyō senshū*, vol. 10 (Tokyo: Daiichi shobō, 1977–78), p. 769.

[15] William Lee, "Chikamatsu and Dramatic Literature in the Meiji Period," in *Inventing the Classics: Cannon Formation, National Identity, and Japanese* Literature, ed. Haruo Shirane and Tomi Suzuki (Stanford, CA: Stanford University Press, 2001), p. 187.

Shōyō began translating Shakespeare in 1884 (when he published his translation of *Julius Caesar*), and this would become a lifelong project. He completed his translation of the complete works in 1928, timed to coincide with the opening of the Waseda Theater Museum. At the same time, Shōyō also turned his attention to Chikamatsu, forming the Chikamatsu Study Group (Chikamatsu Kenkyūkai) in 1887 to re-evaluate the playwright's work from the perspective of a new literary history.

In the case of dramatic authorship, in particular, the specter cast by the West had a specifically archival dimension. In 1896, a year before *Curio Magazine* published its article on the writing desk, Shōyō would address the challenges facing a history of playwriting in two essays published in the magazine *Taiyō* (*The Sun*). In the first, "The Extant Play Scripts of our Country as Literature," Shōyō contrasted the fate of kabuki scripts made for use by actors and not published—"until quite recently hidden away in the dressing rooms, only rarely made public"[16]—with the tradition of publishing play scripts in England going back to the Elizabethan era when playwrights were "celebrated among the reading public."[17] In a subsequent essay, Shōyō wrote how this circumstance of closely held scripts had a second-order effect for the historian of drama:

> Today when there is nothing to help with investigating kabuki's past outside of piecemeal records such as chronologies and works such as impressionistic essays, researching old playwrights and their work is an exceedingly trying task. As I have said previously, because old play scripts were not published but left as manuscripts that have been scattered, it is a great endeavor simply to collect them; but as it is often the case that the works are not signed, it is an unimaginable headache to refer to such miscellanies as the *Chronology of Kabuki* (*Kabuki nendaiki*) and *On the Writing of Plays* (*Genkyō sakusho*) and look up their dates one by one and match work to author.[18]

For Shōyō, the headaches caused by the archive were not orthogonal to the question of the status of drama as a form of literature but part of the constituent problem of the very nature of dramatic authorship during the Edo period. Moreover, the archive of kabuki scripts was not only scattered and fragmentary but

---

[16] Tsubouchi Shōyō, "Bungaku toshite no waga zairai kyakuhon," in *Shōyō senshū*, vol. 10 (Tokyo: Daiichi shobō, 1977–78), p. 215.

[17] Tsubouchi Shōyō, "Bungaku toshite no waga zairai kyakuhon," in *Shōyō senshū*, vol. 10, p. 221. As recent scholarship on Elizabethan theater has shown, the relationship between manuscript and print in Shakespeare's time was considerably more complex than Shōyō had imagined a century ago. See, e.g. Paul Werstine, *Early Modern Playhouse Manuscripts and the Editing of Shakespeare* (Cambridge: Cambridge University Press, 2013) and James Purkis, *Shakespeare and Manuscript Drama: Canon, Collaboration, and Text* (Cambridge: Cambridge University Press, 2016).

[18] Tsubouchi Shōyō, "Kyū kyōgen sakusha oyobi kyū kyakuhon," in *Shōyō senshū*, vol. 10 (Tokyo: Daiichi shobō, 1977–78), p. 227.

also marred by "manuscripts of poor quality rife with added characters, copyist mistakes, and substituted characters."[19]

There is a further problem which Shōyō does not address in these essays, and it would prove more vexing still: the collaborative and corporate nature of authorship which, by the eighteenth century, had become the basic form of dramatic composition. Indeed, as Nakamura Tetsurō has written, playwriting was a kind of "construction site" in which an ensemble of writers worked together to fashion the play.[20]

In this archival context, it is easy to understand the appeal of a figure like Chikamatsu, for in the 1680s, he became one of the first playwrights to sign his name as author to published plays. His works were widely published during his lifetime, and within two years of his death, he had already come to be known as the "patron god of authors."[21] All of the complexities of collation, attestation, and attribution could fall away and the historian, or critic, in search of what Shōyō would call the playwright's "nature and genius" could encounter Chikamatsu's work directly, the product of a single and singular author, alone at his desk.[22]

If this conception of authorship seems quintessentially modern, deeply entwined with ideas of singular authorial genius, there is another way of approaching the figure of Chikamatsu as author formed by a genealogy of interest in the traces of his life that extends back to the opening of the nineteenth century. Indeed, if Chikamatsu was rediscovered—or, to borrow Ihara Toshirō's suggestive phrase, "resurrected"—at the end of the nineteenth century, he had already been recovered at the beginning of that century, and the idea of authorship that emerged from the 1890s forward can, in many ways, be counterpointed to a conception of authorship that had emerged *circa* 1800.[23] At that time, too, the interest in Chikamatsu as author was intimately bound up with the surviving traces of his life and, just as it would be at the end of the century, his image was refracted through the prism of a foreign playwright.

## II Archaeology of the Author's Trace

Although it was Chikamatsu's writing desk that captured Tsubouchi Shōyō's imagination when he visited Matsuyama Yonetarō in 1917 (he would describe the desk in a letter as "difficult to forget"), Shōyō was also interested in a hanging scroll

---

[19] Tsubouchi Shōyō, "Kyū kyōgen sakusha oyobi kyū kyakuhon," in *Shōyō senshū*, vol. 10, p. 227.
[20] Nakamura Tetsurō, *Kabuki no kindai: sakka to sakuhin* (Tokyo: Iwanami Shoten, 2006), p. 5.
[21] This was Nishizawa Ippū's phrase (*sakusha no ujigami*) in his 1727 *Ima mukashi ayatsuri nendaiki*. For a reprint of the text, see Nishizawa Ippū, *Jōruri kenkyū bunken shūsei*, ed. Engeki Bunken Kenkyūkai, Vol. 2 of *Nihon engeki bunken shūsei* (Tokyo: Hokkō Shobō, 1944). Doi: 10.11501/1125481.
[22] Tsubouchi Shōyō, "Chikamatsu to Shēkusupiya," in *Shōyō senshū*, vol. 8 (Tokyo: Daiichi shobō, 1977–78), pp. 769–70.
[23] Ihara Seiseien [Toshirō], "Chikamatsu no fukkatsu," *Kabuki* 22 (March 1902), 1–5.

that Matsuyama owned. The scroll bore a portrait of Chikamatsu drawn in 1723 (shortly before his death at the beginning of the following year) together with an inscription in Chikamatsu's hand reflecting on his own impending death. Like the image of Chikamatsu at his writing desk from *A Souvenir of Naniwa*, this image of the aged playwright would circulate widely in the Meiji period, based on a copy of the painting that appeared in print in an 1807 miscellany titled the *Notes Taken upon Waking Up* (*Suiyo shōroku*).

More than the desk, it is this portrait of Chikamatsu, together with two other hanging scrolls that bear inscriptions in Chikamatsu's hand, that connect the antiquarian and historical impulses of Matsuyama, Shōyō, and their contemporaries to a genealogy of interest in the playwright extending back to the beginning of the nineteenth century: a separate scroll bearing Chikamatsu's death poem (without the portrait) and a painting of a courtesan thought to be done by Chikamatsu's son Sugimori Tamon with an inscription in Chikamatsu's hand. While Matsuyama Yonetarō's father, the art dealer Matsuyama Kitarō, appears to have obtained the death portrait of Chikamatsu in 1895, at the height of the Meiji Chikamatsu boom as the playwright's work was being rediscovered and reprinted, these two other scrolls came into the possession of Takemoto Settsu-Daijō, one of the great chanters of the puppet theater during the Meiji period.[24] Settsu-Daijō died in October 1917, just months after Shōyō visited Matsuyama, and the scrolls (and a collection of other materials related to the puppet theater) then passed into the hands of his adopted son Futami Bunjirō. According to Mizutani Futō's 1904 biography of Settsu-Daijō, the chanter himself had been adopted into the Futami house as a child in the early 1840s. For his part, Bunjirō was intended to become heir to the master chanter, but poor eyesight caused him to abandon the theater as a calling; he would eventually work in the cotton trade after attending Keiō Gijuku.[25]

In 1922, the two scrolls would briefly appear together with Matsuyama's portrait and the writing desk when they were shown at an exhibition of historical Chikamatsu materials in advance of the two hundredth anniversary of the playwright's death. In addition to the portrait of Chikamatsu, the centerpiece of the exhibition, and the writing desk, Matsuyma had also lent a famous letter from 1716 in Chikamatsu's hand known as the "Imose nori no shōsoku," in which Chikamatsu describes the success of his play *The Battles of Coxinga*. The exhibition also featured seventeen items from Futami Bunjirō including the scroll of the courtesan painting, described in the catalogue as "a treasure of the late Settsu-Daijō."

Matsuyama's portrait of Chikamatsu and the writing desk were at the center of the exhibition, but it is the two scrolls owned by Futami Bunjirō that are more interesting from an historical perspective for it is through these two objects that we can trace an interest in the playwright that extends back a century earlier. In

---

[24] Waseda Daigaku Engeki Hakubutsukan, ed., *Engeki hakubutsukan shiryō monogatari*, p. 239.
[25] Mizutani Futō, *Takemoto Settsu-Daijō* (Tokyo: Hakubunkan, 1904), pp. 206–07.

the early years of the nineteenth century, the death poem and the portrait of the courtesan bearing Chikamatsu's inscription both surface *in print*. One of the earliest references to their existence comes at the very end of Kyokutei Bakin's 1804 *Tales Told by Rain* (*Saritsu udan*), the published account of Bakin's 1802 journey to Kyoto and Osaka.[26] In his unpublished journal, Bakin would write that the two scrolls were the only traces of Chikamatsu's hand extant in Osaka.[27]

In *Tales Told by Rain*, Bakin's encounter with the traces of Chikamatsu's hand takes place at the nexus of what we might think of as various strands of nineteenth-century sociability: some private, others public; some direct encounters with objects of the past, others mediated by the printed page. Bakin's account begins with a short biography of Chikamatsu, the details of which, Bakin reveals, he had learned upon visiting the playwright Namiki Shōzō II and examining his "Valuable Notes on Playwriting" ("Kezairoku"). Shōzō II had completed his treatise on dramatic composition in 1801, but it circulated only in manuscript for a century until it was published in 1909 as part of the larger project of recovering and publishing the literary and cultural record of the Edo period described in Chapter 2.[28] Bakin notes that he had then visited the owner of the scrolls, a wealthy merchant named Kumanoya Hikokurō. Although Bakin made a copy of the inscriptions, he does not reproduce them in his text but rather suggests that the copy was for his friend and mentor Santō Kyōden, who intended to write about them at a later date.[29] But Kyōden, who had just begun his turn toward the work that would lead to *Thoughts on Extraordinary Things of Recent Times* (1804), appears never to have written about the scrolls, and Bakin's own copy of the inscriptions would remain in manuscript until 1885 when the text of his "A Miscellany of my Travels" ("Kiryo manroku"), the manuscript account of his journey on which *Tales Told by Rain* was based, was published and in which the two inscriptions were reproduced.[30]

The contents of the scrolls, however, did circulate during the Edo period, somewhat piecemeal. The death poem, for example, appears on the portrait of Chikamatsu published in the *Notes Taken upon Waking Up* (*Suiyo shōroku*; 1807) and a century later, that portrait would be used by Tsubouchi Shōyō and his students as a frontispiece for their collection of Chikamatsu's "masterpieces" published by Waseda University Press in 1910 and which contains the text of Shōyō's lecture on Chikamatsu and Shakespeare.

But it is the painting of the courtesan that is, in many ways, more interesting still for understanding Bakin's own encounter with Chikamatsu in 1802 and for the

---

[26] Kyokutei Bakin, "Chosakudō issekiwa," in Nihon Zuihitsu Taisei Henshūbu ed. *Nihon zuihitsu taisei*, vol. 5, ser. 1 (Tokyo: Yoshikawa Kōbunkan, 1927), p. 711.

[27] Kyokutei [Takizawa] Bakin, *Kiryo manroku*, ed. Atsumi Seikan, vol. 3 (Tokyo: Isandō, 1885), p. 42.

[28] Namiki's name is also romanized as Namiki Shōza; I have used Shōzō because the romanization is more common in English-language materials.

[29] Kyokutei Bakin, "Chosakudō issekiwa," p. 711.

[30] Kyokutei [Takizawa] Bakin, *Kiryo manroku*, vol. 3, pp. 40–42.

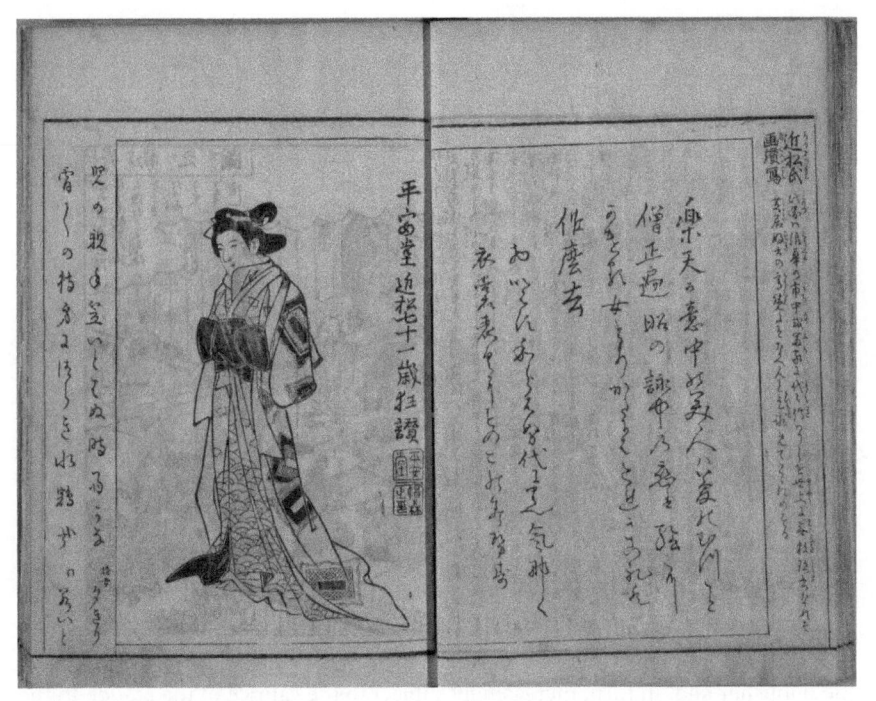

**Figure 4.2** Shōkōsai Hanbē, copy of the image of a courtesan bearing an inscription by Chikamatsu Monzaemon, *Shibai gakuya zue shūi*, 1800.
Source: National Diet Library, Tokyo.

ways in which that encounter would become a touchstone for imagining authorship in the nineteenth century. By the time Bakin visited Osaka in 1802, a copy of the painting and the inscription had already appeared in print, published earlier that year in *An Illustrated Guide to the Dressing Room: A Supplement*, the compendium of theatrical material which includes the image of the Dutch visitor to Dōtonbori (Figure 4.2).[31] It is difficult to imagine that Bakin was unaware of this book: he was a knowledgeable fan of kabuki and widely read in its sources. More importantly, *An Illustrated Guide to the Dressing Room* had been published by Kawachiya Tasuke, whom Bakin had befriended during his trip to Osaka and who would act as one of the publishers of Bakin's *Tales Told by Rain* in1804. Indeed, the relationship that Bakin formed with the publisher became one of the defining collaborations that helped shape the emergence of a national book market in the early nineteenth century and that marked his own ascent as a writer.[32]

And yet, in Bakin's account, *An Illustrated Guide to the Dressing Room* is completely absent, the published and printed volume elided; instead, we are left with

---

[31] See above Chapter 3.
[32] See Ōtaka Yōji, "Jūkyū seiki teki sakusha non tanjō," *Bungaku* 5, 3 (May 2004), 75ff.

a world of manuscripts and heirlooms, antiquarians and collectors, unmediated by print. Indeed, in writing about the scrolls, Bakin would refer to the inscriptions as examples of Chikamatsu's "own hand" (*nikuhitsu*) and the "traces of his brush" (*bokuseki*), two terms that stress his direct, almost physical encounter with the traces of the great author. This encounter with the authorial trace becomes an occasion for a paean to the great playwright but also an opportunity for Bakin's own self-fashioning as a man of erudition who moved fluently in the literary circles of the early nineteenth century. Bakin, that is, was inventing himself as an author, in part, through his encounter with Chikamatsu.

Bakin's journey to Osaka and the resulting collaboration with Kawachiya Tasuke has long been understood as one of the defining moments of his own career as an author and, more broadly, of the emergence of professional authorship in Japan. Although Bakin had begun his career as a writer a decade earlier, in 1791, it would be in the years after his return to Edo that he began the most spectacularly successful literary career of the nineteenth century. It was in these years that he became one of the first writers to get paid for his words, thus marking what Ōtaka Yōji has called "the birth of the nineteenth-century author."[33]

In many ways, the nineteenth-century literary field is defined by the changing nature of authorship in which the author was, for the first time, paid directly by the publisher and, in turn, increasingly subject to the caprice of the reader, to the demands of publisher, even—as I will explore in Chapter 5—to rivalry with the illustrator. Bakin wrote at length on these subjects, returning to the travails of authorship frequently over his writing life.[34] Of course, not all of these relationships and rivalries would have been visible to Bakin in 1802, and a great deal about the nature of authorship would change over the course of his own career, but much of Bakin's own understanding of authorship seems to have been formed, or at least informed, by his search for and his encounter with, the traces of the author during his journey of 1802.

Chikamatsu as "patron god of authors" would be one point of reference for a conception of authorship; a second was offered by Bakin at the end of his entry on Chikamatsu in *Tales Told by Rain*. There, Bakin notes the existence of an ink stone once owned by Chikamatsu that had been passed down to the mid-eighteenth-century playwright Chikamatsu Hanji bearing a nine-character inscription in Chinese on its lacquer cover: "Take that which is common and use it to propagate righteousness through the promotion of virtue and the castigating of vice."[35] The playwright, that is, should take the world around him and

---

[33] Ōtaka Yōji, "Jūkyū seiki teki sakusha non tanjō," pp. 71–80. On the professionalization of authorship, and the payment system (*junpitsu ryō*) that emerged in this period, see Takada Mamoru, *Takizawa Bakin: Momotose nochino chiin wo matsu* (Kyoto: Mineruva Shobō, 2006), pp. 147–50.

[34] See Hamada Keisuke, "On Booksellers, Authors, and Readers in the Works of Bakin," trans. Peter Kornicki, http://www.sharpweb.org/main/wp-content/uploads/2014/09/Paper_Hamada.pdf. (2014)

[35] Kyokutei Bakin, "Chosakudō issekiwa," pp. 711–12.

transform it into a kind of Manichaean universe in which the good are rewarded and the wicked punished. The phrase, Bakin continues, comes from the preface to Li Yu's *chuanchi* play *The Jade Clasp* (*Yu sao tou*), and Chikamatsu was, Bakin concludes, "truly the Li Yu of our country."[36] Thus, the better part of a century before he would be imagined as the Shakespeare of Japan, Chikamatsu is cast as the Li Yu of Japan. And the image of that Chinese writer—playwright and novelist, publisher and entrepreneur—would exert a powerful influence on nineteenth-century conceptions of authorship.

Bakin appears to have discovered Li Yu a decade earlier when he made a commonplace book into which he copied extended passages from *Strange Tales from China* (*Morokoshi kidan*), Hatanaka Kansai's 1790 primer on Chinese drama that would introduce Li Yu to a generation of Japanese readers (discussed in Chapter 3).[37] In *Strange Tales from China*, however, it is Shi Nai'an and Luo Guanzhong, the Yuan Dynasty novelists to whom the *Water Margin* and the *Romance of the Three Kingdoms* are respectively attributed, that are described as "our country's Chikamatsu Monzaemon" (*wagakuni no Chikamatsu Monzaemon*). It seems to have been Bakin himself who found in Li Yu a more appropriate lens through which to view Chikamatsu and his accomplishments.

After his journey to Osaka, Bakin would begin to use the image of Li Yu for fashioning his own identity as a writer.[38] In part, the choice was meant to aver Bakin's own erudition, his fluency with Chinese culture. But for Bakin, Li Yu also represented a particular ideal of authorship: commercial but not vulgar, a writer who negotiated the changing nature of early modern publishing as well as the political transition from the Ming to Qing courts.[39] In a passage on Li Yu from *Strange Tales from China* that Bakin copied out into his commonplace book, the novelist and playwright is described as "one who had no interest in either personal fortune or official position," who refused appointment by the Kangxi Emperor himself, and who "composed prose, poetry, and drama in his leisure into his old age."[40]

In 1804, the same year that *Tales Told by Rain* appeared, Bakin also wrote *Kyokutei's Chuanqi: The Flowered Clasp* (*Kyokutei denki hanakanzashi*), based on Li Yu's play *The Jade Clasp* and written expressly to mimic the form and conventions of *chuanqi* drama while transposing the setting to Japan during the reign of Ashikaga Yoshiteru in the mid-sixteenth century.[41]

---

[36] Kyokutei Bakin, "Chosakudō issekiwa," p. 712.
[37] Hatanaka Kansai, "Inbon shakubun," manuscript, Waseda University Library Special Collections 04 00600 185, https://www.wul.waseda.ac.jp/kotenseki/html/i04/i04_00600_0185/index.html
[38] See Tokuda Takeshi, *Nihon kinsei shōsetsu to Chūgoku shōsetsu*, vol. 51 (Tokyo: Seishōdō Shoten, 1987), pp. 410ff.
[39] See Patrick Hanan, *The Invention of Li Yu* (Cambridge: Cambridge University Press, 1988).
[40] Hatanaka Kansai, "Inbon shakubun," 5r–5v.
[41] The impetus for this mock play, too, appears to have come from Bakin's 1802 journey. During his extended stay in Nagoya, Bakin befriended the literatus Ryūkatei Ransui. At the time, Ransui was deeply interested in vernacular Chinese drama, himself working on a translation of a seventeenth-century chuanqi play by Xie Hongyi called *Hudie meng* (Butterfly Dream). See Tokuda Takeshi,

As with *Tales Told by Rain*, the preface to *The Flowered Clasp* also posits a comparison between Chikamatsu and Li Yu:

> Li Yu said that in creating a play you awaken the senses of the ignorant; our own Chikamatsu has said that one writes drama to aid the promotion of virtue and the castigation of vice. Are they not the pinnacle of Chinese and Japanese drama for the last century and a half?[42]

But if the 1802 journey to Osaka would profoundly shape his identity as an author, Bakin seems to have understood something of the outline of his own authorial persona in a work he published the year before his journey, *A Puff of Kyokutei's Pipe in the Style of Kyōden* (*Kyokutei ippū Kyōden bari*). That book tells the story of a tobacco pouch and a pipe in love but separated when they are sold to a young man and a courtesan, respectively, to be finally reunited when their owners fall in love.

The book opens with a page depicting the interior of Bakin's home, where he receives his friend and mentor Santō Kyōden, who is accompanied by anthropomorphized versions of the tobacco pouch and the pipe. Kyōden has come both to thank Bakin for promoting his tobacco shop the previous year and to ask if he would do so again this year, presumably in the book that we are now reading (Figure 4.3). The following scene shows the interior of Kyōden's tobacco shop: Kyōden is sitting at his desk, brush in hand; in the foreground, two shop clerks serve customers, one displaying pipes, the other a range of tobacco pouches, setting the scene for the separation of the two objects (Figure 4.4). Kyōden's own figure seems ambiguous: is he surveying the commercial scene in front of him or poised to write as he grips a writing brush? Or, as the blank fan in front of him suggests, is he simply waiting for a customer to commission an autographed folding fan, which he is known to have sold from his shop?

Foregrounded in the book, then, is the interconnectedness of art and commerce: the book itself serves as advertising and Kyōden's tobacco shop provides the premise of the story. And there is no doubt that Kyōden's writing was, especially in the late eighteenth century, deeply connected to his other commercial pursuits.[43] But if we turn back from the commercial space of Kyōden's shop to the

---

"*Kyokutei denki hana no kanzashi ron*," *Meiji Daigaku kyōyō ronbunshū* 118 (1978), 86–87. As Kawai Masumi has pointed out, Bakin not only transplants Li Yu's drama to Japanese soil but also, in the process, incorporates elements from several well-known jōruri plays including Chikamatsu's 1721 *Tsunokuni myōto ike*. See Kawai Masumi, "*Kyokutei denki hana no kanzashi to engeki*," *Yomihon kenkyū shinshū* 5 (2004), 6–24.

[42] Tokuda Takeshi and Yokoyama Kuniharu, eds, *Shigeshige yawa. Kyokutei denki hanakanzashi. Saibara kidan. Toribeyama shirabeno itomichi*, Shin Nihon koten bungaku taikei, vol. 80 (Tokyo: Iwanami Shoten, 1992), p. 129.

[43] See Satō Yukiko, *Santō Kyōden: kokkei share daiichi no sakusha* (Kyoto: Mineruva Shobō, 2009), pp. 129ff.

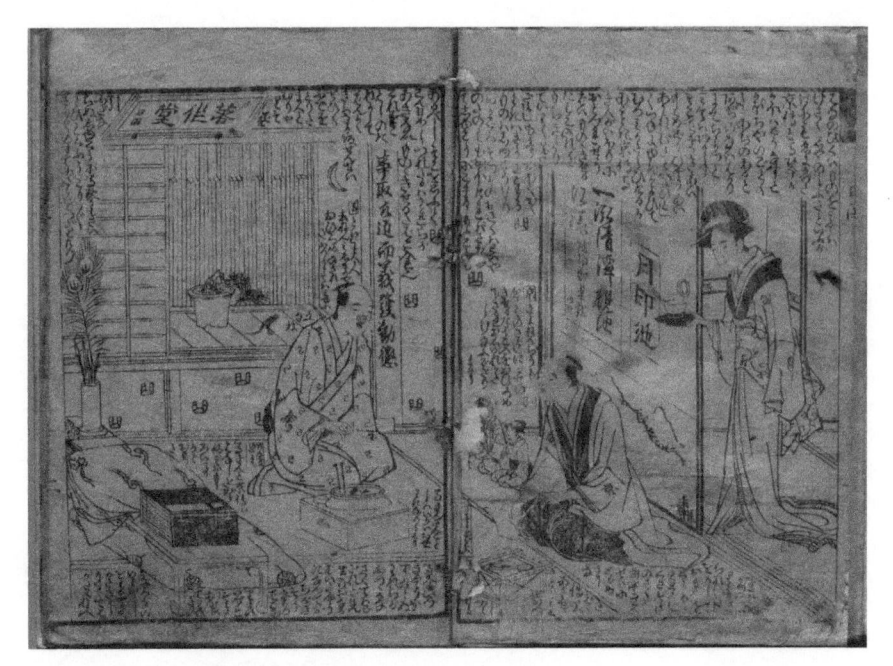

**Figure 4.3** Kitao Shigemasa, Kyokutei Bakin's study from Kyokutei Bakin, *Kyokutei ippū Kyōden bari*, 1801.
Source: National Diet Library, Tokyo.

private space of Bakin's home, it is difficult not to be struck by how different a vision of the writerly life is offered here.

Within this domestic space, the depiction of the interior of Bakin's study is suggestive—the nine-character phrase from the preface to Li Yu's *The Jade Clasp*, which Bakin would use to mark the connection between Chikamatsu and the Chinese writer, appears next to Bakin, running vertically down the edge of a recessed lattice-work window in which a bonsai sits—"Take that which is common and use it to propagate righteousness through the promotion of virtue and the castigating of vice."[44] If the writer is to use the everyday world around him to fashion his work, the placement of the characters along the window is emblematic: the writer may be a creature of the interior, but he draws inspiration from the world beyond. At the far edge of the illustration, to the reader's left, is a writing desk, and beside the desk is a vase with a number of writing brushes but also peacock feathers. A small detail perhaps, but like the nine-character phrase, it becomes a touchstone for a particular ideal of the writing life as it came to be imagined in nineteenth-century Japan.

---

[44] Tokuda Takeshi, *Takizawa Bakin*, Shinchō koten bungaku arubumu (Tokyo: Shinchōsha, 1991), pp. 22–23, quoted in Shiau Han-Chen, "Ri Gyo no *Gyokusōtō denki* to sono honansaku," *Tōkyō daigaku Chūgokugo Chūgoku bungaku kenkyūshitsu kyō* 15 (October, 2012), 127, n. 5.

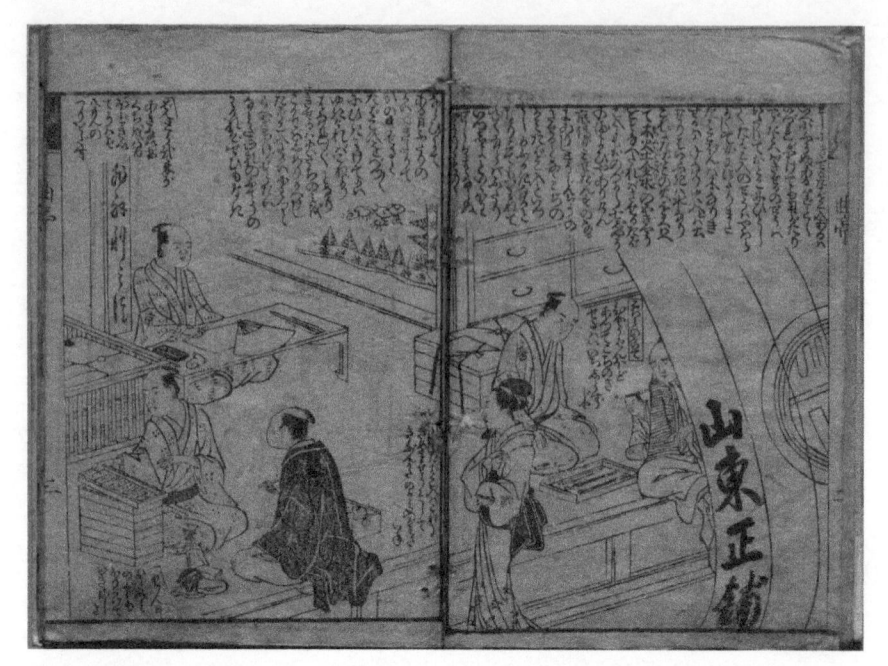

**Figure 4.4** Kitao Shigemasa, Santō Kyōden's shop from Kyokutei Bakin, *Kyokutei ippū Kyōden bari*, 1801.
*Source:* National Diet Library, Tokyo.

In Late Imperial China, a vase with peacock feathers was one of a variety of material objects, what Li Yu called "pleasurable things" (*wanhao zhi wu*) that served as markers of taste and refinement.[45] In late-eighteenth- and nineteenth-century Japan, the feathers in particular came to serve as part of an iconography of the writerly life. Two sources, which both draw on Li Yu's *Casual Expressions of Feelings of Leisure* (*Xianqing ouji*), are central to the emergence of the feather's role as an emblem of authorship.[46] In 1763, Ōeda Ryūhō published a seven-volume compendium on the scholarly life, *A Miscellany of Elegant Pastimes* (*Gayū manroku*), which drew liberally from contemporary Chinese sources including the section on scholarly goods from Li Yu's *Casual Expressions*.[47] The opening section of Ryūhō's book begins with a quotation from the Ming literatus Wu Congxian's *Personal Jottings from My Little Window* (*Xiao chuang qing ji*), and in the book's opening pages, we find two images of studies, the second of which focuses on the

---

[45] See Jonathan Hay, *Sensuous Surfaces: The Decorative Object in Early Modern China* (Honolulu: University of Hawai'i Press, 2010), pp. 8ff. For an example of a scholar at his desk with a decorative peacock feather, see the illustration from *Lu Ban jing* (c. 1600), Hay, *Sensuous Surfaces*, p. 101.

[46] On the reception of *Xianqing ouji* in eighteenth-century Japan, see Yoshida Eri, "Nihon 'bunjinga' kenkyū nōto: Edo chūki no Ri Gyo (Ri Ryūō) no imēji ni kan suru kōsatsu," *Gakushūin Daigaku jinbunkagaku ronshū* 8 (September 1999), 37–41.

[47] Ōeda Ryūhō, *Gayū manroku* (Osaka: Shibukawa Seiemon, 1763), 8r.

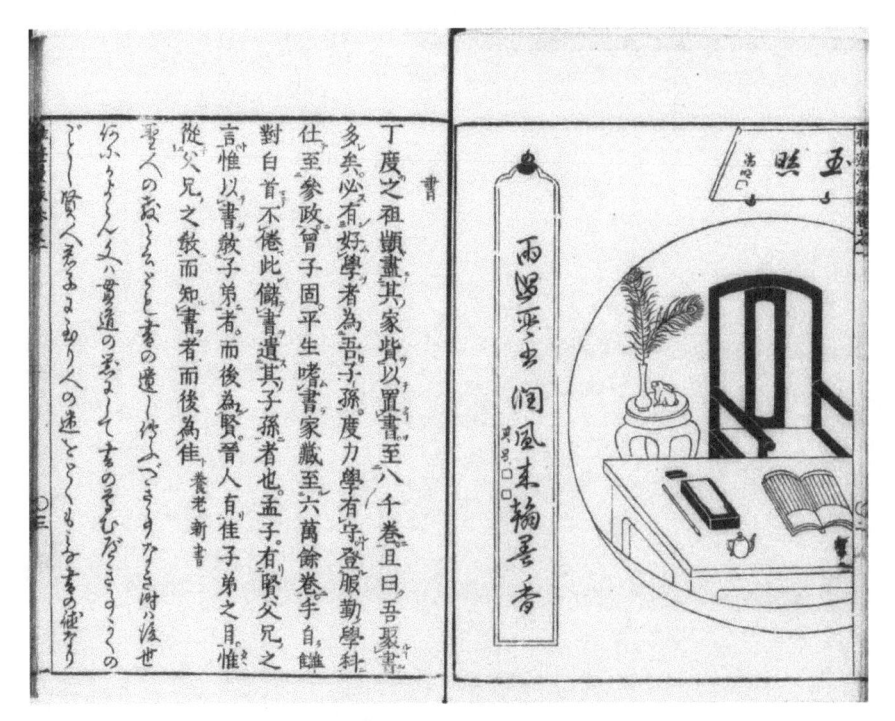

**Figure 4.5** Ōeda Ryūhō, a scholar's writing desk, *Gayū manroku*, 1763.
*Source*: C.V. Starr East Asian Library, University of California, Berkeley.

scholar's writing desk, which holds a composition book, a brush, ink stone, and a dropper for water. Next to the chair is a vase with peacock feathers (Figure 4.5).

More proximate still for Bakin and his circle, the section of Li Yu's own *Casual Expressions* on the accouterments of the scholarly life also became the subject of one of the volumes of *A Thicket of Ancient and Modern Paintings* (*Kokon gasō*) by the Nagasaki painter Sō Shiseki, whose work on Chinese figures was so crucial to *Strange Tales from China*.[48] Sō Shiseki had studied Chinese painting in Nagasaki with Song Ziyan (J. Sō Shigan), who had emigrated to Japan from Zhezhiang Province, where Li Yu had spent a crucial period of his life in the 1650s. After returning to Edo, Sō Shiseki would become one of the best-known painters of the late eighteenth century and would collaborate with Hiraga Gennai. In turn, Gennai would introduce Sō to Shiba Kōkan, who became the painter's most famous pupil. In *A Thicket of Ancient and Modern Paintings*, among the various illustrations of the "pleasurable things" that mark the scholar's study is an image of a table with a vase containing peacock feathers, a folding fan, and a tobacco pipe (Figure 4.6).[49] It is unclear why—among the various "pleasurable things" that we

---

[48] See Chapter 3.
[49] Sō Shiseki, *Kokon gasō*, vol. 6 (Edo: Suharaya Sōbē, 1771), 8v.

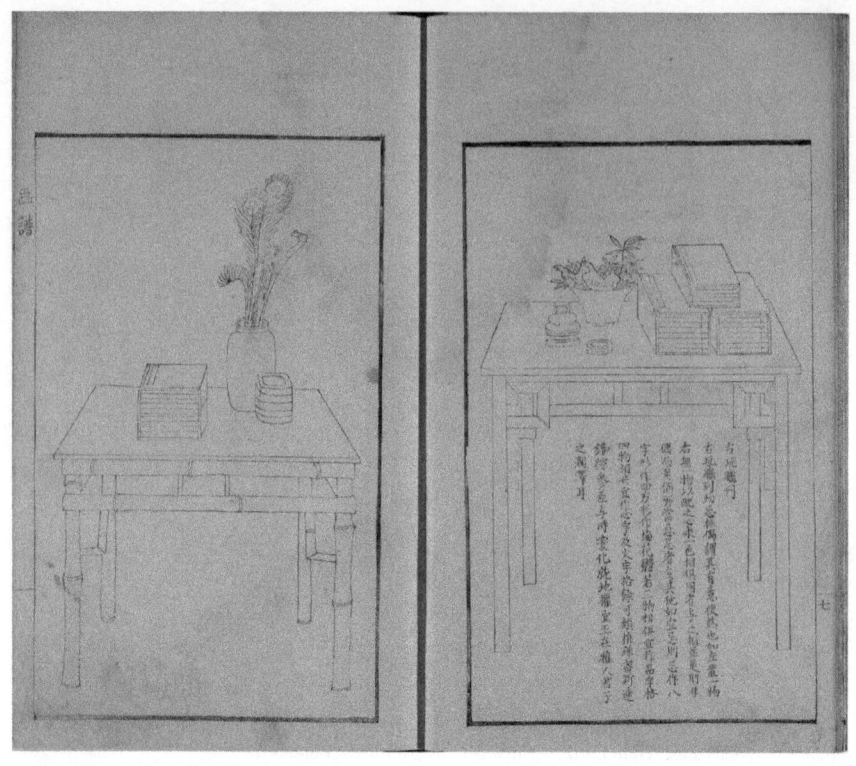

**Figure 4.6** Sō Shiseki, table with vase containing peacock feathers, a folding fan, and a tobacco pipe, *Kokon gasō*, 1770.
Source: Ebi Collection, Art Research Center, Ritsumeikan University.

find in these eighteenth-century images, or in the texts from which they come—it was the peacock feather that came to signify the writerly life, but the bird with its magnificent plumage was a frequent subject of Japanese painters in the eighteenth and early nineteenth centuries, appearing prominently in the work of Itō Jakuchū, Maruyama Ōkyo, and Tani Bunchō.

In the illustration of the interior of Bakin's home from *A Puff of Kyokutei's Pipe in the Style of Kyōden*, the peacock feather as a marker of literary distinction is unobtrusive but seems to inscribe a difference in the habitus of the two writers: one domestic and writerly, gesturing to the refinement of the continental literatus; the other public and commercial, the site of exchange and transaction. To be sure, the two spaces are linked by the figure of Kyōden, who has, after all, come to ask Bakin's help in selling his wares, but even here the commercial nature of the transaction is subsumed under the non-commercial sociability of friendship and obligation.[50]

---

[50] Mizuno Minoru has pointed out that Bakin owed a debt to of gratitude to Kyōden and his brother Kyōzan, who had been of assistance on the anniversary of Bakin's brother's death: Mizuno Minoru *Santō Kyōden nenpukō* (Tokyo: Perikansha, 1991), p. 63 quoted in Satō, *Santō Kyōden*, p. 136.

Much has been written of Bakin's own anxieties over class and status: he was born into a minor samurai family and raised in the home of the Tokugawa bannerman Matsudaira Nobunari; after losing his status as a samurai, Bakin spent the later years of his life selling off his library in an attempt to purchase the status back for his own son, Sōhaku, who tragically died in 1835, a decade before his father. Bakin would write extensively of his family's history and his own frustrations in "A Record of those Dear to Me" ("Aga hotoke no ki"), but one need not become overly invested in biography to see that, beginning *circa* 1800, Bakin envisioned for himself an authorial persona different from Kyōden's and that this self-fashioning is part of what allowed him to navigate the changing literary market of the early nineteenth century in a way that Kyōden could not.[51] If *A Puff of Kyokutei's Pipe in the Style of Kyōden* has often been read as a tableau of the apotheosis of the interdependence of art and commerce at the turn of the nineteenth century, it can also be read as a document of a changing conception of that relationship and of the writer's place within it—a changing conception of authorial identity.

More broadly, the repeated appearance of figurations of the author within the fiction of the late eighteenth century can be read as part of a larger set of reflections that define writing as a pursuit at precisely the moment when authorship as a professional category was emerging in Japan. The images from the opening pages of *A Puff of Kyokutei's Pipe in the Style of Kyōden* seem to offer two visions of the writerly life at this transitional moment: Bakin as professional author, who made his living with his brush, and Kyōden as cultural entrepreneur who cleverly, but also shamelessly, entwined his writing with his other commercial pursuits.

Among fiction writers of the early nineteenth century, Utei Enba was unusual for trying his hand at playwriting. Neither Bakin nor Kyōden, despite the long and abiding interest each had in kabuki, and their liberal use of theatrical themes and images in their fiction, wrote for the stage. *The Flowered Clasp*, Bakin's mock *chuanqi* play that draws on Li Yu's *The Jade Clasp*, was as close as either would come to writing a play of any sort. But if the professional worlds of playwright and novelist remained almost entirely separate across the nineteenth century, the ways in which authorship was understood (i.e. how writers and writing were imagined by writers themselves and by the wider public) shared a in commonality, partaking in the same language and visual tropes. Indeed, the discussion of dramatic authorship in the 1801 "Valuable Notes on Playwrighting," the most important and extensive consideration of the work of the playwright, is framed in relation to a longer history of fiction writing going back to the Heian period (794–1185); it begins with an enumeration of the authors of works ranging from the *The Tale of the Hollow Tree*, *The Tale of the Bamboo Cutter*, and *The Tale of Genji* to the *The Tale of Heikei*, *The Record of the Great Peace*, and *The Record of the Rise and*

---

[51] Ōtaka Yōji, "Jūkyū seiki teki sakusha non tanjō," pp. 78–79.

*Fall of the Genji and Heike*.[52] The construction of authorial identity backstage was always articulated in dialogue with authorship as practiced and imagined in the world of commercial publishing. The nature of dramatic authorship during this period is thus best understood in relation to discourses surrounding authorship more broadly. For playwrights in the nineteenth century, the idea, even ideal, of the autonomous writer sitting at his desk would remain a powerful draw in a world defined by collaboration and compromise, not only partnership with other writers but also negotiation with theater managers and actors. In a stark contrast to the reality of compromise and collaboration, the solitary figure at a desk, marked by a vase of peacock feathers, would become one of the defining images of the playwright in nineteenth-century Japan.

## III Battlefield of the Mind: Playwriting in Early Modern Japan

Although not so well known as the 1738 image of Chikamatsu at his writing desk from *A Souvenir of Naniwa*, a second rendering of the playwright at his desk survives from the early nineteenth century (Figure 4.7). Like many other items related to the playwright's life and career, the painting was shown at the 1922 exhibit and a photo reproduction appears in the catalogue of materials published at the time. The undated image is contained in a forty-two-volume scrapbook of theater ephemera compiled by the playwright and illustrator Hamamatsu Utakuni for the collector Yoshino Goun in the early nineteenth century.[53] Here is the playwright at his desk with his back towards the viewer, seemingly absorbed in the act of reading or writing. To his right are an ink stone, a collection of writing brushes, and a vase with peacock feathers. Before him is a circular window that appears to look out onto a scenic view. The image is undated, but it is likely from the early nineteenth century and suggests something of how Chikamatsu's image had been transformed in the decades after the iconic image of him appeared in *A Souvenir of Naniwa* in 1738. Still alone and at his desk, he is now firmly ensconced in an interior, accompanied by the "pleasurable things" that marked the writerly life of Late Imperial China and, increasingly, of Japan.

Although the source of this image is unknown, it seems likely that one of its points of reference is an illustration labeled simply "Playwright" (*kyōgen sakusha*) appearing in *An Illustrated Guide to the Dressing Room: A Supplement*, the 1800 book that reproduces the courtesan painting with Chikamatsu's handwritten note.

---

[52] Katherine Salzman-Li, *Creating Kabuki Plays: Context for Kezairoku, "Valuable Notes on Playwriting"* (Leiden: Brill, 2010), pp. 173–76.

[53] The albums, known as the "Kyota kyakushokuchō," are housed at the Tsubouchi Memorial Theater Museum and were digitalized in 2018. For a database of images, see https://archive.waseda.jp/archive/subDB-top.html?arg={%22item_per_page%22:20,%22sortby%22:[%22%22,%22ASC%22], %22view%22:%22display-simple%22,%22subDB_id%22:%2291%22}&lang=jp.

**Figure 4.7** Chikamatsu Monzaemon at his writing desk, n.d.
*Source*: Tsubouchi Memorial Theatre Museum, Waseda University.

The image of the playwright in this volume appears just after the description of Chikamatsu and Namiki Shōzō and just before the reproduction of the image of the courtesan and Chikamatsu's inscription from the scroll owned by Kumanoya Hikokurō. In this image, the figuration of the author is intended to be generic rather than a portrait of Chikamatsu himself: here, a playwright sits alone at his writing desk, seemingly deep in contemplation. He is accompanied by the material objects that mark the writing life (brushes and ink stone, and a vase with peacock feathers), and he is positioned in a suggestive way with a sliding door open on the world outside (Figure 4.8).

If the image points, subtly, to the "pleasurable things" of Late Imperial China, it also points to a tradition of authorship within Japan. Indeed, iconographically, the image resembles contemporary depictions of the author of the *Tale of Genji*, Murasaki Shikibu. There is an important lineage of images depicting Murasaki at the Ishiyama Temple—sitting at her desk and gazing out into an exterior—that goes back to the work of painters like Tosa Mitsumoto in the sixteenth century and Tosa Mitsuoki in the seventeenth century.[54] As Satoko Naitō has shown, in the seventeenth and especially eighteenth centuries, this image would circulate

---

[54] See Melissa McCormick, "'Murasaki shikibu ishiyamadera mōde zufuku' ni okeru shomondai: Wa to Kan no sakai ni aru Murasaki zō," trans. Ido Misato, *Kobba* 1434 (April 2015), 5–23.

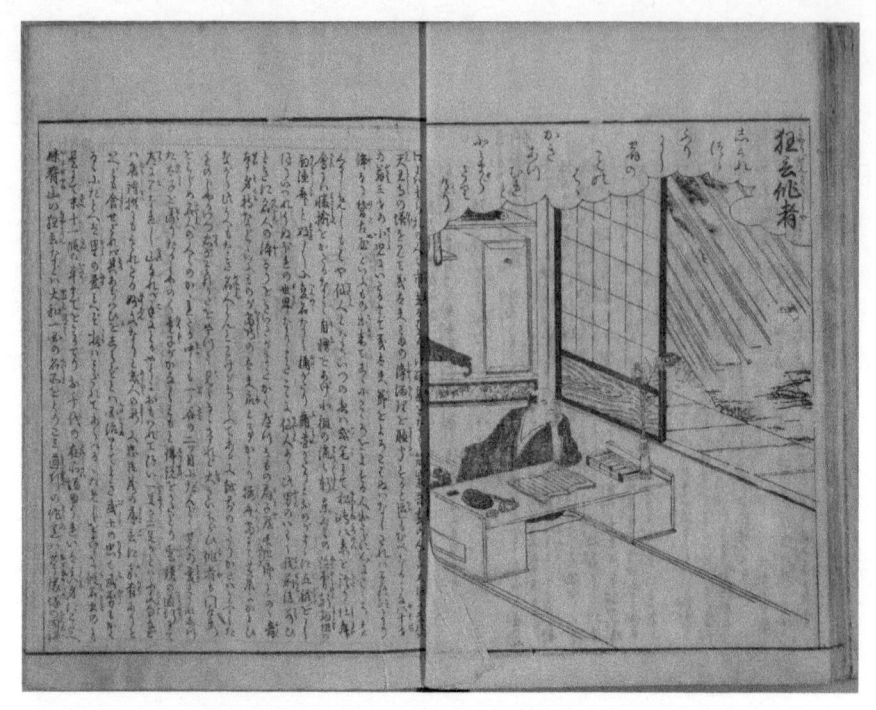

**Figure 4.8** Shōkōsai Hanbē, the playwright from *Shibai gakuya zue shūi*, 1800.
*Source*: National Diet Library, Tokyo.

more broadly in illustrated books and single-sheet prints like Suzuki Harunobu's 1767 print from the series *The Five Virtues* (*Gojō*).[55]

In addition to this iconographic connection to the Heian Court, the image of the playwright also includes, running along the top, a poem in *waka* form that calls to mind the court literature of the distant past. The poem reads:

> Shigure tsutsu
> Furinishi yado no
> Kotonoha ha
> Kakiatsumuredo
> Tomarazarikeri.

Although this *waka* is not marked or attributed in *An Illustrated Guide to the Dressing Room: A Supplement*, "Shigure tsutsu" originally appears in the eleventh-century imperial anthology *A Collection of Gleanings* (*Shūi wakashū*), where it is

---

[55] Satoko Naito, "Beyond the *Tale of Genji*: Murasaki Shikibu as Icon and Exemplum in Seventeenth- and Eighteenth-Century Popular Japanese Texts for Women," *Early Modern Women: An Interdisciplinary Journal* 9, 1 (Autumn 2014), 47–78.

attributed to Nakatsukasa, the daughter of Lady Ise. As Joshua Mostow has noted in his study of Heian court diaries, the original context for the poem in the anthology is Nakatsukasa compiling her mother's verse for *The Collected Poems of Lady Ise* (*Iseshū*). Mostow thus renders the poem into English:

> While I cried with the rains,
> I wrote down all her words,
> Like raking together the leaves
> Of the old house
> And yet there is no stopping.[56]

The proximate source for *An Illustrated Guide to the Dressing Room: A Supplement* is likely an edition of *A Collection of Gleanings* published in Kyoto in 1799, but this poem was neither especially well known nor widely reproduced in the Edo period. While there is a long tradition in Japanese poetics of allusive intertextuality, it seems difficult to imagine that the reader of *An Illustrated Guide to the Dressing Room* was intended to recover the specific allusion to the original context of the poem. Rather, stripped of context, the poem is freed of specific referent and can be read as an almost ahistorical commentary on the work of an author: the endless task of raking together the leaves of words and of the imagination that lay scattered about. But how are we to interpret this image as a product specific to the late-eighteenth- and early-nineteenth-century imagination? The author has been transformed from woman to man, from poet to playwright, no longer a figure of imperial court but of the commercial world of the theater. Like the image of Chikamatsu from the 1738 *A Souvenir of Naniwa*, the playwright is alone, at his desk; but here, he is more clearly situated in an interior, marked by the iconography of the writerly life, seemingly lost in thought in the process of composition. As with other images of authorship, there is an opening onto the world outside the writerly space, which seems to point to the liminal position of the playwright: one who looks (to recall the passage from the preface to Li Yu's *The Jade Clasp* that Bakin quotes) at the world around him and transforms that world into a passion play of good and evil. The theater makes a world in miniature, and the world beyond the sliding door can be understood simply as the stage writ large. As we have seen in Chapter 3, this is a common trope in the late eighteenth century and linked to Chinese drama as it was imagined in Edo Japan.

It thus becomes possible to read this image almost as a palimpsest with various iconographic strata layered atop one another, transforming the playwright imaged in the simple and rough image of Chikamatsu from *A Souvenir of Naniwa* (Figure 4.1) into a figure of some refinement and status, marked with the objects

---

[56] Joshua S. Mostow, *At the House of Gathered Leaves: Shorter Biographical and Autobiographical Narratives from Japanese Court Literature* (Honolulu: University of Hawai'i Press, 2004), p. 26.

of the Chinese literatus, overlain onto an image of the Heian poet. As Katherine Saltzman-Li has argued, one of the defining aspects of the self-fashioning of kabuki playwrights at the turn of the nineteenth century was a preoccupation with questions of legitimacy and lineage.[57] An image such as this can be read as an expression of that anxiety: the playwright situated at the convergence of a long tradition of Japanese writing stretching back the better part of a millennium and a contemporary interest in the late Ming and early Qing dynasties as a site of worldly writerly aspiration.

Saltzman-Li is here writing about the "Valuable Notes on Playwriting," the 1801 manuscript offering a "methodology for playwrights," and this text bears a close relationship with both Bakin's *Tales Told by Rain* and with *An Illustrated Guide to the Dressing Room: A Supplement*, which was composed a year after "Valuable Notes on Playwriting." As Saltzman-Li has pointed out, one of the most important passages from the "Valuable Notes on Playwriting" is addressed to the playwright at his desk:

> As a rule, when at your desk, think of the world as your own, proceed as though no enemy confronts you and handle the actors as if they belonged to you. If you do not act in this way, you will recoil from your brush, hesitation alone will assail you, and you will be unable to move the audience [...] Generally, think of your choice of theme as a tactical decision and the brush as the baton that leads the soldiers. As you confront your enemy—the audience—use that which is currently popular to crush their spirit, and the victory song of critical acclaim will be heard. Even if the brave and talented warrior-actors are talented, if the tactician-playwright's play has not been well prepared for battle, it will be difficult to achieve an outstanding victory.[58]

The author is at a desk but is no longer truly isolated or alone; rather, he sits conjuring a battlefield in his mind. It is tempting to transpose this passage onto the image from *An Illustrated Guide to the Dressing Room: A Supplement*: now the seemingly placid figure of the solitary author raking together the leaves of his imagination is engaged by tactical preparations for a pitched battle, adding yet another layer of depth to this image.

This passage from the "Valuable Notes on Playwriting" in turn reflects back on an earlier passage in that text in which the idea of the playwright as military tactician is first deployed:

> The theater is our castle, the financial backer and the manager are the generals, the actors are the brave soldiers, and the playwrights are the strategists. If the

---

[57] Salzman-Li, *Creating Kabuki Plays*, pp. 75–87.
[58] Salzman-Li, *Creating Kabuki Plays*, p. 77.

strategist does not have authority, the soldiers do not follow orders, and then the preparations for the various battle arrays that we call the play become disordered. Because of this, the enemy—the audience—is unbeatable, and in the end, sadly, we will be as the rank and file, mere fillers for the ditches.[59]

The seemingly tenuous position of the author might well catch our attention. Gone entirely is the conceit of a solitary figure sitting alone at his desk: now, the playwright is enmeshed in a field at once artistic and commercial, caught in various ways between the financial backer and manager, the actor and the audience. It is this image of the playwright as quintessentially *situated*—compromising and compromised—that would come to dominate the ways in which dramatic authorship was figured over the course of the nineteenth century.

These passages are exactly contemporary with the image of the playwright from *An Illustrated Guide to the Dressing Room: A Supplement*, and they suggest how, by 1800, the idea of a solitary author composing alone at his desk, raking together the leaves of his imagination, was already a nostalgic fiction that bore little resemblance to contemporary practice. Indeed, there is a particular poignancy to this image. Furuido Hideo has argued that it was just at the turn of the eighteenth into the nineteenth century that the playwright lost autonomous identity and became but another employee of the theater whose job it was to oversee and manage not only the writing but also the production of the play.[60] At one level, we can see the image in Figure 4.8 in an almost sociological sense, representing a moment of authorship prior to "the fall," as it were, when the author was more a man of letters than an entrepreneur and still outside of the world of the physical theater.

But we might also see the figure differently, as representing an imagined ideal, writing freed of the demands of the market, an image that was always already a fiction or at best a vanishing point. "Valuable Notes on Playwriting," was not the first text to imagine the playwright as military tactician, and the genealogy of that metaphor suggests something of how already, half-a-century earlier, the work of the playwright was understood as hopelessly compromised, damaged beyond repair.

Indeed, the idea of the playwright as tactician marshaling his troops appears in one of the most important eighteenth-century works on the theater, Tada Nanrei's 1750 *A Complete Book of Actors Past and Present* (*Kokon yakusha taizen*) in a section on the playwright (*kyōgen sakusha no koto*):

Authors of a previous era had great authority. They would knit together a three act play entirely in their own minds and while they would privately speak with the manager they would not consult with others. When they assigned roles, no

[59] Salzman-Li, *Creating Kabuki Plays*, p. 75.
[60] Furuido Hideo, "Fukumori Kyūsuke to sono jidai," in Furuido Hideo ed. *Fukumori Kyūsuke kyakuhonshū*, Sōsho Edo bunko vol. 49 (Tokyo: Kokusho Kankōkai, 2001), pp. 54–55.

one would proffer objection. Because the orders of the manager were treated with the obedience and deference shown to a lord and the words of the author as the directions of a military tactician, the play was from top down well constructed and everything from the banner adorning the turret of the theater to the drums are all connected by the plot so that the audience can follow without difficulty and can talk of the play when they return home. In the not too distant past, the author's authority waned and he began holding consultations with everyone, meeting frequently and discussing all manner of things including points of interest from older plays and from there ideas would emerge. He would write while consulting privately with four or five others including the leading actor, the player of villain roles, and the onnagata and began the practice of hon-yomi in which the entire troop was called together and they were read the script and while some would voice their desires it was never the case that the overall play would be affected or ruined. But recently, the leading actor, the villain, and even the onnagata toss around old plays saying, "I want to do this" and "I want to do that"; demand pours in from all directions for the fashioning of the play. Even when the author tries putting it all together and parries by saying "no, no that will not do," because they trifle with the author, he is left to cobble together ideas that did not come from his own bosom and because he must parry their ideas and refashion them the root of the play is splintered and because it has had to be stitched together two or three times the plot does not hang together.[61]

The year is 1750, but already the author has fallen from grace: having lost his authority, his craft lies in ruins. Not satisfied to return to Chikamatsu, at the end of the disquisition on authorship in *A Complete Book of Actors Past and Present*, Nanrei suggests that Murasaki Shikibu herself was the founder of playwriting (*kyōgen sakusha no ganso*), as if one needed to go back to the better part of a millennium to find a figure who might escape the compromised nature of eighteenth-century authorship.[62]

There is something evocative here of the image of the escalator that Raymond Williams uses in his *The Country and the City* to suggest how the horizon of "the fall" seems endlessly to recede, each historical period looking back further to find a moment of perceived wholeness.[63] Even as playwriting became, over the course of the nineteenth century, increasingly a kind of "construction site" (to borrow Nakamura Tetsurō's image), there arose a different vision of playwriting anchored in an ideal of the past, which imagined the author as a noble figure whose work literally linked him to the Heian Court.

---

[61] Tada Nanrei, *Kokon yakusha taizen*, Kabuki Sōsho, vol. 1 (Tokyo: Kinkōdō, 1910), p. 11.
[62] Tada Nanrei, *Kokon yakusha taizen*, p. 12.
[63] Raymond Williams, *The Country and the City* (Oxford: Oxford University Press, 1975), pp. 7ff.

This nostalgic vision, we might imagine, not only cohabited with an understanding of the degraded nature of the author in the mid-nineteenth century but was also, in some sense, its byproduct, as idyllic visions of the past so often are. From this perspective, it is telling that, in nineteenth-century images, the playwright largely ceases to be imagined as a solitary figure, alone at a desk; rather, the most iconic representations of the playwright are of a figure ensconced in the milieu of the actor, backstage. Emblematic of this shift are works like Utagawa Kunisada's 1811 print of the dressing room of the Ichimura-za in which the playwright Narita Yasuke is shown sitting before the great actor, Matsumoto Kōshirō V (Figure 4.9). The author's habitus is reimagined: no longer sitting in a study marked by the "pleasurable things" of the Chinese literatus, the author is now firmly ensconced in the space of the actor. Rather than seated before a window that provides a view of the wider world, the source from which he would draw his inspiration, he is a creature of the interior of the dressing room. The author is no longer alone, lost in contemplation, but a figure of negotiation and compromise, almost emblematically faceless, enclosed by a semi-circle of actors, all of whom face the viewer: Matsumoto Kōshirō V, one of the greatest stars of the age; Bandō Mitsugorō III; and the onnagata Nakayama Tomisaburō I.

When historians in the late nineteenth and early twentieth centuries began to write the history of Japanese drama, it is easy to see why they would recoil from this faceless figure, compromising and compromised, and instead foreground a different vision of dramatic authorship which coalesced around an idea of solitary genius, embodied by Chikamatsu who, alone at his writing desk, composed "those marvelously exquisite passages [. . .] that made millions both past and present feel happiness or anger, laughter or sadness," to recall the *Curio Magazine*. But if the leading playwrights of the day had turned into faceless creatures, starker still was the fate of the minor figures who populated the writers' stable and who worked at the behest of the head writer: the secondary and tertiary writers, many of whose names we now know only through their inclusion on playbills but about whom we know next to nothing. The most systematic attempt to create a "register" of playwrights in the nineteenth century, Mimasuya Nisōji's 1844 manuscript "A Register of Authors" ("Sakusha myōmoku"), records eighty-seven names and notes that "although what we call author (sakusha) is limited to lead authors (tate-sakusha), I shall record as authors the secondary (nimaime) and tertiary writers (sanmaime)."[64] And while entries for the major playwrights of the eighteenth and nineteenth centuries—Sakurada Jisuke, Fukumori Kyūsuke, Namiki Gohei, and Tsuruya Nanboku, for example—give some detail about life and career, for many of the other figures only the barest information is present.

---

[64] Mimasuya Nisōji, "Sakusha myōmoku," in Engei Chinsho Kankōkai ed. *Engeki bunko*, vol. 5 (Tokyo: Engei Chinsho Kankōkai, 1915), p. 2.

**Figure 4.9** Utagawa Kunisada, the dressing room of the Ichimura-za, 1811.
*Source*: National Diet Library, Tokyo.

This manuscript would be bequeathed to Kawatake Mokuami, one of the last great playwrights of the Edo period, who would live through the Meiji Restoration and who would befriend Tsubouchi Shōyō. Like Nisōji, Mokuami, too, left behind an important manuscript on the work of the playwright; from the writing of these two men, we have a detailed account of the practices of nineteenth-century playwriting, including its collaborative, even corporate nature:

> The head playwright consults with the manager and theater owner and decides on the historical setting (*sekai*) of the play; he then creates the plot and explains it to the theater owner. He outlines the plot scene by scene and gives the second and third playwrights those scenes at which they excel in order to compose the whole play. When the draft is done, there is a communal reading and if the same lines have been used more than once, one or the other is cut and revisions made. Then a clean copy is made and that becomes the script.[65]

Mokuami goes into extensive detail over seven manuscript pages to explain the minutiae of the collaborative process including the role that each of the authors played and even how payment was divided.

For modern historians of kabuki, the nature of authorship as a collaborative enterprise has been one of the more vexing subjects for writing a history that treated drama as a literary art. After all, if the history of drama *as literature* is primarily about the plays themselves, as it was for Shōyō and his students and as it would remain for most of the twentieth century, then not really knowing who wrote what creates an enormous dilemma, an almost insoluble problem. If one could talk about the "nature and genius" (to borrow Shōyō's terms) of Shakespeare based on the belief that his plays were his own, how could one talk about the genius of Namiki Gohei, or Sakurada Jisuke, or Tsuruya Nanboku, or Mokuami himself if one was never sure which passages they wrote?[66]

In a pair of essays from 1928, Okamoto Kidō brought out the implications of this problem. Though best remembered for the long-running series of detective stories set in the late Edo period that he wrote from the 1910s through the 1930s, Kidō was himself a playwright of some stature, and his 1911 play *The Tale of Shūzenji* (*Shuzenji monogatari*) is one of the best-known modern kabuki plays. But Kidō was also an amateur historian and wrote at some length about the history of kabuki in the nineteenth century.

---

[65] Hattori Yukio, "Honkoku: 'Kyōgen sakusha kokoroesho,'" *Nagoya Daigaku kokugo kokubungaku* 27 (December 1970), 92.

[66] This understanding of Shakespeare as a solitary genius was, of course, itself ahistorical and, as much recent scholarship has noted, Elizabethan drama, too, needs to be understood within the context of collaboration and corporate authorship. See, e.g. Jeffrey Masten, *Textual Intercourse: Collaboration, Authorship, and Sexualities in Renaissance Drama* Cambridge: Cambridge University Press, 1997) and Brian Vickers, *Shakespeare, Co-author: A Historical Study of Five Collaborative Plays* (Oxford: Oxford University Press, 2002).

In the articles that he wrote in 1928 for the journal *Kabuki Research* (*Kabuki kenkyū*) on the drama of the Bunka and Bunsei periods (1804–1830), Kidō would bring to bear on the problem of authorship something of the forensic imagination that underlay his detective fiction. Central to Kidō's essays was the question of why, during the first decades of the nineteenth century "the world of the play was surpassed by the world of fiction."[67] As Kidō notes, with the exception of Tsuruya Nanboku IV, the dramatists of this age have been largely forgotten; the period is best remembered for the incredible output of a group of fiction writers: Santō Kyōden and Kyokutei Bakin chief among them, but also Shikitei Sanba, Jippensha Ikku, Ryūtei Tanehiko, and Tamenaga Shunsui.

In the second installment of the essay, Kidō makes a striking claim about the effect that the corporate nature of dramatic authorship has had on historiography:

> Had [Kyokutei] Bakin and [Ryūtei] Tanehiko been writers attached to the same theater, Tanehiko's work might have been subsumed under that of Bakin. Or had [Shikitei] Sanba and [Jippensha] Ikku been writers attached to the same theater, Ikku's work might have been subsumed under that of Sanba. When one thinks of this, novelists who each worked independently were fortunate. And playwrights who were imprisoned in a system of corporate authorship were unfortunate.[68]

And Kidō further develops the implications of this line of argument:

> In the scripts of kabuki plays of the past, there was a certain rigid formalism and no matter who was writing it would be fit into the same form but if one examines the details it seems not impossible that one might discover the compositional style and individuality of the hand of each author. But at any rate this would be extremely painstaking work such that no one would undertake it lightly. It is possible that many more scholars like Tomikura [Jirō] will emerge in the future and better account for the abilities of writers like Matsui Kōzō who wielded influence in the shadows.[69]

Here is an interest in the traces of the author's hand, not unlike that shown by Bakin in his journey to Osaka in 1802, but now the interest is filtered through the forensic rather than the antiquarian imagination. By the 1920s, the study of handwriting had become an important element in criminal psychology; it is not hard to imagine how a writer preoccupied with clues and detection would come to imagine the role that an attention to seemingly insignificant details could play in the work of the historian.[70] Indeed, as I shall explore in Chapter 5, a similar impulse

---

[67] Okamoto Kidō, "Kasei jidai no gikyoku," *Kabuki kenkyū*, June 1928, 1.
[68] Okamoto Kidō, "Kaseigeki mandan," *Kabuki kenkyū*, July 1928
[69] Okamoto Kidō, "Kaseigeki mandan."
[70] See Terada Seiichi, *Kagaku to hanzai* (Tokyo: Bunmei shoin, 1918).

was at work among art historians for authenticating works of art. But Kidō's stance is so striking because he means not to authenticate the work of the "genius" (in the sense that Shōyō conceived of authorship) but to recover the work of the minor author, the figure in the shadows, to give credit where credit was due.

In large part, Kidō's vision has gone unrealized and while the advent of big data has made it possible to imagine algorithms that would untangle the hand or style of one author from that of another (the case of Christopher Marlowe being credited as Shakespeare's co-author for *Henry IV* Parts I, II, and III is the most well-known example), the past century has yielded little by way of concrete research on the stylistics of nineteenth-century playwriting in Japan, and we know very little more about the work of minor playwrights in the Edo period than we did a century ago.[71] In part, this is due to the inherent difficulty of what Kidō proposed, a difficulty of which he himself was aware; but in part, the as yet unreclaimed status of the minor author has been dictated by the way that authorship has itself been imagined over the past century and by the impulse to foreground the work of the leading authors in an attempt to claim and reclaim singular literary value for their work.

In this respect, Shōyō's own conception of authorship, and his own preoccupation with drama as a form of literature, is central to the ways that research on dramatic authorship came to be framed in the modern period. In 1902, a quarter of a century before Kidō would imagine a forensic approach to the writer's hand, Tsubouchi Shōyō had been called to give testimony as an expert witness at a trial held in the Tokyo District Court of two men accused of violating the 1887 Kyakuhon Gakufu Jōrei, which extended an idea of intellectual property to dramatic works for the first time. In that trial, Shōyō's vision of authorship would move from an abstract interest in literary history that he had begun to fashion in the 1890s to one that was institutionalized as part of a legal proceeding.

## IV Authorship on Trial

In June 1902, Shōyō was summoned to give ten days of testimony as an expert witness at the trial of two men, Minegishi Denjirō and Kashiwara Isaburō, who were being sued for infringement of the 1887 copyright statute. The suit was brought by Yoshimura Ito, the daughter of Kawatake Mokuami, who had died in 1893, and at its center was the staging of the play *Aoto Fujitsuna, Told in Colored Prints* (*Aoto zōshi hana no nishiki-e*), commonly known as *Benten the Thief* (*Benten kozō*).

---

[71] The only serious attempt to carry out a handwriting analysis of kabuki scripts of which I am aware is the chapter on handwriting in Kawatake Shigetoshi's 1940 *Kabuki Sakusha no kenkyū* (Tokyo: Tōkyōdō, 1940), pp. 276–313. On Shakespeare and Marlowe, see Christopher Shea, "New Oxford Shakespeare Edition Credits Christopher Marlowe as a Co-author," *New York Times*, October 24, 2016, p.3. For an extended analysis of Marlowe's stylistics (and a critique of the New Oxford Shakespeare attribution), see Hartmut Ilsemann, "Christopher Marlowe: Hype and Hoax," *Digital Scholarship in the Humanities* 33, 4 (2018), 788–820.

Mokuami had himself lived through the transformations to the theater world that followed the Meiji Restoration of 1868, and Shōyō's testimony in the case attracted a great deal of attention at a time when the practices that governed the early modern theater were cohabiting uneasily with modern notions of copyright and intellectual property. The *Yomiuri* newspaper ran a three-part article with excerpts of Shōyō's testimony,[72] and the magazine *Kabuki* printed the testimony in full. In explaining their decision to print the full testimony, the editors of *Kabuki* wrote, "As it is a new example without precedent, we believe [the testimony] will become material for theatrical history in the future."[73]

And yet, despite this seemingly prescient note, Shōyō's testimony has not really become a source for theatrical history; it has, instead, been relegated to the status of an anecdote in biographies of Mokuami. The implications of the lawsuit and of Shōyō's participation in it for understanding conceptions of authorship, of intellectual property, and of the status of a text straddling the pre- and post-Meiji divide have gone largely unremarked—perhaps, in part, because some of the most interesting questions surrounding these issues went unasked during the course of the trial and subsequent appeal, and perhaps, too, because they complicate the neat divisions inscribed in the trial (and largely unquestioned since) about the character of authorship and the nature of originality in nineteenth-century kabuki.

The trial, however, stages in a particularly clear way the intersection of drama and print at a moment when many of the modern assumptions surrounding the nature of the theater emerged and attained the force not just of custom but of law. That these assumptions would then guide subsequent scholars in their approach to the theatrical history of this period has made it difficult to see the trial for what it was: an important moment in which a modern understanding of authorship was given particularly forceful voice and applied to a text which had been written at a time when very different legal, institutional, and intellectual conceptions of authorship prevailed. The trial served at once to allow the articulation of this new notion of authorship but also to normalize it, to make it appear natural, as if it had, in some sense, always already been there simply waiting to be recognized. And indeed, since Shōyō would himself go on to be the single most important figure in crafting the historiography of drama in Japan, it is little wonder that his conception of the nature of dramatic authorship would play a critical role in the way in which this subject has been understood for over a century.

The Fukagawa-za, the theater that staged the play which prompted legal action by Mokuami's daughter, had opened in 1897 in the Fukagawa district on the grounds of an earlier theater, the Shinsei-za, and operated in a modern building with a Western façade, seemingly modeled on the Shintomi-za, the first Japanese theater to adopt this architecture. On October 19, 1901, the Fukagawa-za began

---

[72] "Tsubouchi Hakase kanteisho," *Yomiuri shinbun*, August 14–16, 1902.
[73] Tsubouchi Yūzō [Shōyō], "Kyakuhon kanteisho," *Kabuki* 28 (September 1902), 15.

a new program featuring two plays. The main draw was the second half of a very well-known play written by Kawatake Mokuami and first staged in 1862, though both the authorship and the provenance of the play were matters of some dispute in the trial that ensued, and they were two of the issues which Shōyō was called upon to adjudicate.

The years around 1900 marked a time of transition for the kabuki theater, a historical moment during which the institutional, economic, and legal frameworks that defined the theater were changing, and the incidents leading to and constituting the trial can be seen as phenomena occasioned by and, as themselves, part of a series of events that shaped this history. This is the period in which kabuki finally—for the first and only time—achieved a level of real accessibility that would allow us to refer to it as something like a form of popular theater.[74] This critical moment is marked at one end by the abolition of the monopoly system that governed the theater during the early modern period, an abolition that permitted new theaters like the Fukugawa-za to emerge in spaces around the city. Theaters and troupes appeared in rapid succession, shaking to its foundations the economic system that had governed theater for over two-and-a-half centuries.[75] As Ihara Toshirō wrote in 1898, the result was economic chaos and a kind of death spiral with bidding wars over stars, with theaters in Osaka offering 50,000 or 60,000 yen to a single actor for a tour and theater managers acting like sumo wrestlers in loin clothes grappling over backers.[76] "They are obsessed with profit," wrote Ihara, "but think only of the short-term with no far sighted calculations at all."[77]

As the number of competing theaters increased from 1890 onward, "the number of seats exploded" and "theater like kabuki which had remained far beyond the reach of the masses became approachable causing the number of theatergoers to jump quite suddenly."[78] But this moment was short-lived: the audience, which had peaked at about 4.3 million annual theatergoers, declined to 2.8 million in 1903. That year saw the deaths, in rapid succession, of the two great kabuki stars of the age, Onoe Kikugorō V and Ichikawa Danjurō IX, as well as the opening of the first cinema, the Denkikan, in Asakusa.

The Fukagawa-za, with its Western façade, was typical of this moment in which so much of what governed theatrical practice was in flux. The playwrights whom the theater employed, the troupes that put on its plays, the showing of hand-tinted films and of magic acts, were all typical of this transitional moment in theatrical history, which Nakamura Testurō has vividly described as a kind of Janus-like

---

[74] See Aoki Kōichirō, *Meiji Tōkyō shomin no tanoshimi* (Tokyo: Chūō Kōron Shinsha, 2004), pp. 223–24.
[75] See Satō Katsura, *Kabuki no Bakumatsu/Meiji: koshibai no jidai* (Tokyo: Perikansha, 2010), esp. the map on pp. 14–15 that shows the proliferation of "little theaters" from the early 1870s to the early 1880s.
[76] Ihara Seiseien [Toshirō], "Shibai banashi," *Shincho gekkan* 5 (1898), 190.
[77] Ihara Seiseien [Toshirō], "Shibai banashi," 188.
[78] Aoki Kōichirō, *Meiji Tōkyō shomin no tanoshimi*, p. 224.

two-headed eagle, looking both to the past and the future.⁷⁹ And in this period, issues of copyright loomed everywhere. The trial, that is, and Shōyō's testimony, cannot be seen apart from as a specific location in time and space, a moment during which new and lasting conceptions of authorship and intellectual property took shape, both in public discourse in newspapers and in the courtroom.

In June of 1902, when Tsubouchi Shōyō was called to give expert testimony, the trial of Minegishi and Kashiwara had been ongoing for almost a year. The suit was brought by Mokuami's daughter, Ito, under the Kyakuhon Gakufu Jōrei promulgated fifteen years earlier, in December of 1887, and which extended for the first time the idea of intellectual property and copyright protection to play scripts and musical scores. When the law came into effect, Mokuami was still alive, in his early eighties; working with his daughter and his last disciple, Takeshiba Kisui, he began to register his substantial corpus of plays.⁸⁰ Since copyright did not inhere in creation but had actively to be asserted, copies of scripts were deposited with the Ministry of the Interior and Mokuami kept a detailed record of which plays he had registered and when.⁸¹ At the same time, since kabuki scripts were not printed or published during the early modern period, Mokuami also published the versions of the scripts he had registered in order publicly to assert all rights to both performance and publication *as author*. The script of *Benten the Thief* was printed on October 30, 1888, thirteen years to the day before the Fukagawa-za's performance of the play was closed down.

Yet, these "scripts" were in fact little more than digests of the play, in some instances, just single acts. As Iwai Masami has written about the scripts from this era, "Mokuami seems to have fallen into a situation in which he had to turn to a policy of rushing to get copyright and performance rights even if it meant sacrificing the actual content [of the plays] and publishing just the opening act under the play's title."⁸² But even as Mokuami, one of the few playwrights to have been active on both sides of the Meiji Restoration and both before and after the reorganization of intellectual property laws that followed in its wake, set about asserting his rights over plays dating back decades, this system of claiming copyright was easily exploited for purposes of outright piracy and fraud in the years surrounding the trial. In the mid-1890s, an entrepreneurial publisher named Nakanishi Sadayuki began printing compendia which lay legal claim to the rights to vast swathes of Japan's theatrical patrimony and creating chaos among theater troupes, who did not understand how plays from two centuries earlier could now fall under

---

[79] Nakamura Tetsurō, *Kabuki no kindai: sakka to sakuhin*, p. 1.
[80] Wada Osamu, "Kawatake Mokuami no hanken tōroku," *Engeki kenkyū* 17 (1993), 31–48.
[81] Part of the register, "Engeki kyakuhon gakufu hanken tōroku hyō," is reproduced in Waseda Daigaku Engeki Hakubutsukan, ed., *Botsugo hyakunen Kawatake Mokuami: hito to sakuhin* (Tokyo: Waseda Daigaku Tsubouchi Hakushi Kinen Engeki Hakubutsukan, 1993), p. 63. The register itself is still in possession of the Kawatake family.
[82] Iwai Masami, "Mokuami no 'engeki kyakuhon' o megutte," *Kabuki kenkyū to hihyō* 13 (1994), 143.

new copyright statutes.[83] And in 1904, the *Yomiuri* newspaper ran a story about an impresario named Kawakami Kamekichi who similarly tried to lay claim to centuries' worth of popular music, asserting copyright and traveling around the islands of Shikoku and Kyushu demanding payment from traveling musicians and geisha for playing "his" music.[84]

In his own defense, Kashiwara Isaburō, the playwright hired by the Fukagawa-za, argued that Mokuami himself had stolen the play from an earlier script and had even introduced three doctored play scripts into evidence to support his contention; it was this crime of forgery and not the original crime of staging of the play for which Kashiwara would eventually be found guilty of forgery and fined fifty yen.

Shōyō's first charge as expert witness was to determine the authenticity of the four scripts introduced into evidence. While the script of *Benten the Thief*, by means of which Mokuami had asserted his rights over the play, would, unsurprisingly, have a critical role at trial in establishing Ito's claim to her father's authorship, this script would also introduce an important intellectual problem into the case: the "script" that had been filed with the Ministry of the Interior and that Ito introduced into evidence was hardly a script at all. The printed booklet, which contained not just *Benten the Thief* but two other plays as well, was only some forty pages long and contained digests of only the two most famous scenes from *Benten the Thief* covering barely 20 pages of the printed text (printed versions of the play today are about 160 pages). During his testimony, Shōyō would describe this printed text as only the "essential skeletal frame" of the play, from which everything else had been omitted.[85] And yet, despite the skeletal nature of the script, Shōyō would base his argument in favor of Mokuami's authorship of the play almost entirely on a stylistic analysis, an analysis which Shōyō himself acknowledged could not be supported by the text in evidence.[86]

While Shōyō's charge was thus rather narrow, it required the consideration of broader questions about the nature of authorial voice and about the meaning of artistic originality. What Shōyō did not introduce into his discussion of these problems, however, was what it meant to contemplate these questions in relation to a text composed under very different institutional and intellectual conditions than those that would underpin a modern notion authorship with its attendant myth of creative genius. Instead, Shōyō takes as the starting point of his testimony the conviction that one can locate an authentic and original authorial voice—what at

---

[83] See, e.g. "Kōgyōken shingai no saiban," *Asahi shinbun*, November 1, 1895, p. 3, which describes suits filed by Nakanishi against the Asahi-za and the Fukui-za for staging two of the most famous plays in the *kabuki* repertory, *Sugawara and the Secrets of Calligraphy* and *Yoshitsune and the Thousand Cherry Trees*, both dating to the mid-eighteenth century.
[84] "Engeki kyakuhon gakufu no kōgyōken," *Yomiuri shinbun*, August 22, 1904, p. 1.
[85] Tsubouchi Shōyō, "Kyakuhon ni kan suru soshō jiken no kantei," in *Shōyō senshū*, vol. 12 (Tokyo: Daiichi shobō, 1977–78), p. 687.
[86] Tsubouchi Shōyō, "Kyakuhon ni kan suru soshō jiken no kantei," in *Shōyō senshū*, vol. 12, p. 687.

the conclusion of his testimony he would call a "style" (*fudekuse*)—in a play that was actually composed by a team of playwrights working together, and in a text which did not survive in its original form, dating from an era without clear conceptions of intellectual property, when notions of authenticity, originality, and the nature of authorship were all rather different than they would become in the early twentieth century.[87]

What is most intriguing about Shōyō's argument is that not one of the points he makes about Mokuami's distinctive authorial voice is actually supported by the copy of the play filed for copyright purposes and as evidence in the trial, an issue that Shōyō himself acknowledges several times. The text on which Shōyō relies to make the stylistic argument was, in fact, not a play script at all but a work of fiction that Shōyō himself introduced into evidence, an illustrated version of *Benten the Thief* published at the time of the play's premier in March 1862, which Shōyō argued "copied [Mokuami's] original draft word for word."[88] From the 1810s, illustrated fiction (*gōkan*) began to reproduce the stories and even dialogue of plays, becoming something like published play scripts. In the 1820s, playwrights like Tsuruya Nanboku IV and Segawa Jokō II themselves began producing these books, and by the 1850s, they were widespread. While these works were originally published several months after the play's premier, by the late 1850s, it was common for them to appear simultaneously with the play's opening.[89]

Mokuami is listed as the "author" (*sakusha*) on the playbill for the original 1862 performance of *Benten the Thief*, but the illustrated novel uses somewhat different terminology. The cover of the first volume of the text and the colophon note that it was "devised" (*an*) by Kawatake Mokuami, arranged by Yanagiya Umehiko, and illustrated by Utagawa Kunisada. As can be seen from the 1862 playbill, Umehiko, who was responsible for composing the actual text of the novel, was also one of Mokuami's writing team and helped to compose the original play.

Shōyō treats this published novel as a completely transparent vessel for documenting the play with Umehiko becoming a kind of shamanistic medium who channels Mokuami's distinctive style word for word, but the introduction of this text into evidence actually points to a number of complicated questions about the interrelation of fiction, theater, and the printed image. These problems surround the play, and accounting for this complexity will give us a different picture of the nature of authorship. But Shōyō also introduces a second problem in his testimony, the question of what defined a work as *original*. As Shōyō himself conceded in his testimony, "it is not the case that the plot (kyakushoku) of *Benten the Thief* is necessarily original (zanshin)."[90] Like every dramatic work of the time,

---

[87] Tsubouchi Shōyō, "Kyakuhon ni kan suru soshō jiken no kantei," in *Shōyō senshū*, vol. 12, p. 704.
[88] Tsubouchi Shōyō, "Kyakuhon ni kan suru soshō jiken no kantei," in *Shōyō senshū*, vol. 12, p. 687.
[89] See Takahashi Noriko, *Kusazōshi to engeki: yakusha nigao-e sōshiki o chūshin ni* (Tokyo: Kyūko Shoin, 2004), p. 416.
[90] Tsubouchi Shōyō, "Kyakuhon ni kan suru soshō jiken no kantei," in *Shōyō senshū*, vol. 12, p. 688.

*Benten the Thief* drew on a rich vein of narrative history that included stock characters. The five thieves around which the play centered were based on historical figures and had been the subject of numerous works of fiction and oral storytelling: "Depending on one's perspective," Shōyō concedes, "one could see it to some extent as nothing but an adaptation (hon'an) of [plots] heretofore used in the puppet theater, illustrated fiction, and oral storytelling."[91] For Shōyō, then, Mokuami's originality—and authorial originality as such—lay not in the overall plot but in his assemblage of the various parts into a new whole: "it is impossible to doubt that it was [Mokuami's] originality (sō'i) that picked and chose among the common material of such works, that additionally devised new ideas (shin'an), that revised and supplemented and brought together materials, and that so *created a play script in tune with the tastes of its time* called 'Benten the Thief.'"[92]

As part of his explanation of how the play came to be written, Shōyō notes another interesting aspect of Mokuami's play: the claim made in playbills for *Benten the Thief* and repeated in Umehiko's novel that the play was "A tale of righteous thieves which turns Toyokuni's images into kabuki just as they are." The play itself, that is, was a dramatization of a series of prints published in 1859 by Toyokuni III, Utagawa Kunisada, which depicted actors as the thieves of legend who would appear in Mokuami's play. Not only the characters but also some elements of the plot of Mokuami's play were drawn directly from Toyokuni III's prints, which were, in turn, based on earlier versions of the story that circulated in both in oral and written forms.[93]

Yanagiya Umehiko, who fashioned the illustrated novel of *Benten the Thief* and was a disciple and collaborator of Mokuami, had himself lived through the Restoration and was the subject of an interview by the theater critic and historian Ihara Toshirō before his death in 1896 in which he recalled how playwrights as early as the 1850s began to mine the work of professional storytellers for ideas.[94] Umehiko recalled how the first instance of a play based on the work of a storyteller was Segawa Jokō III's "Scarface Yosa" ("Kirare Yosa"), which even features a professional storyteller as a minor character, a device Mokuami would himself use in his 1891 play *Riding the Famous Hot-Air Balloon* (*Fūsen nori uwasa no takadono*) starring Onoe Kikugorō, who had first made his name three decades earlier as Benten Kozō in *Benten the Thief*, a role he would continue to play until his death.

What are we, then, to make of the relationship between Mokuami's play and earlier versions of the narrative mediated as they are through a series of woodblock prints? In what sense can we understand a work such as *Benten the Thief*—so

---

[91] Tsubouchi Shōyō, "Kyakuhon ni kan suru soshō jiken no kantei," in *Shōyō senshū*, vol. 12, p. 688.
[92] Tsubouchi Shōyō, "Kyakuhon ni kan suru soshō jiken no kantei," in *Shōyō senshū*, vol. 12, p. 688.
[93] Tsubouchi Shōyō, "Kyakuhon ni kan suru soshō jiken no kantei," in *Shōyō senshū*, vol. 12, pp. 690–93.
[94] Ihara Seiseien [Toshirō], "Ko Umehiko-ō mukashibanashi," *Waseda bungaku* 24, 1(2) (December 1896), 91.

deeply embedded within a set of tropes that cut across various narrative, theatrical, and visual media—in terms of what Shōyō calls "originality"? In defending Yoshimura Ito's claim to copyright, Shōyō himself seems to have felt compelled to put forth an argument that allowed for the absolute originality of the play as a precondition for the protection afforded by copyright. As he explained in his testimony:

> The copyright of a play script and the copyright of a work that is not a play script need to be completely distinguished from one another [...] Even if there existed a work of storytelling or a novel with a plot similar to that of *Aotozōshi*, or even a work almost exactly the same, [which dated] from before that work, that was an oral tale or a novel and this a script revised to be staged in a theater. As no oral tale or novel can be staged as is, as a matter of course there must emerge a right that applies to the theater and so even if copyright attains to the former, this bears no relation to the rights of the latter. How much more this is the case in regards to works from the past in which copyright did not exist."[95]

What is striking here is the irony that the 1887 law protecting performance rights was originally argued as a means to protect novelists from having their work staged without permission and without compensation and to encourage serious writers to engage in playwriting by properly compensating authors for new plays. And yet, here, Shōyō pushes in the opposite direction, arguing that even if Mokuami had largely borrowed the work of others to compose his play, the play as a particular assemblage ought to be protected by copyright.

In October 1902, just a month before the *Benten the Thief* trial would conclude, Ihara Toshirō recalled the famous case of "The Water Magician" ("Taki no Shiraito") in which the actor and theater manager Kawakami Otojirō was sued by Ozaki Kōyō and Izumi Kyōka in 1895 for staging Kyōka's work without permission. In his essay for *Kabuki* magazine titled "Performance Rights in the West," Ihara described the court's prescription for a public apology by Kawakami in that earlier trial as "very strange" for someone who had "brazenly flouted the law."[96] Copyright had become basically meaningless in protecting works from cross-genre piracy. "There has not been a single case," Ihara writes, "in which a suit has succeeded when a novel has been staged without permission."[97]

Although Ihara writes, at the beginning of his essay, that touching upon the *Benten the Thief* trial directly is "beyond the scope of the current magazine," and the article largely traces questions of intellectual property in relation to British and American theater, he does introduce a set of questions that seem designed

---

[95] Tsubouchi Shōyō, "Kyakuhon ni kan suru soshō jiken no kantei," in *Shōyō senshū*, vol. 12, pp. 694–95.
[96] Ihara Seiseien [Toshirō], "Seiyō no kōgyōken," *Kabuki* 29 (October 1902), 37.
[97] Ihara Seiseien [Toshirō], "Seiyō no kōgyōken," 37.

specifically to interrogate some of the arguments that Shōyō had made in his testimony earlier that year. The first is the question of who really owns the rights to a play when that play is commissioned and paid for by a theater producer. Ihara makes a suggestive analogy:

> To take another example, when a carpenter is hired by a person to construct a house, the house belongs to the person who hired the carpenter but literary works are treated differently for the court claims that the right always lies with the author under any circumstances because copyright law was originally intended to protect the author.[98]

But, Ihara continues, even then, the question is not so simple for "if the producer himself creates the story and hires the writer then in that case the rights belong to the producer." If the author, like a carpenter who hires subcontractors, "hires other authors to help with his own work, then the rights belong to the hiring author."[99] The particular choice of examples by Ihara, despite his claim not to address the *Benten the Thief* trial, directly pertains to the case that was currently in court. First, in the period in which *Benten the Thief* was written, there was no conception of intellectual property as belonging to the author; rather, rights—to performance in the case of a play or to printing in case of a publication—lay in the hands of the theater producer or publisher who *paid* the author. Thus, Mokuami was himself very much like the carpenter in Ihara's example, paid for his labor by the Ichimura-za. But Mokuami was like the carpenter in another way: the play was composed by a team of playwrights working for and under Mokuami. In his own notes on playwriting, "Precepts for Dramatic Composition" ("Kyōgen sakusha kokoroesho"), which have survived in manuscript, Mokuami not only goes into great detail about the collaborative way in which plays were conceived and written but also explains how payment was made by the theater manager to the head playwright, who, in turn, paid his team.[100] Curiously, however, Shōyō not once mentions the corporate nature of authorship in his testimony despite the fact that Yanagiya Umehiko, under whose name the novelized version of *Benten the Thief* appeared, was one of Mokuami's eight assistants on the play.

And the Ichimura-za's theater manager played a critical role in actually conceiving the idea for the play, again a point raised by Ihara. In his memoirs published at the time of his death in 1903, the actor Onoe Kikugorō, who played the thief Benten Kozō in the play's 1862 premier and became famous for the role, recalled that Kunisada's prints had been discovered at a shop in Asakusa by an assistant to Sawada Wasuke, then the theater manager of the Ichimura-za. Sawada brought

---

[98] Ihara Seiseien [Toshirō], "Seiyō no kōgyōken," 37.
[99] Ihara Seiseien [Toshirō], "Seiyō no kōgyōken," 37.
[100] Hattori Yukio, "Honkoku 'Kyōgen sakusha kokoroesho,'" p. 92.

the prints to Mokuami and asked him to draft a play based on the characters in Kunisada's prints.[101]

The images were created by Kunisada, based on picaresque legends that had circulated both orally and in print; intrigued by the images, Sawada, in his capacity as theater manager, then commissioned the play, which was written by Mokuami with the aid of eight other playwrights. The script, as was custom, was not published at the time, but Umehiko, one of Mokuami's team of writers, published an illustrated novel at the time of the play's premier. Using Umehiko's novel as a stand-in for the script, Shōyō argues on behalf of locating Mokuami's distinctive authorial voice and his originality of vision. And yet, despite all of this contingency, Shōyō's view of the nature of authorship would have very long-lasting consequences for the historiography of early modern drama from the specter of which we are only now beginning to emerge.

In this complex set of intersections of image and text, of old material and new craft, of private and public, lie a great number of uncertainties. One need not argue, as Kashiwara did, that Mokuami really stole the play from an earlier author to acknowledge that the ease with which Shōyō argues for Mokuami's stylistic individuality based on Umehiko's novel rather flattens out the problematic nature of authorship in the nineteenth century.

For the historian writing a century on, what is interesting about the trial as its own sort of performance is not the outcome as such—Minegishi, the manager of the Fukagawa-za, was acquitted and Kashiwara, the playwright, fined fifty yen for knowingly falsifying the scripts he introduced into evidence—but rather the implications of the trial for redefining the nature of authorship both as a legal institution and as a concept, giving to Shōyō's conception of authorship not only the authority of the academy but also the force of law. In the decades that followed his involvement in the trial, Shōyō's work on the history of Japanese drama would continue, as would his work as a translator of Shakespeare. But in the middle of the 1910s, Shōyō's work would take a turn toward an area in which he had shown little interest early in his career: the history of images, especially theatrical images, as a form of historical evidence. If an attention to the individuality of the hand would play an important part in the way Shōyō understood authorship, this approach would play an even more central role in early-twentieth-century work in the field of connoisseurship and the emerging discipline of art history. In many ways, even more was at stake in the transnational marketplace for Japanese images that emerged at the end of the nineteenth century than in the national contests of copyright and authorship, for questions of authentication and authenticity hovered over all the objects on which this trade centered. It is to this subject that I shall now turn.

---

[101] Onoe Kikugorō V, *Onoe Kikugorō jiden* (Tokyo: Jiji Shinpōsha, 1903), p. 2.

# 5
# Individuality in an Age of Reproduction
## The Image of the Actor in Nineteenth-Century Japan

### I Image as Document

In the summer of 1925, Tsubouchi Shōyō and his assistant Ōmura Hiroyoshi were photographed in the study of Shōyō's home in the Yochōmachi area of Tokyo (Figure 5.1). The photograph, which Shōyō would later use as one of the frontispieces to Volume 7 of his 1927 *Selected Works*, captures a moment in Shōyō's own career, and in the historiography of Japanese drama more broadly, when the visual record was becoming increasingly central to documenting the theatrical past. The image shows the two men at work cataloging a collection of roughly fifteen thousand prints that Shōyō had arranged for Waseda University to purchase from the collector and dealer Kobayashi Bunshichi in 1916, a group of prints that would later form one of the central collections of the Waseda Theater Museum when it opened in 1928.

In the photograph, both Shōyō and Ōmura appear engrossed in their work, unaware that they are being photographed, though we surely ought to read their attitude as one of staged indifference where the subjects have transformed themselves "in advance into an image."[1] The composition of the photograph too suggests a kind of casualness, even haphazardness, in which the surroundings seem to be captured at random, with frames cut off around the edges and the window behind Ōmura bisected, as is the framed image at the top of the photograph. And then there are the theater prints themselves, the subject of the work being done by Shōyō and Ōmura, which appear, in the photograph, scattered about the edges of the room.

At one level, the image calls to mind the portrait of Utei Enba drawn over a century earlier by Utagawa Kunisada for Shikitei Sanba's 1811 *A Critique of the Audience* (*Kakusha hyōbanki*), an aged figure surrounded by the objects of his antiquarian passions (see Chapter 2, Figure 2.1). Although the prints that Shōyō and Ōmura are cataloging are not Shōyō's, the photograph suggests the scholar's own penchant for collecting: the various masks that hang above the sliding doors

---

[1] Roland Barthes, *Camera Lucida: Reflections on Photography*, reprint edn (New York: Hill and Wang, 2010), p. 10. See also Pierre Bourdieu's remark that "the 'natural' is a cultural ideal which must be created before it can be captured" by the photographer in Bourdieu, *Photography: A Middle-Brow Art*, trans. Richard Nice (Cambridge, MA: Harvard University Press, 1984), p. 81.

**Figure 5.1** Tsubouchi Shōyō in his study, 1925.
Source: Waseda University Library.

and from the cabinet or the small statue of the Buddha that seems to stare back at the viewer. For many years, the Shōyō Memorial Room on the second floor of the Tsubouchi Memorial Theater Museum was adorned with all manner of knick-knacks that Shōyō had collected over the years. Shōyō was himself deeply ambivalent about the work of collecting, what he called the curioification of the past, which was for him the antithesis of historical research. But the photograph begs the question: where are the lines to be drawn between antiquarian and scholar, collector and historian?

The only clue to the origin of the photograph is the date in the caption, summer of 1925, but it is possible to trace the image through a diary entry Shōyō made on Sunday, July 26, 1925, which notes simply that "a reporter from the *Nichinichi Newspaper* came to photograph the sight of our organizing the theater images."[2] The photograph would run on July 28 with a short human-interest story titled "Forgetting the Heat Amid Cataloging Prints—Dr. Tsubouchi."[3]

The better part of a century on, if this photograph is relevant to understanding the history of Japanese drama, it is because the photograph seems to capture, almost unconsciously, so many of the central tensions and ambivalences surrounding the history of printed images in Japan and of their uses in the twentieth century as an historical archive of the theater. In the photograph, for example, the *process* through which the prints are transformed from ephemera into archive is recorded, with Ōmura seemingly caught in the act of pasting the prints onto stock, a gesture that uncannily recalls the process through which Shikitei Sanba too pasted his playbills into albums in an attempt to preserve them as "devices for thinking about the past." But even this simple gesture is freighted, filled with a particular tension as we look about the room at the prints mounted on white stock: where might we draw the line between the prints serving as historical documents and the prints being transformed into aesthetic objects? What separates archivization from museumification?

Then, of course, there is the document that Shōyō is composing, brush in hand, which occupies such a prominent place in the photograph. Indeed, in the photograph, the prints themselves have been pushed to the periphery and at the center is this written document. Shōyō had a penchant for creating charts and diagrams, like the genealogical chart of Japanese theater he had made twenty years earlier for Lafcadio Hearn. On this occasion, Shōyō was creating another taxonomy, one of various types of theatrical prints he would publish later that year in an essay on "Japanese Theater Prints as Historical Documents."[4] The composition of the photograph seems somehow to capture Shōyō's ambivalent attitude toward the use of visual materials in his work, where the image is always subordinated to the written document.

---

[2] Shōyō Kyōkai ed., *Shōyō nikki*, vol. 3, (Tokyo: Shōyō Kyōkai, 2002) p. 210.

[3] "Ukiyo-e no seiri ni atsusa mo wasurete: Tsubouchi Hakase," *Tōkyō nichinichi shinbun*, evening edn, July 28, 1925, p. 1.

[4] See Tsubouchi Shōyō, "Engeki shiryō toshite wa ga kuni no shibai nishiki-e oyobi sono zuhyō," in *Shōyō senshū*, vol. 7 (Tokyo: Daiichi shobō, 1977–78), pp. 317–28.

And there is perhaps a more subtle issue hinted at by the very medium of the photograph: the *reproduction* of the actor prints themselves through their being photographed. It is almost as if the image, somehow unconsciously, is citing the entire history of photographic reproductions of works of art that is so intimately intertwined with the origins of the discipline of art history from the late nineteenth century forward and with its practices across the twentieth century.[5] Even more suggestively, many of the prints can be easily identified and located in the print database of the Waseda Theater Museum pointing to the afterlife of these images in the our digital present, a subject to which I will return in this book's epilogue.

Indeed, in ways of which Shōyō was himself quite conscious, the apparatus of the camera came to structure how he viewed the archival record of printed theater images. Early on in his work on the history of images, Shōyō adopted a particular view on the nature of these prints. They were, he would repeatedly write, documentary in nature, primarily "historical materials" rather than aesthetic objects.[6] Central to Shōyō's conception of these prints was the idea that they constituted a kind of cinematic or proto-cinematic archive, an idea to which he would often return.[7] Such prints, Shōyō would write in the introduction to his 1920 book on Utagawa Toyokuni and his school, "reanimate what really happened on stage like a Kinemacolor film."[8]

Thousands of actor prints survived and could serve as a form of documentary evidence of the past, a record of theatrical history *like* a filmic record—this was a central tenet of Shōyō's understanding of the prints. From here, follow two unarticulated assumptions that govern this understanding of the relationship between these images and their referents. The first derives from the relationship between the film and the profilmic, that which is recorded on film. Shōyō posits an understanding of the image as a straightforward, essentially transparent record of the performance. The images "reanimate" the history of the stage by revivifying the great actors of the eighteenth and nineteenth centuries, drawing explicitly on cinema's much-commented-upon power to bring the dead back to life. The second aspect of Shōyō's likening of these images to a filmic archive is that he subtly substitutes for an iconic understanding of the prints (based on an idea of their resemblance to that which they depict), a view that considers the prints as essentially indexical traces which therefore guarantee the historical character of what they record. To be sure, Shōyō does not imagine that the prints depend on (and thus guarantee) the bodily presence of the actor in the same way as a photograph or

---

[5] Robert S. Nelson, "The Slide Lecture, or the Work of Art 'History' in the Age of Mechanical Reproduction," *Critical Inquiry* 26, 3 (2000), 414–34, https://www.jstor.org/stable/1344289.

[6] Tsubouchi Shōyō, "Engeki shiryō toshite wa ga kuni no shibai nishiki-e oyobi sono zuhyō," in *Shōyō senshū*, vol. 7, pp. 317–28.

[7] See Tsubouchi Shōyō, "Katsudō shashin to wa ga geki no kako," in *Shōyō senshū*, vol. 7 (Tokyo: Daiichi shobō, 1977–78), pp. 299–308.

[8] Tsubouchi Shōyō, "Shibai-e to Toyokuni oyobi sono monka," in *Shōyō senshū*, vol. 7 (Tokyo: Daiichi shobō, 1977–78), p. 10.

moving image, and yet the notion of the actor print as filmic transposes onto these objects the particular truth claims of the camera, that what is depicted really was.

These images, that is to say, become *historical*, as opposed to aesthetic, in character to the extent that they can be seen as documentary: they record that which happened on stage. This stance seems naïve in retrospect but, as Philip Rosen has argued, this basic premise of the indexical nature of historical evidence underlies much of modern historiography, and it allowed Shōyō to open a new way of considering this material which moved away from the subjective, aesthetic appreciation of woodblock prints that pervaded the discourse of collectors and connoisseurs in the early twentieth century.[9] In the process, however, this insistence on the imagined or yearned-for indexicality of these images also created a series of blind spots that, often in subtle ways, still inflect work on theater prints as historical objects even today. For what interested Shōyō was *what* these images represent, not *how* they represent nor how they understood the very idea of representation. And so he was unconcerned with a host of issues surrounding these prints, issues that are themselves both aesthetic and historical in nature: what is meant by the idea of likeness and how can we historicize such an idea; how do we understand the specificity of a body of images that moves freely among different printed media; and, perhaps most vexingly for historians of Japanese prints, how do we understand an idea of stylistic and compositional distinctiveness in a tradition of image making that is often premised, especially in the nineteenth century, on an erasure of stylistic individuality?

And yet these questions are fundamental to the very project Shōyō envisioned— and that the archive of prints he helped collect make possible today—of using these images as a way of thinking historically about the theater in nineteenth-century Japan. In its own way, Shōyō's work on theater prints provides a means of approaching these questions, though it does so in an oblique fashion, not through Shōyō's own statements and arguments but through a series of uncanny resonances and strange silences that appear in his work. These open up a space for re-engaging with these images and in a way that is more strictly historicist than Shōyō's vision.

For all of his attention to detail in his writing on theater prints, Shōyō is also curiously blind to the ways in which Toyokuni's own prints function as pictures, how they often quite self-consciously frame problems of representation, legibility, and reproduction, and thus can serve as meta-pictures that themselves meditate on the role of the image in representing reality. There is a telling moment in Chapter 3 of Shōyō's book on Toyokuni and his school where Shōyō reproduces an illustration by Toyokuni I from a 1793 illustrated satire (*kibyōshi*) by Sakuragawa Jihinari, *Asaina and the Soga Farce* (*Asaina chaban Soga*). Shōyō writes, "I've included

---

[9] Philip Rosen, *Change Mummified: Cinema, Historicity, Theory* (Minneapolis, MN: University of Minnesota Press, 2001).

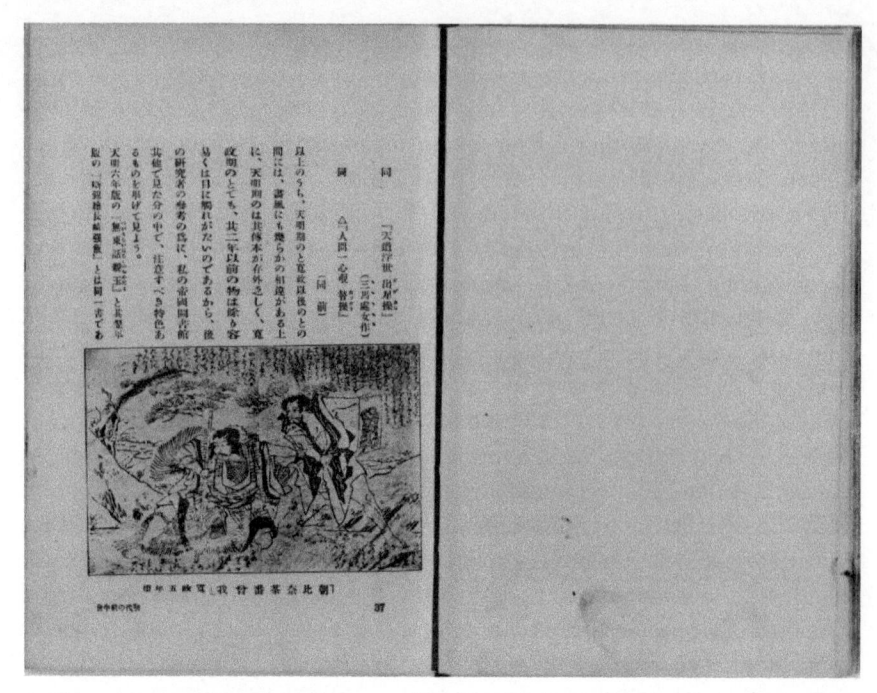

**Figure 5.2** Photo reproduction from Sakuragawa Jihinari's 1793 *Asaina chaban Soga* from Tsubouchi Shōyō's *Shibai-e to Toyokuni oyobi sono monka*, 1920.
*Source*: National Diet Library, Tokyo.

a photo-reproduction of *Asaina and the Soga Farce* as a sample of [Toyokuni's] manner of drawing likeness in his oldest theater prints" (Figure 5.2).[10]

What is especially striking about the illustration, but what goes completely unremarked by Shōyō, is that the image itself contains an image. That image within the image is borne on a scroll held by the character Dainichibō, and it is of the *likeness* of another character in the story, his nephew Kagekiyo (Figure 5.3). The overall composition is, in fact, quite complex, although this scene is tangential to the story of *Asaina and the Soga Farce*: Kagekiyo is in disguise, hiding from Minamoto no Yoritomo and the image that Dainichibō is holding is intended to serve as a marker that reveals his hidden identity. Dainichibō has come to warn Kagekiyo as well as to devise a plan by which Kagekiyo would in fact kill Dainichibō and assume his identity, taking even his own hair as a wig and delivering Dainichibō's severed head as duplicitous proof of Kagekiyo's own demise.[11] The illustration is itself centrally, crucially, about identity both hidden and revealed, about deception and

---

[10] Tsubouchi Shōyō, "Shibai-e to Toyokuni oyobi sono monka," in *Shōyō senshū*, vol. 7, p. 42.
[11] Sakuragawa Jihinari, *Asaina chaban Soga* (Edo: Nishimuraya Yohachi, 1793), 3r–4v.

**Figure 5.3** Utagawa Toyokuni, Kagekiyo and Dainichibō from Sakuragawa Jihinari, *Asaina chaban Soga*, 1793.
Source: National Diet Library, Tokyo.

disguise, and about the power of the image—repeatedly referred to in the text as an *esugata*, a portrait or a likeness—to resemble and to reveal identity.

Shōyō points to this illustration as an early example of one of Toyokuni's actor likenesses (*nigao-e*), but the image itself seems to ask what, precisely, we mean by the term "likeness." At one level, the image within the image of Kagekiyo functions in a straightforward way according to an idea of mimesis: Kagekiyo can be recognized because the image (*esugata*) is a faithful representation that reveals the "truth." But this idea of likeness is embedded in a larger image that plays upon a broader notion of semblance: that the figures of Kagekiyo and Dainichibō are themselves intended to be read as likenesses of actors playing these characters in role. This is, after all, the context in which Shōyō cites this image.

So, we might rightly ask who are these actors and how are we to know? Shōyō, curiously does not address this issue, a stance that suggests a model of transparency functioning like the image within the image. For Shōyō, not only do the actor likenesses function like the image of Kagekiyo in that they can be read directly as mimetic representations of the actors they depict, but also this depiction is essentially transparent; it needs no comment. Shōyō never mentions who these actors are supposed to be.

But on what basis do we judge likeness? Are we intended simply to recognize the actors by the approximation of their faces and, if so, based on what evidence? Already we have arrived at a question about the social nature of these images, of their legibility, and of how these images can only be read in the context of other images: read by Shōyō and by us but also, crucially, by many of Toyokuni's contemporaries. We can recognize Kagekiyo as the great actor Ichikawa Danjūrō V not because we recognize in Toyokuni's image a direct copy of Danjūrō's face (which, of course, we have never seen) but because, in addition to direct signifiers of his identity (his family crest of three nestled boxes), the illustration plays on the iconicity of his image in other depictions of actor and role, images that had become ubiquitous in the satirical genre of *kibyōshi* fiction of the late eighteenth century.[12]

But to the extent that this image refers to actors on stage, there is a gap or distance that would have been recognizable at the time but which is now obscure: the scene depicted in this print was actually staged in 1777, fourteen years before this book was published, when Ichikawa Danjūrō V played Kagekiyo and Dainichibō was played by Ōtani Hiroemon III in a play called *Eternal Spring: The Feathered Mantle of the Soga Brothers* (*Tsukisenu haru hagoromo Soga*), staged at Edo's Ichimura-za. Nakazō had died in 1790 not only before the book was published but also before Toyokuni had begun designing actor prints. Rather than directly depicting a scene on stage, in the manner Shōyō imagined when he invoked the cinematic nature of these representations, Toyokuni's illustration for *Asaina and the Soga Farce* is, in fact, a copy of an earlier image, in this case a print made by Katsukawa Shunshō of the actors in 1777 (Figure 5.4).[13]

The stability of the referentiality of the image that Shōyō assumed begins to crumble: how do we judge the fidelity of this image? As an approximation of these actors? Or of Shunshō's print of these actors? Even as the image within the image, the image of Kagekiyo borne by Dainichibō, suggests that likeness functions on the basis of a straightforward mimetic fidelity, the larger image itself as a whole points in the opposite direction: that we can only *read* this image as a series of signs that point to other images. What is being copied is not nature, as it were, but art. Moreover, these two poles of referentiality—the idea of the direct copy and of the copy of a copy—inhabit an important place both in the discourse surrounding likeness in the nineteenth century (how these images were conceived and talked about) and in the images themselves. Indeed, we have condensed in this image, seemingly chosen at random by Shōyō, all of the central problems of the visual economy of nineteenth-century prints: the role of the individual as creator, originality and artistic genius as analytical categories, and the intersection

---

[12] See Kuroishi Yōko, "Godaime Ichikawa Danjūrō no Kagekiyo: Tenmei nenkan no kibyōshi wo chūshin ni," *Tōkyō gakugei daigaku kiyō* 46, 2 (1995), 265–76.

[13] See Timothy Clark, *The Actor's Image: Print Makers of the Katsukawa School* (Chicago, IL: Art Institute of Chicago, 1994), p. 417.

**Figure 5.4** Katsukawa Shunshō, Ichikawa Danjūrō V as Kagekiyo and Ōtani Hiroemon III as Dainichibō from *Tsukisenu haru hagoromo Soga*, 1777.
Source: Metropolitan Museum of Art.

of text and image and of art and commerce in the visual field of the nineteenth century.

## II  Individuality in an Age of Reproduction

Shōyō's work on Toyokuni and his school can only be understood in relation to a disjuncture between the apprehension of the print designer during his own lifetime and his reputation in the early twentieth century, especially his fate among European connoisseurs and collectors. On the one hand, in the first half of the nineteenth century, Toyokuni's work was widely understood to have ushered in a moment of commercial potential and commodification that transformed the role of the illustrator within a rapidly expanding marketplace of printed matter; on the other hand, from the late nineteenth-century onward, his prints, especially his late work, were regarded as an aesthetic nadir from which Japanese prints would never recover.

At his death in 1825, Toyokuni was memorialized by Santō Kyōden's younger brother Kyōzan as "the crown of recent ukiyo-e masters," whose "name had ascended like the sun";[14] by the time Ernest Fenollosa wrote his *Epochs of Chinese and Japanese Art* in the first decade of the twentieth century, however, Toyokuni's work from the years around 1815 was seen to have "descended into the valley of the shadow of death."[15] His images were "caricatures," marked by "maniacal distortions."[16] In his chapter on Toyokuni in *The Floating World*, a chapter pointedly titled "Must an Artist be Original?," the novelist and collector James Michener would write:

> The Utagawa school, as run by Toyokuni, was a source of positive infection in which every skill calculated to destroy an art was taught. Had the poison he purveyed been typhoid fever or measles he would of course have been arrested, but no one really cares when it is only an art being destroyed. Indeed, at the time, no one recognizes what is happening.[17]

Not only did no one recognize what was happening "at the time," but also it was, indeed, at this very moment in the middle of the second decade of the nineteenth century that Toyokuni's fame was at its height and he was considered the unrivaled master of the actor's likeness.[18] The opening pages of Shōyō's 1920 book on

---

[14] Nakada Tatsunosuke, *Ukiyo-e ruikō* (Tokyo: Iwanami Shoten, 1982), pp. 138–39.
[15] Ernest Fenollosa, *Epochs of Chinese and Japanese Art*, vol. 2 (New York: ICG Muse, Inc., 2000), p. 200.
[16] Fenollosa, *Epochs of Chinese and Japanese Art*, vol. 2, p. 199.
[17] James A. Michener, *The Floating World* (New York: Random House, 1954), p. 187.
[18] Suzuki Jūzō has pointed to this contradiction in our understanding of Toyokuni and suggested the need for a dramatic reevaluation of his prints from the perspective of the world in which they were

Toyokuni and his school offer a way of approaching this contradiction, through the uncanny resonance between an instance of Shōyō's language and the language Toyokuni himself used to talk about his approach to print design in his 1817 *A Quick Guide to Actor Likenesses* (*Yakusha nigao hayageiko*), the one text in which Toyokuni wrote at length about his method. The resonance is to be found in Shōyō's discussion of the problem (which was, by 1920, already quite entrenched in discussions of Toyokuni) of a perceived change, commonly described as a deterioration, of Toyokuni's style in the second decade of the nineteenth century, the very years in which Toyokuni produced *A Quick Guide to Actor Likenesses*. "One can distinguish," Shōyō writes:

> between the prints of the early Bunka period around 1804 and those prints coming after 1811 with a single glance [...] I already knew in broad terms of the change or degradation in Toyokuni's style but it was interesting to be able to grasp this with extreme precision almost spontaneously in the course of my investigations.[19]

Turning his attention from actor prints to the use of actors' likenesses in the illustrated fiction of this period, Shōyō continues:

> I first examined works from the 1790s through the Bunka, Bunsei, and Tenpō periods and put them into a rough order according to chronology. And in doing so I was able to see both the overall changes in patterns of illustration in illustrated fiction taken as a whole and, simultaneously, it became glaringly obvious how and at what point there occurred changes in the *style* of each individual artist.[20]

In this last sentence, Shōyō uses the term *fudekuse* to refer to style, the same term he had used almost two decades earlier in the testimony he gave at the trial of Minegishi Denjirō and Kashiwara Isaburō in support of the claim by Kawatake Mokuami's daughter Ito that the two men had infringed on her father's performance rights to the play *Benten the Thief*.

Here, of course, the idea of the stylistic individuality of the hand, or more literally the brush, has shifted from the literary to the visual, from the individual style discernible within the language of the text to the individual style that could be located in the grammar of the image. But in both instances, the underlying logic is the same: what allowed the critic or historian, or even the court, to make an attribution of an artistic work could be located in a style unique to the individual that would serve almost as a fingerprint.

---

created. See Suzuki Jūzō, *Toyokuni, Kunimasa, Toyohiro, Nidai Toyokuni, hoka*, ed. Takahashi Seiichirō, vol. 9, *Ukiyo-e taikei* (Tokyo: Shūeisha, 1975). p. 74.

[19] Tsubouchi Shōyō, "Shibai-e to Toyokuni oyobi sono monka," in *Shōyō senshū*, vol. 7, p. 12.

[20] Tsubouchi Shōyō, "Shibai-e to Toyokuni oyobi sono monka," in *Shōyō senshū*, vol. 7, p. 13.

Indeed, in the years that separated Shōyō's testimony from the work he began doing on the history of images, there emerged the idea that handwriting could serve as a marker of the individuality, of the identity, of the criminal in precisely the same ways that a fingerprint and this idea became an important subject within forensic science. In a book on "science and crime" published in 1918, the same year Shōyō began writing his essays on Toyokuni and his school, Terada Seiichi, a forensic psychologist and criminologist working at Sugamo Prison, devoted a chapter to the relationship between handwriting and individuality ("Hisseki to kojinsei") and another to the forensic uses of photography, at one point writing that the photographic enlargement of a document could make visible alterations not visible to the "naked eye."[21]

But if Shōyō's use of this term suggests both an assumption of the individuality of artistic genius imprinted on the page *and* a conception of the distinctiveness of the individual derived from the tools of modern forensic science, there is also an interesting resonance between Shōyō's use of this term and the language that Toyokuni himself used to conceptualize the problem of likeness a century earlier in his *A Quick Guide to Actor Likenesses*.

In his own writings on compositional practice, Toyokuni also refers to a notion of distinctiveness or individuality that he designates with the word *kuse*, but in *A Quick Guide to Actor Likenesses* that word is used in a very different sense, referring not to the distinctiveness of the hand of the artist—*fudekuse*—but to the distinctiveness of the face he sought to approximate. Indeed, *kuse* as a marker of physical distinctiveness, peculiarity, or individuality recurs again and again in the several pages of *A Quick Guide* devoted to a discussion of composition and design. In the section of *A Quick Guide* on "The Technique of the Actor's Likeness," Toyokuni writes:

> in all instances, when drawing a face, one must begin with the nose. Then, as this illustration suggests [Figure 5.5], one should draw the mouth second and the eyes third. If one does so then the shape of the face will emerge of its own accord and even a novice at drawing will be able to accomplish it easily. What is especially important is drawing the distinctive features of the face (*kuse*)—since actors' likenesses are colored, even if the resemblance is slight you will be able to tell at a single glance who is whom.[22]

A little later on, Toyokuni again refers to the importance of capturing the individuality of the subject of the likeness: "the width of the mouth should be roughly seven and a half centimeters; each mouth will have its own peculiarity (*kuse*), closed or

---

[21] Terada Seiichi, *Kagaku to hanzai* (Tokyo: Bunmei shoin, 1918).
[22] Utagawa Toyokuni, "Yakusha nigao hayageiko," in *Fukumori Kyusuke kyakuhonshū*, ed. Furuido Hideo (Tokyo: Kokusho Kankōkai, 2001), p. 376.

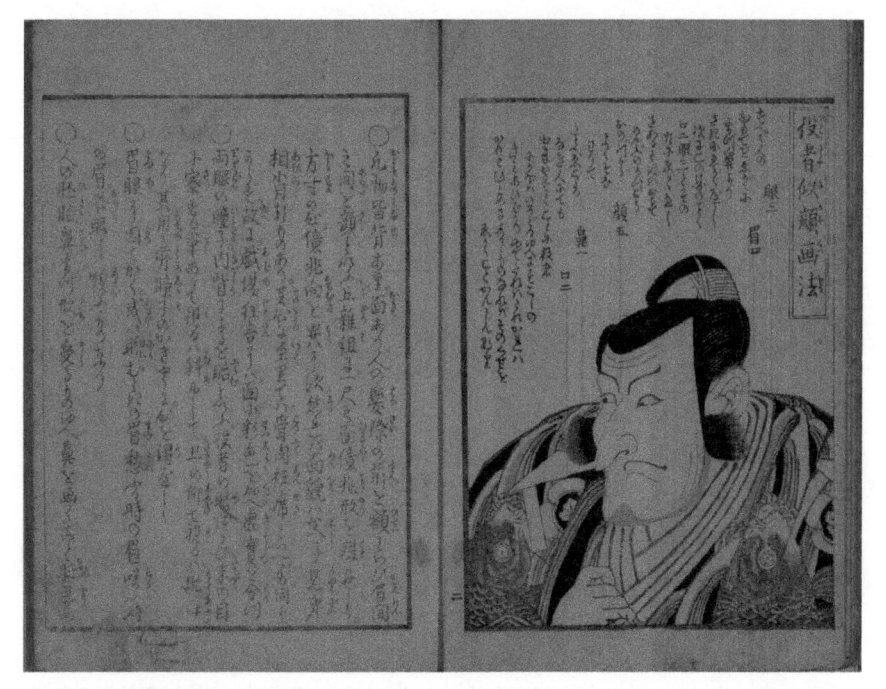

**Figure 5.5** Utagawa Toyokuni, the technique of the actor's likeness, *Yakusha nigao hayageiko*, 1817.
Source: Art Research Center, Ritsumeikan University.

crooked. The mouth should depend on the subject."[23] "Overall," Toyokuni continues, "a face with distinct features (*kuse aru omote*) is easy to approximate and one without distinct features (*kuse naki*) is difficult."[24]

Perhaps, Shōyō's use of *fudekuse* to refer to artistic style is merely a coincidence or a sort of unconscious citation; Shōyō does, after all, discuss *A Quick Guide to Actor Likenesses* in his book. But his use of this term suggests—and very clearly—the way in which the problem of the "artist," as Shōyō calls him, and especially his originality and stylistic individuality came to assume such a crucial place in the historiography of print making, just as it had in discussions of authorship. And yet, this emphasis on originality and stylistic individuality—an emphasis that continues in sometimes subtle ways to influence our understanding of Toyokuni and his age—seems very much at odds with the practice of print design in the early nineteenth century as conceptualized by Toyokuni and his contemporaries. Indeed, the disjunction in the usage of *kuse* from designating the distinctiveness or individuality of the face to be approximated to the individuality of the artist

[23] Utagawa Toyokuni, "Yakusha nigao hayageiko," p. 377.
[24] Utagawa Toyokuni, "Yakusha nigao hayageiko," p. 377.

doing the approximation is emblematic of a shift in emphasis toward the artist or designer as genius which, at least in the early twentieth century, cast a long shadow back over the prints of the previous century.

It is easy to imagine that Toyokuni's reputation in the West (and consequently in Japan) was profoundly impacted by the structural opposition that emerged in European artistic discourse between aesthetic and commercial value, where these two values were often inversely related. That this opposition, and the governing ideology of art for art's sake, emerged at just the moment in Europe when Japanese prints became an object of both aesthetic appreciation and of commerce suggests how deeply connected the history of Japanese prints in the West has been to the emergence of the very aesthetic standards which have then been used to evaluate these images.

At the same time that Shōyō was beginning to grapple with the legacy of this dualistic structure for the understanding of Japanese prints, European art historians, too, were working towards a methodology by which to overcome what, a short time later, Walter Benjamin would call "the fetish of the master's signature."[25] Indeed, the study of the early nineteenth-century world of Japanese printmaking seems to offer a fertile ground for what, in 1915, Heinrich Wölfflin suggestively called "a history of art with no names." In such a history, the individuality of the artist would no longer be the object of historical inquiry but would emerge almost as an impediment to true historical knowledge. "Not everything is possible at all times," Wölfflin writes: "vision itself has a history, and the revelation of these visual strata must be regarded as the primary task of art history."[26] Here, individuality would fade away as an insignificant deviation within a generalized field of possibilities, a "vocabulary of forms."[27] And there is no doubt that at one level, in order to apprehend the work of Toyokuni as a contemporary might have, and so to begin to reclaim the "visual strata" of nineteenth-century Japan, we must begin by shedding the outmoded weight of "the economics of genius" that has dominated the understanding of woodblock prints since the late nineteenth century.[28] This, after all, is what is suggested by the disjuncture between Shōyō's understanding of artistic or stylistic individuality, on the one hand, and Toyokuni's use of *kuse* to refer to the distinguishing characteristics of the face and the individuality of the subject of representation on the other.

This, however, is not the end of the problem but really the beginning. For, while very different from "the economics of genius" that would come to define

---

[25] Walter Benjamin, "Eduard Fuchs, Collector and Historian," in *Walter Benjamin: Selected* Writings, vol. 3 (Cambridge: Belknap Press, 2006), p. 283.

[26] Heinrich Wölfflin, *Principles of Art History: The Problem of the Development of Style in Late Art*, trans. Mary D. Hottinger (New York: Dover Publications, 1950), p. 11.

[27] Ernst Cassierer, *The Logic of the Cultural Sciences*, trans. S. G. Lofts (New Haven, CT: Yale University Press, 2000), p. 116.

[28] Allen Hockley, *The Prints of Isoda Koryūsai: Floating World Culture and Its Consumers in Eighteenth-Century Japan* (Seattle, WA: University of Washington Press, 2003), p. 13.

the value, both artistic and monetary, of Japanese prints as "art" in the twentieth century, Toyokuni and his contemporaries were no less concerned with issues of status, celebrity, and value than later connoisseurs and collectors. Toyokuni would certainly have found van Gogh's idea that Japanese print designers "earned very little money and lived like simple workmen" as foreign and distasteful as Fenollosa's characterization of Toyokuni's work as "degenerate."[29] Indeed, only by understanding how the artist's name functioned within the pictorial economy of nineteenth-century Japan can we properly historicize the function of the name as a marker of aesthetic and economic worth and so approach the structuring of the visual field of Toyokuni and his age.

There is a revealing anecdote, recalled by Kyokutei Bakin in his "Catalogue of Recent Fiction Writers of Edo" ("Kinsei mono no hon Edo sakusha burui"), which suggests the role that Toyokuni saw for his own fame in structuring the market for printed images in the years around 1815:

> Around 1815 or 16, Tsuruya [Kiemon] published a book based on the libretto for the puppet play *Yoshitsune and the Thousand Cherry Trees* which the print designer Toyokuni had drawn using the likenesses of that year's actors but with no text save a preface by [Jippensha] Ikku; when the book did not sell at all, Senkakudō [Tsuruya Kiemon] requested that I add text to the illustrations [...] The book was reprinted in the spring of 1818 and this time when it was published was well received by the public and I've heard that several thousand copies have sold. At the time, many works of fiction illustrated by Toyokuni were very popular and so not satisfied but to rank alongside the authors [*sakusha*], he suggested to those in the book trade the idea of a work of illustrated fiction with no text, thinking that his illustrations alone would sell and wishing to demonstrate as much. The book was published but, with just illustrations and no text, it entertained not even women and children, and Toyokuni, no doubt embarrassed, has not written another such illustrated novel.[30]

Like much that Bakin wrote about his contemporaries, this passage is petty and self-congratulatory. But Bakin was also the most trenchant of observers of nineteenth-century cultural life, and much of what we know of this world we owe to his essays, letters, and diaries. And here we find, presented with Bakin's usual mix of malice and insight, his dearest of subjects: the intersection of aesthetics and commerce and the role that the latter has in shaping the former.

By the middle of the second decade of the nineteenth century, Bakin had grown increasingly frustrated with the role that illustrations and illustrators had come

---

[29] Vincent van Gogh, *Van Gogh on Art and Artists: Letters to Emile Bernard*, trans. Douglas Cooper (New York: Dover Publications, 2003), p. 85.

[30] Kyokutei Bakin, *Kinsei mono no hon Edo sakusha burui: chosha jihitsu hokibon*, ed. Kimura Miyogo (Tokyo: Yagi Shoten, 1988), pp. 85–86.

to play within the literary market.[31] It was not, of course, that Bakin objected to illustrations as such; what he resented was the marginalization of the author, the increasing sense in these years that the author was but one of a number of figures who contributed, in relatively equal weight, to the production of a book.[32] Toyokuni had taken this a step further still; he had essentially eliminated the author. The passage, after all, centers on Toyokuni's status and his desire to "rank alongside the authors," indeed to displace the author by dispensing with the written word and elevating the illustrations as the core of the printed book. Bakin would ungraciously, if cryptically, allude to this in the preface he wrote for the reprinted version of Toyokuni's *Yoshitsune and the Thousand Cherry Trees*: "at the request of Senkakudō, father and son who have been old friends of some thirty years, I have but plucked the strings of the shamisen with my teeth."[33] Bakin is here merely accompanying the main act, Toyokuni, the illustrator.

As he would recall in his "Catalogue of Recent Fiction Writers of Edo," in another passage centered on Toyokuni and his ambitions, this metaphor of instrumental accompaniment was not Bakin's own but had been told to him by his late friend, mentor, and sometime rival Santō Kyōden:

> When [Kyōden's] popularity took off with the publication of *The Complete Tale of Princess Sakura* (*Sakurahime zenden*) [1805] with Toyokuni as his illustrator, he became quite friendly with Toyokuni and Kyōden was more than willing to give the illustrator the lion's share of the credit. Were I to compare it to the puppet theater, Kyōden had said, the illustrator is like the chanter and the author is like the accompanist on the *shamisen*. This goes without saying for illustrated fiction (*gōkan no kusazōshi*) but it is said even historical fiction (*yomihon*) will not sell if the illustrator lacks skill. And Toyokuni was more than happy to believe that he was responsible for his and Kyōden's success and from that point even began putting the illustrator's name above that of the author on the title page and signing the works: illustrated by Toyokuni and written by Kyōden.[34]

In the opening years of the nineteenth century, the "artist's" signature emerges as *the* arbiter of value but very differently from its function at the close of the century. What is crucial is not originality or stylistic distinctiveness but the much more straightforward issue of profit and loss.

Toyokuni's textless version of *Yoshitsune and the Thousand Cherry Trees* and his *A Quick Guide to Actor Likenesses* were both published in the middle years of the

---

[31] See Hamada Keisuke, "On Booksellers, Authors, and Readers in the Works of Bakin," trans. Peter Kornicki, http://www.sharpweb.org/main/wp-content/uploads/2014/09/Paper_Hamada.pdf.

[32] On the marginalization of the author in the early nineteenth century, see Jonathan E. Zwicker, *Practices of the Sentimental Imagination: Melodrama, the Novel, and the Social Imaginary in Nineteenth-Century Japan* (Cambridge, MA: Harvard University Asia Center, 2006), pp. 87–90.

[33] Kyokutei Bakin, *Yoshitsune senbonzakura*, vol. 1 (Edo: Tsuruya Kiemon, 1819), 1r.

[34] Kyokutei Bakin, *Kinsei mono no hon Edo sakusha burui*, p. 151.

second decade of the nineteenth century by Tsuruya Kiemon's publishing house Senkakudō, and the relationship between the two texts is suggestive both of the extent to which Toyokuni's *name* had itself come to function as a marker of value and the role that the actor's image played as a medium in the construction of the graphic economy of nineteenth-century Japan. Jippensha Ikku wrote in his preface to *A Quick Guide to Actor Likenesses*:

> Generation after generation, the way of the image has been practiced and now the Edo-style of ukiyo-e has spread throughout the land. From the time that Utagawa Ichiyōsai [Toyokuni] first created his style (*ichiryū*) of what we know as actor likenesses, they have been greatly admired and everywhere there are many by whom his name (*na*) is cherished.[35]

Toyokuni's version of *Yoshitsune and the Thousand Cherry Trees* takes this logic of the market to its conclusion with the creation of a book with neither words nor author and in which the puppets of the original eighteenth-century play are brought to life by the illustrator in the guise of the leading actors of the day. Kyōden likened Toyokuni to the chanter of the puppet theater: perhaps a more compelling figure might have been the puppeteer, who wordlessly manipulates the dolls for the audience.

## III Reading the Actor's Image

Central to Toyokuni's understanding of compositional practice as he presents it in *A Quick Guide to Actor Likenesses* is the ability of the print designer to capture what is distinctive to the face of the actor he wished to represent. As it is framed in *A Quick Guide*, the individuality of the face is linked to two other interrelated concerns: reproducibility and legibility. The very idea of *A Quick Guide*, of a book on the technique of actor likenesses, is premised on the notion of reproducibility: in the first instance, that the actor's face can be reproduced as a likeness, and a likeness made possible, as Toyokuni stresses, by the existence of individuality and distinctiveness; and in the second instance, that the likeness can be read or recognized and again reproduced by the reader of the book. "Even ignorant women and children can, if they rely upon this book, draw with a level of skill that is achieved with surprising ease."[36] But the local problem of the amateur's ability to reproduce the actor's likeness needs to be seen against the backdrop of a more generalized problem of reproducibility. This has been suggested, for instance, by Craig Clunas's notion of the work of art in the age of woodblock reproduction as he argued

---

[35] Utagawa Toyokuni, "Yakusha nigao hayageiko," p. 375.
[36] Utagawa Toyokuni, "Yakusha nigao hayageiko," p. 375.

in his book on the visual culture of late imperial China.[37] Not only were block-printed actor prints themselves intended to be reproduced on a large scale, but also the actor's image would be more generally reproduced in prints and in book illustrations and in all manner of printed ephemera including a type of broadsheet in which the actor's image was linked to his rank and salary. Within this spectrum of block-printed material, we can see the importance of the distinctiveness of the actor's face: that he can be easily recognized in terms of individuality across a variety of printed media and regardless of who is responsible for the design of any given image. Indeed, the individuality of the face is, in some ways, premised on effacing the individuality of the designer's brush, *the* very problem that is so often pointed to in the stylistic critique of Toyokuni, that his work is indistinguishable from that of many of his students, and especially the work of Toyokuni III (Utagawa Kunisada), which always raises the specter of the inauthentic.

But in conjunction with reproducibility, there is also the problem of legibility, a problem that Toyokuni himself flags in *A Quick Guide to Actor Likenesses* and that also emerges in a variety of writings concerning the actor's image in the early nineteenth century. If the actor's likeness is not legible as the likeness of a specific actor, identifiable by the reproduction of certain distinctive features (Matsumoto Kōshirō's nose or Iwai Hanshirō's curled lower lip), then the likeness itself has no meaning. Or as Toyokuni puts it in *A Quick Guide*, "because a likeness should allow you to distinguish who is who, and the way you draw will depend on little differences in the eyebrows, eyes, nose, and mouth, please savor this book that you might come to a deep understanding of these techniques" (Figure 5.6).[38] Ōkubo Junichi has suggested that this legibility of the face depends not upon a mimetic representation of the actors' features but rather on the coding of these features as signs.[39] This rendering of the face as a semiotic field allows us to situate the problem of the likeness of the face in relation to a broader system of signs; but with the apprehension of the face as a semiotic surface comes an attendant problem of legibility and the specter of misreading.

In his 1920 book on Toyokuni, it is precisely in a discussion of the problem of legibility as convention or, in Shōyō's language "stylization," that Shōyō begins to reframe the question of style in Toyokuni's work. What Shōyō suggests is that there is a relationship between stylization in actor prints after 1810 and the increasing importance of stylization and convention *on the stage* in these years. A discussion of the former, Shōyō argues, cannot be separated from a discussion of the latter. Shōyō never seems completely comfortable with the supposed degeneration

---

[37] See Craig Clunas, *Pictures and Visuality in Early Modern China* (London: Reaktion Books, 1997), pp. 134–48.

[38] Utagawa Toyokuni, "Yakusha nigao hayageiko," pp. 375–76.

[39] Ōkubo Junichi, "*Yakusha nigao-e hayageiko* to sono shūhen," *Bigaku bijutsushi kenkyū ronbunshū* 5 (1987), p. 127.

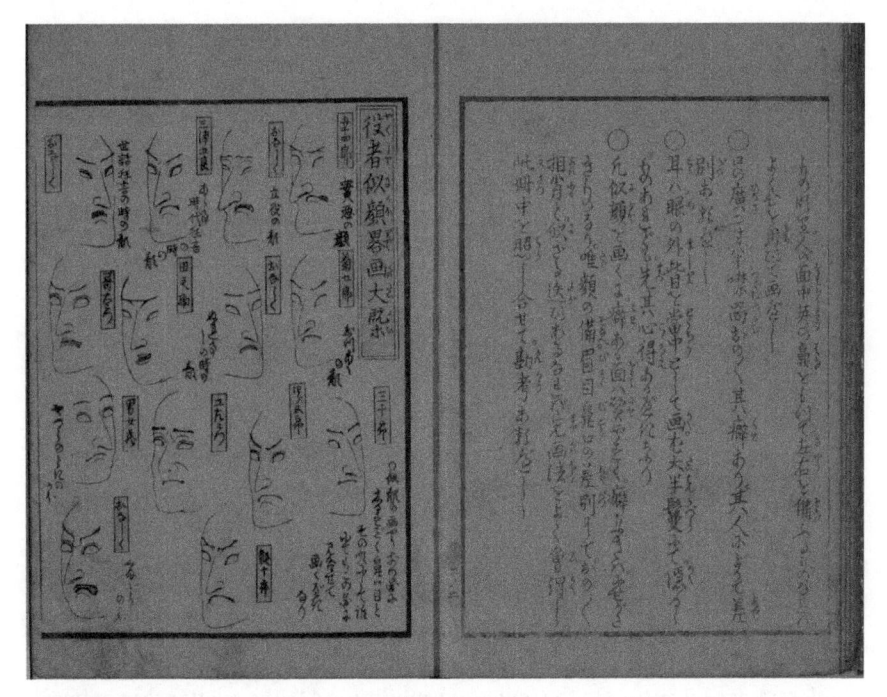

**Figure 5.6** Utagawa Toyokuni, examples of individual actors' faces, *Yakusha nigaoe hayageiko*, 1817.
Source: Art Research Center, Ritsumeikan University.

of Toyokuni after 1810, but neither is he able to escape the basic paradigm of decline which very much structures his discussion of Toyokuni and his school. This tension or unease runs throughout the book, but Shōyō addresses himself to the problem directly when he offers the outlines of a different interpretation of stylistic change, which Shōyō admits is itself indisputable, an interpretation which hinges not on the skill or the intention of the designer but on the content of what is being represented. What Shōyō argues is that a European art historian like Friedrich Succo, who wrote the first book-length study of Toyokuni, was unfamiliar with the history of the Japanese stage in the nineteenth century and could not see that the trend toward convention within actor prints was itself the reflection of a move toward convention *on the stage*. So Shōyō writes that although "of course as pictures their interest and quality declines," the designers of the Utagawa School "strive"—especially after 1810—"directly to copy as well and as objectively as possible the facial features, expressions, and poses of each individual actor." While there is a movement towards stylization in these prints, Shōyō continues, "if one reduces this change in style to a change in attitude toward the subject of actor prints on the part of the artist, then it is only partially right" and "it is necessary to consider the figural style [of these prints] as being born of changes in kabuki itself and in dramatic convention."[40]

Here Shōyō, significantly, shifts his discussion away from addressing the *mode* of representation toward an examination of the *subject* of representation. That is, Shōyō seems intent on rescuing for Toyokuni a place within a history of art dominated by a singular emphasis on mimesis by making the unconventional and highly suggestive argument that the mimetic flaw in Toyokuni's actor prints is due to the non-mimetic nature of what he represented rather than to his technique. If one were faithfully to copy a non-representational art form such as the kabuki of the 1810s, Shōyō argues, one would necessarily come up with a non-representational image regardless of the degree of fidelity one brought to the task. At one level, of course, Shōyō is unable to break out of an obsession with the "imitation of nature"; at another level, however, by pointing toward a homology in the representational strategies of *ukiyo-e* prints and the theater (i.e. between he medium and its subject), Shōyō suggests a novel way of addressing the representational economy of nineteenth-century Japan. He would interrogate the role of convention both on stage and in print as two individuations of a broader concern over legibility in an age of reproduction.

It is in this context that we can understand Toyokuni's own attention in *A Quick Guide to Actor Likenesses* to the issues of legibility and to the relationship between individuality, on the one hand, and type on the other: the importance of capturing the distinctiveness of each actor's face but also the importance of framing this face within the context of readily legible stage conventions including role type. Not only does Toyokuni provide slightly different models for sketching an actor's face in the role of a villain versus as a hero, but he also devotes several pages to the wigs of different roles (Figure 5.7). As he notes in the introduction, the color one will add to the likeness will depend on the make-up used in the role: "There are various distinctions to facial makeup and one should color the face only after careful consideration of the essence of the role." There is thus an intersection in *A Quick Guide*, as indeed in the actor prints themselves, between the individuality of the actor's face and conventions based on role type; but even as distinctiveness and stylization or convention seem in some way antithetical, both are linked to an impulse towards legibility or semiotic clarity. In both instances, it is the emergence of difference against a field of stylization that allows for difference itself to be *read*. The actor's image thus becomes a system of intersecting signs, some of which—patterns of make-up, hairstyle, and costume—point to the actor's role within the drama and on stage and others, which point beyond the stage to the actor himself, his individuality defined in terms of his distinctive facial features, his *kuse*. Properly reading the image involves deciphering both the actor represented and the role he is playing.

[40] Tsubouchi Shōyō, "Shibai-e to Toyokuni oyobi sono monka," in *Shōyō senshū*, vol. 7, pp. 108–09.

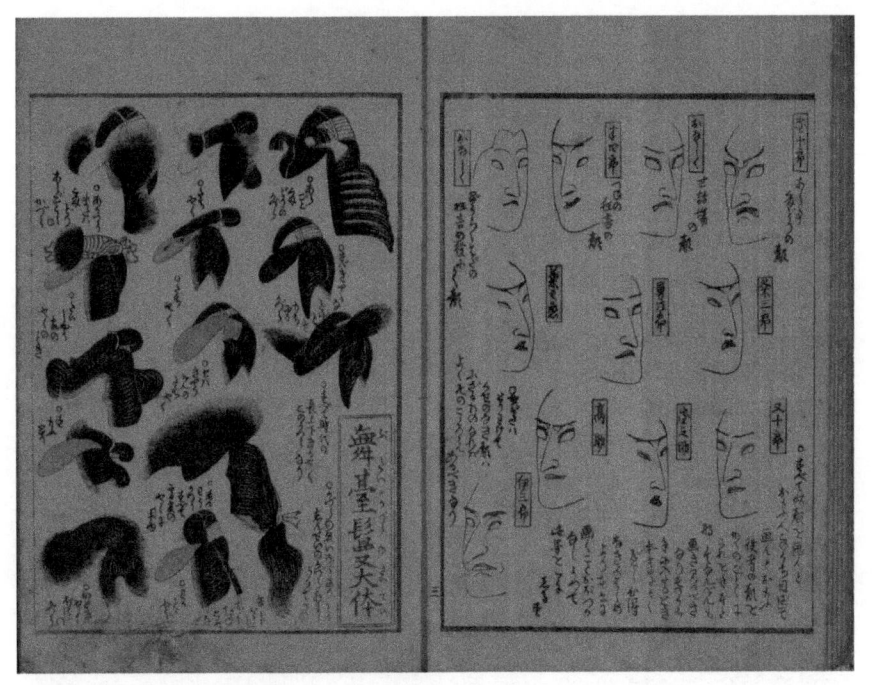

**Figure 5.7** Utagawa Toyokuni, examples of individual actors' faces and wigs based on role type, *Yakusha nigao hayageiko*, 1817.
*Source*: Art Research Center, Ritsumeikan University.

If *A Quick Guide* concerns itself with the semiotics of the actor's image, a host of other works from this period address the grammar of role type. The codification of patterns of make-up, for example, becomes an important subject for early nineteenth-century writings on the culture of the stage, and there emerges in these writings an interesting tension between the preservation of make-up technique as privileged or secret knowledge and the impulse towards making those patterns readily intelligible to the general public. The 1802 *A Magnifying Glass of Thirty-Two Actors' Physiognomies* (*Yakusha sanjūnisō tengankyō*) written by Tōshi Shōkyaku, with a preface by Kyokutei Bakin and illustrated by Toyokuni, provides an extended discussion of theatrical make-up framed as a secret transmission of the physiognomic art of reading complexions. In addition to a general introduction to the principles of physiognomy, with the disclaimer in the preface that "this book is provided for the perusal of the provincial reader and I beg that the theater connoisseurs of Edo not look at it,"[41] *A Magnifying Glass of Thirty-Two Actors' Physiognomies* contains a physiognomic reading of thirty-two actor's faces and a final section titled "A Secret Transmission on Understanding Complexion."

[41] Tōshi Shōkyaku, *Yakusha sanjūnisō tengankyō* (Edo: Gangetsudō and Kōshodō, 1802), 3v.

200 KABUKI'S NINETEENTH CENTURY

Each in its own way, these sections tackle the interpretation of the face and the reading of its features, but the discussion of theatrical make-up in the final section throws into striking relief the issue of legibility in relation to the problem of convention or stylization *within* kabuki as raised by Shōyō. Not only does Shōkyaku provide a general overview of the meanings of different combinations of make-up, but also he includes, mingled in the text, little sketches intended to provide for the reader a basic foundation in *reading* the face as it appears on stage. Shōkyaku begins by explaining that the actor's complexion is "fixed for each role of each act" and then lays out the general guidelines for reading an actor's make-up.[42] Thus, Shōkyaku writes, "A white face with red running down from the eyes is the physiognomy of tragic or romantic hero," and "A face which is a light peach with reddish black wrinkles is the mark of a very old man,"[43] but gradually he becomes more and more specific about the patterns of make-up as they appear on the faces of actors in different roles, adding little sketches to illustrate (Figure 5.8):

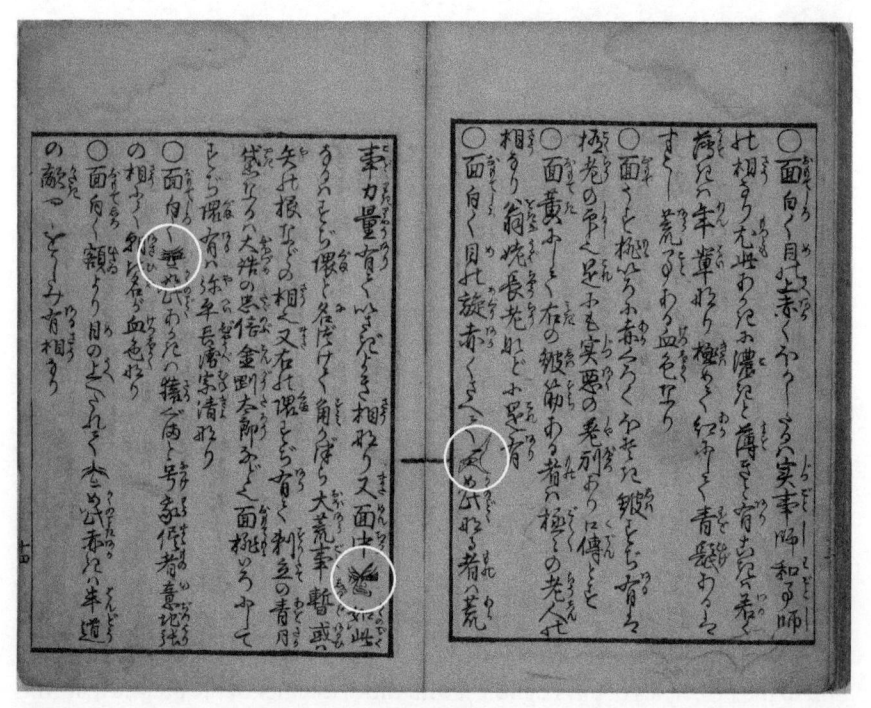

**Figure 5.8** Utagawa Toyokuni, discussion of patterns of makeup from Tōshi Shōkyaku, *Yakusha sanjūnisō tengankyō*, 1802. Indicators of details added by author.
*Source*: Nakai Collection, Art Research Center, Ritsumeikan University.

[42] Tōshi Shōkyaku, *Yakusha sanjūnisō tengankyō*, 16v.
[43] Tōshi Shōkyaku, *Yakusha sanjūnisō tengankyō*, 16v.

A white face on which the eyes are surrounded by red as such (see detail) is the mark of an *aragoto* hero with great strength and heroism. When upon a face you see a pattern like this (see detail), it is known as *sujiguma* or line shadows and is the mark of great *aragoto* hero as in *Just a Minute! (Shibaraku)* or *The Arrow Sharpener (Ya no ne)*. Or when such sinews appear along with a freshly shaven pate, it is the visage of the hero at the end of the play such as Tadanobu or Kongō Tarō. A peach complexion with such sinews is that of a figure like Yaheibyōe Munekiyo.

A white face with a red pattern like this (see detail) is called *sarukuma* or monkey pattern; it is the mark of stubbornness and arrogance; Asaina has this complexion.[44]

The bulk of *A Magnifying Glass of Thirty-Two Actors' Physiognomies* is devoted to the physiognomic description of the faces of individual actors; but here, the emphasis shifts toward a second order of signs, an order that, in a very real sense, forms a layer of convention that rests upon and overlays the individual faces of the actors, incorporating them into the readily legible world of stage convention. There is, in Shikitei Sanba's *Illustrated Dictionary of Theater for Beginners* (*Shibai kinmō zui*), published the following year, 1803, a similar discussion of make-up as physiognomy that counterpoints Shōkyaku's discussion in *A Magnifying Glass of Thirty-Two Actors' Physiognomies* and that also suggests a way of reformulating the problem that Shōyō flags in his discussion of convention, a problem that we might think of as a generalized homology between stylization on the stage and in print.

On the one hand, Sanba refrains from directly addressing the various individual patterns of make-up, noting that "theatrical makeup is something transmitted within acting families and there are many oral and secret transmissions."[45] Thus, in his encyclopedic treatment of the theater that provides an astonishing array of information for the reader, Sanba leaves out make-up almost completely, giving only a brief list of the major styles. And yet, like Shōkyaku in *A Magnifying Glass of Thirty-Two Actors' Physiognomies*, Sanba devotes an extended discussion to the interpretation of make-up couched as a discussion of the physiognomy of complexion. And while this discussion is less detailed than Shōkyaku's and does not provide anything like Shōkyaku's wonderful little sketches to help the reader decipher the visual grammar of make-up, he nonetheless identifies a striking disjuncture or gap between legibility as it functions on stage and as it functions between the stage and the audience. It is in relation to this gap that we can begin to understand stylization both on stage and within prints as two individuations of a larger, more general problem of legibility in the early nineteenth century.

---

[44] Tōshi Shōkyaku, *Yakusha sanjūnisō tengankyō*, 16v–17r.
[45] Shikitei Sanba, *Shibai kinmō zui: Kyōwa 3-nen shohanbon*, Kabuki no Bunken 3 (Tokyo: Nihon Geijutsu Bunka Shinkōkai, 2001), p. 87.

Sanba's discussion of complexion begins similarly to Shōkyaku's, though it is framed as an explication of a foreign land, a device that Sanba uses throughout his encyclopedia.

> The complexions of the people of this land are beautiful, all with white faces. But again, there are those with red faces, either very red or with the whole face covered with a light red or with red sinews. And some faces mix red and blue. These faces are not so because of some illness but were such at birth. Although to an observer from a different land these faces appear quite marvelous, to the residents of this country they are quite ordinary and no one is much surprised by seeing a blue or red face.[46]

But then, turning to the subject of villainy, there is an interesting shift in which the impulse to make the conventions of theatrical make-up legible for the reader gives way to a brilliant discussion of the problem of moral legibility on the stage among characters in the play:

> With blue faces, there are again very blue faces, light blue faces, and faces with blue lines. And there are those on whom only the area around the eyes is blue. People of this hue are exceedingly devious and perverted. But the inhabitants of this land do not seem to notice and often reveal to these people the details of some important matter only later to regret it. Or else, although a person is in fact good, they are doubted and are not confided in. This often causes that person great consternation. Although it is said that one's heart is like one's face meaning that an inconstant heart will be revealed on an inconstant face, there are many in this land with constant faces whose hearts are inconstant [...] At any rate, this is a most confusing country.[47]

Crucial to the dramatic conventions about which Sanba writes is the emergent incommensurability between legibility as it functions on stage and as it functions between the stage and the audience, the ability, that is, of the audience to read the signs and conventions as they appear while the play unfolds. Thus, the audience can read the villainy and virtue of the characters even while these qualities of character remain illegible to the characters on stage. Hence, a gap emerges between the spectator who sees the evil designs quite clearly, and quite literally, written on the villain's face, and the innocent hero or heroine on stage who seems always to misinterpret signs of evil as signs of virtue and signs of virtue as signs of vice.

The problem of legibility—which surfaces in *A Quick Guide to Actor Likenesses* as a question of distinguishing one actor from another—resurfaces in two striking

---

[46] Shikitei Sanba, *Shibai kinmō zui*, p. 95.
[47] Shikitei Sanba, *Shibai kinmō zui*, p. 95.

ways on the stage. First, there is the legibility of the role type on the face of the actor as encoded in make-up; second is the way that all manner of reading and misreading are crucial to the drama of the kabuki theater. In a discussion of stage props in *Illustrated Dictionary of Theater for Beginners*, Sanba suggests how the deployment of various signs within the diegetic world of the play—signs that are invariably misread only, in the end, to be properly deciphered—functions within the plot structure of nineteenth-century drama. He notes, for instance, that there appear in the world of the theater many magical swords with various wondrous powers. Even when hidden away, a magical sword can, by means of its virtuous power, cause a base person to cower in fear and even to faint. But these swords, Sanba notes, are constantly lost, as are, he continues, precious jewels. And seals, which are so often used to forge, and counterfeit, and cheat seem, in this world, stolen with particular ease and are repeatedly lost. And objects once lost or stolen are often then lost or stolen again.[48] Within the plays of the eighteenth and nineteenth centuries, all of these lost and stolen swords, jewels, and seals function as markers that reveal a person's true identity, or their culpability for a crime, or their identity as the long-lost son or daughter of a powerful lord. What we might think of as the drama of legibility is, quite literally, enacted over and again on stage. And to the problem to which Shōyō points, we can add a third layer: it is not simply that the actor prints of Toyokuni need to be seen against the backdrop of stylization and convention on stage but that acting convention, too, has to be seen in relation to a dramatic world which is, in its own way, centered around making identity properly legible. Indeed, when one looks at the culture of the early nineteenth century from the perspective of the intersection of these various elements in which the problem of legibility looms so centrally, it is hard not to see that this culture is, in many ways, structured by a generalized preoccupation with the status of the legible.

In early nineteenth-century Japan, there are, then, two intuitions of legibility. In one, legibility is contingent and thus susceptible to misapprehension; in the other, legibility is unmediated and the specter of misreading has been banished: one cannot misrecognize the sign because its identity is guaranteed by its referent. We might return now to the early image that Toyokuni produced for Sakuragawa Jihinari's 1793 *Asaina and the Soga Farce* of Kagekiyo and Dainichibō. That image usefully frames these two conceptions of likeness. At one level, the overall image (as a representation of actors in role) is highly dependent on the ability of the reader to decipher the visual grammar of the illustration in order properly to read it as the likeness of the historical actors Danjūrō V and Hiroemon III. At another level, the image within the image of Kagekiyo in disguise borne by Dainichibō posits an idea of the mimetic power of the image that can immediately reveal Kagekiyo's identity to all who see it.

---

[48] Shikitei Sanba, *Shibai kinmō zui*, pp. 131–32.

Toyokuni would return to this conceit several times over the course of his career, and we find similar compositions in which images within images function as markers of identity in a way that is completely unmediated, based entirely on mimetic fidelity, suggesting the idea of the power of the image to transcend the fragile contingency of context and aspire to what we might think of as immediate and authentic legibility. Here, we might return to an image that I discussed briefly in Chapter 1, one which is taken from a work of fiction on which Toyokuni collaborated with Shikitei Sanba in 1811, *Shadows of Kabuki Cast by Magic Lantern* (*Sono utsushi-e kabuki no omokage*) (Figure 5.9).

In *Shadows of Kabuki Cast by Magic Lantern*, itself in part based on a kabuki play, we find another image bearing the figures of two characters—Tonoinosuke and Nowakihime—who are in hiding from Kodama Hangan. This image first surfaces in the tableau that Toyokuni creates halfway through the work which, as Sanba writes in the note to the reader, represents a kind of stitch linking together the first and second halves of the narrative by interweaving a series of events that, Sanba claims, could not otherwise be fitted into the book.[49] At the center of the

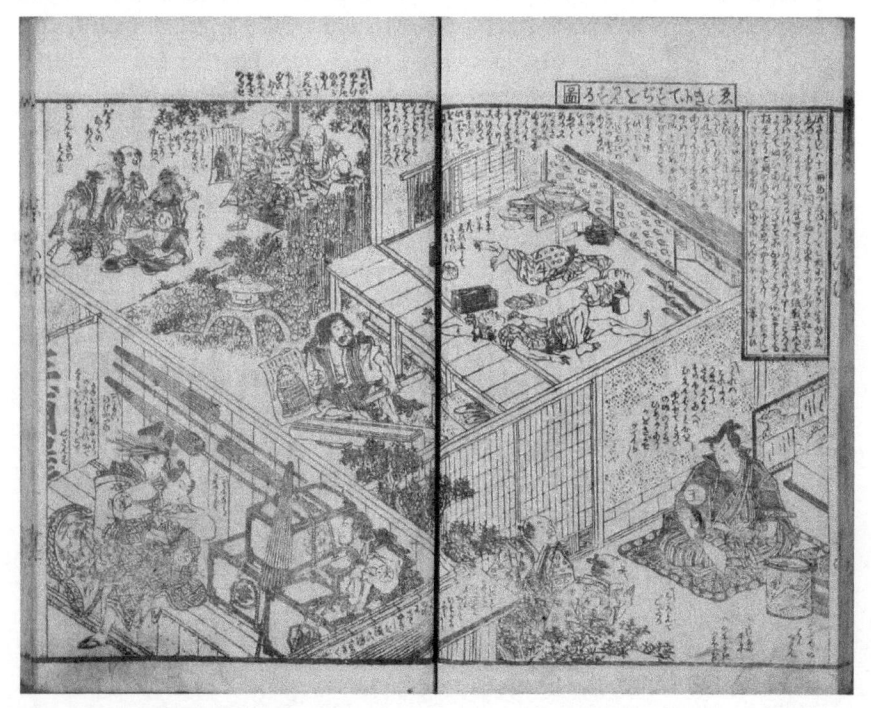

**Figure 5.9** Utagawa Toyokuni, tableau of the plot from Shikitei Sanba, *Sono utsushie kabuki no omokage*, 1811.
Source: Waseda University Library.

---

[49] Shikitei Sanba, *Sono utsushi-e kabuki no omokage* (Edo: Igaya Kan'emon, 1811), 16r.

page, we have the debauched Buddhist priest Hōkaibō in the process of substituting the scroll he has been using to raise funds for a new temple bell for the famed carp scroll. That scroll, the treasure of the Toshima family, done in the hand of the Han Emperor Wu, had been stolen by the retainers of the villain Kodama Hangan. To the lower right, we have Kodama Hangan dispatching his retainers Ihozaki and Gyūhei to search for the fugitive Tonoinosuke, the scion of the Toshima house, and his betrothed Nowakihime, who are shown to the left hiding in the Miuraya and pledging to meet again when the bell tolls midnight. Of course, they are here being overheard by Hōkaibō, hidden in the corner; and above this are Kodama's retainers questioning the wicked Muen Baba and her henchmen while searching for the fugitive couple.

As in the earlier image that Toyokuni produced for *Asaina and the Soga Farce*, there is a homology in this work that revolves around the ways in which likeness is conceptualized and used. First, we have the use of actors' images to illustrate the work, a practice that was already widespread in the second decade of the nineteenth century. Here, as the use of the likeness of Matsumoto Kōshirō V suggests, the images appear to point beyond the page of the book to a real actor in role, even though Kōshirō did not appear in the play on which the work was ostensibly based.

But then there is also the use of likeness within *Shadows of Kabuki Cast by Magic Lantern*, the image-bearing scroll used to search for the fugitive couple, described in the text as a *ninsōgaki* or physiognomic description of a criminal. Here, there is an interesting conceit: while *ninsōgaki* were, indeed, used in the Edo period to search for criminals, these broadsheets simply carried a description of the criminal *in words* with no images. The scroll in *Shadows of Kabuki*, then, is itself a kind of fiction, though one, importantly, with a real efficacy within the story. When Muen Baba discovers Tonoinosuke and Nowakihime hiding along with the courtesan Miyato, it is the scroll that confirms their identities (Figure 5.10).[50] Within the plot, the image is readily legible *as* the likeness of the two figures it depicts and points towards an idea of mimesis: Muen Baba can identify the lovers because, as she says in the story, "It is just as shown here: the young man is the young woman's lover, Tonoinosuke, and the woman is none other than Nowakihime."[51] As with the earlier image of Kagekiyo and Dainichibō, we have a conception of likeness that is transparent: the two figures can be recognized because the scroll faithfully reproduces their images. But, as in that earlier work, likeness is itself set within a context that foregrounds the use of actor likenesses and thus points to a tension between these two conceptions of likeness: one embedded in cultural knowledge and thus contingent on the viewer's ability to read the image; the other premised on an idea of mimetic fidelity as transparent and unmediated.

Moreover, in *Shadows of Kabuki Cast by Magic Lantern*, this question of the legibility of images is itself framed within the larger drama of legibility that Sanba

---

[50] Shikitei Sanba, *Sono utsushi-e kabuki no omokage*, 22r–23v.
[51] Shikitei Sanba, *Sono utsushi-e kabuki no omokage*, 22r–23v.

**Figure 5.10** Utagawa Toyokuni, Muen Baba's discovery of Tonoinosuke and Nowakihime from Shikitei Sanba, *Sono utsushie kabuki no omokage*, 1811
*Source*: Waseda University Library.

had himself outlined in his earlier *Illustrated Dictionary of Theater for Beginners*. Almost all of the stage conventions that Sanba catalogues in his Illustrated Dictionary of Theater for Beginners—lost and stolen objects, disguises, mistaken identities—appear, in one form or another, in *Shadows of Kabuki Cast by Magic Lantern*: there is the carp scroll (stolen twice), which leads to the downfall of the Toshima house; there is the debauched Hōkaibō who disguises himself as Tonoinosuke in an attempt to seduce Nowakihime; and for his part, Tonoinosuke has fallen in love with the courtesan Miyato who, we learn at the very end of the novel, on her death, is actually the long-lost twin sister of his betrothed Nowakihime. What proves her identity is a stick of incense that was left with her when she was abandoned as a baby and which is discovered at her death. As in other works of the nineteenth century, both printed and on stage, the story of *Shadows of Kabuki Cast by Magic Lantern* turns on the dangers of misrecognition, but at its end, all misrecognition and misreading are banished, and it is the light cast by the two magical objects, the statue of Kannon and the carp scroll, that restores the proper moral order, the proper identity of things and their legibility, to the world.

Here are two orders of legibility: one that plays out within the diegetic world of the novel or the play and another that unfolds among the readers, viewers, and the characters in the story. The former is premised on an idea of a misreading of signs that is dispelled as the true nature of the world is revealed by the end of the story. The contingency of meaning (and thus the possibility of misrecognition) is highlighted but only to be dispensed with: we are left with the notion that the true nature of objects always reveals itself.

There is a particularly striking example of how the drama of legibility works in the textless version of *Yoshitsune and the Thousand Cherry Trees* that Toyokuni produced in the years just before publishing *A Quick Guide to Actor Likenesses*. Toyokuni uses the likenesses of contemporary actors-in-role so that, as Bakin would write in his preface to the later edition, "one opening the book will feel just as though he were at the theater and watching the gestures of the actors."[52] But Toyokuni also employs a different technique with which he had begun to experiment in the middle years of the second decade of the nineteenth century, incorporating the stage itself and the audience into representations of the story, dispensing with any conceit of the dramatic action occupying its own, separate space, but heightening the sense of the reader as spectator. In a series of illustrations depicting Act III, Scene 3, one of the dramatic highlights of the play, Toyokuni guides the viewer through that very movement from misrecognition to recognition that is crucial to the nineteenth-century drama of legibility.

The first illustration depicts the audience watching two of the leading actors of the day, Ichikawa Omezō and Asao Kuzaemon, in character on the *hanamichi* as the general Kajiwara Kagetoki and Yazaemon, proprietor of the Tsurube sushi shop (Figure 5.11). Kagetoki searches for the fugitive Taira no Koremori whom Yazaemon is hiding. This image is followed by a depiction of the actor Matsumoto Kōshirō V as Igami no Gonta, Yazaemon's son, receiving a war mantle from Kagetoki as a reward for betraying Koremori and turning in Koremori's severed head along with Wakaba no Naishi and Rokudai, Koremori's wife and son. The final illustration in the series, which concludes Act III of the play and the second volume of the three-volume book, shows the real Koremori, very much alive, with Wakaba and Rokudai. The caption reads:

> Igami no Gonta has switched his own wife and child for Wakaba no Naishi and Rokudai Kimi and pretended that the severed head in the sushi tub was Lord Koremori's and reveals his true motive. Yazaemon, who did not know this, has stabbed Gonta and, as Gonta is on his final breath, Koremori solves the riddle contained in the verse of the war mantle: you must become a priest.[53]

Gonta, moved by his father's devotion to Koremori, has sacrificed his own wife and child for Wakaba and Rokudai, but this is all revealed too late: Yazaemon has compounded the tragedy by killing his own son, Gonta.

---

[52] Kyokutei Bakin, *Yoshitsune senbonzakura*, 1r.
[53] Kyokutei Bakin, *Yoshitsune senbonzakura*, 35r.

**Figure 5.11** Utagawa Toyokuni, Ichikawa Omezō as Kajiwara Kagetoki and Asao Kuzaemon as Yazaemon from Kyokutei Bakin, *Ehon Yoshitsune senbonzakura*, 1819.
*Source*: Art Research Center, Ritsumeikan University.

Over the course of these three illustrations, it is as if the drama of legibility is enacted before our eyes. The first image sets up a disjuncture between the stage and the audience, marking the gap of legibility to which Sanba had pointed in his *Illustrated Dictionary of Theater for Beginners*. Then comes the great moment of misreading, where it appears that Gonta has betrayed his father's vow to protect Koremori, Wakaba, and Rokudai. Finally comes the revelation of Gonta's "true motive," but, of course, this comes too late. Gonta has sacrificed his wife and son in the service of Koremori, and Yazaemon too, in stabbing Gonta, has taken the life of his own son.

In the preface that he wrote to the later edition of Toyokuni's illustrated *Yoshitsune and the Thousand Cherry Trees*, Bakin noted that this was the most "remarkable" (*myō*) scene in the play: "Gonta's transformation from pure evil to pure good completely fools the audience." "This scene," Bakin continues, "is the origin of the technique of deceiving the audience which is now widely employed by writers of romances."[54] Here, Bakin points to a suggestive tension in the mechanics of a scene which depends for its dramatic effect on the deception of the audience,

---

[54] Kyokutei Bakin, *Yoshitsune senbonzakura* vol.1 (Edo: Tsuruya Kiemon, 1819), 1r.

on the collapsing of the semiotic gap between how the audience interprets what it sees and how the characters within the play read each other. The audience is fooled by Gonta just as Yazaemon is. Yet, by the early nineteenth century, this very "technique" of deception and revelation has itself become a common and widely deployed narrative device, really *the* narrative device of early nineteenth-century drama and fiction, endlessly repeated in the plays and novels of this period. Deception and revelation, that is, are built into the narrative fabric of the early nineteenth century; the aesthetic of this period is unthinkable without this technique. Whatever the power of this device to "deceive" audiences in the 1740s when *Yoshitsune and the Thousand Cherry Trees* was first staged, by the time Bakin was writing in the second decade of the nineteenth century the efficacy of this scene was surely quite different. It was no longer dependent on the successful deception of the audience but almost the reverse, for the audience is aware of the gap between what it sees and what the characters on stage see. They watch the tragedy of the scene unfold before their eyes but are powerless to stop it.

Or we might imagine that this scene functioned quite differently depending on the capacity of the playgoer correctly to decipher the various levels of signs encountered in the staging of the drama. To borrow the distinction from the preface to *A Magnifying Glass of Thirty-Two Actors' Physiognomies*, the "provincial" playgoer might indeed be fooled, but for the "theater connoisseur of Edo" a more complicated drama of recognition was at work. The constant invocation of the figure of an almost mythical provincial traveler—so perfectly embodied by Sanba's Inakamono Tarōzaemon in his 1806 *Theater Chic This Side of the Curtain* (*Kejō suigen maku no soto*)—overwhelmed by the signs and surfaces he encounters in the metropolis suggests the degree to which the problem of legibility had come, in the opening decades of the nineteenth century, to be intimately bound up not only with status and class as they are conventionally understood but also with a geography of difference.

It is tempting, then, to see the problem of legibility as it appears again and again in the culture of the theater of early nineteenth-century Japan as in some ways directly related to the issue of the broadening base of consumption. Early-nineteenth-century texts themselves, after all, often turn to the subject of what we might think of as unauthorized or illegitimate consumption; the provincial playgoer unable to decipher an actor print is just one instance of this figuration. In many ways, this is essentially the argument that is made about Toyokuni: that, beginning in the second decade of the nineteenth century, his work deteriorates precisely because he is pandering to a widening market of consumers, that he sacrifices art to commerce, and that he is content with abasing himself before the "popular eye."[55] But this view of Toyokuni is never put forward by his contemporaries despite the fact that writers like Bakin and Sanba—both of whom

---

[55] Nakada Tatsunosuke, *Ukiyo-e ruikō*, p. 140.

often collaborated with Toyokuni—frequently address this very subject in the context of the fiction market.[56] Indeed, to see legibility as solely, or even primarily, a question of making available to one set of socially constituted dispositions codes that are already operative for another is fundamentally to misunderstand the problem of legibility as it is figured within the culture of the early nineteenth century. The crucial gap in legibility that, for writers like Sanba and Bakin, exists between the connoisseur and the amateur or provincial, a gap that is often exploited for comic purposes, is itself a sort of repetition of the gap between what the audience sees and what the characters on stage see. Sanba points obliquely to this in his *Illustrated Dictionary of Theater for Beginners*, and Toyokuni dramatizes it in his illustrations to *Yoshitsune and the Thousand Cherry Trees*. But the existence of the gap is itself not the crucial issue; it is the fact that the gap makes visible—by highlighting and by dramatizing the breakdown of the process of semiosis—the fundamental contingency of *all* legibility.[57]

The emergence, then, of legibility as such a crucial matter *within* the culture of the early nineteenth century suggests an anxiety over ambiguity, even the problem of intelligibility, an anxiety central to the staging of the drama of legibility within kabuki, an anxiety that cultural codes once legible, or what is more probably the case, codes that were *imagined* to have been once clearly and naturally legible, are understood to be imbedded, contingent, and ambiguous. That the drama of this time so often revolves around the mistaken interpretation of a sign which is later clarified suggests a nostalgic impulse toward a lost or imagined world of authentic legibility, a world from which misinterpretation and misreading are banished.

Early-nineteenth-century understandings of representation seem caught between these poles, between an open acknowledgement of the codes that make representation possible, on the one hand, and a not yet entirely abandoned ideal of a representation that transcends the fragile contingency of the viewer and aspires to authentic, unmediated legibility on the other. Toyokuni's 1817 *A Quick Guide to Actor Likenesses*, with its emphasis on piecing together the individuality of the actor through a sort of bricolage of noses, eyes, hairstyles, and make-up, is a text that not only acknowledges representation as a kind of code but also provides the tools for the code to be both deciphered and reproduced.

Beginning in the early twentieth century, the tension that existed in nineteenth-century aesthetics between an understanding of representation as convention and a contrapuntal impulse towards an affective efficacy that exceeds and complicates that very understanding, would grow increasingly opaque to interpreters of the prints of Toyokuni and his contemporaries. The latter would be overwhelmed by

---

[56] See Jonathan E. Zwicker, *Practices of the Sentimental Imagination: Melodrama, the Novel, and the Social Imaginary in Nineteenth-Century Japan*, pp. 85–90.

[57] See Pierre Bourdieu, *Distinction: A Social Critique of the Judgment of Taste*, trans. Richard Nice (Cambridge, MA: Harvard University Press, 1984), p. 2.

the former and Toyokuni would be, like so many others, charged with a kind of "dumbing down" of the aesthetic heights of early *ukiyo-e* printmakers.[58] In the late nineteenth century, however, there remained a rather different interpretation of Toyokuni and his work, one that accentuated rather than elided the not-easily-reconciled tension between a foregrounding of conventionality, on the one hand, and the positing of an authentic realm of emotion on the other.

One of the most suggestive examples of this tension comes from an anecdote recorded by Iijima Kyoshin in his *Lives of the Utagawa Ukiyo-e Masters* (*Ukiyoeshi Utagawa retsuden*) compiled in the 1890s. Like most of the legends that surround Toyokuni, we know very little of the origins of this story: it is likely apocryphal, of uncertain date, perhaps a piece of self-fashioning by Toyokuni himself, perhaps part of posthumous reframing of his life and work. The story centers on a commission Toyokuni received to paint a portrait of a wealthy merchant. Toyokuni accepts the commission but as the months go by, he produces nothing. When the merchant sends a young servant girl to check on the progress of the portrait, Toyokuni has sketched the outline but left it completely blank. Then the story takes an unexpected twist as the servant precociously asks that Toyokuni produce a portrait of her as well. "You," Toyokuni responds to her request, "what would you need a portrait for?" The servant explains that she is from a distant province and has not seen her parents for three years:

> Weeping she says: "I thought if I could but send them my portrait how happy they would be." Hearing this, Toyokuni was himself brought to tears, deeply moved by her feelings. Straight away he took up his brush and had the girl sit and painted her portrait, lavishly colored on a beautiful piece of silk.

When the merchant learns of this, he is understandably angry and confronts Toyokuni over his excessive procrastination.[59] Toyokuni answers:

> What you believe is reasonable but I have not been dallying. I often pick up my brush with the intention of painting but am unable to. In truth, your portrait (*shōzō*) is difficult to paint. In general, to paint a portrait one must first observe the subject's nature and conduct but if you are unable to draw these then the portrait will not be realistic (*shin wo utsusu koto atawazaru*). For example, if one is loyal, then I must grasp that feeling of loyalty as I draw; if one is filial then I must grasp that feeling of filial piety and so forth. Yet when I observe your everyday comportment, you are simply too ordinary, there is nothing at all particular about you. And so, there is nothing on which I can focus my attention and so I have made no progress at all. I have already completed the outline of the portrait but

---

[58] On "dumbing down," see Allen Hockley's analysis in *The Prints of Isoda Koryūsai*, pp. 64–68.

[59] Iijima Kyoshin, *Ukiyoeshi Utagawa retsuden*, ed. Tamabayashi Seirō (Tokyo: Unebi Shobō, 1941), pp. 111–12.

without something on which to focus my attention I am unable to add the colors. As for your servant, her face is brimming with true filial piety and so is quite easy to draw and so I was able to finish drawing that image quite quickly.[60]

In *A Quick Guide to Actor Likenesses*, representation is premised on the physical distinctiveness or peculiarities of the face: "a face with individuality is easy to approximate and one without individuality is difficult." Here, the matter is rather different: no mention is made of the contours of lips or noses; instead, the emphasis has shifted to using the portrait to express the inner feelings of the subject, themselves expressed in the face, like the servant's devotion to her parents: brimming with filial piety, she is the very picture of unaffected innocence. She can be drawn because of her very artlessness, though the artless and sincere servant girl is herself one of the great archetypes of nineteenth-century literary and theatrical culture.

The merchant, on the other hand, is a sort of "man without qualities": he can be represented only in outline but the details are blank, the very embodiment of Marx's idea of money as "the general overturning of *individualities*."[61] Indeed, the entire anecdote turns on the negation of money: the merchant can commission a portrait but cannot, in the end, buy one; the servant girl, on the other hand, cannot pay Toyokuni but can be embodied in an image. Here, images are removed from the commercial arena, a total disavowal of that aspect of Toyokuni's work that was most pronounced during his life, his ability to turn the reproduction of likeness into a currency.

This anecdote recalls an earlier legend surrounding Toyokuni's talent, one that was created by Toyokuni himself, with Santō Kyōden's help. The story is first recorded in the preface Kyōden wrote to *Opening the Canister for Morning Tea* (*Asa chanoyu chotto kuchikiri*, 1812), a work of illustrated fiction on which he collaborated with Toyokuni:

> Utagawa Toyokuni's father Kurahashi Gorobē was a dollmaker by trade and was quite talented at making dolls that resembled actors. There is thus a natural connection with Toyokuni's now taking actor's likenesses as his own trade. There is a doll of the late Ichikawa Danjūrō V made by Toyokuni's late father in the role of Ya no ne Gorō. Toyokuni had been keeping this doll as a memento of his father but when he showed the doll to the current Danjūrō, the actor was so overwhelmed at seeing his grandfather's likeness before him that he was moved to tears. Toyokuni was touched and gave the doll to Danjūrō and it is now in his possession.[62]

[60] Iijima Kyoshin, *Ukiyoeshi Utagawa retsuden*, pp. 112–15.
[61] Karl Marx, "Economic and Philosophic Manuscripts of 1844," in *The Marx–Engels Reader*, ed. Robert C. Tucker (New York: Norton, 1978), p. 105.
[62] Santō Kyōden, *Asa chanoyu chotto kuchikiri* (Edo: Eirakuya Tōshirō, 1812), 1r.

It is impossible to tell whether this anecdote is apocryphal, but as a piece of self-fashioning it is extremely revealing. There are two crucial elements of the story that Kyōden tells: the ability of Toyokuni's father's doll to elicit Danjūrō's tears and the ascription of the affective power of Toyokuni's own images to inheritance rather than to learning.

Both Kyoshin's anecdote from the end of the nineteenth century and the story of the puppet of Ichikawa Danjūrō recorded by Kyōden at the beginning of that century hinge on tears. Tears serve a particular function, marking a space free from money and the fungibility of things: both anecdotes, that is, disavow money in favor of the gift. It is as if even Toyokuni, the great champion of the image as commodity and certainly the most commercially successful print designer of his day, was unable, ultimately, to abandon the ideal of a mode of representation that escaped the powers of money. Or, one imagines, it was that a figure like Toyokuni, who *could* finally embrace the full potential of the commercialization of the image, would, after his death, be reinterpreted so that he could be integrated into an aesthetic system fraught with ambivalence toward print and profit. But these anecdotes also share a third link: each centers not on a printed image but on a singular object as if, at the very moment that images attain their greatest potential as commercial objects through the intersection of convention as a mode of representation and print as a manner of reproduction, something else pushes in the opposite direction: an epistemology of representation that disavows both convention and commerce and which is based not on reproduction but on singularity.

To grasp the aesthetic of Toyokuni and his age is to come to terms with this seemingly paradoxical embrace of the commercial potential of the image, on the one hand, and a profound ambivalence toward print and commerce on the other, an ambivalence marked by a lingering anxiety over the status of the authentic and how individuality is articulated in an age of reproduction. For professional print designers and authors, these anxieties were both a matter of practical concern and an occasion for self-reflection. In an 1833 essay on the relationship between woodblock prints and painting, Toyokuni's contemporary and fellow print designer Keisai Eisen argued strenuously against what he saw was an artificial distinction made between *ukiyo-e* prints and Japanese-style paintings (*Yamato-e*), based solely on the fact that the former were printed and sold and the latter produced by officially sponsored ateliers:

> It is not as if it were only ukiyo-e designers who produced printed images; there is nothing other than printing to transmit images to posterity. For someone beginning to learn to paint these are of the greatest benefit and there are hundreds of volumes of collections of every master of Chinese painting. Moreover, there are dozens of books in Japan that reproduce the hand of Chinese painters

like Li Yu's *Mustard Seed Garden Manual of Painting* and there are hundreds of volumes published of Japanese-style painters in the Kanō style such as Ōoka Shunboku and Tachibana Morikuni [...] Is it not a great fortune due to receiving the favor of heaven and good karma that today prints can be sold as among the most celebrated products of Edo? In this sense, is it not mistaken to distinguish between officially patronized painters and those who paint for pleasure and those who do so to make a living?[63]

For the better part of two centuries now, Eisen's questions have gone unanswered. The space that had been opened in the early nineteenth century to interrogate these problems had closed with the end of that century. With the emergence of the modern discipline of art history in Japan in the late nineteenth century, the split between block printed images and painted images would be reified and institutionalized.[64] While prints would come to be comprehended as "art," this was itself premised on a negation of their most immediate commercial dimensions and an accompanying museumification.

Only recently have we turned toward a recovery of the commercial history of woodblock prints, which has held out the promise of understanding the complexity that marked these objects in the nineteenth century as products of both aesthetic and commercial impulses. For Eisen, the problem is not how to reconcile art and commerce but what such terms might mean in an age dominated by print and in which the making of pictures is freed from structures of patronage, for the first time becoming a profession. The historian of these prints, then, is confronted by a seemingly paradoxical situation: the woodblock prints of Toyokuni and his age cannot be understood through conventional categories of art and commerce not because they are both aesthetic and commercial, and thus blur the distinctions between the two, but because what it meant to be aesthetic or commercial in nineteenth-century Japan can only be grasped by interrogating the history of representation of which these images are themselves a part. In his 1920 book on Toyokuni, Tsubouchi Shōyō had seen these prints as an entirely transparent medium, as a means to "reanimate what really happened on stage like a Kinemacolor film." Shōyō was deeply resistant to the aestheticization of woodblock prints, which risked transforming the historical record into objects for aesthetic contemplation; but in looking toward the prints as a documentary source, Shōyō did not grasp what is essentially historical about the prints: not what they represent but *how* they represent and ultimately how they grapple with representation itself. If the prints of Toyokuni and his contemporaries are to be likened to the cinema, it is

---

[63] Nakada Tatsunosuke, *Ukiyo-e ruikō*, p. 25.

[64] On the emergence of art history as a modern academic discipline, see Kitazawa Noriaki, *Me no shinden* (Tokyo: Bijutsu shuppansha, 1989); Satō Dōshin, *"Nihon bijutsu" tanjō: kindai Nihon no "kotoba" to senryaku* (Tokyo: Kōdansha, 1996); Satō Dōshin, *Modern Japanese Art and the Meiji State: The Politics of Beauty*, trans. Hiroshi Nara (Los Angeles, CA: Getty Research Institute, 2011).

not in their ability transparently to capture reality but rather in the question they raise of how any medium is situated within a social and historical context, how representation is always also a problem of legibility.

## IV Photographing the Stage/Staging the Photograph

The episode about Toyokuni and the servant girl was first recorded by Iijima Kyoshin in the mid-1890s, and there are two crucial stories to be told about the fate of the actor's image in the final decade of the nineteenth century that help make sense of the historicity of this anecdote. The first is the role that an international market for Japanese prints, centered on Europe and America, played in structuring the ways in which these prints came to be valued, both aesthetically and commercially, in Japan itself. The second is how the photograph emerged as its own medium of likeness in relation to the theater, a medium that was seen first as a commodity and, eventually, as an archival tool, a means of reproducing and preserving earlier, woodblock printed images. Three decades later, both of these strands would come together in the 1925 photograph of Shōyō in his study surrounded by actor prints, the photograph with which I began this chapter.

During the course of writing his essays on theater prints in the late 1910s, Shōyō repeatedly visited two prominent dealers from whom he purchased a number of prints: Kobayashi Bunshichi and Kawaura Kenichi. Both men had begun their careers in the 1890s and were intimately involved in the international trade in Japanese prints during that decade.

Kobayashi worked closely with Iijima Kyoshin and, in 1893, published two books by Kyoshin, his biography of Katsushika Hokusai and a brief guide to *ukiyo-e* print designers (*Ukiyo eshi benran*). In the years that followed, Kobayashi would play a critical role in the global trade in Japanese prints, a position he occupied until his death in 1923, and he would help to shape the tastes of great collectors of Gilded Age America such as Isabella Stuart Gardner and Charles Lang Freer. In 1916, Shōyō helped to facilitate Kobayashi's sale of some 15,000 theater prints to the Waseda University Library, a collection that would eventually form the basis of the collection of the Theater Museum when it opened in 1928. It was these prints that Shōyō was cataloging when he was photographed in his study in 1925.

In 1893, the same year that Kobayashi published Kyoshin's guide to print designers, a dealer named Sakai Matsunosuke also produced a guide to collecting woodblock prints, *A Handbook for Purchasing Antique Ukiyo-e* (*Kodai ukiyo-e kaiire hikkei*). Sakai's book is a fascinating document of this period: written "as a handbook for those purchasing antique ukiyo-e to export abroad,"[65] it contains

---

[65] Sakai Matsunosuke, *Kodai ukiyo-e kaiire hikkei* (Tokyo: Yoshizawa Shōho, 1893), p. 1.

extensive advice on what kinds of prints are valued by foreign collectors (above all, hand-painted images and illustrated books) as well as what kinds of items a dealer might offer in exchange for prints (helpfully sold by the book's publisher, Yoshizawa Shōho): Western chromolithographs and color lithograph reproductions of Utamaro prints. Sakai's book, moreover, provides a clear picture of the fate to which the actor's image was consigned in the late nineteenth century:

> Although actor likenesses that are at least a century old and that correspond to diagrams eight and above are acceptable, those corresponding to diagrams nine and forward have very little value. Moreover, there are many buyers who will not purchase prints by certain designers regardless of price and even prints corresponding to diagrams eight and above are worth only about half of what you can get for a print of a beauty (*bijinga*).[66]

The advice for the collector and dealer is presented in quintessentially economic terms, terms, moreover, shaped by foreign taste. The dividing line between those actor prints of some value and those of no value at all is set a century earlier, at the end of the eighteenth century, and thus the actor's likeness ceases to have any value just as Toyokuni's career begins to take off. Even older prints from the eighteenth century (by designers of the Torii and Katsukawa schools) are assigned only minimal value if their subject is the stage.

The diagrams referred to repeatedly in the text, which appear at the beginning of the handbook (Figure 5.12), are little sketches of various women's hairstyles that are intended to reveal the approximate date of the print's composition. Here, we find a faint echo of Toyokuni's own sketches of hairstyles from *A Quick Guide to Actor Likenesses* but with a very different import. In Toyokuni's text, the actors' wigs were intended to suggest role type and, crucially, to be a kind of fungible sign that could be employed by any number of print designers to designate the role not only in prints but also in fiction or emblazoned on decorative objects. The same marker is here transformed into a clue to be used for authentication and to assign value, the hair as key to dating.

The most suggestive aspect of Sakai's handbook, however, is to be found in the circumstances under which it was published. The pamphlet was issued by a small import–export firm, Yoshizawa Shōho, which was at the time centrally involved in the trade in various decorative and artistic objects, curios in the sense that Tsubouchi Shōyō would use that term. *A Handbook for Purchasing Antique Ukiyo-e* contains, for example, an advertisement for objects that Yoshizawa Shōho was seeking to purchase and to sell overseas, including old postage stamps, pearls, and shells, but above all the *inrō*, *netsuke*, and incense boxes that were in great demand at the World Fair then taking place in Chicago. But the importance of Yoshizawa

---

[66] Sakai Matsunosuke, *Kodai ukiyo-e kaiire hikkei*, p. 21.

**Figure 5.12** Hairstyles used for dating prints from Sakai Matsunosuke, *Kodai ukiyo-e kaiire hikkei*, 1893.
Source: National Diet Library, Tokyo.

Shōho for the history of Japanese images lies elsewhere. By 1894, the year after *A Handbook for Purchasing Antique Ukiyo-e* was published, Yoshizawa Shōho had merged with another firm, Marukawa Shōten, and assumed the new name of Yoshizawa Shōten. It was around this time that Yoshizawa came to be run by Kawaura Kenichi and began to specialize in selling imported magic lantern slides and projectors, which had been Marukawa's main business.[67]

In 1897, Kawaura purchased one of the first cinématographes brought to Japan; and, in the decade-and-a-half that followed, Yoshizawa Shōten, under Kawaura, would play a central role in the development of the early film industry in Japan. When Kawaura left the cinema entirely in 1912, after helping to establish the Nikkatsu Corporation, he returned to dealing in woodblock prints and published several books based on the prints in his collection.[68] But in 1899, Kawaura worked with Inoue Takejirō, the manager of the Kabuki-za Theater, to arrange for his

[67] Iriguchi Yoshirō, "Yoshizawa Shōten-shu: Kawaura Kenichi no ashiato (1)," *Tōkyō kokuritsu kindai bijutsukan kenkyū kiyō* 18 (2014), 32–63.
[68] Iriguchi, "Yoshizawa Shōten-shu: Kawaura Kenichi no ashiato (1)."

cameraman, Shibata Tsunekichi, to shoot a sequence from the kabuki play *Maple Viewing* (*Momijigari*) starring Ichikawa Danjūrō VII and Onoe Kikugorō V. That film is now the oldest surviving Japanese film, and in 2009, it became the first film designated as an Important Cultural Property by the Agency for Cultural Affairs. I will return to the history of this film and its role in imagining the utopian possibilities of an archive of performance in the epilogue, but first I would like to consider the development of photography and its uses, especially from the mid-1890s forward, as a tool for the preservation of the actor's image and for the preservation of images of the actor.

The earliest photographs of kabuki actors were taken by Uchida Kuichi and date to the 1860s.[69] It is remarkable to realize that roughly a decade before this pioneer of photography in Japan took his iconic photograph of the Emperor Meiji in Western military dress in 1873, Uchida had made portraits of these men who were, at the time, still legally outcasts. By the mid-1870s, studios like the Moriyama Shashinkan and the Genrokukan specializing in actor portraits had begun to operate in the vicinity of theaters, and albumen prints of actors were sold as *cartes de visite* both directly by the studios and within the theaters.[70] Like actor prints, these photographs were conceptualized as commodities and collectibles, and, like those prints, at the time they came to be especially linked to female desire and female consumption.

Indeed, although the print and the photograph appear in some ways as distinct—even potentially antithetical—modes of representation, for well over a quarter of a century, both forms of likeness not only coexisted but also occupied a murky and porous "borderland": images taken as photographs were routinely turned into lithographs or etchings in order to make them more easily reproducible (hence, more easily commodifiable), but they were also turned into oil paintings, seeming to push in the opposite direction, transforming one of the harbingers of the age of mechanical reproduction into the singular and unique.[71] At the same time, woodblock prints, like an 1870 series of actor likenesses by Ochiai Yoshiiku, were designed to evoke the aesthetic composition of the actor photograph, in some ways mimicking lithograph copies of *cartes de visite* but now as "copies" without an original.[72]

Suggestively, Iijima Kyoshin first recorded the anecdote about Toyokuni and the servant girl precisely in the middle of the 1890s when, as Murashima Ayaka has argued, there is a moment in which both the photograph and the actor print

[69] Murashima Ayaka, "Bakumatsu/Meiji-ki no Nihon ni okeru engeki shashin no hatten to hensen: kabuki yakusha hishatai toshita mono o chūshin ni," *Engekigaku ronbunshū* 52 (2011), 68.

[70] Murashima, "Bakumatsu/Meiji-ki no Nihon ni okeru engeki shashin no hatten to hensen," 68.

[71] On the idea of the photographic "borderland," see Hamano Shiho, *Shashin no bōdārando: x sen/shinrei shashin/nensha* (Tokyo: Seikyūsha, 2015), pp. 13–17. On the coexistence of photographs and prints, see Murashima, "Bakumatsu/Meiji-ki no Nihon ni okeru engeki shashin no hatten to hensen," 63–64 and Kamiyama Akira, *Kindai engeki no raireki: kabuki no "isshin nisei"* (Tokyo: Shinwasha, 2006), pp. 110ff.

[72] See Okatsuka Akiko and Wagatsuma Naomi, *Ukiyo-e kara shashin e: shikaku no bunmei kaika* (Tokyo: Seigensha, 2015).

occupy a shared, overlapping space in the representational economy of the theater.[73] What are we to make of this (temporal) coincidence? How, we might ask, can we read Kyoshin's recounting of that episode as itself a story about this fraught moment in Japanese visual culture when the woodblock print and the photograph begin finally to diverge, a divergence that comes just as the Western aestheticization of the Japanese print helps to remake the understanding of Japan's own visual past?

Two elements are central to the story as Kyoshin records it: the first is that likeness has been completely removed from the commercial sphere; the second is that likeness is no longer a question of rendering a mimetic copy of surface but of expressing an "interiority" that, as Karatani Kōjin noted in his *Origins of Modern Japanese Literature*, was just being "discovered" in Japan at this very moment.[74] It is as if, freed by the camera from the drudgery of approximating likeness, the work of a printmaker like Toyokuni can be truly artistic, judged not in relation to a normative conception of fidelity (which itself is historical and shifts over the course of the nineteenth century) but in relation to aesthetic ideals (which no less have a history also shifting across the nineteenth century), ideals which are here themselves cordoned off from the market that loomed so prominently at the end of the nineteenth century.

If the relationship between the photographic and xylographic production of likeness was reimagined in the 1890s, it was in part because technological changes provided a context in which the truth claim of photography could be reconceptualized. The claim made in 1903 by Kawajiri Seitan writing for the magazine *Kabuki*—that the photograph could be a particularly useful tool for the archiving and preservation of the theater—was emblematic of this shift toward the archival:

> There has been a tendency until now for the majority of the photographs of actors in various roles to be treated as playthings for women and children who are fans but in truth it goes without saying that [photographs] can provide a not inconsiderable object of reference for future generations.[75]

As an archival tool, the photograph was only as good as its truth claim; its ability to capture that which transpired on stage needed to be conceptualized before it could be taken for granted, that is, naturalized. This, in turn, depended on freeing the camera from the confines of the portrait studio, allowing the illusion of the photograph as documentary trace.

As Murashima Ayaka has pointed out, the 1890s marked a critical turning point in this history of the actor photograph. Until the 1890s, actor photographs were taken as portraits in studios and sold as *cartes de visite*.[76] These photographs were

---

[73] Murashima, "Bakumatsu/Meiji-ki no Nihon ni okeru engeki shashin no hatten to hensen," 64.
[74] See Karatani Kōjin, *The Origins of Modern Japanese Literature*, trans. Brett de Barry (Durham, NC: Duke University Press, 1993), pp. 45–75.
[75] Quoted in Kamiyama, *Kindai engeki no raireki*, p. 117.
[76] Murashima, "Bakumatsu/Meiji-ki no Nihon ni okeru engeki shashin no hatten to hensen," 64ff.

emblematically "staged": long exposure times meant that the subject needed to be frozen in place for as long as twenty seconds. By the 1890s, the situation had radically changed: shutter speeds had increased to one-twentieth of a second and the invention of the dry collodion process meant that the time between taking and developing the photograph could be extended, freeing the camera from the studio and making it more mobile. This new mobility of the camera combined with the introduction of electric lighting to kabuki when the Kabuki-za opened in 1889 meant that, for the first time, the photographic apparatus could cross the threshold into the theater itself. This, in turn, had a profound effect on the ways in which the actor photograph would be conceptualized in the decade that followed: now no longer a *staged* image, the photograph could be imagined as an indexical trace of the ephemeral performance of the actor *on stage*. This was, to be sure, a utopian vision of the possibilities of the photograph as archival tool, but this conception of the truth claim of the photograph would have a powerful effect not just on the practices of photography but on how photographic evidence was imagined as a tool for the theater historian.[77]

One of the most striking examples of how the photograph was reimagined as a document of performance is the iconic photograph of the actor Ichikawa Danzō VII in the role of Nikki Danjō taken by the photographer and editor Abe Yutaka in 1908 and first published in the magazine *Engei gahō*. The photograph was republished in 1912, just after Danzō's death, in the book *Flowers of the Stage* (*Butai no hana*), which collects the photographs that Abe had taken of actors beginning in 1907.[78]

In *Flowers of the Stage*, the photograph of Danzō is accompanied by a caption that reads: "The late Ichikawa Danzō as Nikki Danjō from the play *The Disputed Succession* (*Meiboku sendai hagi*) at the Kabuki-za, April 1908." The caption suggests that the photograph captures Danzō on stage in one of his most famous roles but, as Murashima Ayaka has noted, Abe had, in fact, asked Danzō to pose specifically for the photograph, which then captures and makes iconic his interpretation of the role and his *mie*—the frozen moment that is, in fact, frozen by the camera itself.[79]

Indeed, Kamiyama Akira has argued that rather than simply capturing and preserving that which transpired on stage, the camera helps to ensure, even to invent, the iconicity of the pose, which is all the more iconic because of its preservation and reproduction.[80] But we can go further still, for Danzō's pose, here recreated for the benefit of the camera, and Abe's composition both draw on the iconography of the actor print, especially the "close up"-like *ōkubie* most closely identified with Tōshūsai Sharaku's late-eighteenth-century actor prints, which had come to

---

[77] Kamiyama, *Kindai engeki no raireki*, p. 118.
[78] Abe Yutaka, *Butai no hana* (Tokyo: Engei gahōsha, 1912).
[79] Murashima, "Bakumatsu/Meiji-ki no Nihon ni okeru engeki shashin no hatten to hensen," 74–76.
[80] Kamiyama, *Kindai engeki no raireki*, p. 118.

be especially valuable (both aesthetically and commercially) by the late nineteenth century. The iconographic similitude has a strange double effect for it both lends to Abe's photograph an artistic aura—setting it off from the much more frequent wide-angle shots that show the entire figure of the actor on stage—and seems to "confirm" in Sharaku's work an essentially mimetic quality, lending his images the patina of photographic realism.

In all of his work, Abe would foreground the conceit that his photographs captured the actor *on stage*. In the decade following the publication of *Flowers of the Stage*, Abe would produce a series of books of photographs of individual actors under the title *On Stage* (*Butai no omokage*) that purported to show the actor's "visage on stage." But how are we to understand the claim of these books and their photographs when the very presence of the actor "on stage" needs to be staged for the camera? Indeed, while Abe's work advances an idea of the photograph as a documentary record of the stage based on a truth claim fundamentally different from the actor print (that the indexicality of the photograph points directly to existence of the body of the actor on stage whose trace it inscribes), there is the sleight of hand fundamental to Abe's work through which the *staged* photograph of the actor posing for the camera stands in for the unphotographed presence of the actor on stage. In this process, the very artfulness of the photograph is erased and it comes to appear as a natural, unmediated record of what transpired on stage.

Almost all of the photographs that Abe published in the 1910s and early 1920s play on this perception of the photograph as document of performance, but in 1923, he published a book of photographs of the great Meiji era actor Ichikawa Danjūrō IX that draws on this rhetoric of the photograph as documentary record but is, in many ways, quite different from Abe's earlier books for the simple reason that Danjūrō IX had died in 1903, before Abe had begun his career as a photographer.

Rather than presenting his own work, the book, *Danjūrō on Stage* (*Butai no Danjūrō*), reproduces hundreds of photographs of the actor taken across his career by a variety of photographers including many by Kajima Seibei at his studio (the Genrokukan in Kobiki-chō).[81] Here, the work of others is refashioned and presented as a record of the actor "on stage." With the help of historian Ihara Toshirō and Danjūrō's adopted son Ichikawa Sanshō, Abe identified the photographs of Danjūrō with particular historical performances, and the photographs are presented in *Danjūrō on Stage* as documents of these performances. It is as if lacking a photographic archive of the stage from photography's earliest years in Japan, Abe has to completely reimagine what these early photographs of the actor taken in the studio in fact represented, blurring further the already blurry line between the "staged" photograph and the photograph "on stage."

---

[81] Ihara Seiseien [Toshirō] and Abe Yutaka ed., *Butai no Danjūrō* (Tokyo: Butai no Danjūrō kankōkai, 1923).

The framing of the photographs as documents of the actor on stage is, moreover, further complicated by a series of photographs that Abe includes at the end of the book capturing Danjūrō out of role and in private life. These photographs are mainly portraits taken at studios, the earliest of which date to 1868. The repetition of the "unadorned" (*sugao*) face of the actor seems almost to insist on a unity of identity not dissimilar to Toyokuni's own intuition that the individuality of the actor's face becomes the guarantor of identity regardless of how it is represented. Indeed, at one level, the apparatus of the camera takes this logic to its natural conclusion, for these twenty-five portraits, taken over a quarter of a century by various photographers, seem unequivocally to demonstrate an individuality of the face that overwrites the individuality of the hand behind the camera.

In addition to these portraits, *Danjūrō on Stage* also includes a handful of photographs taken of Danjūrō among family and friends; these photographs are strikingly different from the others in the album not just in subject matter but also in composition. Several of the photographs are taken outdoors and they seem to have been taken by an amateur, possibly a member of Danjūrō's family. A pair of these late photographs allow us to return to a number of the themes that I have considered over the course of this chapter ranging from questions about the individuality or distinctiveness of the actor's face and the nature of likeness to the relationship between the actor and role or, indeed, to the very place of the camera itself within the economy of reproduction in the late nineteenth century.

These three photographs (Figure 5.13) were taken in 1894 and they seem to mark the moment at which the camera becomes truly mobile. The subject is no longer tethered to the studio, nor does he need to sit or pose for the photograph; indeed, as the latter two photographs suggest, he does not even need to be aware that he is being photographed. But what is shown in these photographs? Danjūrō, of course, although even such a simple statement is significantly more complex than it may at first seem. Central to both photographs, certainly more central than Danjūrō himself and seemingly the subject of the composition, is his eldest daughter Jitsuko. The caption tells us that the photographs were taken in April 1894 on an outing to the Satake Villa, a public garden in Mukōjima, to celebrate Jitsuko's recovery from illness. In the bottom two photographs, to Danjūrō's right, is the figure of what appears to be a woman gazing out over the lake who, we are told by the caption, is the *onnagata* Ichikawa Shinzō V; the young man whose gaze seems a mirror image of Danjūrō's is the actor Ichikawa Shakoroku. But if these figures are the subject of the photograph, there is something else denoted by these photos: the very movement of the camera out of the studio and into the spaces of private life.

In contrast to the *staged* photographs of Danjūrō in role, these images seem to offer access to the private and the personal, to a *reality* which was not more real because of the photograph's powers of mimetic fidelity but because it seems to capture an unscripted moment that is, for that reason, all the more telling. What

**Figure 5.13** Photograph of Ichikawa Danjūrō IX in 1894 from Abe Yutaka. ed., *Butai no Danjūrō* (1923).
Source: National Diet Library, Tokyo.

these photographs of Danjūrō suggest is that what was truly novel about the camera was not its promise to capture likeness more fully than the woodblock print but its promise to denote reality as such. By highlighting the unscripted nature of the moment, the photographs achieve a kind of "reality effect" by which the very ordinariness of the scene as a moment in everyday life becomes central to that which is depicted. If it were Abe's discovery that the photograph could serve as an archive of performance, these final images from *Danjūrō on Stage* show a very different idea of what a photograph as archive might mean.

We might return here to the figure of Danjūrō himself. His suit, and his beloved English foxhound Charlie, seem to project a modernity that mirrors the modernity of the medium and that set him apart from the other figures in the photographs, who all wear Japanese dress. The suit appears emblematic of the ambiguities, complexities, and contradictions of the man and his career: the greatest actor of his age, Danjūrō is now best remembered as the figure most closely identified with the failed project of "modernizing" kabuki and with the strange archaisms that resulted, especially the so-called "living history" (*katsureki*) plays that attempted to portray current historical events within the context of kabuki's formalism. But are we certain that this figure is Danjūrō?

To be sure, the face is unmistakable—we *recognize* him from other photographs of the actor, suggesting a unity of identity derived from the indexicality of the photograph, that it points directly to the body it has captured. And yet, in his book on the "phantom of the body" in Japanese performing arts, the critic Watanabe Tamotsu has suggested a way of thinking about the identity of the performer as threefold. Watanabe calls these the three "I"s of the actor in the Japanese tradition: the man who is born (here, Horigoshi Hideshi, born in the city of Edo in 1838); then the actor as a member of an acting lineage who has assumed a new name (here, Ichikawa Danjūrō IX, a name he assumed in 1874 and bore until his death in 1903); and finally, the role he played on stage at any given moment (Kamakura Gongorō, for example, from the play *Just a Minute!* (*Shibaraku*), a role for which he was particularly famous).[82] The actor as represented in the great body of actor prints, the archive that Shōyō imagined could serve as a proto-cinematic record of the theatrical past which recorded what happened on stage, seems to rest at some point between the second and third of these identities. In most—although not all—instances, the depiction is of an actor in role: Danjūrō V as Kagekiyo, for example, from Toyokuni's 1793 illustration for *Asaina and the Soga Farce*. There is also a long tradition, going back to the 1780 picture book *Fuji in Summer* (*Natsu no Fuji*), of depicting actors beyond the stage curtain, out of role and in private life, and we find numerous examples of this in printed images and illustrated books across the nineteenth century. But the photographs of Danjūrō in private life from *Danjūrō on Stage* are again different for they seem to rest somewhere between the identity of this figure as actor (Danjūrō IX) and as man (Horigoshi Hideshi), his "unadorned" face the marker of a somatic presence that precedes (or lies beneath) the identity of Danjūrō IX.

I am not arguing that it is possible, or even useful, to try to disentangle these identities (identities that Watanabe describes as "delicately intertwined"),[83] much less to posit a border where one ends and another begins (the whole of these photographs seems to push against such an idea), but rather to suggest that what sets these photographs apart from the hundreds of other photographs that appear in Abe's volume, or of the block-printed images of the actor that were produced over the course of his career, is the sense that here we have a man who is quintessentially not "on stage," a record of the private life of a figure who had lived his life in the public eye since the age of seven, when he assumed his first acting name, Kawarazaki Chōjūrō, in 1845, and who had been known in public life as Danjūrō IX—or often just "the Ninth" (*kyūdaime*)—for two decades by the time this photograph was taken.

Indeed, it is these photographs rather than the photographs of the actor in role that seem truly to distinguish the novel promise of the photographic medium: not

---

[82] See Watanabe Tamotsu, *Shintai wa maboroshi* (Tokyo: Genki shobō, 2014), pp. 17–18.
[83] Watanabe, *Shintai wa maboroshi*, p. 21.

that it was better than the woodblock print at capturing likeness but that the likeness it was able to capture, under certain circumstances, held out the promise of greater authenticity according to a certain way of understanding authenticity. It is hard not to feel that these two unscripted photographs show us more of Danjūrō than the hundreds of images of the actor in role reproduced in Abe's volume because they show him as himself.

But what do we mean by this *as himself*? After all, there is a long tradition, going back to the late eighteenth century, of woodblock prints purporting to show actors out of make-up and in private life. Famously, the picture book *Fuji in Summer*, which Katsukawa Shunshō published in 1780, became a sensation because it seemed to offer access to the actor beyond the stage, unadorned, like the peak of Mount Fuji in summer, no longer covered with snow. But if these images promised to allow a glimpse of the actor in private life (like the image in *Fuji in Summer* of Danjūrō's great grandfather Danjūrō V at his home, brush in hand as he inscribes a poem on a fan), they were, in most instances, no less than the images of the actor on stage or in role, published and public, meant to be sold and to be bought, commodities of the imagination. These photographs of Danjūrō, by contrast, show us that which we were never meant to see, a private moment which we have somehow glimpsed without the knowledge of the subjects, none of whom acknowledge the presence of the camera.

And here we might return to the anecdote about Toyokuni's portrait of the servant girl that Iijima Kyoshin first recorded just at the time this photograph of Danjūrō was taken in the mid-1890s. That anecdote, too, revolves around the idea of an image that cannot be commoditized, an image marked by its essentially private nature as a gift, a memory, for the girl's parents in the countryside. It is surely no coincidence that this anecdote revolving around the portrait as keepsake should surface at precisely the moment when the photograph extended to the masses, and for the first time, the idea of portraiture. But whereas the camera indiscriminately reproduces whatever surfaces it is trained upon, Toyokuni (as "artist") is only able to depict the subject whose interiority, whose depth, allows for the expression of individuality.

Abe had asked Tsubouchi Shōyō to write a preface to *Danjūrō on Stage*, and in his brief prefatory remarks, Shōyō too begins to articulate a form of this question but from a very different perspective. If the photographs collected in this book can be thought of as documents of the history of the theater, what, Shōyō wonders, becomes of that which goes unarchived, that which has not been saved from predations of ephemerality:

> Truly, imagine if the glare of Danjūrō IX's great big eyes had been realistically photographed in the same way as today's Matsumoto Kōshirō VII? Imagine if those great, full lips of his had been photographed in the manner of Onoe Baikō VI in *The Earth Spider* (*Tsuchigumo*) or as a demoness. Or imagine if he had

recorded that clear voice of his, that controlled intonation, onto a gramophone and we could hear it today just as it was.

Oh, that clear voice. That famous style of his that reverberated with such vigor and such force to every corner of the boxes on the balcony until the early 1890s.[84]

During his lifetime, Danjūrō had been photographed and even captured on film, but his voice had never been recorded, so now the voice becomes a marker of that which has not been preserved, that element of performance lost to the archive and to be recalled only in the mind, only in the memory, of those who heard it. In this sense, the voice becomes a symptom of a much larger problem, a problem felt keenly by Japanese intellectuals in the late teens and early twenties: what becomes of a past that has not been preserved? What is the role of the archive or the museum when what it preserves is always partial and fragmentary, an awareness particularly keen among those, like Shōyō, who had lived through the great transition of the late nineteenth century.

For Shōyō, the idea of creating a museum of theatrical history that would situate Japan's own dramatic past within a history of world theater was intimately bound up with the history of images and with the idea of the cinema. Shōyō first mentions the creation of a theater museum in 1916, in a note about ideas for future projects, just at the time Shōyō comes to be increasingly interested in woodblock prints as a set of documents providing what he called historical or documentary evidence of theatrical history. Central to Shōyō's conception of these prints was the idea that they constituted a kind of cinematic or proto-cinematic archive, an idea to which he would return repeatedly in the 1910s.

It was in 1915, a year before he began to imagine a future museum of the theater, that Shōyō first conceptualized the nature of the printed archive of theater images as cinematic in an essay he published on "Motion Pictures and the Past of Japanese Drama" ("Katsudō shashin to waga geki no kako"). In explaining the emergence of long-form illustrated fiction that used actors' images, for example, Shōyō argued that "From at least a hundred and thirty or forty years ago, production of a kind of film that we could consider a primitive motion picture began in Japan, and gradually the scale was increased so that roughly a century ago even extremely long-form films began to be produced."[85] This is the printed page reimagined as filmic print. But what is most important about this conception of a theatrical history, in which theater prints become a proto-cinematic archive, is that it flattens kabuki out in a particular way. If this archive is able to capture the history of kabuki in an essentially documentary fashion, it is able to do so, Shōyō argues, because kabuki was

[84] Tsubouchi Shōyō, "*Butai no Danjūrō jō*," in *Shōyō senshū*, vol. 7 (Tokyo: Daiichi shobō, 1977–78), p. 296.

[85] Tsubouchi Shōyō, "Katsudō shashin to waga geki no kako," in *Shōyō senshū*, vol. 7, p. 302.

primarily gestural: "In the case of Japanese drama, it goes without saying that for the puppet theater and kabuki [. . .] with the exception of certain instances from the puppet theater, there is very little that needs to be heard with the ears."[86] This is because, Shōyō explains, kabuki placed importance on "appealing directly to the eyes." Here, not only the actor's voice in both spoken dialogue and dramatic recitation (*tsurane*) but also vocal and instrumental music fade into the background as inessential elements of a drama that would come to be literally embodied in "frozen moments" (*mie*), the dramatic poses and gestures that have come to define the way kabuki has been imagined as a dramatic art.

And yet, in 1923, when he was asked to write a preface to Abe's book of photographs of Danjūrō, Shōyō not only returns to the voice but also foregrounds it as a particular problem, a marker of the inherent gaps and lacunae that necessarily characterize the historical record. If the printed archive—an archive that by 1923 included not just woodblock prints but photographic and film prints, even voices imprinted on pressed shellac—was the basis on which a history of the theater could be written, the archive of memory stood as a strange marker, even to Shōyō, of the limits of this historical project.

Like the 1894 photographs of Danjūrō and his family, the 1925 photograph of Shōyō at work in his study with which I began this chapter brings us to a set of questions about reproduction and authenticity and the private space made public. To be sure, in this instance, it was the making public of the private space of the study that was at the center of the photograph and of the article with which it appeared. The studied indifference of Shōyō and his assistant Ōmura Hiroyoshi posits a different relationship between the camera and its subject than that suggested by the photographs of Danjūrō and his daughter taken thirty years earlier. But more suggestive still are the actor prints, which have been in some sense "accidentally" photographed by the cameraman from the *Tokyo Nichinichi Newspaper* capturing Shōyō at work in his study. These prints were the prints that had been sold to Waseda by Kobayashi Bunshichi and that would eventually form an important part of the holdings of the Waseda Theater Museum when it opened in 1928. The better part of three-quarters of a century later, they would be photographed again when the print collection of the Museum was digitized as part of a project of creating a database of theater images that Akama Ryō began in 1993.[87]

That database makes it possible, without too much difficulty, to identify these images that are, in several senses, peripheral to the photograph. We might take as an example a sequence of prints designed by Toyokuni's pupil Utagawa Kunisada that appear just to the viewer's right of Shōyō which illustrate an 1839 staging of

---

[86] Tsubouchi Shōyō, "Katsudō shashin to waga geki no kako," in *Shōyō senshū*, vol. 7, p. 300.
[87] Akama Ryō and Kaneko Takaaki, "Ukiyo-e dejitaru ākaibu no genzai," *Jōhō shorigakkai kenkyūkai kenkyū hōkoku* 78 (May 2008), pp. 37–44.

the play *Gosho ōgi masago no shiranami* at the Ichimura-za. Just beyond Shōyō's shoulder are the first two sheets: on the left, closer to Shōyō, is the actor Ichikawa Kyūzō II in the role of Hisayoshi and, to the right, the actor Arashi Kichisaburō III in the role of Ishikawa Goemon. Above the image of Kyūzō is a third print from the sequence showing Iwai Tojaku as the courtesan Masagoji. It was in an attempt to distinguish the work of Toyokuni and Kunisada (Toyokuni III) that Shōyō first began to write about actor prints in 1918, and so these prints themselves bear an intimate relationship to Shōyō's art historical turn and to his book on Toyokuni and his school.

Or we might take the print of Ichikawa Danjūrō VII, Danjūrō IX's father, that lies just below these prints, in the lower right-hand corner of the photograph. Here, Danjūrō VII is in the role of Banzui Chōbei in another print designed by Kunisada, this one dating to 1819. In this instance, the Waseda Theater Museum's Database for Theater Research contains records for four separate copies of this print and so we are immediately confronted with yet another problem: which of the copies of this print do we see in the photograph of Shōyō and under what circumstances would the answer to that question matter?

And we can go further, for is not the subject of these prints also an occasion to meditate on questions of original and copy, and, indeed, of copies of a copy? Here, after all, we have the depiction of an actor who is himself the seventh in a line of actors stretching back to the late eighteenth century and forward to our present, drawing on the conventions of a role that has been repeatedly performed over generations. The 1925 photograph of Shōyō in his study captures a specific copy of a specific print of one actor in a role that he played in a specific play in a specific year, but as the architecture of the database makes clear, makes, in some ways, unavoidable, this is only one of hundreds of images of Danjūō VII and one of dozens of images of various actors playing this character.

Today, with an ease unimaginable to Shōyō himself, we can call forth these images and compare and collate them; we can, indeed, transport these images once more beyond the walls of the museum, back, as it were, to the privacy of the study, at least as images on screen if no longer as the printed objects that Shōyō and Ōmura were cataloguing in 1925. And we might recall once more the figure of Ōmura, one hand lifting up the edge of a print, the other using a brush to apply paste to the underside of the print, the very physicality of the print heightened by the strange circumstances of the photograph, which projects a three-dimensionality. We can glimpse the surface of the print, but it is hard not to focus on the print's underside, which is not visible but which is the focus of Ōmura's attention and thus strongly, emblematically, present in its absence. And that unmarked surface will become ever less accessible to the viewer once the print is pasted onto stock and again when it has become a digital image on a screen. Ōmura's freighted gesture inadvertently focuses our attention on the very thingness of these images, their material instantiation on paper, this seemingly insignificant detail which was captured accidentally by the camera, frozen in place as a reminder that the surface of the image is itself only one dimension of the physical artifact of the print.

Today more than ever, historical research on Japan's theatrical past is guided by images, but in a way much broader and more profound than Shōyō could have imagined a century ago. For it is not just images in a traditional sense (theater and actor prints) but digital images of all manner of texts, playbills and broadsheets, maps and guidebooks, almanacs and encyclopedias that have come to define the work of the theater historian in the early twenty-first century. More material is available more easily than ever before, but in these circumstances, the very nature of research—its spaces, its physical forms—has begun to change. It is to a consideration of the nature of these changes and their implications for writing a history of kabuki in an age of print that I would like now to turn in this book's epilogue.

# Epilogue

Stage and Print in the Digital Age

When Abe Yutaka compiled *Danjūrō on Stage* (*Butai no Danjūrō*) in 1923, he was given access to the family's collection of photographs of the great actor by Danjūrō's son-in-law, Ichikawa Sanshō V. In 2010, a copy of Abe's book was digitized by the National Diet Library, and now these once private photographs can be viewed by anyone in the world with an internet connection. The fate of this book and its photographs are broadly suggestive. Today, with relative ease and from the comfort of one's own home, the historian can search for and access an astonishing array of texts and images, ephemera and maps. The images can be manipulated, enlarged, made newly legible, overlain on other images to facilitate comparison, sorted into sets by year, or by genre, or by author (or artist). This transformation of the historical record into a vast and labyrinthine library without walls that can be searched and saved, downloaded and annotated, has profound implications for humanist scholars. In the case of the materials with which I have worked, the fact that the transformation has largely taken place over the course of the writing of the book has highlighted for me both the nature of this transformation of access and its impact on the ways in which I have thought about, done research for, and written *Kabuki's Nineteenth Century*.

The digitization of *Danjūrō on Stage* is emblematic. In 2009, the National Diet Library in Tokyo undertook a large-scale expansion of its digitization efforts, increasing its budget one-hundredfold from the previous year.[1] This rush to build on ongoing efforts in the creation of a digital archive came as a recognition that Japan was relatively late in using digital tools to preserve and make accessible its printed past, pushing to the forefront of public discourse questions about the nature of this printed past and its relationship to the digital present and future.[2] In very concrete ways, these questions touch on a number of themes that I have addressed over the course of this book from the rights of authors in a changing publishing landscape, to questions of owning the published past, to issues of preservation and access. But there is also at stake another question, a new question

---

[1] Wada Atsuhiko, *Dokusho no rekishi o tou: shomotsu to dokusha no kindai* (Tokyo: Shinyōsha, 2011), p. 94.

[2] See Sawabe Kin's interview with Nakayama Masaki, then the head of the National Diet Library's Digital Information Department, in Sawabe Kin "Kokurtitsu Kokkai Toshokan dejitaru ākaibu kōsō," *Zu bon: toshokan to media no hon* 17 (December 2011), 87.

about the relationship between the physical book and its digital image and what it might mean for the historian to examine an archive that is increasingly accessible in dematerialized, disembodied form.

Let us return once more to the 1894 photograph of the actor Ichikawa Danjūrō IX and his family from Abe's 1923 book that I discussed at the end of Chapter 5 (see Figure 5.13). What, we might ask, are we looking at when we view this image? Not a "photograph" in the traditional sense of an image imprinted on a light-sensitive surface or, of course, an "original" print of the image, which likely no longer exists—the book was published shortly before the Great Kanto Earthquake in 1923, and it is likely that we have this image only because it was reproduced in Abe's book. Rather, we are looking at an image of an image, but even this is the beginning, rather than the end, of considering the digitized version of the photograph.

We might turn to Abe's afterword to his 1923 book, where he wrote in great detail about the laborious process through which the book was itself constructed:

> As is well known, until [Danjūrō] began to be photographed at [Kajima Seibei's] Genrokukan Studio [in 1895], the photographs were all in the form of *cartes de visite* which have not only yellowed over the years but half of which have faded. Even many of the later photographs had completely changed color and it was not possible to reproduce them as they were. In order to pass them down as vibrantly and artistically and as true to life as possible, I used the most recent airbrush techniques on the four-hundred and seventy photographs, re-photographed them to make new negatives and then retouched these negatives. Among the photographs there were a number that needed to be retouched and re-photographed three or four times before they were ready to be used.[3]

There are several striking elements in Abe's description of the labor of producing *Danjūrō on Stage*: first is the fact that the photographs, rather than serving as a given and transparent vessel to document and preserve the past, must themselves be collected and saved from the effects of time—archived; then there is the airbrushing and retouching of the photographs that seem to go to the very core of the photograph's truth claim, and they are a reminder that, as scholars like Geoffrey Batchen and Tom Gunning have argued, the manipulation of photographs has a long history predating the digital.[4]

---

[3] Abe Yutaka, "Hashigaki," in *Butai no Danjūrō*, ed. Ihara Seiseien [Toshirō] and Abe Yutaka (Tokyo: Butai no Danjūrō kankōkai, 1923).

[4] Geoffrey Batchen, "Phantasm: Digital Imaging and the Death of Photography," *Aperture* 136 (Summer), 46–51; Tom Gunning "What Is the Point of an Image; or Faking Photographs?," in *Still Moving: Between Cinema and Photography*, ed. Karen Beckman and Jean Ma (Durham, NC: Duke University Press, 2008), pp. 23–40.

For Abe, the painstaking task of airbrushing and retouching the photographs was aimed at restoring them to their "original" condition so that they might better convey the "truth" of what they show; but for us, living in the age of Photoshop, the retouching and manipulation of photographs has come to be a central concern over what, precisely, we mean by the truthfulness of images. There is, moreover, an important distinction, an important disjuncture, between the photograph as surface image and the photograph as image-bearing surface, a disjuncture, that is, between the *image* of Danjūrō—preserved within the book and now in digital form—and its material instantiation, the early albumen prints of the actor, most of which have been lost.

Even before its digitization, what the 1923 book preserved was images of images, photographs of photographs that were again re-photographed when the book was digitized in 2010. What we see when we view this photograph, which seems to show us Danjūrō "as he was," is thus the digitization of a print of a reproduction of a photograph which has been repeatedly airbrushed and retouched and rephotographed, the "original" of which (held at the time of the 1923 Great Kanto Earthquake by Danjūrō's son-in-law) likely no longer exists, a ghostly reminder of the fact that many of the photographic images of Danjūrō survive now only because they were reproduced in *Danjūrō on Stage*. Under such circumstances, how are we to think about the seeming *authenticity* of the photographs of Danjūrō among his family? In what does this authenticity inhere?

One approach to this question is offered by another sequence of images of Danjūrō captured at the end of the nineteenth century, a short film shot by the cameraman Shibata Tsunekichi in 1899, the only moving images taken of the actor before his death in 1903. That film, *Maple Viewing* (*Momijigari*), is rightly famous as the oldest surviving film shot by a Japanese cameraman; in 2009, the same year that the National Diet Library undertook the expansion of its digital archives, it became the first film designated an Important Cultural Property by Japan's Agency for Cultural Affairs.

*Maple Viewing* has long occupied a critical place within the history of Japanese cinema, a point of origin for what would become one of the largest and most important film industries in the world. But if the place of *Maple Viewing* in the history of Japanese film is relatively well understood, we might ask of its place within the history of Japanese drama or, relatedly, of its place within the long—and ongoing—history of documenting and preserving the history of Japanese drama. Indeed, the designation of the film as an important cultural property, coming as it does amid a debate over the meaning of digital media for the future of film preservation, raises a series of questions about the nature of archival practices in the digital age, but it also reminds us that many of the questions surrounding these practices were posed a century earlier when film itself came to be imagined in almost utopian terms as a recording medium that might, for the first time, allow for an archive of movement. And if, as Mary Ann Doane has argued, cinema "directly confronts the problematic question of the *representability* of the ephemeral, the archivability of presence,"⁵ its significance "lies in its apparent capacity to perfectly represent the contingent, to provide the pure record of time" and thus—for performance, "promise the archiving of ephemerality itself."⁶

What is so striking about the1894 photograph of Danjūrō among his family is the way it seems to capture the actor in an entirely unscripted moment, but *Maple Viewing* is quintessentially *staged*. For histories of cinema, the subject of the play has been incidental: it is treated almost as a kind of actuality, a happening that gets caught on film, and there has long been a debate within film history over whether the film should be classified as a documentary or as fiction, a question that hinges on the vexed relationship between the film and its subject, the play.⁷ The play was, of course, staged for the camera and, as I will explore below, part of the motive for that staging was the idea that what was filmed would be preserved in perpetuity, a document of the two great actors of the age but also a document of kabuki at the fin de siècle, a document for a new age.

In this context, the choice of preserving *Maple Viewing* is suggestive in several ways: the kabuki play was an adaptation of a *nō* play by the late fifteenth-century playwright Kanze Nobumitsu; it tells the story of the late-Heian warrior Taira no Koremochi's hunting excursion among the autumn foliage used as a premise to vanquish a demon appearing in the guise of the beautiful Sarashinahime. When it was chosen for preservation by the new technology of film, this pseudo-classical play, set in the distant Heian past and invoking the dramatic heritage of the *nō* theater, was meant to cast a particular afterimage. Indeed, in the context of the late nineteenth century, *Maple Viewing* can be seen as belonging to a contested moment in the history of the struggle over the nature of kabuki's identity as a representational medium. Rewritten for kabuki by Kawatake Mokuami in 1887, *Maple Viewing* was, from very early on, part of an effort to "preserve" kabuki. In 1889, it was included in a program of plays by the Japan Entertainment Society (*Nihon Engei Kyōkai*), which had adopted the concept of "preservation" or "*hozon*" from work being done on the history of Japanese art by figures like Okakura Tenshin and Ernest Fenollosa.⁸

The play itself, which would become an object of preservation through film, was intimately bound up with the idea of cultural preservation and so it became a kind of overdetermined object of the impulse to preserve. *Maple Viewing* emphasizes kabuki's place as a "traditional" art form and, in turn, it anchors the new

---

⁵ Mary Ann Doane, *The Emergence of Cinematic Time: Modernity, Contingency, the Archive* (Cambridge, MA: Harvard University Press, 2002), p. 25.

⁶ Doane, *The Emergence of Cinematic Time*, p. 22.

⁷ On this point, see the analysis by Komatsu Hiroshi, "Questions Regarding the Genesis of Non-fiction Film," Yamagata International Film Festival: Documentary Box #5, 1994, http://www.yidff.jp/docbox/5/box5-1-e.html.

⁸ See Kamiyama Akira, *Kindai engeki no raireki: kabuki no "isshin nisei"* (Tokyo: Shinwasha, 2006), pp. 94–108.

photographic technology of the cinema in a broad cultural framework imbued with a sense of tradition.

One of the most detailed accounts of the events surrounding the shooting of *Maple Viewing* can be found in a newspaper clipping which is preserved in a scrapbook collected by the silent film narrator Komada Kōyō (1877–1935) and now housed at the Tsubouchi Memorial Theater Museum:

> Having successfully shot a shinpa play, the Katsudō Shashin Shōkai decided to film a kabuki dance sequence of Dan[jūrō] and Kiku[gorō] and straightaway began negotiations with Inoue Takejirō, the then manager of the Kabuki-za. Inoue agreed right away and offered to provide not just the actors but costumes, props, and musicians all free of charge. Instead, what he wanted was to preserve a copy of the film in perpetuity at the Kabuki-za and asked that he receive a copy of the film. With their discussions coming together, the two men decided on filming Dan[jūrō] and Kiku[gorō]'s hit *Maple Viewing*.
>
> However, while Kikugorō agreed without reservation, Danjūrō, who was a difficult personality, would not agree. While Inoue was unsure how best to proceed and seemed quite put out, the producer Ogasahara Shinbē said "It's ok. I will take over and make things work." Although Inoue tended to worry he entrusted the job to Ogasahara. While Inoue was fretting over having entrusted this job to Ogasahara, Danjūrō suddenly agreed to appear in *Maple Viewing* and to be filmed.
>
> Having been such quick work, Inoue was surprised and called Ogasahara: "what did you say to convince Danjūrō?" to which Ogasahara calmly replied: "Nothing special. I simply told him that the U.S. Ambassador was coming to the Kabuki-za and would like to introduce the visage of a Japanese star to the world and would like to put a photograph of that star in a magazine and that we wanted to use Kikugorō and his *Maple Viewing* and so would let him take the highlights with a high-speed camera. Danjūrō considered for a moment and then said 'hmmm, you can take a photograph even of someone moving? The power of modernity is extraordinary. Perhaps I shall have one of these taken of me as a memento for after my death' and he quickly agreed."[9]

There are several striking elements in this account. The first is the clipping itself: it has been cut out of a newspaper and preserved in a scrapbook, but it is taken out of its original context so that we know nothing of its origin, when it was printed, and how long after the events described. Further, Komada's scrapbooks were digitized by the Tsubouchi Memorial Theater Museum around 2014; for the database, each item was digitized discreetly and a gap opens up between the clipping as it is

---

[9] See the newspaper clipping, "Katsudō shashin," in vol. 6 of the scrapbooks of the *benshi* Komada Kōyō, now housed at the Waseda University Theater Museum: "Komada Kōyō sukappubukku," manuscript, Tsubouchi Memorial Theater Museum, Waseda University, 16758-1-6.

preserved in the scrapbook, pasted on a page with other bits of ephemera, and the way it has been digitized as a single record with no sense of its location—or situatedness—within Kōyō's albums. Although the database of Kōyō's scrapbooks was briefly public, it has now disappeared, all that remains of it is the ghostly presence of a broken link and a capture on the Internet Archive's Wayback Machine.[10] I will return to this question of the nature of the digital archive, but first I would like to consider the way in which this clipping itself meditates on film's dual role as both an archival medium which preserves that which it captures and as an archival object, a medium that needs to be "preserved in perpetuity" for its content to have any archival life.

Central to this account is the way the film was imagined by Danjūrō as a medium by which to make present that which would be absent in death. This ghostliness of the film was one of the aspects that would be most commented upon when the film was shown in the early twentieth century. When *Maple Viewing* was first shown in public in 1903, the film seemed to bring the actors to life before the eyes of the audience: "It felt," wrote a reporter for the *Osaka Asahi* Newspaper, "as if [the actors] were there and as if we were watching their extraordinary skill."[11]

But in conjunction with this role that Danjūrō imagines that the film might play as a personal memento for after his death, *Maple Viewing* was also imagined as broadly archival in nature, with a copy to be "preserved in perpetuity" at the Kabuki-za. The preservation of the (physical) film and the preservation of the actors in role captured by the film are intimately bound together. Indeed, an ambiguity emerges over the very object of preservation, and that ambiguity has resurfaced as digital technology has allowed for the content and the medium to be severed. We now live in an age when digital content no longer relies on the physical medium of film in order to preserve and reproduce the actors and their gestures; like the photographs of Danjūrō preserved in Abe's book, it is possible to imagine a ghostly afterlife of a film like *Maple Viewing* that exists only as a digital presence were its embodiment on film to disappear.

And here we might return to the designation of *Maple Viewing* as an Important Cultural Property; Tochigi Akira has pointed out that "what received the designation of Important Cultural Property was neither the work (*sakuhin*) called *Maple Viewing* nor all the copies of the film *Maple Viewing* but the particular film given to the National Film Center by Nikkatsu Corporation in 2006."[12] It is the physical *print* of the film, the strip of 35 millimeter Kodak nitrocellulose film, just under 105 meters in length, that has been imagined as part of Japan's cultural heritage, pointing to a further disjuncture between this fragile and flammable object—preserved

---

[10] See https://web.archive.org/web/20150315095827/http://www.enpaku.waseda.ac.jp/db/komada/index_kmd.php.

[11] Quoted in Ueda Manabu, *Nihon eiga sōsōki no kōgyō to kankyaku: Tōkyō to Kyōto o chūshin ni* (Tokyo: Waseda Daigaku Shuppanbu, 2012), pp. 175–77.

[12] Tochigi Akira, "Eiga *Momijigari* no jūyō bunkazai no shitei ni tsuite," *Eiga terebi gijutsu* 684 (August 2009), 26.

in the National Film Center's storage facility housed on a former US Army base outside of Tokyo—and the moving images of Danjūrō IX and Kikugorō V that the film had itself been intended to preserve.

But like the photograph of Danjūrō with his family reproduced in Abe's 1923 book, what survives today is not an "original" print of the film but a copy of the print made by Nikkatsu Corporation in 1927 in the aftermath of the Great Kanto Earthquake when much of the Japanese past seemed suddenly so fragile. When we view *Maple Viewing* on YouTube or look at the photograph of Danjūrō among his family on the website of the National Diet Library's Digital Collections, we are looking at images that at some basic level have been severed from their material instantiations, and we might recognize this disembodiment as significant. Indeed, it seems to me that, at least for scholars who use digitized materials, there is always a recognition of the gap between the real and the virtual, a recognition that reifies the *absence* of the authentic object and that suggests its auratic *presence* elsewhere, seemingly just on the other side of the screen.

But what do we mean by *presence*? If we think of the two images of Danjūrō—both of which make a claim to a straightforward indexicality (as afterimages of a body imprinted by light on a physical surface)—neither exists in its "original" form; in both instances, the object that has been preserved and digitized is a copy dating to the 1920s, two decades after the actor's death. These are, of course, particular instances, but both suggest the sometimes too comfortable, if often unarticulated, distinction between the real and the virtual, the original and the copy. To what extent, we might ask, are we more proximate to the real when we hold a copy of Abe's book in our hands at the National Diet Library or when we have a chance to see the 35 mm print of *Maple Viewing* (it was shown at the National Film Center in 2015) than when we view these objects on a computer screen from our home or office?

The very idea of designating film as a tangible Important Cultural Property recognized by the state coincides precisely with the moment when "the long privilege of the analog image and the technology of analog image production has been almost completely replaced by digital simulations and digital processes"—as if the idea of film as *tangible* cultural property is premised on the historical erasure of that tangibility:

> The celluloid strip with its reassuring physical passage of visible images, the noisy and cumbersome cranking of the mechanical film projector or the Steenbeck editing table, the imposing bulk of the film canister are all disappearing one by one into a virtual space, along with the images they so beautifully recorded and presented.[13]

But what is this virtual space? On the one hand, this "disappearing" of the physical can be thought of as an uncanny re-enactment of the virtuality of film as an

---

[13] D. N. Rodwick, *The Virtual Life of Film* (Cambridge, MA: Harvard University Press, 2007), p. 8.

imaginary signifier: "a little rolled up perforated strip which 'contains' vast landscapes, fixed battles, the melting of ice on the River Neva, and whole life-times, and yet can be enclosed in the familiar round metal tin, of modest dimensions, clear proof that it does not 'really' contain all that."[14] What has changed, then, is the disappearance of those final material traces—the "little rolled up perforated strip" and the "familiar round metal tin, of modest dimensions"; but in their place we do not have "nothing" but a different kind of materiality. For just as that perforated strip and round metal tin remained invisible to the viewer who sat in the cinema, so too the virtual worlds, increasingly part of our everyday as well as scholarly lives, are embodied in very real, physical infrastructures, even if we rarely think about them as we look at our screens.[15]

If we take this line of thought seriously, that any encounters we might have with the seemingly disembodied images of Danjūrō IX on our computer screens are (no less than our encounters with these images in the library or archive) *situated*, dependent on, and shaped by infrastructures of which we are often unconscious, it is obvious that what is most important about the changes brought about by the emergence of the digital archive is a question of situatedness, the situatedness of the material, to be sure, but also, and perhaps more profoundly, our own situatedness as scholars: that we can now access an astonishing array of material without ever getting on a plane, without ever setting foot in a physical library, without ever leaving home.

The research that I conducted for this book has one foot in this digital world but the other decidedly in the analog. When I began doing my preliminary research, almost none of the materials that I consulted had yet been digitized; by the time I came to write this epilogue, very little that I needed had yet to be digitized. That this book was written over a period of time that saw the emergence of large online databases and repositories of digitized materials has heightened, for me, a consciousness of what has been called "the space/time coordinates of reading early modern books," and I would like to offer some thoughts on the nature of digital archive and its implications for the work we do in the humanities by way of two experiences I had during the course of writing *Kabuki's Nineteenth Century*.[16]

\*\*\*

One of the first pieces of research that I conducted (before I had a very clear idea of what this book would be about) was an examination of the scrapbooks of theater programs and storytelling ephemera that Shikitei Sanba had compiled in 1815. I first read about Sanba's habits as a collector, and the scrapbooks that he compiled, in an article that Hattori Yukio had published in the *Nihon kosho tsūshin*

---

[14] Christian Metz, *The Imaginary Signifier: Psychoanalysis and the Cinema* (Bloomington, IN: Indiana University Press, 1986), pp. 43–44.
[15] See Alexander Galloway, *The Interface Effect* (Cambridge: Polity, 2012), p. 64.
[16] See Bruce R. Smith, "Getting Back to the Library, Getting Back to the Body," in *Shakespeare and the Digital World*, ed. Christine Carson and Peter Kirwan (Cambridge: Cambridge University Press, 2014), p. 25.

newsletter;[17] on the basis of that article, I arranged to travel to Tokyo to see the materials at the National Diet Library. Since I first consulted those albums, they have been digitized and can be accessed with an ease that was then barely imaginable.

The digitization of such materials is important for both researcher and repository: in terms of access, the materials can be viewed anywhere in the world, and in terms of preservation, they are not subject to the normal wear and tear of use. But it is difficult to imagine that something is not lost in the bargain, our access to the original object in all its materiality, its thingness.[18] The scrapbooks open this problem in a compelling way. First, there is a physical dimension to the albums that does not come across easily on the two-dimensional screen: the clear distinction, for example, between the pages of Sanba's albums and the ephemera pasted onto them; or, in the case of "The Origins of the Revival of Storytelling" ("Otoshibanashi chūkō raiyu"), the physical structure of the album which opens in accordion-style and in both directions: there is no clear front or back. When this scrapbook was digitized, however, it was necessary to flatten out the album, and in consequence, it is impossible to discern on the computer screen the original form and its open-endedness—neither front nor back, neither beginning nor ending.

As I have earlier discussed, Sanba's scrapbooks are themselves challenging objects for thinking about questions of original and copy: they are singular objects composed entirely of printed material, an original fashioned out of copies. To view these albums now on a screen, where they are transformed into "pictures of themselves,"[19] is to raise again a set of questions about originals and copies of which Sanba and his contemporaries were already well aware. Indeed, one of the points I have argued across the chapters of this book is that the culture of the early nineteenth century cannot be understood apart from a set of anxieties over the nature of the real and its representations in print, anxieties that manifest themselves in many different ways from the prizing, in certain instances, of manuscript culture over print to the uncertain capacity of print to capture the ephemeral nature of the performance on stage.

Sanba's scrapbooks foreground the question of preservation: he was intent on *preserving* these materials as "devices for thinking about the past," and his habits as a collector cannot be understood apart from this impulse. But no less interesting is the question of *access* that the albums raise: if the hand-made or hand-copied, the manuscript and the singular, came to have a certain value for writers in the opening years of the nineteenth century, was it not in part because of access, the

---

[17] Hattori Yukio, "Shikitei Sanba no shibai banzuke no shūshū," *Nihon kosho tsūhin* 49, 2 (February 1984), 4.

[18] See Smith, "Getting Back to the Library, Getting Back to the Body," p. 27.

[19] See Lisa Gitelman, *Paper Knowledge: Toward a Media History of Documents* Durham, NC: Duke University Press, 2014), p. 114.

question of who and when and in what context these materials might be viewed? The printed broadsheet once removed from circulation became an object of a particular kind of antiquarian sociability symbolized by groups like the Unchakai.

But there is another story to tell about the imbrication of these albums in a particular kind of sociability, a sociability that relates to the fate of the albums once they left Sanba's hands. Both Sanba's scrapbook of storytelling ephemera and his albums of theater programs would eventually find their way into the collection of the Imperial Library in Ueno, the pre-war incarnation of the National Diet Library. "Programs of Edo's Three Theaters" ("Edo sanshibai monbanzuke"), Sanba's collection of theater programs, was purchased by the library in 1912. "The Origins of the Revival of Storytelling," Sanba's album of storytelling ephemera, by contrast, did not make its way into the library's collections until 1918 and had, by that time, passed through the hands of a number of other collectors, and it bears an endpaper note detailing its provenance.

This note is itself an immensely rich object for thinking about this scrapbook and the work of collecting: how the materials were originally collected and how, in turn, the scrapbook itself became an object of collection in a genealogy of collecting that extends across the nineteenth century. And the endpaper is that much more intriguing for its account beginning with Shibue Chūsai, the nineteenth-century physician, bureaucrat, collector, and bibliophile around whom Mori Ōgai would construct one of the great historical novels of modern Japanese literature and who would become famous in English through Edwin McClellan's *Woman in the Crested Kimono*.[20]

Chūsai had evidently acquired the scrapbook sometime after Sanba's death; after Chūsai's death, Sanba's scrapbook changed hands several times before it was acquired by the Imperial Library. Ōgai had published his biographical novel on Chūsai in 1917, a year before the scrapbook was acquired, and although the novel contains a wonderful description of Ōgai tracking down Chūsai's identity in the reading room of the old Imperial Library, Ōgai had missed Sanba's scrapbook by a year or so.

In reading Ōgai's novel after having had a chance to look at Sanba's scrapbooks in the rare book room at the National Diet Library, I could not help but reflect on a genealogy that connected Sanba to Chūsai to Ōgai and ultimately, the better part of a century after Ōgai, to my own experience of looking at these materials and in some fashion making them part of the archive that I was collecting. "He had once walked along the same path as me," Ōgai writes of Chūsai;[21] I suppose that is how I felt about both Ōgai and Chūsai. Even more striking than the uncanny sense that both Chūsai and Ōgai had preceded me was Ōgai's trajectory in the novel from

---

[20] Edwin McClellan, *Woman in the Crested Kimono: The Life of Shibue Io and Her Family* (New Haven, CT: Yale University Press, 1985).
[21] Mori Ōgai, *Shibue Chūsai*, rev. edn (Tokyo: Iwanami Shoten, 1999), p. 24.

a concern with collecting historical documents, to use in his fiction, to an exploration of the collector Chūsai and his world. This was, after all, how I had myself become interested in Sanba as a collector of theater ephemera: what Sanba pasted into his albums became, very quickly for me, only of secondary interest. More compelling was the collector himself, the historical practices he represented, and the constitution of the albums as documents. What Ōgai sensed in Chūsai was a way of recasting the history of the nineteenth century not as a history of great men and great events but as a record of the everyday, the ephemeral, the commonplace. Chūsai was, to borrow Marvin Marcus's suggestive phrase, a "paragon of the ordinary," but he has become now one of the defining figures of Japan's nineteenth century.[22]

*Shibue Chūsai* marks a rupture in Ōgai's historical fiction between his earlier work that focused on history as event—one thinks here of his 1914 "Incident at Sakai" ("Sakai jiken")—and his turn toward the ordinary and the everyday in the years following his encounter with Chūsai. But even as Chūsai is the subject of Ōgai's novel, he is not its protagonist as such: that figure, the reader begins gradually to understand, is Ōgai himself as historian. Ōgai's novel is about the work of the historian and, recalling Kyōden's self-portrait in the preface to *Thoughts on Extraordinary Things of Recent Times* (*Kinsei kisekikō*) or the figure of the "antiquarian" from Sanba's *A Critique of the Audience* (*Kakusha hyōbanki*), the novel recounts how Ōgai visits graveyards and rummages through old documents to recover the forgotten life of Chūsai. As the novel recovers Chūsai's life in painstaking detail, Ōgai as the I-narrator (*watakushi*) begins to occupy an increasingly important role in the novel. It is difficult, indeed, not to read *Shibue Chūsai* as a strange kind of "I-novel," even as a kind of a "confessional" novel where the very subject of confession becomes the historian's craft.

Looking back on my own first encounter with Sanba's scrapbooks, mediated now by the passage of time but also by a heightened sense of the role of the digital in historical research, I cannot help but be struck by how my approach to doing research for and writing this book was shaped by a perhaps unconscious sense of situatedness. One of Ōgai's great insights in *Shibue Chūsai* was seeing the object of his inquiry with a sort of double vision by which Chūsai appeared at once to belong to a different world that lay just beyond recovery and simultaneously to inhabit the same spaces as Ōgai—doppelganger or secret sharer. "Had he been my contemporary," Ōgai writes of Chūsai, "we would no doubt have rubbed sleeves over a drain cover in some back alley."[23] For me, Ōgai, who had done his research in the pre-war Imperial Library, played a similar role: it was hard not to have a sense that his specter lingered in the library and that my own approach to my work was very much shaped by the insights that I took from his novel.

---

[22] See Marvin Marcus, *Paragons of the Ordinary: The Biographical Literature of Mori Ōgai* (Honolulu: University of Hawai'i Press, 1993).

[23] Mori Ōgai, *Shibue Chūsai*, p. 24.

Sanba himself (whose work as a collector and historian of the quotidian forms the kernel of this experience) was intimately aware of questions of specters and haunting and the relationship between the real and its representations, the shadows cast by the real. In one of the first materials that I discuss in this book, Sanba's 1811 *Shadows of Kabuki Cast by Magic Lantern* (*Sono utsushi-e kabuki no omokage*), Sanba meditates on the way that the printed book appears as a kind of shadow of the play it purports to represent on the page, but he also questions the very duality of real and shadow, original and copy. If, at one level, this work of fiction can be thought of as a shadow cast by the play, the book as a separate narrative and as a physical object that can be held in the hand of the reader becomes its own reality rather than merely the disembodied play (existing now only in the form of the shadows it has cast on various printed objects) that seems to stand in a spectral relationship to our reality.

This insight from two centuries ago seems to present a very useful way to think about the spectral nature of the digital archive and its relationship to *things* of which it appears as a shadow. And just as Sanba's own work is marked by a deep ambivalence, a sense of mourning for the loss of an (imagined) authentic experience as well as an acknowledgement that shadows may, in fact, be more real than the objects which cast them, so too is our digital age defined by a similar set of anxious ambivalences that both embrace the power and the potential of the digital record and posit a sense of nostalgia for the lost authenticity of the experiences of the (scholarly) past. And just as Ōgai was writing, in the second decade of the twentieth century, when the proximity of the past allowed him to see quite clearly this double vision, so too the writing of this book across a period that spanned the great digital divide has heightened, for me, the very processes of research that often remain unconscious (and unacknowledged) by the scholar.

In a strange and completely unexpected way, Sanba's *Shadows of Kabuki Cast by Magic Lantern* played a pivotal role in my thinking about these problems as I finished writing this book. I had first come across the book's title in the catalogue of materials owned by the Hayashi household in Tsumago, and my access to the book was provided by a copy that had been digitized by Waseda University Library. But in the course of finishing this book, I decided to travel to Tsugamo to examine the copy that had been held in the Hayashi family library as well as other materials that I treat in this book. At that point, I had written through the body of the book and had begun to think seriously about the question of what it meant to be writing in a moment very much defined by the ease of access brought about by digitization.

When I finally made arrangements to see the books, I did so in the context of a specific lack of access: the books, though catalogued, had remained in the storehouse of the Hayashi household and had never been photographed or digitized. To see them meant to travel to Tsumago, to make arrangements with the museum, and to be granted access by Hayashi Bunji, the current head of the Hayashi house, which still owns the books (and the storehouse).

At the level of *content*, I knew what was contained in almost all of the materials in the collection; but these books and playbills were distinct, in part, precisely because they were something to which I did not have easy access, a subject that demanded a particular kind of attention and planning. Their singularity lay in their situatedness: in place and in space, in a storehouse in the mountains, as part of a collection, as objects that had been owned and read by a specific person, and perhaps, I hoped, had been marked by her hand in some way that would be meaningful, the traces of a reader that would open up a different horizon of interpretation. In an age defined by digitization and ease of access to all kinds of materials, there was something fascinating about the objects which had not yet been digitized, singular not in their content but in their location and in the *uses* someone had made of them.

Several things then unfolded: first, try as I might, I was unable to locate a number of items in the catalogue despite the fact that apparently no one had looked at the collection again since it was first catalogued. The book I most wanted to see, the copy of *Shadows of Kabuki Cast by Magic Lantern* housed in the collection, was one of the books I simply could not find. And many of the playbills collected across the nineteenth century were also missing. Having traveled to Tsumago with the hope of finding some specific way of addressing, of thinking about these unique copies and what they meant for a particular reader (and then for myself as a historian), I was left quite literally empty-handed. At the same time, as I worked through the collection I was confronted with various traces of the historical reader. There were hand-colored kimono, there was a beast whose head had been removed as it was struck by a hero, there were doodles (a set of armor and a kind of phallic-looking beast), and someone practicing their handwriting, even, within the pages of one book a leaf that had been perfectly preserved for a century-and-a-half. But most of the manuscript markings were unintelligible except in the most basic sense: they marked the presence of a reader, but which reader and when, these were lost to history. Most of the books bear stamps from commercial lending libraries, sometimes more than one, and it is never clear whether the markings we are encountering today can be attributed to a specific historical reader like Hayashi Kuni—a theater-mad young woman of the provinces—or were the remnant of these books' prehistories as objects that circulated widely in the collections of lending libraries.

In retrospect, what strikes me most about this experience was how it was itself an uncanny repetition of one of the central themes of both Sanba's book and of my own: the relationship between the ephemerality of performance and its record as a kind of shadow. Was my own relationship to the missing book, and to the digitized version of Shōyō's copy that became my stand-in, not, in its own way, a repetition of the ghostly relationship of a text to the ephemerality of performance?

The digitized version of Shōyō's copy of *Shadows of Kabuki Cast by Magic Lantern* is not an adequate substitute for the missing copy from the Hayashi library; it is not a substitute at all. But that is really Sanba's own point: if the book is a shadow cast by the stage, it is not at the level of substitution that the process works but something perhaps more like "surrogation," what Joseph Roach has described as "the doomed search for originals by continuously auditioning stand-ins."[24] Indeed, just as "performance [...] stands in for an elusive entity that it is not but that it must vainly aspire both to embody and to replace," so are the relationships between text and performance or between the text and its digitization part of this continual process.[25] If we see the digitized document not primarily as a copy (of the original, whose richness it always fails adequately to represent) but as itself a stage in this process of surrogation, we can more fully engage in the complexity of what the digital archive represents for the scholar.

In one of the final scenes of *Shadows of Kabuki Cast by Magic Lantern*, the ghosts of the debauched priest Hōkaibō and of his victim, Miyato, the long-lost twin of Nowakihime, are driven away by the light cast from two magical objects, a statue of Kannon from the Sensōji Temple in Asakusa and a carp scroll in the hand of the Emperor Wu of Han China. As I have suggested in my discussion of this work, this final drama of light and shadow, of ghostly presence and its foretold absence, is immensely rich for thinking about Sanba's own intuition of the relationship between print and performance, page and stage—a subject which itself hangs over Sanba's work like a ghostly presence. But here, I would like to focus not on *Shadows of Kabuki Cast by Magic Lantern* itself but on a minor detail of the copy of the work that was digitized by Waseda University (and that once belonged to Tsubouchi Shōyō). Just at the place in the text where this scene unfolds, someone has written by hand repeatedly, and in the voice of the ghosts, "*urameshii*" and "*urameshiya*," an expression of resentment to the world, a haunting lament (Figure 6.1). There is a strange doubleness to this lament for it also marks the ghostly presence of the reader, a reader now lost to history other than in his or her marginalia, which has been preserved in a way that reader could never have imagined, by digitization, a ghostly embodiment of "the enduring ephemeral" of our digital age.[26] The lament is also a reminder of the *singularity* of the individual book, a block-printed text that, in ways similar to Sanba's scrapbooks, has been made unique by an intervention of the human hand. And it is hard, at this point, not to recall the missing copy of the same book from the Hayashi collection: what traces that text may have borne have, at least for now, disappeared.

If this uncanny presence of the historical reader in the voice of the textual ghost is useful for reflecting back on the themes I have tried to elucidate over the course of this book, it is because it is a reminder of the very complexities of any attempt

---

[24] Joseph Roach, *Cities of the Dead: Circum-Atlantic Performance* (New York: Columbia University Press, 1996), p. 3.
[25] Roach, *Cities of the Dead*, p. 3.
[26] Wendy Hui Kyong Chun, "The Enduring Ephemeral, or the Future Is a Memory," *Critical Inquiry* 35 (Autumn 2008), 148–71.

**Figure 6.1** Utagawa Toyokuni, the ghosts of Hōkaibō and Miyato from Shikitei Sanba, *Sono utsushie kabuki no omokage*, 1811.
Source: Waseda University Library.

to interrogate the historical record. Writing about surrogation, Roach suggests that "the fit cannot be exact," that "the intended substitute either cannot fulfil expectations, creating a deficit, or actually exceeds them, creating a surplus."[27] The digitization of Shōyō's copy of *Shadows of Kabuki Cast by Magic Lantern* seems, quite literally, to embody this dynamic: it is an inadequate substitute for the missing book in the Hayashi library, on the one hand, and yet the haunting voice of the reader, recorded toward the end of the volume, is suspended indefinitely as precisely this ghostly surplus on the other. Two centuries ago, Sanba's own work seemed to anticipate this very problem: the published book, he suggests, is a shadow cast by the play but, as I have noted earlier, *Shadows of Kabuki Cast by Magic Lantern* itself is structured in such a way that it *exceeds* the play in characters and in plot. Or we might recall the scrapbooks that Sanba would compile in the years after writing this work: the blank pages he left at the end of both albums signify, simultaneously, missing objects that he had intended to add but also the impossibility completing his enterprise.

[27] Roach, *Cities of the Dead*, p. 2.

I have returned so often to Sanba in the course of this book, as I did in the course of my research, because it seems to me there is something worth bearing in mind about earlier meditations on printed archives as devices for "thinking about the past." Sanba's scrapbooks are now more accessible than ever, but the basic problem to which they draw attention remains largely unchanged: there will always be more material to gather, the scholarly enterprise will always remain provisional, incomplete.

# Character List

Abe Yutaka 安部豊
akubasho 悪場所
Akutagawa Ryūnosuke 芥川龍之介
Aoto zōshi hana no nishiki-e 青砥稿花紅彩画
aragoto 荒事
Arai Hakuseki 新井白石
Arashi Kichisaburō 嵐吉三郎
Asa chanoyu chotto kuchikiri 朝茶湯一寸口切
Asaina 朝比奈
Asaina chaban Soga 朝比奈茶番曽我
Asao Kuzaemon 浅尾工左衛門
ayatsuri ningyō 操人形
Bandō Mitsugorō 坂東三津五郎
Banzui Chōbē 幡随長兵衛
banzuke 番付
benshi 弁士
Benten Kozō 弁天小僧
Boshin Sensō 戊辰戦争
Bunmeiron no gairyaku 文明論之概略
Butai no Danjūrō 舞台之團十郎
Butai no hana 舞台之華
Butai no omokage 舞台のおもかげ
Buyō Inshi 武陽隠士
canggu (J. sōkotsu) 蒼鶻
Chidaruma 血達磨
Chijin godai 地神五代
Chikamatsu Hanji 近松半二
Chikamatsu Kenkyūkai 近松研究会
Chikamatsu Monzaemon 近松門左衛門
Daikoku no zu 大極図
Dainichibō 大日坊
dan 旦
Danjūrō shichise no mago 団十郎七世嫡孫
dengaku 田楽
Denkikan 電気館
dōchūki 道中記
Edo nanshoku saiken 江戸男色細見
Edo sanshibai monbanzuke 江戸三芝居紋番附
Edo-chō 江戸町
ehon banzuke 絵本番付
Eitaijima 永代島
Ejima Ikushima jiken 江島生島事件

Engei gahō 演芸画報
engeki 演劇
esugata 絵姿
etoki 絵解
fudekuse 筆癖
Fujikawa Heikurō 藤川平九郎
Fujiwara Sadamoto 藤原貞本
Fukagawa 深川
Fukagawa taizen 深川大全/巽大全
Fukiya-chō 葺屋町
Fukiya-chō Gaidō 葺屋町街道
Fukuchi Ōchi 福地桜痴
Fukumori Kyūsuke 福森久助
Fukunoya Uchinari 福廼屋内成
Fukuyama 福山
Fukuzawa Yukichi 福沢諭吉
Fūsen nori uwasa no takadono 風船乗評判高閣
Futami Bunjirō 二見文次郎
Fuwa Banzaemon 不破伴左衛門
Gakushū 楽州
Gakuya Shinmichi 楽屋新道
Gekijō ikkan mushimegane 劇場一観顕微鏡
Gekijō kuni 劇場国
Genkyō sakusho 言狂作書
Genrokukan 玄鹿館
Gepponkoku 月本国
gesaku 戯作
gesakusha 戯作者
Geza ken 下座県
gōkan 合巻
Goryūtei Tokushō 五柳亭徳升
Gosho ōgi masago no shiranami 館扇面真砂白浪
Goyō no matsu 五葉松
Gunji Masakatsu 郡司正勝
Gunsho Ruijū 群書類従
Gyōki 行基
Hachimonjiya 八文字屋
Haiyūkō 俳優考
Hamamatsu Utakuni 浜松歌国
Hana no Edo kabuki nendaiki 花江都歌舞妓年代記
Hana no Edo kabuki nendaiki zoku hen 花江都歌舞妓年代記続編
hanamichi 花道
Hanawa Hokiichi 塙保己一
harikomichō 貼込帖
Hasegawa Kanbē 長谷川勘兵衛
Hatanaka Kansai 畠中観斎
Hayashi Bunji 林文二
Hayashi Kamejurō 林亀寿郎
Hayashi Kuni 林くに

hiiki renjū 贔屓連中
Hikōden (C. Feihong chuan) 飛虹伝
Hinaya Ryūho 雛屋立圃
Hiraga Gennai 平賀源内
Hisayoshi 久吉
Hishikawa Moronobu 菱川師宣
Hisseki to kojinsei 筆跡と個人性
Hōkaibō 法界坊
Honbu ken 本舞県
Honjin 本陣
Honjo 本所
Horie-chō 堀江町
Horigoshi Hideshi 堀越秀
Hōseidō Kisanji 朋誠堂喜三二
hozon 保存
Ichijima Kenkichi 市島謙吉
Ichikawa Danjūrō 市川團十郎
Ichikawa Jitsuko 市川実子
Ichikawa Kyūzō 市川九蔵
Ichikawa Omezō 市川男女蔵
Ichikawa Sanshō 市川三升
Ichikawa Shakoroku 市川蝦蛄六
Ichikawa shichisei kyogen nendaiki 市川七世狂言年代記
Ichikawa Shinzō 市川新蔵
Ichimura Uzaemon 市村羽左衛門
Ichimura-za 市村座
Igami no Gonta いがみの権太
Ihara Toshirō 伊原敏郎
Iijima Kyoshin 飯島虚心
Ikushima Shingorō 生島新五郎
Ima mukashi ayatsuri nendaiki 今昔操年代記
Imose nori no shōsoku 妹背海苔の消息
Inakamono Tarōzaemon 田舎者太郎左衛門
Inari ken 稲荷県
Inari-michi 稲荷道
Inazuma byōshi 稲妻表紙
Inoue Takejirō 井上竹次郎
Iseshū 伊勢集
Ishikawa Goemon 石川五右エ門
Ishizuka Hōkaishi 石塚豊芥子
Iwai Hanshirō 岩井半四郎
Iwai Tojaku 岩井杜若
Izumi Kyōka 泉鏡花
jing 浄
Jippensha Ikku 十返舎一九
jitsuaku 実悪
jōruri 浄瑠璃
Jūni bungō 十二文豪
Kabuki dōchū zue 歌舞伎道中図絵

Kabuki kaidō ki 歌舞伎街道記
Kabuki kenkyū 歌舞伎研究
Kabuki shinpō 歌舞伎新報
Kabuki-za 歌舞伎座
Kagekiyo 景清
kagema jaya 陰間茶屋
Kaigai kidan 海外奇談
Kajima Seibē 鹿島清兵衛
Kajiwara Kagetoki 梶原景時
kakekotoba 掛詞
Kakusha hyōbanki 客者評判記
Kamakura Gongorō 鎌倉権五郎
Kamigata 上方
Kanadehon chūshingura 仮名手本忠臣蔵
Kanda Myōjin 神田明神
Kanō Hinasuke 叶雛助
Kansei Reforms 寛政改革
Kanze Nobumitsu 観世信光
Kariganeya Gisuke 雁金屋儀助
Kashiwara Isaburō 柏原伊三郎
Katakiyaku 敵役
Katō Ebian 加藤曳尾庵
Katsukawa Shundō 勝川春童
Katsukawa Shunshō 勝川春章
katsureki 活歴
Katsushika Hokusai 葛飾北斎
Kawajiri Seitan 川尻清潭
Kawajiya 河内屋
Kawakami Kamekichi 川上亀吉
Kawakami Otojirō 川上音二郎
Kawarazaki Chōjūrō 河原崎長十郎
Kawarazaki-za 河原崎座
Kawatake Mokuami 河竹黙阿弥
Kawaura Kenichi 河浦謙一
Keiō Gijuku 慶應義塾
Keisai Eisen 渓斎英泉
Keiten Yoshi 経典余師
Kejō suigen maku no soto 戯場粋言幕乃外
Kezairoku 戯財録
kibyōshi 黄表紙
Kiku no sono 菊の園
Kikuchi Mohē 菊地茂兵衛
Kimura Mokurō 木村黙老
Kimura Senshū 木村仙秀
kinchakuya 巾着屋
Kinmō zui 訓蒙図彙
Kinsei kiseki kō 近世奇跡考
Kinsei mono no hon Edo sakusha burui 近世物之本江戸作者部類
Kirare Yosa 切られ与三

Kiso 木曽
Kitagawa Morisada 喜田川守貞
Kitagawa Tsukimaro 喜多川月麿
Kobayashi Bunshichi 小林文七
Kobiki-chō 木挽町
Kodai ukiyo-e kaire hikkei 古代浮世絵買入必携
Kodama Hangan 児玉判官
Kogaku 古学
Kokon shibai irokurabe hyakunin isshu 古今四場居百人一首
Kokon yakusha taizen 古今役者大全
Kokugaku 国学
Kokuseiya chūgiden 國姓爺忠義傳
Kokusho Kankōkai 国書刊行会
Komada Kōyō 駒田好洋
Kongō Tarō 金剛太郎
Kōraiya 高麗屋
koshibai 小芝居
kottō 骨董
Kottō zasshi 骨董雑誌
Kottōnetsu 骨董熱
Kottōshū 骨董集
Kumanoya Hikokurō 熊野屋彦九郎
Kurahashi Gorobē 倉橋五郎兵衛
kusazōshi 草双紙
Kyakuhon Gakufu Jōrei 脚本楽譜条例
Kyakusha hyōbanki 客者評判記
Kyakushoku 脚色
Kyō-machi 京町
kyōgen kuni 狂言国
kyōgen sakusha 狂言作者
Kyōgen sakusha kokoroesho 狂言作者心得書
kyōka 狂歌
Kyokutei Bakin 曲亭馬琴
Kyota kyakushoku chō 許多脚色帖
Li Yu (J. Ri Gyo) 李漁
Magome 馬籠
Manji Takao 万治高尾
Maruhon 丸本/院本
Masagoji 真砂路
Matsumoto Kōshirō 松本幸四郎
Matsunoya 松廼舎
Matsuyama Kitarō 松山喜太郎
Matsuyama Yonetarō 松山米太郎
Meiboku sendai hagi 伽羅先代萩
Meisetsu jijoden 鳴雪自叙伝
meisho zue 名所図会
Mie 見栄/見得
Mimasuren 三升連
Mimasuya Nisōji 三升屋二三治

Minami-za 南座
Minegishi Denjirō 峰岸傳次郎
minkan no zatsuji 民間の雑事
Minyūsha 民友社
Miyatake Gaikotsu 宮武外骨
Miyato 宮戸
Mizutani Futō 水谷不倒
Momijigari 紅葉狩
Mori Ōgai 森鴎外
Morisada mankō 守貞謾稿
Morishima Chūryō 森島中良
Morita Kanya 森田/守田勘彌
Morita-za 森田座
Moriya Jihē 森屋治兵衛
Moriyama Shashinkan 森山写真館
Morokoshi kabuki kyogen 唐土歌舞伎狂言
Morokoshi kidan 唐土奇談
Motoori Norinaga 本居宣長
Muen-baba 無縁姥婆
Murayama Matasaburō 村山又三郎
Nagano 長野
Nagiso-machi 南木曽町
Naitō Meisetsu 内藤鳴雪
Naka-no-chō 仲之町
Nakamura Kanzaburō 中村勘三郎
Nakamura Nakazō 中村仲蔵
Nakamura Shikan 中村芝翫
Nakamura Utaemon 中村歌右衛門
Nakamura-za 中村座
Nakanishi Sadayuki 中西貞行
Nakao Choken 中尾樗軒
Nakasendō 中山道
Nakatsukasa 中務
Nakayama Tomisaburō 中山富三郎
Nakazawa Dōni 中沢道二
Namiki Gohei 並木五瓶
Namiki Shōzō 並木正三
Naniwa miyage 難波土産
Narita Yasuke 成田屋助
Natsu no Fuji 夏の富士
nendaiki 年代記
nigao-e 似顔絵
Nihon Bijutsu Kyōkai 日本美術協会
Nihonbashi 日本橋
Nikki Danjō 仁木弾正
nimaime 二枚目
Ningyō-chō 人形町
Ninkōjō 任興帖
ninsōgaki 人相書

Nishizawa Ippū 西沢一風
Nowakihime 野分姫
nukihon 抜本
O ki ni mesu mama お気に召すまま
Ochazuke no aji お茶漬けの味
Ochiai Yoshiiku 落合芳幾
Ogasahara Shinbē 小笠原新兵衛
Ogyū Hokkei 荻生北渓
Ogyū Korenori 荻生維則
Ogyū Sorai 荻生徂徠
Ōishi Yoshio 大石良雄
Okamoto Kidō 岡本綺堂
ōkubie 大首絵
Ōkuma Shigenobu 大隈重信
Ōmon 大門
ōmoto 大綱
Ōmura Hiroyoshi 大村弘毅
ōmuseki 鸚鵡石
onnagata 女形
Onoe Baikō 尾上梅幸
Onoe Kikugorō 尾上菊五郎
Ōoka Shunboku 大岡春卜
ōshibai 大芝居
Ōta Nanpo 大田南畝
Ōtani Hiroemon 大谷廣右衛門
Ōtani Jicchō 大谷十町
Ōtaya Sakichi 太田屋佐吉
Otoshibanashi chūkō raiyu 落話中興来由
Ozaki Kōyō 尾崎紅葉
Ozu Yasujirō 小津安二郎
Rokudai 六代
Ryōgoku 両国
Ryūtei Enshi 柳亭燕枝
Ryūtei Tanehiko 柳亭種彦
saiken 細見
Saitō Gesshin 斎藤月岑
sajiki 桟敷
Sakai jiken 堺事件
Sakai Matsunosuke 酒井松之助
Sakai-chō 堺町
Sakano Kyūjirō 坂野久次郎
Sakurada Jisuke 桜田治助
Sakuragawa Jihinari 桜川慈悲成
Sakurahime zenden 桜姫全伝
sakusha 作者
Sakusha myōmoku 作者名目
Sanbasō 三番叟
Sanja Daigongen 三社大権現
sanmaime 三枚目

Sanmon gosan no kiri 山門五三桐
Sanshibai gakuya zassho 三芝居楽屋雑書
Sanshibai yakusha saiken 三芝居細見
Sanshōtei Karaku 三笑亭可楽
Santai no kigen 三台紀原
Santō Kyōden 山東京伝
Santō Kyōzan 山東京山
Sanza butai fūkei no zu 三舞台風景之図
Sanza Daigongen 三座大権現
Saritsu udan 簔笠雨談
Sarugaku 申楽/猿楽
saruwaka mai 猿若舞
Saruwaka saiken zu 猿若細見図
Saruwaka-chō 猿若町
Satō Kōichi 佐藤功一
Satsuma-za 薩摩座
Sawada Wasuke 沢田和助
Sawamura Sōjūrō 沢村宗十郎
Segawa Jokō 瀬川如皐
Segawa Kikunojō 瀬川菊之丞
Seikyoku ruisan 声曲類纂
seishi 正史
Seji kenmon roku 世事見聞録
sekai 世界
Senba Tarōbē 仙波太郎兵衛
Senjimon seiko no yanagi 千字文西湖の柳
Senkakudō 仙鶴堂
Shēkusupiya kenkyū shiori シエークスピヤ研究栞
Shen zhong lou 蜃中樓
sheng 生
Shibai chōhōsho 劇場重法書
Shibai kinmō zui 劇場訓蒙図彙
Shibai saiken sanbasō 芝居細見三葉草
Shibaraku 暫
Shibata Tsunekichi 柴田常吉
Shibue Chūsai 渋江抽斎
Shikankoku ichiran 芝翫国一覧
Shikitei Sanba 式亭三馬
Shimeizen 四鳴蝉
Shin Gunsho Ruijū 新群書類従
Shin Izumi-chō 新和泉町
Shin Yoshiwara 新吉原
shina 等
Shingaku 心学
Shinkoku yakusha kōmoku 新刻役者綱目
Shinsei-za 新盛座
Shinshi Saruwaka nendaiki 新梓猿若年代記
Shinshū 信州
Shintomi-chō 新富町

Shintomi-za 新富座
shirabyōshi 白拍子
shiryō 史料
shō 証
Shōhi chiriki 娼妃地理記
Shōnen jidai ni mita kabuki no tsuioku 少年時代に観た歌舞伎の追憶
shōzō 肖像
Shūi wakashū 拾遺和歌集
shunga 春画
Shunshokudai 春色台
Shuzenji monogatari 修禅寺物語
Song Ziyan (J. Sō Shigan) 宋紫岩
Sono utsushie kabuki no omokage 其寫絵劇倪
sugao 素顔
Sugimori Tamon 杉森多門
sugoroku 双六
Suiyo shōroku 睡余小録
sujiguma 筋隈
Sumi-chō 角町
Sumida River 隅田川
Sumidagawa gonichi no omokage 隅田川続倪
Sumiyoshi-chō 住吉町
surimono 刷物
Suzuki Harunobu 鈴木春信
Tachibana Morikuni 橘守国
Tachiyaku 立役
Tada Nanrei 多田南嶺
Tadanobu 忠信
Taira no Koremori 平維盛
Taira no Masakado 平将門
Taishū 台州
Taiyō 太陽
Takara awase 宝合
Takemoto Settsu-Daijō 竹本摂津大掾
Takeshiba Kisui 竹柴其水
Taki no Shiraito 瀧の白糸
Tamenaga Shunsui 為永春水
Tamura Nariyoshi 田村成義
Tani Bunchō 谷文晁
Tanki manroku 耽奇漫録
Tankikai 耽奇会
Tatesakusha 立作者
Temae miso 手前味噌
tenchi ichidai gijō 天地一大戯場
tenchi kaibyaku 天地開闢
Tenjin shichidai 天神七代
Tenpō Kaikaku 天保改革
Tōkai dōchū hizakurige 東海道中膝栗毛
Tōkaidō 東海道

Tōkyō Senmon Gakkō 東京専門学校
Torii Kiyonobu 鳥居清信
Tosa Mitsumoto 土佐光元
Tosa Mitsuoki 土佐光起
Tōshi Shōkyaku 東子樵客
Tōshūsai Sharaku 東洲斎写楽
Tsubouchi Shōyō 坪内逍遥
Tsuchigumo 土蜘
Tsuga Teishō 都賀庭鐘
Tsuji banzuke 辻番付
Tsukagoshi Yoshitarō 塚越芳太郎
Tsukudajima 佃島
Tsumago 妻籠
tsurane つらね
Tsuruya Kiemon 鶴屋喜衛門
Tsuruya Nanboku 鶴屋南北
uchigōshi 内格子
ugachi 穿
Ukan jigi 羽勘字義
Ukan sandai zue 羽勘三台図絵
Ukiyo 浮世
Ukiyo-e 浮世絵
Ukiyo eshi benran 浮世絵師便覧
Ukiyoeshi Utagawa retsuden 浮世絵歌川列伝
Unchakai 雲茶会
Unchaten 雲茶店
Utagawa Kunisada 歌川国貞
Utagawa Kuniyoshi 歌川国芳
Utagawa Yoshifuji 歌川芳藤
Utei Enba 烏亭焉馬
Wakaba no Naishi 若葉の内侍
Wakan sansai zue 和漢三才図会
wakashu 若衆
Waki honjin 脇本陣
Wu shuang pu 無雙譜
Ya no ne 矢の根
Ya no ne Gorō 矢の根五郎
Yaheibyōe Munekiyo 弥平兵衛宗清
yakusha hyōbanki 役者評判記
Yakusha jinkokuki 役者人国記
Yakusha kuchi jamisen 役者口三味線
Yakusha meisho zue 戯子名所図会
Yakusha meisho zue (hyōbanki) 役者名所図会
Yakusha nigao hayageiko 役者似顔早稽古
Yakusha sanjūnisō tengankyō 俳優卅二相點顔鏡
Yakusha saraekō 役者時習講
Yakuwari banzuke 役割番付
Yamaguchiya Tōbē 山口屋藤兵衛
Yamamur-za 山村座

Yamanaka Sadajirō 山中定次郎
Yamato-e 大和絵
Yamazaki Yoshinari 山崎美成
Yanagibashi 柳橋
Yanagiya Umehiko 柳屋梅彦
yarō 野郎
yarō hyōbanki 野郎評判記
Yarō sanza taku 野良三座詫
Yasuda Zenjirō 安田善次郎
Yazaemon 弥左衛門
Yobukodori waka sanchō zenzu 呼子鳥和歌三町全図
yomihon 読本
Yōryū Shujin 揚柳主人
Yoshi-chō 芳町
Yoshimura Ito 吉村いと
Yoshino Goun 吉野五運
Yoshitsune senbon zakura 義経千本桜
Yoshiwara saiken 吉原細見
Yoshizawa Ayame 芳澤あやめ
Yoshizawa Shōho 吉沢商舗
Yoshizawa Shōten 吉沢商店
yūjo hyōbanki 遊女評判記
Yūki-za 結城座
Yu saotou 玉搔頭
Yushima Seidō 湯島聖堂
Zaju 雑劇
Zare-e 戯絵
Zhu Peizhang (J. Shu Haishō) 朱佩章

# Biographical Appendix

Abe Yutaka 安部豊 (1886–1957). Journalist, editor, and photographer. Abe produced a series of albums of photographs of actors beginning in 1912 with *Flowers of the Stage* (*Butai no hana*) and, with Ihara Toshirō, edited a collection of photographs of the actor Ichikawa Danjūrō IX in 1923.

Chikamatsu Hanji 近松半二 (1725–83). Playwright. Hanji was one of the most successful playwrights for the puppet theater (*jōruri*) in the second half of the eighteenth century. Many of his plays are still performed in both the *jōruri* and kabuki repertories.

Chikamatsu Monzaemon 近松門左衛門 (1653–1725). Playwright. Chikamatsu wrote for both the puppet theater (*jōruri*) and for kabuki and is considered Japan's greatest dramatist. His works still form an important part of the *jōruri* repertory and have been widely translated.

Fukumori Kyūsuke 福森久助 (1767–1818). Playwright. Active as a kabuki playwright from the 1780s through his death, Kyūsuke has been largely overshadowed by his more successful contemporary Tsuruya Nanboku IV. His play *A Song of the Dream Yoshiwara* (*Sono kouta yume no Yoshiwara*) is still performed as part of the kabuki repertory.

Hanagasa Bunkyō 花笠文京 (1758–1860). Playwright. Bunkyō was a minor kabuki playwright who was a disciple of Tsuruya Nanboku IV (1755–1829).

Hatanaka Kansai 畠中観斎 (1752–1801). Poet. Along with Ōta Nanpo, Kansai was one of the most prominent writers of comic verse in the late eighteenth century. His 1790 *Strange Tales from China* (*Morokoshi kidan*) played a central role in introducing Chinese stage conventions to Japan.

Hayashi Kuni 林くに (dates unknown). The daughter of a prominent family in Tsumago, Kuni collected fiction and theater ephemera in the mid-nineteenth century. Little is known of Kuni's life, but part of her collection is on view at the Nagisomachi Museum in Tsumago, Nagano Prefecture.

Hōseidō Kisanji 朋誠堂喜三二 (1735–1813). Fiction writer. Born into a samurai family, Kisanji wrote primarily comic fiction from the late 1770s through the beginning of the 1790s.

Ichikawa Danjūrō V 市川團十郎 (1741–1806). Actor. The son of Ichikawa Danjūrō IV, Danjūrō V made his debut at the age of four and would become the leading actor of the late eighteenth century.

Ichikawa Danjūrō VII 市川團十郎 (1791–1859). Actor. The grandson of Ichikawa Danjūrō V on his mother's side, Danjūrō VII was adopted by his uncle Danjūrō VI shortly after his birth and made his debut as Ichikawa Shinnosuke at the age of four. After Danjūrō VI's unexpected death in 1799 at the age of twenty-two, the then Shinnosuke ascended to the name of Danjūrō VII in 1800 at the age of ten and, along with Matsumoto Kōshirō V and the *onnagata* Iwai Hanshirō IV, became one of the greatest actors of the first half of the nineteenth century.

Ichikawa Danjūrō IX 市川團十郎 (1838–1903). Actor. The fifth son of Danjūrō VII, Danjūrō IX was adopted at birth by Kawarazaki Gonnosuke VI, the proprietor of the Kawarazaki-za theater. In 1874, the actor, then known as Kawarazaki Sanshō, returned to the Ichikawa family and assumed the hereditary name of Danjūrō IX. Along with Onoe Kikugorō V, Danjūrō IX became one of the most important actors of the Meiji period and a central figure in efforts to reform and modernize kabuki.

Ihara Toshirō 伊原敏郎 (1870–1941). Theater critic and historian who wrote under the pen name Seiseien (青々園). In 1900, Ihara founded the magazine *Kabuki* with Miki Takeji, the younger brother of the novelist Mori Ōgai.

Ishizuka Hōkaishi 石塚豊芥子 (1799–1861). A spice merchant by trade, Hōkaishi was a bibliophile, collector, and theater enthusiast who compiled the continuation of Utei Enba's *Chronology of Kabuki*, covering the period between 1819 and 1859.

Iwai Hanshirō V 岩井半四郎 (1776–1847) Actor. The son of the *onnagata* (player of female roles) Iwai Hanshirō IV, Hanshirō V made his debut in 1787, at the age of eleven, and became the most famous *onnagata* of the first half of the nineteenth century.

Kawatake Mokuami 河竹黙阿弥 (1816–93). Playwright. Often considered the last great kabuki playwright, Mokuami was active between 1835 and shortly before his death in 1893. Many of his plays are still part of kabuki's repertory.

Kawatake Shigetoshi 河竹繁俊 (1889–1967) Historian of kabuki. Born Ichimura Shigetoshi, he assumed the surname Kawatake after being adopted by Kawatake Mokuami's daughter, Yoshimura Ito, in 1911. Kawatake served as the director of the Tsubouchi Memorial Theater Museum at Waseda University from 1934–60.

Kimura Mokurō 木村黙老 (1774–1857). A samurai from the Takamatsu Domain on the island of Shikoku, Mokurō was a bibliophile and collector who wrote several important works on the history of kabuki and fiction writing in the early nineteenth century.

Kitamura Morisada 喜田川守貞 (1810–?). A sugar merchant by trade, Morisada compiled a thirty-five-volume manuscript detailing the customs and daily life of nineteenth-century Japan.

Kobayashi Bunshichi 小林文七 (1861–1923). Collector and dealer of ukiyo-e prints. Through his friendship with Ernest Fenollosa, Kobayashi played a prominent role in selling Japanese prints in America. In 1916, he sold roughly 15,000 theater prints to Waseda University, which are now part of the Tsubouchi Memorial Theater Museum.

Kyokutei Bakin 曲亭馬琴 (1767–1848). Author. Born into a minor samurai family, Bakin became active in publishing satirical and comic fiction in the early 1790s as a disciple of Santō Kyōden. By the early nineteenth century, Bakin had turned to the composition of a genre of historical fiction known as *yomihon* and would become one of the central literary figures of the first half of the nineteenth century.

Li Yu (J. Ri Gyo) 李漁 (1611–1680). Author and playwright. Active from the late Ming to the early Qing periods, Li Yu published widely in fiction, essays, and drama during his lifetime and became well known in Japan beginning in the late eighteenth century.

Matsumoto Kōshirō V 松本幸四郎 (1764–1838). Actor. The son of Matsumoto Kōshirō IV, Kōshirō made his debut on stage at the age of six in 1770 under the name Ichikawa Sumizō and assumed the name Kōshirō V in 1801. A player of both protagonists and villains, Kōshirō V was one of the most popular and famous actors of the first decades of the nineteenth century.

Naitō Meisetsu 内藤鳴雪 (1847–1926). Haiku poet. Meisetsu was a student and close friend of the much younger Masaoka Shiki (1867–1902), one of the central figures in the development of modern haiku poetry.

Nakamura Kanzaburō I 中村勘三郎 (1598–1658). Originally a practitioner of the Ōkura school of kyōgen drama from the area near Kyoto, Kanzaburō traveled to Edo in 1622. Under the name Saruwaka Kanzaburō, he founded the first of Edo's kabuki theaters in 1624, the Saruwaka-za, later the Nakamura-za.

Nakamura Nakazō III 中村仲蔵 (1809–86). Actor. For most of his career, Nakazō III performed under the name Nakamura Tsuruzō and took the name Nakazō III only in 1865. Today, Nakazō is best remembered for his memoir *Self Praise* (*Temae miso*) written from 1855–73.

Nakamura Utaemon III 中村歌右衛門 (1778–1838). Actor. Active primarily in Osaka, Utaemon III, also known by his poetic name Shikan, was one of the greatest actors of the late eighteenth and early nineteenth centuries. His journey to appear in Edo in 1808 was an enormous event.

Nakamura Utaemon IV 中村歌右衛門 (1798–1852). Actor. Born in Edo, Utaemon IV was adopted by Utaemon III when the latter traveled to Edo from Osaka in 1808. Utaemon IV spent his career in Edo and was one of the most important actors of the 1820s and '30s.

Namiki Gohei 並木五瓶 (1747–1808). Playwright. Originally active in Osaka and Kyoto, Gohei moved to Edo in 1794 and is credited with introducing many of the elements of the Osaka stage to Edo. His 1778 *The Golden Gate and the Paulownia Crest* (*Sanmon gosan no kiri*) is still widely performed.

Namiki Shōzō II 並木正三 (?–1807). Playwright. Although a minor playwright, Shōzō's "Valuable Notes on Playwrighting" ("Kezairoku"; 1801) is one of the most important documents about the work of the playwright in the eighteenth and nineteenth centuries. His name is also romanized as Namiki Shōza.

Onoe Kikugorō V 尾上菊五郎 (1844–1903). Actor. Along with Ichikawa Danjūrō IX and Ichikawa Danzō I, Kikugorō V was one of the leading actors of the Meiji period. One of his most famous roles was as the thief Benten Kozō in Kawatake Mokuami's 1862 *Aoto Fujitsuna, Told in Colored Prints* (*Aoto zōshi hana no nishiki-e*). Kikugorō's autobiography was published in 1903.

Ōta Nanpo 大田南畝 (1749–1823). Poet, essayist, and shogunal bureaucrat. Born to a minor samurai family in Edo, Nanpo became a central figure in literary circles in the late nineteenth and early twentieth centuries. In 1804 he served as the magistrate of Nagasaki, during which time he collected a large number of Chinese and Dutch objects.

Santō Kyōden 山東京伝 (1761–1816). Author and illustrator. Kyōden began his career as an illustrator under the name Kitao Masanobu and started writing comic fiction in the late 1770s. By the early nineteenth century, Kyōden was widely regarded as the leading fiction writer of Edo.

Shibue Chūsai 渋江抽斎 (1805–1858). Physician and collector. The subject of Mori Ōgai's biographical novel *Shibue Chūsai* (1916), Chūsai was a kabuki enthusiast and friend of Ishizuka Hōkaishi. Together with Hōkaishi and Nagashima Juami, Chūsai was part of a group known as the *Megane-ren* (Glasses Circle) because all three were nearsighted and wore glasses to the theater.

Shikitei Sanba 式亭三馬 (1776–1822). Sanba was a prolific fiction writer whose career spanned the period from the end of the eighteenth century through his death in 1822.

Today, he is best remembered for his comic fiction (*kokkeibon*). Sanba was also an avid collector of theater ephemera.

Tamura Nariyoshi 田村成義 (1851–1920). Theater proprietor. Tamura worked as a lawyer in the 1870s before becoming involved with theater management in the 1880s. From 1908 until his death in 1920, Tamura ran the Ichimura-za, the city's oldest theater, with a history going back to the seventeenth century. Tamura also compiled the final section of the *Chronology of Kabuki*.

Tsubouchi Shōyō 坪内逍遥 (1859–1935). Critic, novelist, translator, historian, and playwright. Shōyō was a translator of Shakespeare and wrote widely on both European and Japanese drama. Shōyō also promoted the academic study theater and founded the Tsubouchi Memorial Theater Museum at Waseda University in 1928. Shōyō's *A Single Paulownia Leaf* (*Kiri hitoha*), written between 1894 and 1895 and first staged in 1904, was one of the first attempts to write a modern kabuki play.

Tsuruya Nanboku IV 鶴屋南北 (1755–1829). Playwright. Born into a merchant family, Nanboku apprenticed to the playwright Sakurada Jisuke in 1776 and spent over a quarter of a century working on the teams of other playwrights before becoming the leading author in 1803. Nanboku would go on to become the leading playwright of the first decades of the nineteenth century, and many of his masterpieces are still part of the kabuki repertory.

Utagawa Kunisada 歌川国貞 (1786–1865). Print designer. A disciple of Utagawa Toyokuni I, Kunisada also produced prints as Toyokuni III. Like Toyokuni I, Kunisada produced prints in a wide variety of genres but is especially well known for his actor prints.

Utagawa Toyokuni I 歌川豊国 (1769–1825). Print designer. The son of a dollmaker, Toyokuni apprenticed with the print designer Utagawa Toyoharu (1735–1814), the founder of the Utagawa school. Toyokuni began designing prints and book illustrations in the 1780s and rose to prominence in the 1790s with his actor prints.

Utei Enba 烏亭焉馬 (1743–1822). The son of a carpenter, Enba was a prominent figure in the literary and theatrical worlds of the late eighteenth and early nineteenth centuries. Enba compiled the first historical chronology of kabuki in Edo and was a central figure in the Mimasu-ren, a group of theater fans that supported the actor Ichikawa Danjūrō V. A writer of comic fiction and verse, Enba also played an important role in the revival of comic storytelling (*otoshibanashi*, later known as *rakugo*) in the early nineteenth century.

Yamazaki Yoshishige 山崎美成 (1796–1856). Essayist and collector. Born into a family of pharmacists, Yoshishige became a central figure in the world of curiosity and collecting in the 1820s, hosting monthly meetings of the Society of Curiosity Lovers (Tankikai) which were attended by intellectuals including Kyokutei Bakin and the painter Tani Bunchō (1763–1841).

Yasuda Zenjirō II 安田善次郎 (1879–1936). Collector. Yasuda's father, Zenjirō I (1838–1921), was one of the pioneers of banking and insurance in the Meiji period. While working for his father's companies, Zenjirō II was a bibliophile and collector. Zenjirō II's scrapbooks, now housed at the Tsubouchi Memorial Theater Museum at Waseda University, contain a large collection of theater ephemera.

Yoshimura Ito 吉村いと (1849/50–1924) The daughter of the kabuki playwright Kawatake Mokuami, Ito played an important role in asserting her father's copyright claims over his dramatic work. In 1911, at the suggestion of Tsubouchi Shōyō, she adopted Ichimura (later Kawatake) Shigetoshi as her heir.

# Bibliography

Abe Yutaka, 安部豊, *Butai no hana* 舞台之華 (Tokyo: Engei gahōsha, 1912).
Abe Yutaka, "Hashigaki" in *Butai no Danjūrō*, ed. Ihara Seiseien [Toshirō] and Abe Yutaka (Tokyo: Butai no Danjūrō kankōkai, 1923).
Abrams, Richard, "Oldys, Motteux and 'the Play'rs Old Motto': The 'Totus Mundus' Conundrum Revisited," *Theatre Notebook* 61, 3 (2007), 122–31.
Adorno, Theodor W., *The Jargon of Authenticity* (Evanston, IL: Northwestern University Press, 1973).
Adorno, Theodor W., *Prisms* (Cambridge, MA: MIT Press, 1981).
Akama Ryō 赤間亮, "Kabuki no shuppanbutsu (4): Kabuki no engekisho" 歌舞伎の出版物 (4):歌舞伎の演劇書, in *Kabuki bunka no shosō* 歌舞伎文化の諸相, vol. 4 of Iwanami Kōza Kabuki/Bunraku 岩波講座歌舞伎・文楽, ed. Akama Ryō (Tokyo: Iwanami Shoten, 1998), pp.55–60.
Akama Ryō 赤間亮, ed., *Kabuki bunka no shosō* 歌舞伎文化の諸相, vol. 4 of 'Iwanami Kōza Kabuki/Bunraku 岩波講座歌舞伎・文楽 (Tokyo: Iwanami Shoten, 1998).
Akama Ryō 赤間亮, *Zusetsu Edo no engekisho: Kabuki hen* 図説江戸の演劇書:歌舞伎編 (Tokyo: Yagi Shoten, 2003).
Akama Ryō 赤間亮 and Kaneko Takaaki 金子貴昭, "Ukiyo-e dejitaru ākaibu no genzai" 浮世絵デジタルアーカイブの現在, *Jōhō shorigakkai kenkyūkai kenkyū hōkoku* 情報処理学会研究報告 78 (May 2008), 37–44.
Altick, Richard, *The English Common Reader: A Social History of the Mass Reading Public, 1800–1900* (Columbus, OH: Ohio State University Press, 1998).
Anderson, Benedict, *The Spectre of Comparisons: Nationalism, Southeast Asia, and the World* (London: Verso, 1998).
Aoki Kōichirō 青木宏一郎, *Meiji Tōkyō shomin no tanoshimi* 明治東京庶民の楽しみ (Tokyo: Chūō Kōron Shinsha, 2004).
Arai Hakuseki 新井白石, "Haiyūkō" 俳優考, in *Arai Hakuseki zenshū* 新井白石全集, vol. 6, ed. Kokusho Kankōkai 国書刊行会 (Tokyo: Kokusho Kankōkai,1907) pp.524–35.
Barthes, Roland, *Camera Lucida: Reflections on Photography*, reprint edn (New York: Hill and Wang, 2010).
Batchen, Geoffrey, "Phantasm: Digital Imaging and the Death of Photography," *Aperture* 136 (Summer 1994), 46–51.
Benjamin, Walter, *The Arcades Project*, trans. Howard Eiland and Kevin McLaughlin (Cambridge, MA: Belknap Press, 2002).
Benjamin, Walter, "Eduard Fuchs, Collector and Historian," in Marcus Bullock Michael W. Jennings eds. *Walter Benjamin: Selected Writings*, vol. 3 (Cambridge, MA: Belknap Press, 2006), pp. 260–302.
Bergson, Henri, *Laughter: An Essay on the Meaning of the Comic*, trans. Cloudesley Brereton and Fred Rothwell (Mineola, NY: Dover Publications, 2005).
Berry, Mary Elizabeth, *Japan in Print: Information and Nation in the Early Modern Period* (Berkeley, CA: University of California Press, 2006).

Bhabha, Homi K., "Of Mimicry and Man: The Ambivalence of Colonial Discourse," in Homi K. Bhabha, *The Location of Culture*, Routledge Classics (London: Routledge, 2004), pp.121–31.

Blair, Ann M., *Too Much to Know: Managing Scholarly Information before the Modern Age* (New Haven, CT: Yale University Press, 2010).

Bourdaghs, Michael, *The Dawn That Never Comes: Shimazaki Tōson and Japanese Nationalism* (New York: Columbia University Press, 2003).

Bourdieu, Pierre, *Distinction: A Social Critique of the Judgement of Taste*, trans. Richard Nice (Cambridge, MA: Harvard University Press, 1984).

Bourdieu, Pierre, *Photography: A Middle-Brow Art*, trans. Shaun Whiteside (Stanford, CA: Stanford University Press, 1996).

Brandon, James R., *Kabuki's Forgotten War 1931–1945* (Honolulu: University of Hawai'i Press, 2009).

Brandt, Kim, *Kingdom of Beauty: Mingei and the Politics of Folk Art in Imperial Japan* (Durham, NC: Duke University Press, 2007).

Brantlinger, Patrick M., *The Reading Lesson: The Threat of Mass Literacy in Nineteenth-Century British Fiction* (Bloomington, IN: Indiana University Press, 1998).

Bratton, Jacky, *New Readings in Theatre History* (Cambridge: Cambridge University Press, 2003).

Burns, Susan L., *Before the Nation: Kokugaku and the Imagining of Community in Early Modern Japan* (Durham, NC: Duke University Press Books, 2003).

Buyō Inshi, *Lust, Commerce, and Corruption: An Account of What I Have Seen and Heard, by an Edo Samurai*, ed. and trans. Mark Teeuwen and Kate Wildman Nakai (New York: Columbia University Press, 2014).

Carlson, Marvin, *The Haunted Stage: The Theater as Memory Machine* (Ann Arbor, MI: University of Michigan Press, 2001).

Cassierer, Ernst, *The Logic of the Cultural Sciences*, trans. Steve G. Lofts (New Haven, CT: Yale University Press, 2000).

Chartier, Roger, *The Cultural Origins of the French Revolution*, trans. Lydia G. Cochrane (Durham, NC: Duke University Press Books, 1991).

Chartier, Roger, "Popular Appropriations: The Readers and Their Books," in Roger Chartier, *Forms and Meanings: Texts, Performances, and Audiences from Codex to Computer* (Philadelphia, PA: University of Pennsylvania Press, 1995), pp.83–97.

Chartier, Roger, *Inscription and Erasure: Literature and Written Culture from the Eleventh to the Eighteenth Century*, trans. Arthur Goldhammer (Philadelphia, PA: University of Pennsylvania Press, 2007).

Chun, Wendy Hui Kyong, "The Enduring Ephemeral, or the Future Is a Memory," *Critical Inquiry* 35 (Autumn 2008), 148–71. Doi: https://doi-org.libproxy.berkeley.edu/10.1086/595632.

Clark, Timothy, "Edo Kabuki in the 1780s," in *The Actor's Image: Print Makers of the Katsukawa School*, ed. Timothy Clark (Chicago, IL: Art Institute of Chicago, 1994), pp. 27–48.

Clark, Timothy, ed., *The Actor's Image: Print Makers of the Katsukawa School* (Chicago, IL: Art Institute of Chicago, 1994).

Clark, Timothy J., *The Painting of Modern Life: Paris in the Art of Manet and His Followers* (Princeton, NJ: Princeton University Press, 1999).

Clunas, Craig, *Pictures and Visuality in Early Modern China* (London: Reaktion Books, 1997).

Crary, Jonathan, "Spectacle, Attention, Counter-Memory," October 50 (1989), 96–107. Doi: https://doi.org/10.2307/778858.

Crary, Jonathan, *Techniques of the Observer: On Vision and Modernity in the 19th Century* (Cambridge, MA: MIT Press, 1992).

Creighton, Millie, "The Heroic Edo-Ic: Traveling the History Highway in Today's Tokugawa Japan," in *Japanese Tourism and Travel Culture*, ed. Sylvie Guichard-Anguis and Okpyo Moon (London: Routledge, 2011), pp. 37–75.

Darnton, Robert, *The Forbidden Best-Sellers of Pre-Revolutionary France* (New York: W. W. Norton & Co., 1996).

Debord, Guy, *The Society of the Spectacle* [1967], trans. Ken Knabb (Berkeley, CA: Bureau of Public Secrets, 2014).

Derrida, Jacques, *Archive Fever: A Freudian Impression*, trans. Eric Prenowitz (Chicago, IL: University of Chicago Press, 1997).

Doane, Mary Ann, *The Emergence of Cinematic Time: Modernity, Contingency, the Archive*, (Cambridge, MA: Harvard University Press, 2002).

Dōgedō Shiten 童戯堂四囀, *Shibai hyakunin isshu* 芝居百人一首, ed. Ihara Toshirō 伊原敏郎 (Tokyo: Engei Chinsho Kankōkai, 1914). Doi: 10.11501/1088269.

Dōrosai Hyakki 洞露斎百喜, *Shikankoku ichiran* 芝翫国一覧 (Osaka: Morimoto Tasuke, 1815). Doi: 10.20730/100080434.

Eisenstein, Elizabeth L., *The Printing Press as an Agent of Change* (Cambridge: Cambridge University Press, 1980).

"Engeki kyakuhon gakufu no kōgyōken" 演劇脚本楽譜の興行権, Yomiuri shinbun 読売新聞, August 22, 1904, p. 1.

Fenollosa, Ernest, *Epochs of Chinese and Japanese Art*, 2 vols (New York: ICG Muse, Inc., 2000).

Fujii Otoo 藤井乙男, "*Gedai kagami* oyobi *Ayatsuri nendaiki* no ihan" 外題年鑑及び操年代記の異版 in Fujii Otoo, *Edo bungaku sōsetsu* 江戸文学叢説 (Tokyo: Iwanami Shoten, 1931). Doi: 10.11501/1223497.

Fukuoka, Maki, *The Premise of Fidelity: Science, Visuality, and Representing the Real in Nineteenth-Century Japan* (Stanford, CA: Stanford University Press, 2012).

Fukuzawa, Yukichi, *An Outline of a Theory of Civilization*, trans. David Dilworth and G. Cameron Hurst (New York: Columbia University Press, 2009).

Furuido Hideo 古井戸秀夫, "Fukumori Kyūsuke to sono jidai" 福森久助とその時代, in Furuido Hideo *Fukumori Kyūsuke kyakuhonshū* 福森久助脚本集, Sōsho Edo bunko 叢書江戸文庫 vol. 49 (Tokyo: Kokusho Kankōkai, 2001), pp.454–77.

Galloway, Alexander, *The Interface Effect* (Cambridge: Polity, 2012).

Gitelman, Lisa, *Paper Knowledge: Toward a Media History of Documents* (Durham, NC: Duke University Press, 2014).

Geinōshi Kenkyūkai 芸能史研究会, ed., *Nihon shomin bunka shiryō shūsei* 日本庶民文化史料集成, 16 vols (Tokyo: Sanichi Shobō, 1973).

"Gekijō onko hakurankai" 劇場温故博覧会, Asahi shinbun 朝日新聞, February 27, 1897, p. 3.

"Gekijō onko hakurankai ga kaijō" 劇場温故博覧会が開場, Yomiuri shinbun 読売新聞, Feburary 26, 1897, p. 3.

Gerstle, C. Andrew, "Kabuki Culture and Collective Creativity," in *Kabuki Heroes on the Osaka Stage, 1780–1830*, ed. C. Andrew Gerstle (Honolulu: University of Hawai'i Press, 2005), 10–19.

Gerstle, C. Andrew, *Kabuki Heroes on the Osaka Stage, 1780–1830* (Honolulu: University of Hawai'i Press, 2005).

Gillies, John, *Shakespeare and the Geography of Difference* (Cambridge: Cambridge University Press, 1994).
Gluck, Carol, "The Invention of Edo," in *Mirror of Modernity: Invented Traditions of Modern Japan*, ed. Stephen Vlastos (Berkeley, CA: University of California Press, 1998), pp. 262–84.
Goree, Robert, "Publishing Kabukiland: Late Edo Culture and Kyokutei Bakin's Yakusha Meisho Zue," in Keller Kimbrough and Satoko Shimazaki ed. *Publishing the Stage: Print and Performance in Early Modern Japan*, Boulder Books on Asian Studies 1 (Boulder, CO: Center for Asian Studies, University of Colorado Boulder, 2011), https://www.colorado.edu/cas/sites/default/files/attached-files/robert_goree_hr.pdf.
Goree, Robert, *Printing Landmarks: Popular Geography and Meisho Zue in Late Tokugawa Japan* (Cambridge, MA: Harvard University Press, 2020).
Goryūtei Tokushō 五柳亭徳升, *Sanshibai yakusha saiken* 三芝居役者細見 (Edo: Moriya Jihē and Yamaguchiya Tōbē, 1826).
Gouhier, Henri, *Le Théâtre et Les Arts À Deux Temps* (Paris: Flammarion, 1989).
Gōyama Kiwamu 合山究, "Minmatsu Shinsho ni okeru 'jinsei wa dorama de aru' no setsu" 明末清初における「人生はドラマである」の説, in *Chūgoku tetsugakushi ronshū kenkyū* 中国哲学史論集研究, ed. Aoki Kyōju Taikyū Kinenkai 青木教授退休記念会 (Fukuoka: Asahi Shobō, 1982).
Gunji Masakatsu 郡司正勝, "Atogaki" あとがき, in *Nakamura Nakazō* 中村仲蔵, *Temae miso* 手前味噌, ed. Gunji Masakatsu (Tokyo: Seiabō, 2009).
Gunning, Tom, "What Is the Point of an Image; or Faking Photographs?," in *Still Moving: Between Cinema and Photography*, ed. Karen Beckman and Jean Ma (Durham, NC: Duke University Press, 2008), pp. 23–40.
Hachimonjiya Jishō 八文舎自笑, ed., *Shinkoku yakusha kōmoku* 新刻役者綱目, 2 vols (Kyoto: Hachimonjiya Hachizaemon, 1771). Doi: 10.11501/2554385.
Hamada Keisuke 浜田啓介, "Kokkeibon toshite no gekisho" 滑稽本としての劇書, in Hamada Keisuke 浜田啓介, *Kinsei shōsetsu: eii to yōshiki ni kansuru shiken* 近世小説:営為と様式に関する私見 (Kyoto: Kyōto Daigaku Gakujutsu Shuppankai, 1993), pp. 205–08.
Hamada Keisuke, "On Booksellers, Authors, and Readers in the Works of Bakin," trans. Peter Kornicki, 2014. http://www.sharpweb.org/main/wp-content/uploads/2014/09/Paper_Hamada.pdf.
Hamano Shiho 浜野志保, *Shashin no bōdārando: x sen/shinrei shashin/nensha* 写真のボーダーランド：X線・心霊写真・念写(Tokyo: Seikyūsha, 2015).
Hanan, Patrick, *The Invention of Li Yu* (Cambridge, MA: Harvard University Press, 1988).
Harley, John B. and John H. Andrews, *The New Nature of Maps: Essays in the History of Cartography*, ed. Paul Laxton, new edn (Baltimore, MD: Johns Hopkins University Press, 2002).
Hatanaka Kansai 畠中観斎, *Morokoshi kidan* 唐土奇談 (Kyoto: Kōseikaku, 1933). Doi: 10.11501/1194861.
Hatanaka Kansai 畠中観斎, "Inbon shakubun" 院本釈文. Manuscript, Waseda University Library Special Collections イ04 00600 185, https://waseda.primo.exlibrisgroup.com/permalink/81SOKEI_WUNI/7jeksk/alma991000399289704032.
Hattori Yukio 服部幸雄, "Honkoku: 'Kyōgen sakusha kokoroesho'" 翻刻・『狂言作者心得書』, *Nagoya Daigaku kokugo kokubungaku* 名古屋大学国語国文学27 (December 1970), 89–94.
Hattori Yukio 服部幸雄, "Shikitei Sanba no shibai banzuke shūshū" 式亭三馬の芝居番付蒐集, *Nihon kosho tsūhin* 日本古書通信 49, 2 (February 1984), 4.

Hattori Yukio 服部幸雄, "Shibaihon taishūka no seiki (1)" 芝居本大衆化の世紀 (1), *Nihon kosho tsūhin* 日本古書通信 58, 10 (October 1993), 10–11.

Hattori Yukio 服部幸雄, "Shibaihon taishūka no seiki (2)" 芝居本大衆化の世紀 (2), *Nihon kosho tsūhin* 日本古書通信 58, 11 (November 1993), 8–10.

Hattori Yukio 服部幸雄, "Kaidai" 解題, in Shikitei Sanba 式亭三馬 *Shibai kinmo zui: Kyōwa sannen shohanbon* 戯場訓蒙図彙：享和三年初版本, Kabuki no Bunken 3 (Tokyo: Nihon Geijutsu Bunka Shinkōkai, 2001), pp.1–6.

Hattori Yukio 服部幸雄, *Ōinaru koya: Edo kabuki no shukusai kūkan* 大いなる小屋：江戸歌舞伎の祝祭空間 (Tokyo: Kōdansha, 2012).

Hay, Jonathan, *Sensuous Surfaces: The Decorative Object in Early Modern China* (Honolulu: University of Hawai'i Press, 2010).

Hayashi Kimio 林癸未夫, "Engeki Hakubutsukan no keikaku" 演劇博物館の計画, Asahi shinbun 朝日新聞, February 22, 1927.

Hirano, Katsuya, *The Politics of Dialogic Imagination: Power and Popular Culture in Early Modern Japan* (Chicago, IL: University of Chicago Press, 2013).

Hirose Chisako 広瀬千紗子, "Hachimonjiya gekisho no seiritsu: 'Shinsen kokon yakusha taizen' wo megutte" 八文字屋劇書の成立:[新撰古今役者大全]をめぐって], *Geinōshi kenkyū* 芸能史研究 45 (1974), 44–64.

Hirose Chisako 広瀬千紗子, "Hana no Edo kabuki nendaiki no seiritsu" 花江都歌舞妓年代記の成立, *Kinsei bungei* 近世文芸 41 (1984), 40–60.

Hirosue Tamotsu 広末保, *Shinpen akubasho no hassō* 新編悪場所の発想 (Tokyo: Chikuma Shobō, 1988).

Hockley, Allen, *The Prints of Isoda Koryūsai: Floating World Culture and Its Consumers in Eighteenth-Century Japan* (Seattle, WA: University of Washington Press, 2003).

Horkheimer, Max and Theodor W. Adorno, *Dialectic of Enlightenment*, trans. John Cumming, (New York: Continuum, 1972).

Hōseidō Kisanji 朋誠堂喜三二, *Ukan sandai zue* 羽勘三台図絵, Kabuki no Bunken 歌舞伎の文献 vol. 4 (Tokyo: Kokuritsu Gekijō,1971).

Hurley, Erin, *Theatre and Feeling* (New York: Palgrave, 2010).

Hutcheon, Linda, *Irony's Edge: The Theory and Politics of Irony* (London: Routledge, 1994).

Hutcheon, Linda, *A Theory of Parody: The Teachings of Twentieth-Century Art Forms* (Urbana, IL: University of Illinois Press, 2000).

Ihara Seiseien [Toshirō] 伊原青々園 [敏郎], "Ko Umehiko-ō no mukashibanashi" 故梅彦翁昔話 *Waseda bungaku* 早稲田文学24, 1(2) (December 1896), 91.

Ihara Seiseien [Toshirō] 伊原青々園 [敏郎], "Shibai banashi" 芝居ばなし, *Shincho gekkan* 新著月刊5 (1898), 187–93.

Ihara Seiseien [Toshirō] 伊原青々園 [敏郎], "Chikamatsu no fukkatsu" 近松の復活, *Kabuki* 歌舞伎22 (March 1902), 1–5.

Ihara Seiseien [Toshirō] 伊原青々園 [敏郎], "Seiyō no kōgyōken" 西洋の興行権, Kabuki 歌舞伎 29 (October 1902), 37.

Ihara Seiseien [Toshirō] 伊原青々園 [敏郎] and Abe Yutaka 安部豊, eds, *Butai no Danjūrō* 舞台之團十郎 (Tokyo: Butai no Danjūrō kankōkai, 1923).

Iijima Kyoshin 飯島虚心, *Ukiyoeshi Utagawa retsuden* 浮世絵師歌川列伝, ed. Tamabayashi Seirō 玉林晴朗 (Tokyo: Unebi Shobō, 1941). Doi: 10.11501/1239939

Ikegami, Eiko, *Bonds of Civility: Aesthetic Networks and the Political Origins of Japanese Culture* (Cambridge: Cambridge University Press, 2005).

Ilsemann, Hartmut, "Christopher Marlowe: Hype and Hoax," *Digital Scholarship in the Humanities* 33, 4 (2018), 788–820. Doi: 10.1093/llc/fqy001.

Iriguchi Yoshirō 入江良郎, "Yoshizawa Shōtenshu: Kawaura Kenichi no ashiato (1)" 吉澤商店主・河浦謙一の足跡 (1), *Tōkyō kokuritsu kindai bijutsukan kenkyū kiyō* 東京国立近代美術館研究紀要18 (2014), 32–63.

Ishizuka Hōkaishi 石塚豊芥子, *Hana Edo kabuki nendaiki zokuhen* 花江都歌舞妓年代記続編, ed. Mizutani Futō 水谷不倒 and Ichijima Kenkichi 市島謙吉, vol. 4, Shin Gunsho Ruijū (Tokyo: Kokusho Kankōkai, 1907). Doi: 10.11501/991629.

Itō Sōhei 伊藤漱平, "Ri Ryū ō no shōzōga" 李笠翁の肖像画, *Kyūko* 汲古14 (1988) 49–53 and 15 (1989) 62–8.

Ivy, Marilyn, *Discourses of the Vanishing: Modernity, Phantasm, Japan* (Chicago, IL: University of Chicago Press, 1995).

Iwai Masami 岩井眞實, "Mokuami no 'engeki kyakuhon' o megutte 黙阿弥の[演劇脚本]をめぐって," *Kabuki kenkyū to hihyō* 歌舞伎研究と批評13 (1994), 143–67.

Jack, Belinda, *The Woman Reader* (New Haven, CT: Yale University Press, 2012).

Jardine, Lisa and Anthony Grafton, "'Studied for Action': How Gabriel Harvey Read His Livy," *Past & Present* 129 (1990), 30–78.

Jones, Stanleigh, *The Bunraku Puppet Theatre of Japan: Honor, Vengence, and Love in Four Plays of the 18th and 19th Centuries* (Honolulu: University of Hawai'i Press: 2013).

Kaguraoka Yōko 神楽岡幼子, *Kabuki bunka no kyōju to tenkai: kankyaku to gekijō no naigai* 歌舞伎文化の享受と展開:観客と劇場の内外 (Tokyo: Yagi Shoten, 2002).

Kaguraoka, Yōko, "Osaka Kabuki Fan Clubs and Their Obsessions," in *Kabuki Heroes on the Osaka Stage, 1780–1830*, ed. C. Andrew Gerstle (Honolulu: University of Hawai'i Press, 2005) 30–5.

Jones, Stanleigh, *The Bunraku Puppet Theatre of Japan: Honor, Vengence, and Love in Four Plays of the 18th and 19th Centuries* (Honolulu: University of Hawai'i Press: 2013).

*Kamakura ezu* (Kamakura: Ōsakaya Magobē, n.d.), http://www.wul.waseda.ac.jp/kotenseki/html/bunko10/bunko10_08464/index.html.

Kamiyama Akira 神山 彰, *Kindai engeki no raireki: kabuki no "isshin nisei"* 近代演劇の来歴:歌舞伎の[一身二生](Tokyo: Shinwasha, 2006).

Karatani Kōjin, *The Origins of Modern Japanese Literature*, trans. Brett de Barry (Durham, NC: Duke University Press, 1993).

Kastan, David Scott, *Shakespeare and the Book* (Cambridge: Cambridge University Press, 2001).

Katsurajima Nobuhiro 桂島宣弘, "Ikkokushi no seiritsu"一国史の成立, in *Seiki tenkanki no kokusai chitsujo to kokumin bunka no keisei* 世紀転換期の国際秩序と国民文化の形成, ed. Nishikawa Nagao 西川長夫 and Watanabe Kōzō 渡辺公三 (Tokyo: Kashiwa Shobō, 1999) 103–26.

Kawai Masumi 河合眞澄, "Kyokutei denki hana no kanzashi to engeki" 『曲亭伝奇花釵児』と演劇, *Yomihon kenkyū shinshū* 読本研究新集5 (2004), 6–24.

Kawatake Shigetoshi 河竹繁俊, *Kabuki sakusha no kenkyū* 歌舞伎作者の研究 (Tokyo: Tōkyōdō, 1940).

Kawazoe Yū 川添祐, "Gakujustu bunkoban kaisetsu" 学術文庫版解説, in *Ōinaru koya: Edo kabuki no shukusai kūkan* 大いなる小屋:江戸歌舞伎の祝祭空間, ed. Hattori Yukio 服部幸雄 (Tokyo: Kōdansha, 2012) pp.396–400.

Kern, Adam, *Manga of the Floating World: Comic Book Culture and the Kibyōshi of Edo Japan.* (Cambridge, MA: Harvard University Press, 2006).

Kimura Mokurō 木村黙老, "Gekijō ikkan mushimegane" 劇場一観顕微鏡, in Engeki bunko 演劇文庫, ed. Engei Chinsho Kankōkai, reprint, vol. II (Tokyo: Gannandō Shoten, 1973).

Kimura Senshū 木村仙秀, "Matsunoya Bunko no zōsho" 松廼舎文庫の蔵書, in Kimura Sutezō 木村捨三 ed., *Kimura Senshū shū* 木村仙秀集, Nihon Shoshigaku Taikei 日本書誌学大系, vol. 31-3 (Tokyo: Seishōdō Shoten, 1983), pp. 115–48.

Kitagawa Morisada 喜田川守貞, *Morisada mankō* 守貞謾稿, ed. Asakura Haruhiko 朝倉治彦 and Kashikawa Shūichi 柏川修一, 5 vols (Tokyo: Tōkyōdō Shuppan, 1992).

Kitazawa Noriaki 北澤憲昭, *Me no shinden: bijutsushi juyōshi nōto* 目の神殿:美術受容史ノート (Tokyo: Bijutsu shuppansha, 1989).

"Ko Danjūrō Enshi no koto" 故談洲楼燕枝の事, Asahi shinbun 朝日新聞, Feburary 13, 1900, p. 5.

"Kōgyōken shingai no saiban" 興行権侵害の裁判, Asahi shinbun 朝日新聞, November 1, 1895, p. 3.

Koide Masahiro 小出昌洋, "Tanki manroku kaidai" 耽奇漫録解題, in *Tanki manroku* 耽奇漫録, ed. Nihon Zuihitsu Taisei Henshūbu 日本随筆大成編輯部, *Nihon zuihitsu taisei: bekkan* 日本随筆大成:別巻, vol. 1 (Tokyo: Yoshikawa Kōbunkan, 1994) 1–10.

Koizumi, Setsuko, *Reminiscences of Lafcadio Hearn* (New York: Houghton Mifflin, 1918).

"Komada Kōyō sukappubukku" 駒田好洋スクラップブック, manuscript, Tsubouchi Memorial Theater Museum, Waseda University, 16758-1-6.

Komatsu Hiroshi, "Questions Regarding the Genesis of Nonfiction Film," Yamagata International Film Festival: Documentary Box #5, 1994, http://www.yidff.jp/docbox/5/box5-1-e.html.

Kornicki, Peter, *The Book in Japan: A Cultural History from the Beginnings to the Nineteenth Century* (Leiden: Brill, 1998).

Kornicki, Peter, "Literacy Revisited: Some Reflections on Richard Rubinger's Findings," *Monumenta Nipponica* 56, 3 (2001), 381–95. Doi:10.2307/3096792.

Kornicki, Peter, *Languages, Scripts, and Chinese Texts in East Asia* (Oxford: Oxford University Press, 2018).

Kornicki, Peter, "Women, Education, and Literacy," in *The Female as Subject: Reading and Writing in Early Modern Japan*, ed. Peter F. Kornicki, Mara Patessio, and Gaye. Rowley (Ann Arbor, MI: University of Michigan Press, 2010), pp. 7–37.

"Kōsei shinkoku Saruwaka saiken zu" 校正新刻猿若細見図, in *Waseda Daigaku Engeki Hakubutsukan shozō Yasuda Bunko kyūzō kinsei kindai fūzoku shiryō harikomichō* 早稲田大学演劇博物館所蔵安田文庫旧蔵近世・近代風俗史料張込帖, vol. 2, 14 microfilm reels (Tokyo: Yūshōdō Shuppan, 2001), R-2, 8–036.

Kuchiki Yuriko 朽木ゆり子, *Hausu obu Yamanaka: Tōyō no shihō wo Ōbei ni utta bijutsushō* ハウス・オブ・ヤマナカ:東洋の至宝を欧米に売った美術商 (Tokyo: Shinchōsha, 2013).

Kumata Atsumi 熊田淳美, *Sandai hensanbutsu: Gunsho ruijū, Koji ruien, Kokusho sōmokuroku no shuppan bunkashi* 三大編纂物:群書類従・古事類苑・国書総目録の出版文化史 (Tokyo: Bensei Shuppan, 2009).

Kurahashi Masae 倉橋正恵, "Ishizuka Hōkaishi 'Kakōto kabuki nendaiki zokuhen': kinsei kōki ni okeru kabuki kōgyō kiroku no ichi yōsō" 石塚豊芥子『花江都歌舞妓年代記続編』：近世後期における歌舞伎興行記録の一様相, *Ronkyū nihonbungaku* 論究日本文学 100 (2014), 111–26.

Kuroishi Yōko 黒石陽子, "Godaime Ichikawa Danjūrō no Kagekiyo: Tenmei nenkan no kibyōshi o chūshin ni" 代目市川團十郎:天明年間の黄表紙を中心に, *Tōkyō gakugei daigaku kiyō* 東京学芸大学紀要46, 2 (1995), 265–76.

"Kyō kaikanshiki no Engeki Hakubutsukan" 今日開館式の演劇博物館, Yomiuri shinbun 読売新聞, October 27, 1928.

Kyokutei Bakin 曲亭馬琴, *Yoshitsune senbonzakura* 義経千本桜, 3 vols (Edo: Tsuruya Kiemon, 1819). Doi: 10.20730/100130898.

Kyokutei Bakin 曲亭馬琴, "Chosakudō issekiwa" 著作堂一夕話, in *Nihon zuihitsu taisei* 日本随筆大成, vol. 5, ser. 1 (Tokyo: Yoshikawa Kōbunkan, 1927), 643–712. Doi: 10.11501/1217400.

Kyokutei Bakin 曲亭馬琴, *Kinsei mono no hon Edo sakusha burui: chosha jihitsu hokibon* 近世物之本江戸作者部類:著者自筆本, ed. Kimura Miyogo 木村三四吾(Tokyo: Yagi Shoten, 1988).

Kyokutei Bakin 曲亭馬琴, *Bakin no yakusha meisho zue o yomu* 馬琴の戯子名所図会を読む, ed. Daichō o Yomu Kai 台帳を読む会, Chikamatsu Kenkyūjo Sōsho 4 (Osaka: Izumi Shoin, 2001).

Kyokutei [Takizawa] Bakin 曲亭[滝沢]馬琴, *Kiryo manroku* 羇旅漫録, ed. Atsumi Seikan 渥美正幹, 3 vols (Tokyo: Isandō, 1885). Doi: 10.11501/888907.

"Kyū Yasuda Bunko zōsho no fukugen" 旧安田文庫蔵書の復元, *Kagami* かがみ32/33 (1998), 58–170.

Lee, William, "Chikamatsu and Dramatic Literature in the Meiji Period," in *Inventing the Classics: Cannon Formation, National Identity, and Japanese Literature*, ed. Haruo Shirane and Tomi Suzuki (Stanford, CA: Stanford University Press, 2001), pp. 179–98.

Leiter, Samuel, ed., *A New Kabuki Encyclopedia* (Westport, CT: Greenwood Press, 1997).

Leiter, Samuel, ed., *A Kabuki Reader: History and Performance* (Armonk, NY: M. E. Sharpe, 2002).

Leupp, Gary, *Male Colors: The Construction of Homosexuality in Tokugawa Japan* (Berkeley, CA: University of California Press, 1997).

Liu, Lydia, *The Clash of Empires: The Invention of China in Modern World Making* (Cambridge, MA: Harvard University Press, 2004).

Maeda, Tsutomu 前田勉, *Edo no dokushokai: kaidoku no shisōshi* 江戸の読書会: 会読の思想史 (Tokyo: Heibonsha, 2012).

Marcus, Marvin, *Paragons of the Ordinary: The Biographical Literature of Mori Ōgai* (Honolulu: University of Hawai'i Press, 1993).

Maruyama Masao, *Studies in the Intellectual History of Tokugawa Japan*, (Tokyo: University of Tokyo Press, 1974).

Marx, Karl, "Economic and Philosophic Manuscripts of 1844," in *The Marx–Engels Reader*, ed. Robert C. Tucker (New York: Norton, 1978), pp. 66–125.

Masten, Jeffrey, *Textual Intercourse: Collaboration, Authorship, and Sexualities in Renaissance Drama* (Cambridge: Cambridge University Press, 1997).

McClellan, Edwin, *Woman in the Crested Kimono: The Life of Shibue Io and Her Family* (New Haven, CT: Yale University Press, 1985).

McCormick, Melissa, "'Murasaki shikibu ishiyamadera mōde zufuku' ni okeru shomondai: Wa to Kan no sakai ni aru Murasaki zō" [紫式部石山詣図幅]における諸問題: 和と漢の境にある紫式部像, trans. Ido Misato 井戸美里, *Kokka* 国華 1434 (April 2015), 5–23.

Michener, Jamese A., *The Floating World* (New York: Random House, 1954).

Metz, Christian, *The Imaginary Signifier: Psychoanalysis and the Cinema* (Bloomington, IN: Indiana University Press, 1986).

Miki Sadanari 三木貞成, *Namiwa miyage* 難波土産, Jōruri kenkyū bunken shūsei 浄瑠璃文献集成, Engeki Bunken Kenkyūkai 演劇文献研究会 ed., *Nihon engeki bunken shūsei* 日本演劇文献集成, vol. 2 (Tokyo: Hokkō Shobō, 1944). Doi: 10.11501/1125481.

Mimasuya Nisōji 三升屋二三治, "Sakusha myōmoku" 作者名目, in Engei Chinsho Kankōkai ed. *Engeki bunko* 演劇文庫, vol. 5 (Tokyo: Engei Chinsho Kankōkai, 1915). Doi: 10.11501/948799.

Miyatake Gaikotsu 宮武外骨, *Kottō zasshi* 骨董雑誌, vol. 17 of *Miyatake Gaikotsu kono naka ni ari* 宮武外骨此中にあり (Tokyo: Yumani Shobō, 1994).

Mizuno Minoru 水野稔, *Santō Kyōden nenpukō* 山東京伝年譜稿 (Tokyo: Perikansha, 1991).

Mizutani Futō 水谷不倒, *Takemoto Settsu-Daijō* 竹本摂津大掾 (Tokyo: Hakubunkan, 1904). Doi: 10.11501/992061.

Momokawa Takahito 百川敬仁, *Uchinaru Norinaga* 内なる宣長 (Tokyo: Tōkyō Daigaku Shuppankai, 1987).

Mordell, Albert, *The Erotic Motive in Literature* (New York: Boni and Liveright, 1919).

Mori Ōgai 森鴎外, *Shibue Chūsai* 渋江抽斎, rev. edn (Tokyo: Iwanami Shoten, 1999).

Morishige Noburō 守重信郎, "Wagakuni hatsu honkakuteki daigaku hakubutsukan no tanjō ni tsuite" わが国初の本格的大学博物館の誕生について, *Nihon Daigaku Daigakuin Sōgō Shakai Jōhō Kenkyūka kiyō* 日本大学大学院総合社会情報研究科紀要 11 (2010), 129–38.

Mostow, Joshua S., *At the House of Gathered Leaves: Shorter Biographical and Autobiographical Narratives from Japanese Court Literature* (Honolulu: University of Hawai'i Press, 2004).

Murashima Ayaka 村島彩加, "Bakumatsu/Meiji-ki no Nihon ni okeru engeki shashin no hatten to hensen: kabuki yakusha hishatai toshita mono wo chūshin ni" 幕末・明治期の日本における演劇写真の発展と変遷, *Engekigaku ronbunshū* 演劇学論文集 52 (2011), 63–83. Doi: https://doi.org/10.18935/jjstr.52.0_63.

Naff, William E., *The Kiso Road: The Life and Times of Shimazaki Tōson*, ed. J. Thomas Rimer (Honolulu: University of Hawai'i Press, 2010).

Nagatomo Chiyoji 長友千代治, *Kinsei Kamigata jōruribon shuppan no kenkyū* 近世上方浄瑠璃本出版の研究 (Tokyo: Tōkyōdō Shuppan, 1999).

Nagatomo Chiyoji 長友千代治, *Edo jidai no shomotsu to dokusho* 江戸時代の書物と読書 (Tokyo: Tōkyōdō Shuppan, 2001).

Najita, Tetsuo, "Method and Analysis in the Conceptual Portrayal of Tokugawa Intellectual History," in *Japanese Thought in the Tokugawa Period, 1600–1868: Methods and Metaphors*, ed. Tetsuo Najita and Irwin Scheiner (Chicago, IL: University of Chicago Press, 1978), 3–38.

Najita, Tetsuo, "History and Nature in Eighteenth-Century Japanese Thought," in *The Cambridge History of Japan Volume 4. Early Modern Japan*, ed. John Whitney Hall and James L. McClain, The Cambridge History of Japan (Cambridge: Cambridge University Press, 1991) pp.596–659.

Nakada Tatsunosuke 仲田勝之助, ed., *Ukiyo-e ruikō* 浮世絵類考 (Tokyo: Iwanami Shoten, 1982).

Nakamura Nakazō III 中村仲蔵, *Temae miso* 手前味噌, ed. Gunji Masakatsu (Tokyo: Seiabō, 2009).

Nakamura Tetsurō 中村哲郎, *Kabuki no kindai: sakka to sakuhin* 歌舞伎の近代:作家と作品, (Tokyo: Iwanami Shoten, 2006).

Nakano Junya 中野順哉, *Utakata: Nanadaime Tsurusawa Kanji ga mita bunraku* うたかた:鶴澤寛治が見た文楽 (Nishinomiya: Kansai Daigaku Shuppankai, 2019).

Naitō Meisetsu 内藤鳴雪, *Meisetsu jijoden* 鳴雪自叙伝 (Tokyo: Okamura Shoten, 1922). Doi: 10.11501/971903.

Naito, Satoko, "Beyond the *Tale of Genji*: Murasaki Shikibu as Icon and Exemplum in Seventeenth- and Eighteenth-Century Popular Japanese Texts for Women," *Early Modern Women: An Interdisciplinary Journal* 9, 1 (Autumn 2014), 47–78, https://www.jstor.org/stable/26431282.

Nelson, Robert S., "The Slide Lecture, or the Work of Art 'History' in the Age of Mechanical Reproduction," *Critical Inquiry* 26, 3 (2000), 414–34, https://www.jstor.org/stable/1344289.

Nishizawa Ippū 西沢一風, *Ima mukashi ayatsuri nendaiki* 今昔操年代記, *Jōruri kenkyū bunken shūsei* 浄瑠璃文献集成, ed. Engeki Bunken Kenkyūkai 演劇文献研究会, Vol. 2 of *Nihon engeki bunken shūsei* 日本演劇文献集成 (Tokyo: Hokkō Shobō, 1944). Doi: 10.11501/1125481.

Nishizawa Ippū 西沢一風, 難波土産 in Engeki Bunken Kenkyūkai 演劇文献研究会 ed. *Nihon engeki bunken shūsei* 日本演劇文献集成vol.2 (Tokyo: Hokkō Shobō, 1944). Doi: 10.11501/1125481.

Nobuhiro Shinji 延広真治, *Rakugo wa ikani shite keiseisaretaka* 落語はいかにして形成されたか (Tokyo: Heibonsha, 1986).

Ōeda Ryūhō 大枝流芳, *Gayū manroku* 雅遊漫録 (Osaka: Shibukawa Seiemon, 1763).

Okada Hidenori 岡田秀則, *Eiga to iu "buttai X": firumu ākaibu no me de mita eiga* 映画という《物体X》:フィルム・アーカイブの眼で見た映画 (Tokyo: Rittōsha, 2016).

Okamoto Kidō 岡本綺堂, "Kasei jidai no gikyoku" 化政時代の戯曲, *Kabuki kenkyū* 歌舞伎研究, June 1928, 1–3.

Okamoto Kidō 岡本綺堂, "Kaseigeki mandan" 化政劇漫談, *Kabuki kenkyū* 歌舞伎研究, July 1928, 123–26.

Okamoto Shiro, *The Man Who Saved Kabuki: Faubion Bowers and Theatre Censorship in Occupied Japan*, trans. Samuel Leiter (Honolulu: University of Hawai'i Press, 2001).

Okatsuka Akiko 岡塚章子 and Wagatsuma Naomi 我妻直美, *Ukiyo-e kara shashin e: shikaku no bunmei kaika* 浮世絵から写真へ:視覚の文明開化 (Tokyo: Seigensha, 2015).

Ōkubo Junichi 大久保純一, "*Yakusha nigao-e hayageiko* to sono shūhen" 『役者似顔画早稽古』とその周辺, *Bigaku bijutsushi kenkyū ronbunshū* 美学美術史研究論集5 (1987), 121–48. Doi: 10.11501/7957546.

Okumura Kayoko 奥村佳代子, "Chūgokugo yaku *Chūshingura* no shosō: *Kagai kidan* no honyakusha zō to honyaku taido shotan" 中国語訳[忠臣蔵]の諸相:『海外奇談』の翻訳者像と翻訳態度初探, *Kansai Daigaku tōzai gakujutsu kenkyūjo kiyō* 関西大学東西学術研究所紀要 43 (April 2010), 131–42.

Onoe Kikugorō V 尾上菊五郎, *Onoe Kikugorō jiden* 尾上菊五郎自伝 (Tokyo: Jiji Shinpōsha, 1903). Doi: 10.11501/1870335.

Ōta Nanpo 大田南畝, "Ichiwa ichigen"一話言, in Hamada Giichirō 浜田義一郎ed., *Ōta Nanpo zenshū* 大田南畝全集, vol. 16 (Tokyo: Iwanami Shoten, 1988), pp. 89–111.

Ōtaka Yōji 大高洋司, "Jūkyū seiki teki sakusha non tanjō"一九世紀的作者の誕生, *Bungaku* 文学5, 3 (May 2004), 71–80.

Ōtsuka Takanobu 大塚高信, "Gurōbu-za: sono fukugen mokei to kōshō" グローブ座:その復元模型と考証, in *Engeki hakubutsukan shiryō monogatari* 演劇博物館資料ものがたり, ed. Waseda Daigaku Engeki Hakubutsukan 早稲田大学演劇博物館 (Tokyo: Waseda Daigaku Tsubouchi Hakushi Kinen Engeki Hakubutsukan, 1988), pp. 312–18.

Pflugfelder, Gregory M., *Cartographies of Desire: Male–Male Sexuality in Japanese Discourse, 1600–1950* (Berkeley, CA: University of California Press, 2007).

Phelan, Peggy, *Unmarked: The Politics of Performance* (London: Routledge, 2003).

Piper, Andrew, *Book Was There: Reading in Electronic Times* (Chicago, IL: University of Chicago Press, 2012).

Pollack, David, "Making Desire: Advertising and Sexuality in Edo Literature, Drama, and Art," in *Gender and Power in the Japanese Visual Field*, ed. Joshua S. Mostow, Norman Bryson, and Maribeth Graybill (Honolulu: University of Hawai'i Press, 2003), pp. 71–88.

Poulton, M. Cody, *A Beggar's Art: Scripting Modernity in Japanese Drama, 1900–1930* (Honolulu: University of Hawai'i Press, 2010).

Purkis, James, *Shakespeare and Manuscript Drama: Canon, Collaboration, and Text* (Cambridge: Cambridge University Press, 2016).

Raleigh, Walter Alexander, Sidney Lee, and Charles T. Onions, eds, *Shakespeare's England; an Account of the Life & Manners of His Age. An Introduction to Shakespeare for Japanese Students* (Oxford: Clarendon Press, 1916).

Rath, Eric C., *The Ethos of Noh: Actors and Their Art* (Cambridge, MA: Harvard University Asia Center, 2004).

Raz, Jacob, "The Audience Evaluated. Shikitei Samba's Kyakusha Hyobanki," *Monumenta Nipponica* 35, 2 (1980), 199–221. Doi: 10.2307/2384338.

Raz, Jacob, *Audience and Actors: A Study of Their Interaction in the Japanese Traditional Theatre* (Leiden: Brill, 1983).

Roach, Joseph, *Cities of the Dead: Circum-Atalantic Performance* (New York: Columbia University Press, 1996).

Roach, Joseph, *It* (Ann Arbor, MI: University of Michigan Press, 2007).

Rodwick, David N., *The Virtual Life of Film* (Cambridge, MA: Harvard University Press, 2007).

Rose, Jonathan, *The Intellectual Life of the British Working Classes* (New Haven, CT: Yale University Press, 2010).

Rosen, Philip, *Change Mummified: Cinema, Historicity, Theory* (Minneapolis, MN: University of Minnesota Press, 2001).

Rubinger, Richard, *Popular Literacy in Early Modern Japan* (Honolulu: University of Hawai'i Press, 2007).

Sakai Matsunosuke 酒井松之助, *Kodai ukiyo-e kaiire hikkei* 古代浮世絵買入必携 (Tokyo: Yoshizawa Shōho, 1893). Doi: 10.11501/850571.

Sakuragawa Jihinari 桜川慈悲成, *Asahina chaban Soga* 朝比奈茶番曽我 (Edo: Nishimuraya Yohachi, 1793). Doi: 10.11501/9892753.

Saltzman-Li, Katherine, *Creating Kabuki Plays: Context for Kezairoku, "Valuable Notes on Playwriting"* (Leiden: Brill, 2010).

Sand, Jordan, *Tokyo Vernacular: Common Spaces, Local Histories, Found Objects* (Berkeley, CA: University of California Press, 2013).

Santō Kyōden 山東京伝, *Asa chanoyu chotto kuchikiri* 朝茶湯一寸口切 (Edo: Eirakuya Tōshirō, 1812). Doi: 10.20730/100307207.

Santō Kyōden 山東京伝, "Kinsei kisekikō" 近世奇跡考, in Nihon Zuihitsu Taisei Henshūbu ed. 日本随筆大成編輯部 *Nihon zuihitsu taisei* 日本随筆大成, ser. 2, vol. 6 (Tokyo: Yoshikawa Kōbunkan, 1974) pp. 263–377.

Santō Kyōden 山東京伝, *Kottōshū* 骨董集, vol. 3 (Edo: Tsuruya Kiemon, 1815).

Satō Chino 佐藤知乃, "Yakusha hyōbanki no kaihan: *Yakusha saraekō* shoshi hoi" 役者評判記の改板：『役者時習講』書誌補遺, *Engeki kenkyūkai kaihō* 演劇研究会報41 (May 2015), 20–30.

Satō Dōshin 佐藤道信, "*Nihon bijutsu*" tanjō: kindai Nihon no "kotoba" to senryaku 〈日本美術〉誕生:近代日本の[ことば]と戦略 (Tokyo: Kōdansha, 1996).

Satō Dōshin 佐藤道信, *Modern Japanese Art and the Meiji State: The Politics of Beauty* trans. Hiroshi Nara (Los Angeles, CA: Getty Research Institute, 2011).

Satō Katsura 佐藤かつら, *Kabuki no bakumatsu/Meiji: koshibai no jidai* 歌舞伎の幕末・明治:小芝居の時代 (Tokyo: Perikansha, 2010).

Sato, Masayuki, "A Social History of Japanese Historical Writing," in *The Oxford History of Historical Writing*, vol. 3, ed. Daniel Woolf and Axel Schneider (Oxford: Oxford University Press, 2011), pp. 80–102. Doi:10.1093/acprof:osobl/9780199219179.003.0005.

Satō Miyuki 佐藤深雪, "Santō Kyōden: tenkaki no kōshōka" 山東京伝転換期の考証家, *Kokubungaku kaishaku to kanshō* 57, 3 (1992), 145–50.

Satō Yukiko 佐藤至子, *Edo no shuppan tōsei: danatsu ni honrō sareta gesakushatachi* 江戸の出版統制:弾圧に翻弄された戯作者たち (Tokyo: Yoshikawa Kōbunkan, 2017).

Satō Yukiko 佐藤至子, *Santō Kyōden: kokkei share daiichi no sakusha* 山東京伝:滑稽洒落第一の作者 (Kyoto: Mineruva Shobō, 2009).

Sawabe Kin 沢辺均, "Kokurtitsu Kokkai Toshokan dejitaru ākaibu kōsō" 国立国会図書館デジタルアーカイブ構想, *Zu bon: toshokan to media no hon* ず・ぼん:図書館とメディアの本 17 (December 2011), 86–99.

Screech, Timon, *Sex and the Floating World: Erotic Images in Japan, 1700–1820* (Honolulu: University of Hawai'i Press, 1999).

Screech, Timon, *The Lens within the Heart: The Western Scientific Gaze and Popular Imagery in Later Edo Japan* (Honolulu: University of Hawai'i Press, 2002).

Screech, Timon, *Tokyo before Tokyo: Power and Magic in the Shogun's City of Edo* (London: Reaktion Books, 2020).

Sekita Kaoru 関田かおる, "Tsubouchi Shōyō to Koizumi Yakumo: shinshiryō kara mite" 坪内逍遥と小泉八雲:新資料からみて, *Kokubungaku kaishaku to kyōzai no kenkyū* 国文学解釈と教材の研究 43, 8 (1998), 78–87.

"Senba-shi no shindaikagiri" 仙波氏の身代限, *Asahi shinbun* 朝日新聞, December 20, 1891, p. 1.

Shakespeare, William, *Okinimesumama* お気に召すまゝ, trans. Tsubouchi Shōyō 坪内逍遥(Tokyo: Waseda Daigaku Shuppanbu, 1920). Doi: 10.11501/962971.

Shea, Christopher, "New Oxford Shakespeare Edition Credits Christopher Marlowe as a Co-author," New York Times, October 24, 2016, 3.

Shiau Han-Chen 蕭涵珍, "Ri Gyo no Gyokusōtō denki to sono honansaku" 李漁の『玉搔頭伝奇』とその翻案作, *Tōkyō daigaku Chūgokugo Chūgoku bungaku kenkyūshitsu kyō* 東京大学中国語中国文学研究室紀要 15 (October, 2012), 125–39, https://doi.org/10.15083/00035251.

Shiau Han Chen 蕭涵珍, "Ri Gyo no sōsaku to juyō" 李漁の創作とその受容, doctoral thesis, Division of Asian Studies, Graduate School of Humanities and Sociology, University of Tokyo, 2013. Doi: https://doi.org/10.15083/00006193.

"Shibai chōhōsho" 芝居重法書, in *Waseda Daigaku Engeki Hakubutsukan shozō Yasuda Bunko kyūzō kinsei kindai fūzoku shiryō harikomichō* 早稲田大学演劇博物館所蔵安田文庫旧蔵近世・近代風俗史料張込帖, vol. 5, 14 microfilm reels (Tokyo: Yūshōdō Shuppan, 2001), R-5, 31–005.

Shikitei Sanba 式亭三馬, "Edo sanshibai monbanzuke" 江戸三芝居紋番付, manuscript, Kotenseki Shiryōshitsu, National Diet Library, http://dl.ndl.go.jp/info:ndljp/pid/1288373?__lang=en.

Shikitei Sanba 式亭三馬, "Otoshibanashi chūkō raiyu" 落話中興来由, 1815, manuscript, Kotenseki Shiryōshitsu, National Diet Library, https://dl.ndl.go.jp/info:ndljp/pid/1288373/1.

BIBLIOGRAPHY 273

Shikitei Sanba 式亭三馬, *Sono utsushi-e kabuki no omokage* 其寫絵劇俤 (Edo: Igaya Kanemon, 1811).

Shikitei Sanba 式亭三馬, "Shikitei zakki" 式亭雑記, in *Zoku enseki jusshu* 続燕石十種, ed. Ichijima Kenkichi 市島謙吉 and Iwamoto Kattōshi 岩本活東子, vol. 1 (Tokyo: Kokusho Kankōkai, 1908), pp. 44–81. Doi: 10.11501/991279.

Shikitei Sanba 式亭三馬, "Kakusha hyōbanki" 客者評判記, in *Nihon shomin bunka shiryō shūsei* 日本庶民文化史料集成, ed. Geinōshi Kenkyūkai 芸能史研究会, vol. 6 (Tokyo: Sanichi Shobō, 1973), 479–529.

Shikitei Sanba 式亭三馬, "Otoshibanashi kaizuri echō" 落話会刷画帖 in in *Nihon shomin bunka shiryō shūsei*日本庶民文化史料集成, ed. Geinōshi Kenkyūkai 芸能史研究会, vol. 8 (Tokyo: Sanichi Shobō, 1976) 127–39.

Shikitei Sanba 式亭三馬, *Ukiyoburo; Kejō suigen maku no soto; Daisen sekai gakuyasagashi*, 浮世風呂・戯場粋言幕の外・大千世界楽屋探, ed. Satake Akihiro 佐竹昭広, Shin Nihon Koten Bungaku Taikei 新日本古典文学大系, vol. 86 (Tokyo: Iwanami Shoten, 1989).

Shikitei Sanba 式亭三馬, *Shibai kinmo zui: Kyōwa sannen shohanbon* 戯場訓蒙図彙: 享和三年初版本, Kabuki no Bunken 3 (Tokyo: Nihon Geijutsu Bunka Shinkōkai, 2001).

Shimazaki, Satoko, *Edo Kabuki in Transition: From the Worlds of the Samurai to the Vengeful Female Ghost* (New York: Columbia University Press, 2016).

Shimazaki, Satoko, "Stage Sounds for the Eyes: Performance and Visual-Textual Space of Gōkan," in *Graphic Narratives from Early Modern Japan: The World of Kusazōshi*, ed. Laura Moretti and Satō Yukiko (Leiden and Boston, CA: Brill, forthcoming).

Shimazaki Tōson, *Before the Dawn*, trans. William E. Naff, reprint edn (Honolulu: University of Hawai'i Press, 1988).

Shinoda Kinji 篠田金治, *Kuraishō* 藏意抄 (Edo: Nishimura Genroku, 1813). Doi: 10.11501/8929485.

"Shinpan sanshibai gakuya zassho" 新版三芝居楽屋雑書, in *Waseda Daigaku Engeki Hakubutsukan shozō Yasuda Bunko kyūzō kinsei kindai fūzoku shiryō harikomichō* 早稲田大学演劇博物館所蔵安田文庫旧蔵近世・近代風俗史料張込帖, vol. 5, 14 microfilm reels (Tokyo: Yūshōdō Shuppan, 2001), R-5, 31–006.

*Shinpo Yamato nendai kōki eshō* (Kyoto: Fushimiya Hyōaemon et al., 1692), http://www.wul.waseda.ac.jp/kotenseki/html/ri04/ri04_00923/index.html.

"Shinshi Saruwaka nendaiki" 新梓猿若年代記, in *Waseda Daigaku Engeki Hakubutsukan shozō Yasuda Bunko kyūzō kinsei kindai fūzoku shiryō harikomichō* 早稲田大学演劇博物館所蔵安田文庫旧蔵近世・近代風俗史料張込帖, vol. 5, 14 microfilm reels (Tokyo: Yūshōdō Shuppan, 2001), R-5, 31–010.

Shively, Donald H., "Bakufu Versus Kabuki," *Harvard Journal of Asiatic Studies* 18, 3/4 (1955), 326–56.

Shōkōsai Hanbē 松好齋半兵衛, *Shibai gakuya zue shūi* 戯場樂屋圖會拾遺, 2 vols (Osaka: Kawajiya Tasuke, 1800), https://dl.ndl.go.jp/info:ndljp/pid/2605334.

Shōyō Kyōkai 逍遥協会, ed., *Mikan Tsubouchi Shōyō shiryōshū* 未刊坪内逍遥資料集 6 vols (Tokyo: Shōyō Kyōkai, 2001).

Simmel, Georg, "Fashion," in *Georg Simmel on Individuality and Social Forms*, ed. Donald N. Levine (Chicago, IL: University of Chicago Press, 1971), pp294-323.

Smith, Bruce R. "Getting Back to the Library, Getting Back to the Body," in *Shakespeare and the Digital World*, ed. Christine Carson and Peter Kirwan (Cambridge: Cambridge University Press, 2014), pp. 24–32. Doi: https://doi.org/10.1017/CBO9781107587526.

Sō Shiseki 宋紫石, *Kokon gasō* 古今画藪, 13 vols (Edo: Suharaya Sōbē, 1771).

Stevenson, Elizabeth, *The Grass Lark: a Study of Lafcadio Hearn* (New Brunswick, NJ: Transaction Publishers, 1999).
Stewart, Susan, *On Longing: Narratives of the Miniature, the Gigantic, the Souvenir, the Collection* (Durham, NC: Duke University Press, 1993).
Suwa Haruo 諏訪春雄, "Kaiga shiryō ni miru shoki kabuki no geitai: wakashū kabuki no kaiga" 絵画資料に見る初期歌舞伎の芸態:若衆歌舞伎, *Kokugo to kokubungaku* 国語と国文学 50, 5 (1973). 42–56.
Suzuki Hiroyuki 鈴木廣之, *Kōkokatachi no jūkyūseiki: Bakumatsu Meiji ni okeru "mono" no arukeorojī*, 好古家たちの19世紀―幕末明治における"物"のアルケオロジー (Tokyo: Yoshikawa Kōbunkan, 2003).
Suzuki Hiroyuki, *Antiquarians of Nineteenth-Century Japan: The Archaeology of Things in the Late Tokugawa and Early Meiji Periods*, trans. Maki Fukuoka (Los Angeles, CA: Getty Research Institute, 2022).
Suzuki Jūzō 鈴木重三, *Toyokuni, Kunimasa, Toyohiro, Nidai Toyokuni, hoka* 豊国: 国政, 豊広, 豊春, 二代豊国ほか, ed. Takahashi Seiichirō 高橋誠一郎, vol. 9, *Ukiyo-e taikei* 浮世絵大系 (Tokyo: Shūeisha, 1975).
Suzuki Toshiyuki 鈴木俊幸, ed., *Kinsei kōki ni okeru shoseki/sōshi nado no shuppan/ryūtsu/kyōju ni tsuite no kenkyū: Kiso Tsumago Hayashike zōsho oyobi Kiso Uematsu Rinsenji shozō hangi no chōsa o chūshin ni* 近世期における書物・草紙等の出版・流通・享受についての研究:木曽妻籠林家蔵書及び木曽上松臨川寺所蔵板木の調査を中心に (Hachiōji: Chūō Daigaku Bungakubu, 3833 Kenkyūshitsu, 1996).
Suzuki Toshiyuki 鈴木俊幸, *Edo no dokushonetsu: jigakusuru dokusha to shoseki ryūtsū* 江戸の読書熱:自学する読者と書籍流通, (Tokyo: Heibonsha, 2007).
Suzuki Toshiyuki 鈴木俊幸, "'Nendaiki' oboegaki" [年代記]覚書, in *Mō hitotsu no kotenchi: zenkindai Nihon no chi no kanōsei* もう一つの古典知:前近代日本の知の可能性, ed. Maeda Masayuki 前田雅之 (Tokyo: Bensei shuppan, 2012), pp. 215–20.
Tada Nanrei 多田南嶺, *Kokon yakusha taizen* 古今役者大全, Kabuki Sōsho 歌舞伎叢書, vol. 1 (Tokyo: Kinkōdō, 1910). Doi: 10.11501/858205.
Takada Mamoru 高田衛, ed., *Tsuga Teishō/Itami Chinen shū* 都賀庭鐘・伊丹椿園集, Edo kaii kisō bungei taikei 江戸怪異綺想文学大系, vol. 2 (Tokyo: Kokusho Kankōkai, 2001).
Takada Mamoru 高田衛, *Takizawa Bakin: Momotose nochino chiin o matsu* 滝沢馬琴:百年以後の知音を俟つ (Kyoto: Mineruva Shobō, 2006).
Takahashi Noriko 高橋則子, *Kusazōshi to engeki: yakusha nigao-e sōshiki o chūshin ni* 草双紙と演劇:役者似顔絵創始期を中心に (Tokyo: Kyūko Shoin, 2004).
Takahashi, Yūichirō, "Kabuki Goes Official: The 1878 Opening of the Shintomi-Za," in *A Kabuki Reader: History and Performance*, ed. Samuel L. Leiter (Armonk, NY: M. E. Sharpe, 2002), pp. 123–51.
Tamura Nariyoshi 田村成義, Zokuzoku kabuki nendaiki 続々歌舞伎年代記 (Tokyo: Ichimura-za, 1922). Doi: 10.11501/1870465
Tanahashi Masahiro 棚橋正博, *Shikitei Sanba: Edo no gesakusha* 式亭三馬:江戸の戯作者 (Tokyo: Perikansha, 1994).
Tanaka, Stefan, *Japan's Orient: Rendering Pasts into History* (Berkeley, CA: University of California Press, 1995).
Tanihata Akio 谷端昭夫, *Cha no yu jinbutsushi* 茶の湯人物誌 (Kyoto: Tankōsha, 2012).
Terada Seiichi 寺田精一, *Kagaku to hanzai* 科学と犯罪 (Tokyo: Bunmei shoin, 1918).
Terada Shima 寺田詩麻, "Engeki Hakubutsukan shozō no 'Zoku zoku kabuki nendaiki' ni tsuite" 演劇博物館所蔵の『続々歌舞伎年代記』について, *Engeki kenkyū* 演劇研究 19 (1995), 13–27.

Tessō Dōjin 徹桑土人, "Kyōhō nenjū Fukami shirabegaki" 享保年中深見調書, in "Kaihyō ibun" 海表異聞, manuscript, Dōshisha University Library, Komuro-Sawabe Bunko, Co81.K5 vol. 38 (n.d.), https://dgcl.doshisha.ac.jp/digital/collections/MD00000040/?lang=0.

Tochigi Akira とちぎあきら, "Eiga *Momijigari* no jūyō bunkazai no shite ni tsuite" 映画『紅葉狩』の重要文化財の指定について, *Eiga terebi gijutsu* 映画テレビ技術684 (August 2009), 26-29.

Tokuda Takeshi 徳田武, "*Kyokutei denki hana no kanzashi* ron" 『曲亭伝奇花釵児』論, *Meiji Daigaku kyōyō ronbunshū* 明治大学教養論集118 (1978), 77-99, http://hdl.handle.net/10291/4879.

Tokuda Takeshi 徳田武, *Nihon kinsei shōsetsu to Chūgoku shōsetsu* 日本近世小説と中国小説, *Nihon shoshigaku taikei* 日本書誌学大系, vol. 51 (Tokyo: Seishōdō Shoten, 1987).

Tokuda Takeshi 徳田武, *Takizawa Bakin* 滝沢馬琴, Shinchō koten bungaku arubumu 新潮古典アルバム (Tokyo: Shinchōsha, 1991).

Tokuda Takeshi 徳田武 and Yokoyama Kuniharu 横山邦治, eds, *Shigeshige yawa. Kyokutei denki hanakanzashi. Saibara kidan. Toribeyama shirabeno itomichi* 繁野話. 曲亭伝奇花釵児. 催馬楽奇談. 鳥辺山調綾, Shin Nihon koten bungaku taikei 新日本古典文学t大系 vol. 80 (Tokyo: Iwanami Shoten, 1992).

Tōshi Shōkyaku 東子樵客, *Yakusha sanjūnisō tengankyō* 俳優卅二相點顏鏡 (Edo: Gangetsudō and Kōshodō, 1802).

"Tsubouchi Hakase kanteisho" 坪内博士鑑定書, Yomiuri shinbun 読売新聞, August 14-16, 1902.

Tsubouchi Shōyō 坪内逍遥, "Bungaku toshite no waga zairai kyakuhon" 文学としての我が在来脚本 in *Shōyō senshū* 逍遥選集, vol. 10 (Tokyo: Daiichi shobō, 1977-78), pp.215-226.

Tsubouchi Shōyō 坪内逍遥, "*Butai no Danjūrō* jō" 舞台の團十郎 in *Shōyō senshū* 逍遥選集, vol. 7 (Tokyo: Daiichi shobō, 1977-78), p. 293-98.

Tsubouchi Shōyō 坪内逍遥, "Chikamatsu tai Shēkuspiya tai Ibusen" 近松対シェイクスピヤー対イプセン in *Shōyō senshū* 逍遥選集, vol. 10 (Tokyo: Daiichi shobō, 1977-78), pp. 769-814.

Tsubouchi Shōyō 坪内逍遥, "Chikamatsu to Shēkusupiya" 近松とシェイクスピヤー in *Shōyō senshū*逍遥選集, vol. 8 (Tokyo: Daiichi shobō, 1977-78), pp. 769-78.

Tsubouchi Shōyō 坪内逍遥, "Engeki shiryō toshite no wa ga kuni no shibai nishiki-e narabi sono zuhyō" 演劇史料としての我が国の芝居錦絵並び其の図表 in *Shōyō senshū* 逍遥選集, vol. 7 (Tokyo: Daiichi shobō, 1977-78), pp.317-28.

Tsubouchi Shōyō 坪内逍遥, "Katsudō shashin to wa ga geki no kako" 活動写真と我が劇の過去, in *Shōyō senshū* 逍遥選集, vol. 7 (Tokyo: Daiichi shobō, 1977-78), pp.299-308.

Tsubouchi Shōyō 坪内逍遥, "Kottōnetsu" 骨董熱 in *Shōyō senshū* 逍遥選集, vol. 2 (Tokyo: Daiichi shobō, 1977-78), p. 803, p.787-808.

Tsubouchi Shōyō 坪内逍遥, "Kyakuhon ni kan suru soshō jiken no kantei" 脚本に関する訴訟事件の鑑定, in *Shōyō senshū* 逍遥選集, vol. 1 (Tokyo: Daiichi shobō, 1977-78), pp.685-814.

Tsubouchi Shōyō 坪内逍遥, "Ky ū kyogen sakusha oyobi ky ū kyakuhon" 旧狂言作者及び旧脚本, in *Shōyō senshū* 逍遥選集, vol. 10 (Tokyo: Daiichi shobō, 1977-78), pp. 227-244.

Tsubouchi Shōyō 坪内逍遥, *Ninkōjō* 任興帖 (Tokyo: Daiichi Shobō, 1936), https://archive.wul.waseda.ac.jp/tomon/tomon_18727/tomon_18727_0001/tomon_18727_0001_p0028.jpg.

Tsubouchi Shōyō 坪内逍遥, *Shēkusupiya kenkyū shiori* シェークスピヤ研究栞 (Tokyo: Waseda Daigaku Shuppanbu, 1928). Doi: 10.11501/1180529.

Tsubouchi Shōyō 坪内逍遥, "Shibai-e to Toyokuni oyobi sono monka" 芝居絵と豊国及び其の門下 in *Shōyō senshū* 逍遥選集, vol. 7 (Tokyo: Daiichi shobō, 1977–78), pp.1-268.

Tsubouchi Shōyō 坪内逍遥, "Shibai nishikie shūsei' jo" 「芝居錦絵集成」序 in *Shōyō senshū* 逍遥選集, vol. 7 (Tokyo: Daiichi shobō, 1977–78), pp.291-92.

Tsubouchi Shōyō 坪内逍遥, "Shōnen jidai ni mita kabuki no tsuioku" 少年時代に見た歌舞伎の追憶, in *Shōyō senshū* 逍遥選集, vol. 12 (Tokyo: Daiichi shobō, 1977–78), pp. 53–292.

Tsubouchi Shōyō 坪内逍遥, *Shōyō senshū* 逍遥選集, 17 vols (Tokyo: Daiichi shobō, 1977–78).

Tsubouchi Shōyō 坪内逍遥, *Tsubouchi Shōyō shokanshū* 坪内逍遥書簡集, ed. Shōyō Kyōkai 逍遥協会, 6 vols (Tokyo: Waseda Daigaku Shuppanbu, 2013).

Tsubouchi Shōyō 坪内逍遥 and Tsunashima Ryōsen 綱島梁川, eds, *Chikamatsu no kenkyū* 近松の研究 (Tokyo: Shunyōdō, 1900). Doi: 10.11501/991478.

Tsubouchi Yūzō [Shōyō] 坪内雄蔵[逍遥], "Kyakuhon kanteisho" 脚本鑑定書, *Kabuki* 歌舞伎28 (September 1902), 15–24. Doi: 10.11501/3545636.

Tsukagoshi Yoshitarō 塚越芳太郎, *Chikamatsu Monzaemon* 近松門左衛門 (Tokyo: Kenyūsha, 1894). Doi: 10.11501/872073.

Ueda Manabu 上田学, *Nihon eiga sōsōki no kōgyō to kankyaku: Tōkyō to Kyōto o chūshin ni* 日本映画草創期の興行と観客:東京と京都を中心に (Tokyo: Waseda Daigaku Shuppanbu, 2012).

Ukai Nobuyuki 鵜飼信之, *Kokuseiya chūgiden* 國姓爺忠義傳 (Kyoto: Tanaka Shōbē, 1717). Doi: 10.20730/200017184.

"Ukiyo-e no seiri ni atsusa mo wasurete: Tsubouchi hakase" 浮世絵の整理に熱さも忘れて: 坪内博士, *Tōkyō nichinichi shinbun* 東京日々新聞, evening edn, July 28, 1925, p. 1.

Utagawa Toyokuni 歌川豊国, "Yakusha nigao hayageiko" 役者似顔早稽古, in *Fukumori Kyusuke kyakuhonshū* 福森久助脚本集, ed. Furuido Hideo 古井戸秀夫 (Tokyo: Kokusho Kankōkai, 2001), pp.319–81.

Utei Enba 烏亭焉馬, *Shibai saiken sanbasō* 芝居細見三葉草 (Edo: Moriya Jihē and Yamaguchiya Tōbē, 1817). Doi: 10.20730/100080689.

Utei Enba 烏亭焉馬, *Shibai saiken sanbasō* 芝居細見三葉草, 6 vols (Edo: Moriya Jihē and Yamaguchiya Tōbē, 1832). Doi: 10.20730/100344980.

Utei Enba 烏亭焉馬, *Hana no Edo kabuki nendaiki* 花江都歌舞妓年代記 (Tokyo: Kabuki Shuppanbu, 1926). Doi: 10.11501/1764922.

Utei Enba 烏亭焉馬, "Kabuki dōchu zue" 歌舞伎道中図絵, in *Waseda Daigaku Engeki Hakubutsukan shozō Yasuda Bunko kyūzō kinsei kindai fūzoku shiryō harikomichō* 早稲田大学演劇博物館所蔵安田文庫旧蔵近世・近代風俗史料張込帖, vol. 5, 14 microfilm reels (Tokyo: Yūshōdō Shuppan, 2001), R–5, 31–002.

van Gogh, Vincent, *Van Gogh on Art and Artists: Letters to Emile Bernard*, trans. Douglas Cooper (New York: Dover Publications, 2003).

Vickers, Brian, *Shakespeare, Co-author: A Historical Study of Five Collaborative Plays* (Oxford: Oxford University Press, 2002).

Wada Atsuhiko 和田敦彦, *Ekkyō suru shomotsu: henyōsuru dokusho kankyō no naka de* 越境する書物:変容する読書環境の中で (Tokyo: Shinyōsha, 2011).

Wada Atsuhiko 和田敦彦, "Shomotsu to basho no rekishigaku" 書物と場所の歴史学, in *Ekkyō suru shomotsu: henyōsuru dokusho kankyō no naka de* 越境する書物:変容する読書環境の中で (Tokyo: Shinyōsha, 2011), pp.11-20.

Wada Atsuhiko 和田敦彦, *Dokusho no rekishi wo tou: shomotsu to dokusha no kindai* 読書の歴史を問う:書物と読者の近代 (Tokyo: Kasama Shoin, 2014).

Wada Osamu 和田修, "Kawatake Mokuami no hanken tōroku" 河竹黙阿弥の版権登録, *Engeki kenkyū* 演劇研究 17 (1993), 31–48.

Waseda Daigaku Engeki Hakubutsukan 早稲田大学演劇博物館, ed., *Engeki hakubutsukan gojūnen* 演劇博物館五十年 (Tokyo: Waseda Daigaku Tsubouchi Hakushi Kinen Engeki Hakubutsukan, 1978).

Waseda Daigaku Engeki Hakubutsukan 早稲田大学演劇博物館, ed., *Engeki hakubutsukan shiryō monogatari* 演劇博物館資料ものがたり (Tokyo: Waseda Daigaku Tsubouchi Hakushi Kinen Engeki Hakubutsukan, 1988).

Waseda Daigaku Engeki Hakubutsukan 早稲田大学演劇博物館, ed., *Botsugo hyakunen Kawatake Mokuami: hito to sakuhin* 没後百年河竹黙阿弥:人と作品 (Tokyo: Waseda Daigaku Tsubouchi Hakushi Kinen Engeki Hakubutsukan, 1993).

Watanabe Tamotsu 渡辺保, *Shintai wa maboroshi* 身体は幻 (Tokyo: Genki shobō, 2014).

Werstine, Paul, *Early Modern Playhouse Manuscripts and the Editing of Shakespeare* (Cambridge: Cambridge University Press, 2013).

Wigen, Kären, *The Making of a Japanese Periphery, 1750–1920* (Berkeley, CA: University of California Press, 1995).

Williams, Raymond, *The Country and the City* (Oxford: Oxford University Press, 1975).

Wölfflin, Heinrich, *Principles of Art History: The Problem of the Development of Style in Late Art*, trans. Mary D. Hottinger (New York: Dover Publications, 1950).

Yamamoto Harufumi 山本陽史, "Santō Kyōden no kōshō zuihitsu to gesaku" 山東京伝の考証随筆と戯作, *Kokugo to kokubungaku* 国語と国文学 63, 10, 1986, 50–65;

Yamamoto Harufumi 山本陽史, "Kaidai: takara awase kai to 'Kyōbun takara awase no ki'" 解題:宝合会と[狂文宝合記], in *"Kyōbun takara awase no ki" no kenkyū* 『狂文宝合記』の研究, ed. Kobayashi Fumiko 小林ふみ子 and Nobuhiro Shinji 延広真治 (Tokyo: Kyūko Shoin, 2000).

Yamamoto Kazuaki 山本和明, "Santō Kyōden to 'kōshō'" 山東京伝と[考証], in 中西智海先生還暦記念論文集刊行会Nakanishi Chikai Sensei Kanreki Kinen Ronbunshū Kankōkai ed. *Bukkyō to ningen* 仏教と人間 (Kyoto: Nagata Bunshōdō, 1994), pp. 229–46.

Yanai Kenji 矢内賢二, *Meiji no kabuki to shuppan media* 明治の歌舞伎と出版メディア (Tokyo: Perikansha, 2011).

"Yobukodori waka sanchō zenzu" 呼子鳥和歌三町全図, in *Waseda Daigaku Engeki Hakubutsukan shozō Yasuda Bunko kyūzō kinsei kindai fūzoku shiryō harikomichō* 早稲田大学演劇博物館所蔵安田文庫旧蔵近世・近代風俗史料張込帖, vol. 2, 14 microfilm reels (Tokyo: Yūshōdō Shuppan, 2001), R–2, 8–037.

Yonemoto, Marcia, *Mapping Early Modern Japan: Space, Place, and Culture in the Tokugawa Period, 1603–1868* (Berkeley, CA: University of California Press, 2003).

Yoshida Eri 吉田恵理, "Nihon 'bunjinga' kenkyū nōto: Edo chūki no Ri Gyo (Ri Ryū ō) no imēji ni kan suru kōsatsu" 日本[文人画]研究ノート:江戸中期の李漁(李笠翁)イメージに関する一考察, *Gakushūin Daigaku jinbunkagaku ronshū* 学習院大学人文科学論集8 (September 1999), 37–41, http://hdl.handle.net/10959/1927.

Zwicker, Jonathan E., *Practices of the Sentimental Imagination: Melodrama, the Novel, and the Social Imaginary in Nineteenth-Century Japan* (Cambridge, MA: Harvard University Asia Center, 2006).

# Index

Figures are indicated by *f* following the page number

Abe Yutaka 安部豊 220, 223*f*, 230, 257
*An Account of What I Have Seen and Heard* (Buyō Inshi) 29
Adorno, Theodor W. 36, 63
Akama Ryō 15, 35, 57, 227
Akutagawa Ryūnosuke 芥川龍之介 67
*Aoto Fujitsuna, Told in Colored Prints* 169–78
*Aoto zōshi hana no nishiki-e* 青砥稿花紅彩画 *see Aoto Fujitsuna, Told in Colored Prints*
Arai Hakuseki 新井白石 125
Arashi Kichisaburō 嵐吉三郎 228
*As You Like It* 36
*Asa chanoyu chotto kuchikiri* 朝茶湯一寸口切 *see Opening the Canister for Morning Tea*
*Asaina chaban Soga* 朝比奈茶番曽我 *see Asaina and the Soga Farce*
*Asaina and the Soga Farce* 183–85

banzuke 番付 4, 36, 43, 51
*A Beauty Contest of One Hundred Actors Past and Present* 47
Benjamin, Walter 16, 57, 63, 192
*Benten kozō* 弁天小僧 *see Aoto Fujitsuna, Told in Colored Prints*
*Benten the Thief see Aoto Fujitsuna, Told in Colored Prints*
Berry, Mary Elizabeth 43, 48
*The Bloodstained Bodhidharma* 3
Bratton, Jacky 6, 18
*Butai no Danjūrō* 舞台之團十郎 *see Danjūrō on Stage*
Buyō Inshi 武陽隠士 29, 31–33

*Catalogue of Recent Fiction Writers of Edo* (Kyokutei Bakin) 68, 193
Chartier, Roger 64–65
*Chidaruma* 血達磨 *see The Bloodstained Bodhidharma*
Chikamatsu Hanji 近松半二 150, 257
Chikamatsu Monzaemon 近松門前門 123, 139–53, 158–59, 161, 164–65, 257
*A Chronology of the Kabuki of Flowering Edo* (Utei Enba) 41, 42*f*, 47*f*

*A Chronology of the Kabuki of Flowering Edo Part II* (Ishizuka Hōkaishi) 68
*A Chronology of Puppetry Past and Present* (Nishizawa Ippū) 45
*Chūshingura: The Storehouse of Loyal Retainers* 50, 129
Clunas, Craig 79, 195
*The Collected Poems of Lady Ise* 161
*A Collection of Curiosities* (Santō Kyōden) 59
*A Complete Book of Actors Past and Present* (Tada Nanrei) 44, 163
Crary, Jonathan 32–33
*A Critique of the Audience* (Shikitei Sanba) 23, 23*f*, 38, 39*f*, 179, 240
*A Critique of Patrons* (Utei Enba) 38
"Curio Fever" (Tsubouchi Shōyō) 71

Dainichibō 大日坊 184–86, 187*f*, 203, 205
*Danjūrō on Stage* (Abe Yutaka) 221, 223*f*, 230
"Danjūrō shichise no mago" 団十郎七世嫡孫 (Utei Enba) 43
Debord, Guy 32–33
*Denki sakusho see On the Writing of Plays*
detailed view 49, 85, 86, 95, 98, 113
*A Detailed View of the Actors of the Three Theaters* 98, 100*f*
*Detailed View of Edo Male Love* (Hiraga Gennai) 93
*A Detailed View of Saruwaka* 86, 86*f*
*A Detailed View of the Theater: The Three-Leafed Clover* (Utei Enba) 95, 95*f*, 97*f*
*A Disquisition on the Customs of Actors* 94, 116, 116*f*

*Edo nanshoku saiken* 江戸男色細見 *see Detailed View of Edo Male Love*
"Edo sanshibai monbanzuke" 江戸三芝居紋番附 *see "Programs of Edo's Three Theaters"*
Ejima-Ikushima Affair 50

*Facts about Actors, Newly Printed* (Hachimonjiya Jishō) 122
Fenollosa, Ernest 188, 233

*The Flavor of Green Tea over Rice* (Ozu Yasujirō) 3
Friedrich Succo 74, 197
fudekuse 筆癖 174, 189–91
*Fuji in Summer* (Katsukawa Shunshō) 224
Fujikawa Heigorō 128, 128
Fukagaw-za 深川座 170–72, 178
Fukiya-chō 葺屋町 22, 81, 93, 94, 96, 98, 107, 108
Fukuchi Ōchi 福地桜痴 137
Fukumori Kyūsuke 福森久助 165, 257
Fukuzawa Yukichi 福沢諭吉 62

*Gekijō ikkan mushimegane* 劇場一観顕微鏡 see *A View of the Theater through a Microscope*
*Genkyō sakusho* 言狂作書 see *On the Writing of Plays*
gesaku 戯作 8, 29
gōkan 合巻 101, 174, 194
Goryūtei Tokushō 五柳亭徳升 98–100, 128
Gunji Masakatsu 郡司正勝 2
*Gunsho Ruijū* 群書類従 68

*Hana no Edo kabuki nendaiki* 花江都歌舞妓年代記 see *A Chronology of the Kabuki of Flowering Edo*
*Hana no Edo kabuki nendaiki zoku hen* 花江都歌舞妓年代記続編 see *A Chronology of the Kabuki of Flowering Edo Part II* 68
Hanawa Hokiichi 塙保己一 68
Hatanaka Kansai 畠中観斎 124, 128f, 151, 257
Hattori Yukio 3, 15, 118, 237
Hayashi Kuni 林くに 6, 13, 24, 28, 29, 37, 242, 257
Hearn, Lafcadio 72, 181
Hinaya Ryūho 雛屋立圃 49, 59
Hiraga Gennai 平賀源内 92, 155
Hishikawa Moronobu 菱川師宣 49, 59
Hōkaibō 法界坊 25, 205, 206, 243, 244f
Hōseidō Kisanji 朋誠堂喜三二 81, 105, 106, 125f, 257

Ichijima Kenkichi 市島謙吉 69, 70, 73
Ichikawa Danjūrō 市川團十郎
 Ichikawa Danjūrō I 39–40, 42, 42f, 45
 Ichikawa Danjūrō II 39–40, 106
 Ichikawa Danjūrō V 106, 111, 143, 186, 187f, 212–13, 224–25, 257
 Ichikawa Danjūrō VII 20, 43, 134, 134f, 218, 228, 257
 Ichikawa Danjūrō IX 137, 143, 171, 186, 212–13, 221–28, 231–36, 257
Ichikawa Jitsuko 市川実子 222

Ichikawa Komazō V 100f, 128
Ichikawa Omezō 市川男女蔵 111, 207, 208f
Ichikawa Sanshō 市川三升 221, 230
Ichimura Uzaemon 市村羽左衛門 107, 111
Ichimura-za 市村座 25, 85, 107, 108, 165, 166f, 177, 186, 228
Ihara Seiseien see Ihara Toshirō
Ihara Toshirō 伊原敏郎 47, 171, 175, 176, 221, 258
Iijima Kyoshin 飯島虚心 211, 215, 218, 225
Ikushima Shingorō 生島新五郎 50, 143
*An Illustrated Collection of Actors* (Kyokutei Bakin) 110, 110f, 111, 117f
*Illustrated Dictionary of Theater for Beginners* (Shikitei Sanba) 22, 81, 112, 201
*An Illustrated Encyclopedia of U and Kan's Three Stages* (Hōseidō Kisanji) 81, 106, 109f, 115f
*Ima mukashi ayatsuri nendaiki* 今昔操年代記 see *A Chronology of Puppetry Past and Present*
*Imose nori no shōsoku* (Chikamatsu Monzaemon) 妹背海苔の消息 147
"Incident at Sakai" (Mori Ōgai) 240
Inoue Takejirō 井上竹次郎 217, 234
*Iseshū* 伊勢集 see *The Collected Poems of Lady Ise*
Ishizuka Hōkaishi 石塚豊芥子 51, 67, 88, 88f, 258
Iwai Hanshirō V 岩井半四郎 20, 196, 258

*The Jade Clasp* (Li Yu) 151
Jippensha Ikku 十返舎一九 168, 193, 195,
jōruri 浄瑠璃 14, 16, 17, 85, 126, 129
*Just a Minute!* 111, 143, 201, 224

Kabuki-za 歌舞伎座 3, 68, 217, 220, 234, 235
*Kagekiyo* 景清 184–186, 187f, 203, 205, 224
kagema jaya 陰間茶屋 92
*Kakusha hyōbanki* 客者評判記 see *A Critique of the Audience*
Kamiyama Akira 137, 138, 220
*Kanadehon chūshingura* 仮名手本忠臣蔵 see *Chūshingura: The Storehouse of Loyal Retainers*
Kangxi Emperor 123, 151
Kansei Reforms 寛政改革 101
Katsukawa Shundō 勝川春童 109f, 115, 115f
Katsukawa Shunshō 勝川春 186, 187f, 225
Katsushika Hokusai 葛飾北斎 215
Kawachiya Tasuke 149, 150
Kawakami Otojirō 川上音二郎 176
Kawarazaki-za 河原崎座 8, 85, 88

Kawatake Mokuami 河竹黙阿弥 68, 137, 167, 169, 171, 174, 189, 258
Kawaura Kenichi 河浦謙一 215, 217
Keisai Eisen 渓斎英泉 213
*Kejō suigen maku no soto* 戯場粋言幕乃外 see *Theater Chic This Side of the Curtain*
*Kezairoku* 戯財録 see *Valuable Notes on Playwriting*
kibyōshi 黄表紙 183, 186
Kimura Mokurō 木村黙老 132, 134f, 136f, 258
*Kinsei kiseki kō* 近世奇跡考 see *Thoughts on Extraordinary Things of Recent Times*
*Kinsei mono no hon Edo sakusha burui* 近世物之本江戸作者部類 see *Catalogue of Recent Fiction Writers of Edo*
Kitagawa Morisada 喜田川守貞 89, 90f, 92f, 93f, 114f
Kitagawa Tsukimaro 喜多川月麿 101, 102f
Kobayashi Bunshichi 小林文七 179, 215, 227, 258
Kobiki-chō 木挽町 7, 98, 108, 221
*Kokon shibai irokurabe hyakunin isshu* 古今四場居百人一首 see *A Beauty Contest of One Hundred Actors Past and Present*
*Kokon yakusha taizen* 古今役者大全 see *A Complete Book of Actors Past and Present*
Kokugaku 国学 59, 61
Komada Kōyō 駒田好洋 234
koshibai 小芝居 8
*Kottōnetsu* 骨董熱 see "Curio Fever"
*Kottōshū* 骨董集 see *A Collection of Curiosities*
Kyakuhon Gakufu Jōrei 脚本楽譜条例 169, 172
*Kyakusha hyōbanki* 客者評判記 see *A Critique of Patrons*
"Kyōgen sakusha kokoroesho" 狂言作者心得書 see "Precepts for Dramatic Composition"
kyōka 狂歌 50, 130
Kyokutei Bakin 曲亭馬琴 61, 63, 64, 80, 110, 117f, 126, 132, 153f, 154f, 168, 193, 199, 208f, 258

*Latter-Day Reflections of the Sumida River* 25
Li Yu (J. Ri Gyo) 李漁 122–24, 126, 140, 151–55, 157, 161, 214, 258

*A Magnifying Glass of Thirty-Two Actors' Physiognomies* (Tōshi Shōkyaku) 199, 200f
*Maple Viewing* (Shibata Tsunekichi) 218, 232
Matsumoto Kōshirō 松本幸四郎: Matsumoto Kōshirō V 20, 25, 97, 97f, 100f, 111, 117, 121, 128, 134, 134f, 165, 196, 205, 207, 258

Matsumoto Kōshirō VII 225
Matsuyama Kitarō 松山喜太郎 144, 147
Matsuyama Yonetarō 松山米太郎 144, 146, 147
*Meisetsu jijoden* 鳴雪自叙伝 (Naitō Meisetsu) 4, 8–9
meisho zue 名所図会 110, 110f, 111
Mimasuren 三升連 43, 143
Mimasuya Nisōji 三升屋二三治 165
Miyatake Gaikotsu 宮武外骨 141
Mizutani Futō 水谷不倒 69, 147
*Miscellaneous Notes from Behind the Stage of the Three Theaters* 81, 82f
*The Mirage Tower* (Li Yu) 122
*Momijigari* 紅葉狩 see *Maple Viewing*
Mori Ōgai 森鴎外 239, 240
"Morisada mankō" 守貞謾稿 see "Morisada's Miscellany"
"Morisada's Miscellany" (Kitagawa Morisada) 89, 90f, 93f, 113, 114f
Morishima Chūryō 森島中良 58, 65, 123
Morita Kanya 森田/守田勘彌 111
Morita-za 森田座 2, 7
*Morokoshi kidan* 唐土奇談 see *Strange Tales from China*
Motoori Norinaga 本居宣長 59
Murasaki Shikibu 159, 164
Murashima Ayaka 218, 219, 220

Nagatomo Chiyoji 16, 45
Naitō Fusanoshin 4
Naitō Meisetsu 内藤鳴雪 4, 8, 259
Nakamura Kanzaburō 中村勘三郎 41, 44, 47, 107, 111, 143, 259
Nakamura Nakazō III 中村仲蔵 1, 8, 9, 259
Nakamura Shikan 中村芝翫 see Nakamura Utaemon III
Nakamura Tetsurō 146, 164
Nakamura Utaemon 中村歌右衛: Nakamura Utaemon II 128
  Nakamura Utaemon III 4, 20, 130–32, 259
  Nakamura Utaemon IV 4, 5f, 20, 259
Nakamura-za 中村座 39, 47, 85, 107, 108, 143
Nakatsukasa 中務 161
Namiki Gohei 並木五瓶 165, 167, 259
Namiki Shōza see Namiki Shōzō
Namiki Shōzō 並木正三 148, 159, 259
*Naniwa miyage* 難波土産 see *A Souvenir of Naniwa*
Narita Yasuke 成田屋助 165
*Natsu no Fuji* 夏の富士 see *Fuji in Summer*
*A Newly Printed Chronology of Saruwaka* 81

Nishizawa Ippū 西沢一風 45, 145
Notes Taken upon Waking Up 147, 148

O ki ni mesu mama お気に召すまま see As You Like It
Ochazuke no aji お茶漬けの味 see The Flavor of Green Tea over Rice
Ochiai Yoshiiku 落合芳幾 218
Ōeda Ryūhō 154, 155f
Ogyū Hokkei 荻生北渓 125
Ogyū Korenori 荻生維則 65
Ogyū Sorai 荻生徂徠 125
Okamoto Kidō 岡本綺堂 167
On the Writing of Plays (Nishizawa Ippū) 145
onnagata 女形 42, 45, 103, 127, 135, 164, 165
Onoe Baikō 尾上梅幸 225
Onoe Kikugorō 尾上菊五郎 128, 171, 175, 177, 218, 259
Opening the Canister for Morning Tea (Shikitei Sanba) 212
"The Origins of the Revival of Storytelling" (Shikitei Sanba) 52, 56f, 238
Ōta Nanpo 大田南畝 49, 50, 65
Ōtani Hiroemon 大谷廣右衛門 186, 187f
Ōtani Jicchō 大谷十町 50
"Otoshibanashi chūkō raiyu" 落話中興来 see "The Origins of the Revival of Storytelling"
Ozaki Kōyō 尾崎紅葉 176
Ozu Yasujirō 小津安二郎 3

"Precepts for Dramatic Composition" (Kawatake Mokuami) 177
"Programs of Edo's Three Theaters" (Shikitei Sanba) 52, 239

A Quick Guide to Actor Likenesses (Utagawa Toyokuni I) 189, 191f, 199f

"A Register of Authors" (Mimasuya Nisōji) 165
Ryūtei Enshi 柳亭燕枝 143
Ryūtei Tanehiko 柳亭種彦 168

saiken 細見 see detailed view
Saitō Gesshin 斎藤月岑 91
"Sakai jiken" 堺事件 see "Incident at Sakai"
Sakai Matsunosuke 酒井松之助 215, 217f
Sakai-chō 堺町 22, 81, 93–99, 107, 108
Sakurada Jisuke 桜田治助 2, 165, 167
Sakuragawa Jihinari 桜川慈悲成 184f, 203
"Sakusha myōmoku" 作者名目 see "A Register of Authors"

Sanshibai gakuya zassho 三芝居楽屋雑書 see Miscellaneous Notes from Behind the Stage of the Three Theaters
Sanshibai yakusha saiken 三芝居役者細見 see A Detailed View of the Actors of the Three Theaters
Sanshōtei Karaku 三笑亭可楽 55, 56f
Santō Kyōden 山東京伝 38, 49–51, 58, 64, 123, 126, 148, 152, 154f, 168, 188, 194, 212, 259
Santō Kyōzan 山東京山 123
Saritsu udan 蓑笠雨談 see Tales Told by Rain
Saruwaka saiken zu 猿若細見図 see A Detailed View of Saruwaka
Saruwaka-chō 猿若町 1–4, 7, 9, 81, 84–91, 94–95, 101–2, 113
Satsuma-za 薩摩座 85
Segawa Jokō II 瀬川如皐 174
Segawa Jokō III 瀬川如皐 2, 175
Seji kenmon roku 世事見聞録 see An Account of What I Have Seen and Heard
Self Praise (Nakamura Nakazō III) 1–8, 10
Senjimon seiko no yanagi 千字文西湖の柳 see Thousand Character Classic Willow of the West Lake
Shadows of Kabuki Cast by Magic Lantern (Shikitei Sanba) 23–26, 204f, 206f, 242–44, 244f
Shen zhong lou 蜃中樓 see The Mirage Tower
Shibai chōhōsho 劇場重法書 see A Treasury of the Theater
Shibai kinmō zui 劇場訓蒙図彙 see Illustrated Dictionary of Theater for Beginners
Shibai saiken sanbasō 芝居細見三葉草 see A Detailed View of the Theater: The Three-Leafed Clover
Shibaraku 暫 see Just a Minute!
Shibata Tsunekichi 柴田常吉 218, 232
Shibue Chūsai 渋江抽斎 68, 239, 240, 259
Shibue Chūsai 渋江抽斎 (Mori Ōgai) 239, 240
Shikankoku ichiran 芝翫国一覧 see A View of the Land of Shikan
Shikitei Sanba 式亭三馬 19, 23f, 38, 39f, 54f, 76, 80, 81, 105, 112, 114f, 168, 179, 181, 201, 204, 206f, 237, 244f, 259
Shimazaki Tōson 12, 27
Shin Gunsho Ruijū 新群書類従 68
Shin Yoshiwara 新吉原 68, 85–87, 95–98, 101, 106–8
Shinkoku yakusha kōmoku 新刻役者綱目 see Facts about Actors, Newly Printed

282  INDEX

*Shinshi Saruwaka nendaiki* 新梓猿若年代記 *see A Newly Printed Chronology of Saruwaka*
shunga 春画  29
Sō Shiseki 宋紫石  155, 156f
Song Ziyan (J. Sō Shigan) 宋紫岩  155
*Sono utsushie kabuki no omokage* 其寫絵劇俤 *see Shadows of Kabuki Cast by Magic Lantern*
*A Souvenir of Naniwa* (Miki Sadanari)  141, 142f
*Strange Tales from China* (Hatanaka Kansai)  124, 128f, 151
Sugimori Tamon 杉森多門  147
*Suiyo shōroku* 睡余小録 *see Notes Taken upon Waking Up*
*Sumidagawa gonichi no omokage* 隅田川続俤 *see Latter-Day Reflections of the Sumida River*
Suzuki Harunobu 鈴木春信  160
Suzuki Toshiyuki  13, 28, 31, 34

Takemoto Settsu-Daijō 竹本摂津大掾  147
Takeshiba Kisui 竹柴其水  172
Takizawa Bakin *see* Kyokutei Bakin
*Tales Told by Rain* (Kyokutei Bakin)  148
Tamura Nariyoshi 田村成義  51, 67–69, 260
Tani Bunchō 谷文晁  65, 156
"Tanki manroku" 耽奇漫録  65
Tankikai 耽奇会  65, 68
*Temae miso* 手前味噌 *see Self Praise*
*Theater Chic This Side of the Curtain* (Shikitei Sanba)  19, 209
*Thoughts on Extraordinary Things of Recent Times* (Santō Kyōden)  58, 240
*Thousand Character Classic Willow of the West Lake*  124, 126
Torii Kiyonobu 鳥居清信  47
Tosa Mitsumoto 土佐光元  159
Tosa Mitsuoki 土佐光起  159
Tōshi Shōkyaku 東子樵客  199, 200f
Tōshūsai Sharaku 東洲斎写楽  220
*A Treasury of the Theater*  81, 83f, 108
Tsubouchi Shōyō 坪内逍遥  10, 36, 43, 64, 69–71, 77, 141, 143–44, 146, 167, 169, 172, 179, 180If, 184f, 214, 216, 225, 243, 260
Tsuga Teishō 都賀庭鐘  129
Tsumago 妻籠  12, 13, 34, 37, 241, 242
Tsuruya Kiemon 鶴屋喜衛門  193–95

Tsuruya Nanboku 鶴屋南北  165, 167, 168, 174, 260

*Ukan sandai zue* 羽勘三台図絵 *see An Illustrated Encyclopedia of U and Kan's Three Stages*
Unchakai 雲茶会  49, 50–51, 65, 106, 239
Utagawa Kunisada 歌川国貞  4, 38, 95f, 97f, 99, 99f, 100f, 134, 134f, 136f, 165, 166f, 174, 175, 179, 196, 227, 260
Utagawa Kuniyoshi 歌川国芳  4, 5f
Utagawa Toyokuni I 23f, 24, 36, 39f, 110, 110f, 117f, 121, 139, 182, 185f, 191f, 197f, 199f, 200f, 204f, 206f, 208f, 212, 244f, 260
Utagawa Toyokuni III *see* Utagawa Kunisada
Utagawa Yoshifuji 歌川芳藤  84
Utei Enba 烏亭焉馬  38, 41, 42f, 47f, 64, 77, 95, 95f, 97f, 100, 101, 102f, 105, 143, 157, 179, 260

*Valuable Notes on Playwriting*  148
*A View of the Land of Shikan*  130, 131f, 132f
*A View of the Theater through a Microscope* (Kimura Mokurō)  93, 132, 134f, 136f

yakusha hyōbanki 役者評判記  38, 44, 91, 94, 105
*Yakusha nigao hayageiko* 役者似顔早稽古 *see A Quick Guide to Actor Likenesses*
*Yakusha sanjūnisō tengankyō* 俳優卅二相點顔鏡 *see A Magnifying Glass of Thirty-Two Actors' Physiognomies*
*Yakusha saraekō* 役者時習講 *see A Disquisition on the Customs of Actors*
Yamazaki Yoshishige 山崎美成  58, 65, 260
Yanagiya Umehiko 柳屋梅彦  174, 175, 177
Yasuda Zenjirō II 安田善次郎  81, 83, 95, 260
Yobukodori waka sanchō zenzu 呼子鳥和歌三町全図  84, 85f, 88f
Yonemoto, Marcia  81, 105, 106, 119
Yoshimura Ito 吉村いと  169, 176, 260
*Yoshitsune and the Thousand Cherry Trees*  208f
*Yoshitsune senbonzakura* 義経千本桜 *see Yoshitsune and the Thousand Cherry Trees*
Yoshiwara saiken 吉原細見  91, 92, 95
Yoshizawa Shōho 吉沢商舗  216, 217
Yūki-za 結城座  85
*Yu saotou* 玉搔頭 *see The Jade Clasp*